MW01119479

T

# RUNAWAY AND HOMELESS YOUTH

# SOCIAL ISSUES, JUSTICE AND STATUS SERIES

**Risk and Social Welfare**
*Jason L. Powell and Azrini Wahidin*
*(Editors)*
2009. ISBN: 978-1-60741-691-3

**Risk and Social Welfare**
*Jason L. Powell and Azrini Wahidin*
*(Editors)*
2009. ISBN: 978-1-60876-798-4 (E-book)

**Low Incomes: Social, Health
and Educational Impacts**
*Jacob K. Levine*
*(Editor)*
2009. ISBN: 978-1-60741-175-8

**Handbook on Social Change**
*Brooke H. Stroud and Scott E. Corbin*
*(Editors)*
2009. ISBN: 978-1-60741-222-9

**Handbook on Social Change**
*Brooke H. Stroud and Scott E. Corbin*
*(Editors)*
2009. ISBN: 978-1-60876-776-2
(E-book)

**Social Development**
*Lynda R. Elling (Editor)*
2009. ISBN: 978-1-60741-612-8

**Social Development**
*Lynda R. Elling (Editor)*
2009. ISBN: 978-1-60876-688-8
(E-book)

**Handbook of Social Justice**
*Augustus Kakanowski and Marijus
Narusevich (Editors)*
2009. ISBN: 978-1-60741-713-2

**Doctoring Medical Governance: Medical
Self-Regulation in Transition**
*John M. Chamberlain*
2009. ISBN: 978-1-60876-119-7

**Social Epileptology: Understanding
Social Aspects of Epilepsy**
*Jaya Pinikahana and Christine Walker*
*(Editors)*
2009. ISBN: 978-1-60876-228-6

**Who Pays the Price? Foreign Workers,
Society, Crime and the Law**
*Mally Shechory, Sarah Ben-David
and Dan Soen (Editors)*
2010. ISBN: 978-1-60876-320-7

**Race and Ethnicity: Cultural Roles,
Spiritual Practices
and Social Challenges**
*Jonathan K. Crennan (Editor)*
2010. ISBN: 978-1-60692-099-2

**Race and Ethnicity: Cultural Roles,
Spiritual Practices
and Social Challenges**
*Jonathan K. Crennan (Editor)*
2010. ISBN: 978-1-61668-535-5 (E-book)

**Youth Violence and Juvenile Justice:
Causes, Intervention
and Treatment Programs**
*Neil A. Ramsay and Colin R. Morrison
(Editors)*
2010. ISBN: 978-1-61668-011-4

**Issues and Lessons for Incarcerated
and Released Parents**
*Jonathan T. Swift (Editor)*
2010. ISBN: 978-1-60692-961-2

SOCIAL ISSUES, JUSTICE AND STATUS SERIES

# RUNAWAY AND HOMELESS YOUTH

JOSIAH HUGHES
AND
ISIAH WRIGHT
EDITORS

Nova Science Publishers, Inc.
*New York*

For permission to use material from this book please contact us:
Telephone 631-231-7269; Fax 631-231-8175
Web Site: http://www.novapublishers.com

## NOTICE TO THE READER

The Publisher has taken reasonable care in the preparation of this book, but makes no expressed or implied warranty of any kind and assumes no responsibility for any errors or omissions. No liability is assumed for incidental or consequential damages in connection with or arising out of information contained in this book. The Publisher shall not be liable for any special, consequential, or exemplary damages resulting, in whole or in part, from the readers' use of, or reliance upon, this material. Any parts of this book based on government reports are so indicated and copyright is claimed for those parts to the extent applicable to compilations of such works.

Independent verification should be sought for any data, advice or recommendations contained in this book. In addition, no responsibility is assumed by the publisher for any injury and/or damage to persons or property arising from any methods, products, instructions, ideas or otherwise contained in this publication.

This publication is designed to provide accurate and authoritative information with regard to the subject matter covered herein. It is sold with the clear understanding that the Publisher is not engaged in rendering legal or any other professional services. If legal or any other expert assistance is required, the services of a competent person should be sought. FROM A DECLARATION OF PARTICIPANTS JOINTLY ADOPTED BY A COMMITTEE OF THE AMERICAN BAR ASSOCIATION AND A COMMITTEE OF PUBLISHERS.

**Library of Congress Cataloging-in-Publication Data**
Runaway and homeless youth / editors, Josiah Hughes and Isiah Wright.
    p. cm.
  Includes index.
  ISBN 978-1-60741-521-3 (hardcover)
  1. Runaway teenagers--United States. 2. Homeless youth--United States. 3. Runaway teenagers--Service for--United States. 4. Homeless youth--Service for--United States. I. Hughes, Josiah. II. Wright, Isiah.
  HV1431 .R86
  362.74--dc22
                                                                                        2009038414

*Published by Nova Science Publishers, Inc.* ✦ *New York*

# CONTENTS

# PREFACE

There is no single definition of the term "runaway youth" or "homeless youth". However, both groups of youth share the risk of not having adequate shelter and other provisions, and may engage in harmful behaviors while away from a permanent home. The precise number of homeless and runaway youth is unknown due to their residential mobility and overlap among the populations. Determining the number of these youth is further complicated by the lack of a standardized methodology for counting the population and inconsistent definitions of what it means to be homeless or a runaway. Estimates of the homeless youth exceed one million. Thus homelessness among adolescents and young adults is a major social concern in the United States. In this book, the authors cite research indicating that youth may be the single age group most at risk of becoming homeless, yet comparatively little research has been done in the past decade on this vulnerable population. After reviewing the characteristics of homeless youth, the authors review recent research findings on the homeless youth population and interventions developed to address their housing and service needs. These include interventions directed at youth themselves (education, employment, social skills training) as well as family-focused strategies. The authors conclude with future directions for both research and practice. This book consists of public documents which have been located, gathered, combined, reformatted, and enhanced with a subject index, selectively edited and bound to provide easy access.

Chapter 1 - In this paper, the authors cite research indicating that youth may be the single age group most at risk of becoming homeless, yet comparatively little research has been done in the past decade on this vulnerable population. Some important progress has been made, including longitudinal studies on youth "aging out" of foster care. After reviewing the characteristics of homeless youth, the authors review recent research findings on the homeless youth population and interventions developed to address their housing and service needs. These include interventions directed at youth themselves (education, employment, social skills training) as well as family-focused strategies. The authors conclude with future directions for both research and practice.

Chapter 2 - Youth homelessness has profound consequences reaching well beyond individual youth and their immediate families. Indeed, negative impacts from youth homelessness enter into the very fabric of our communities and the nation as a whole. Research suggests that as many as 1.6 million young people may be homeless at some point during the year. When youth leave their homes and enter the homeless population, they are in jeopardy of engaging in anti-social and risky behaviors as well as becoming one of the most severely victimized groups in our society.[1] Alarmingly, an increasing amount of research on the chronic homeless population notes a correspondence of homelessness experienced in youth to subsequent adult experiences of homelessness.

Chapter 3 - There is no single definition of the term "runaway youth" or "homeless youth." However, both groups of youth share the risk of not having adequate shelter and other provisions, and may engage in harmful behaviors while away from a permanent home. These two groups also include "thrownaway" youth who are asked to leave their homes, and may include other vulnerable youth populations, such as current and former foster youth and youth with mental health or other issues.

The precise number of homeless and runaway youth is unknown due to their residential mobility and overlap among the populations. Determining the number of these youth is further complicated by the lack of a standardized methodology for counting the population and inconsistent definitions of what it means to be homeless or a runaway. Estimates of the homeless youth exceed one million. Estimates of runaway youth — including "thrownaway" youth (youth asked to leave their homes) — are between one million and 1.7 million.

Chapter 4 - The Runaway and Homeless Youth Act (RHYA) was signed into law in 1974 as Title III of the Juvenile Justice and Delinquency Prevention Act (P.L. 93-415). RHYA authorizes funding for programs to support runaway and homeless youth, as well as related training, research, and other activities. These programs and activities are administered by the Family and Youth Services Bureau (FYSB) in the Department of Health and Human Services' (HHS) Administration for Children and Families.

In the second session of the 110th Congress, Congress passed and the President signed into law the Reconnecting Homeless Youth Act of 2008 (P.L. 110-378) to extend existing programs and establish new activities under RHYA for FY2009 through FY2013. The law represents a compromise between provisions that were included in two bills introduced in the 110th Congress: H.R. 5524 and S. 2982. On March 4, 2008, Representative John Yarmuth introduced H.R. 5524, the Reconnecting Homeless Youth Act of 2008, which passed the House on June 9, 2008. On May 6, 2008, Senator Patrick Leahy introduced S. 2982, the Runaway and Homeless Youth Protection Act, which passed the Senate on September 25, 2008. The House approved S. 2982 on September 26, and the President signed it into law as P.L. 110-378 on October 8, 2008.

This report discusses P.L. 110-378 and includes a table with a side-by-side comparison of its provisions to those in H.R. 5524, as well as to the law and regulations as they existed prior to the enactment of S. 2982. The new law amends and adds provisions related to program funding, requirements, and accountability. It extends the authorization of appropriations for the three programs under RHYA that provide direct services to youth: the Basic Center Program (BCP), Transitional Living Program (TLP), and Street Outreach Program (SOP). Unlike prior law, P.L. 110-378 enables HHS to reallot any unused BCP funds from one state to other states and permits youth to remain in BCP and TLP shelters for a longer period. Another change made by the law requires HHS to regularly submit a report to Congress that describes the incidence and prevalence of runaway and homeless youth. The law also directs the Government Accountability Office to report to Congress on the process by which HHS awards BCP, TLP, and SOP grants.

Chapter 5 features a transcript of a hearing before the U. S. House of Representatives.

Chapter 6 features a transcript of a hearing before the U. S. Senate.

In: Runaway and Homeless Youth
Editors: Josiah Hughes and Isiah Wright

ISBN: 978-1-60741-521-3
© 2010 Nova Science Publishers, Inc.

*Chapter 1*

# HOMELESS YOUTH IN THE UNITED STATES: RECENT RESEARCH FINDINGS AND INTERVENTION APPROACHES*

## *Paul A. Toro, Amy Dworsky and Patrick J. Fowler*

## ABSTRACT

In this paper, the authors cite research indicating that youth may be the single age group most at risk of becoming homeless, yet comparatively little research has been done in the past decade on this vulnerable population. Some important progress has been made, including longitudinal studies on youth "aging out" of foster care. After reviewing the characteristics of homeless youth, the authors review recent research findings on the homeless youth population and interventions developed to address their housing and service needs. These include interventions directed at youth themselves (education, employment, social skills training) as well as family-focused strategies. The authors conclude with future directions for both research and practice.

## INTRODUCTION

Homelessness among adolescents and young adults is a major social concern in the United States. Robertson and Toro (1999) concluded that youth may be the single age group most at risk of becoming homeless. Nevertheless, most of the research that has been conducted over the last two decades has focused on homeless adults, including those with mental disorders and substance abuse problems. Studies that have examined homelessness among adolescents and young adults as well as other age groups, have often cast the problem as one of individual vulnerabilities rather than as a social phenomenon involving transactions between individuals and their environments (Haber & Toro, 2004; Shinn, 1992; Toro et al.,

---

* This is an edited, reformatted and augmented version of a National Symposium on Homelessness Research publication dated March 2007.

1991). This research has also been of limited value with respect to the development of public policies or empirically based interventions that either assist youth who are currently homeless or prevent homelessness among adolescents and young adults who are at risk (Shinn & Baumohl, 1999; Toro, Lombardo, & Yapchai, 2002).

These problems notwithstanding, some progress has been made since Robertson and Toro reviewed the literature on homeless youth over eight years ago for the 1998 National Symposium on Homelessness Research. Longitudinal studies, including research on youth "aging out" of foster care, have been an important source of information. Our knowledge about what works when it comes to prevention and programs that target homeless youth has also increased, although significant gaps remain. After briefly discussing some definitional issues and describing the homeless youth population and its constituent subgroups along a number of dimensions, we summarize what has been learned in recent years.

## Definitional Issues

We begin with a fundamental question. What does it mean to say that a youth is homeless? Alternatively, who does the population of homeless youth include? The Runaway and Homeless Youth Act (RHYA) defines homeless youth as individuals who are "not more than 21 years of age ... for whom it is not possible to live in a safe environment with a relative and who have no other safe alternative living arrangement." Implicit in this definition is the notion that homeless youth are not accompanied by a parent or guardian (Haber & Toro, 2004). The McKinney-Vento Homeless Assistance Act, the primary piece of federal legislation pertaining to the education of homeless children, provides a somewhat different definition. According to Subtitle B of Title VII of that legislation, youth are homeless if they "lack a fixed, regular, and adequate nighttime residence." In contrast to the RHYA, McKinneyVento applies not only to unaccompanied youth but also to those who are homeless or doubled up with their families. Because homeless families with children are the focus of another paper in this Symposium, we will adopt a more restrictive definition that excludes youth who are homeless with a parent or other guardian and youth who are wards of the state.

Homeless youth can be distinguished from two other homeless populations: single adults, who are predominantly male and do not have children in their custody; and homeless families, typically comprising a mother and her children.[1] Homeless youth include runaways, who have left home without parental permission, *throwaways*, who have been forced to leave home by their parents, and *street youth*, who have spent at least some time living on the streets as well as *systems youth*—i.e., young people who become homeless after aging out of foster care or exiting the juvenile justice system (Farrow, et al., 1992). Although these categories reflect important distinctions among youth with respect to the reasons they are homeless and their experiences while homeless, they are neither static nor mutually exclusive (Hammer, Finkelhor, & Sedlak, 2002), and it can be difficult to determine which label best applies. Youth may perceive themselves as being thrown out by their parents, while parents may perceive their son or daughter as running away. In other cases, youth may be removed from their home by child welfare authorities and then run away from their out-of-home care placement or leave home by mutual agreement with their parents. Street youth often spend significant amounts of time in adult caregivers' homes, shelters, and temporary quarters with friends or other family (Greenblatt & Robertson, 1993). The one thing homeless youth have in common is that they are on their own without the supervision of an adult caretaker (Haber & Toro, 2004). In order to allow review of the full array of relevant literature, the present paper uses a broad definition, including all youth ages 12 to 25 who fit either the RHYA or McKinney-Vento definition (so long as they are "homeless on their own").

# HOMELESS YOUTH: A BRIEF SUMMARY OF THE EXISTING RESEARCH LITERATURE

In this section, we briefly review how homeless youth have been studied in the past and what is known about homeless youth from this research (for a more comprehensive review, see Robertson & Toro, 1999).

Haber and Toro (2004) describe four basic approaches used by researchers to sample homeless youth. The first approach is to survey large groups of youth in the general population and identify those with a history of homelessness (e.g., Ringwalt et al., 1998; Windle, 1989). These methods may misrepresent the total homeless youth population because they do not include youth who are currently homeless, who may well have longer histories of homelessness and other negative characteristics. The second draws youth from service settings such as inner-city clinics (Kipke, Montgomery, & MacKenzie, 1993; Yates et al., 1988). Of course, youth seeking services may be different from those who do not seek help. The third approach samples youth from shelters (e.g., McCaskill, Toro, & Wolfe, 1998). Some of the youth these facilities serve have been brought to the shelter by their families or third parties such as the police. Many have never spent a night on the streets. Such youth are often younger and less likely to have extensive histories of homelessness than street youth (Robertson & Toro, 1999). The fourth approach involves sampling from street locations where homeless youth are known to congregate and/or from drop-in centers designed to serve street youth (e.g., Cauce et al., 1994; Kipke, O'Connor, Palmer, & MacKenzie, 1995; Roy et al., 1998). This method often yields a sample biased toward youth who are engaged in a variety of deviant behaviors, especially if the sample includes many youth who are 18 or older. Some recent studies have combined the four methods in an effort to obtain more representative samples (e.g., Heinze, Toro, & Urberg, 2004; Paradise et al., 2001; Toro & Goldstein, 2000; Unger et al., 1998; Whitbeck, Hoyt, & Yoder, 1999; Witken et al., 2005).

## Prevalence and Geographical Distribution of Youth Homelessness

Just how many youth are homeless in a given year is difficult to know. Estimates vary widely depending on how "homeless" is defined and the age range that is used. Different sampling and estimation techniques can also yield different results. For example, Ringwalt and colleagues analyzed data collected from a representative U.S. household sample of nearly 6,500 youth, ages 12 to 17, as part of the Youth Risk Behavior Survey (YRBS) and found that approximately 7.6 percent had been homeless for at least one night during the past 12 months (Ringwalt et al., 1998). This would translate into approximately 1.6 million homeless youth each year. Similarly, the Second National Incidence Study of Missing, Abducted, Runaway and Thrownaway Children (NISMART II), which combined data from three different surveys (the National Household Survey of Adult Caretakers, the National Household Survey of Youth, and the Juvenile Facilities Study) estimated that approximately 1.7 million youth experienced a runaway or throwaway episode in 1999 (Hammer, Finkelhor, & Sedlack, 2002). Other studies have looked at the likelihood of ever becoming homeless during adolescence. According to one estimate, 15 percent of youth will become homeless at least once before age 18 (Ringwalt, Greene, & Iachan, 1994).

Homeless youth can be found in urban, suburban, and rural areas throughout the U.S., but tend to be most visible in major cities (Robertson & Toro, 1999). Moreover, although they may be an understudied population, homeless youth in rural areas have proven difficult to recruit (e.g., Heinze, Toro, & Urberg, 2004; Thrane & Yoder, 2000). Nevertheless, few differences have been found when urban, suburban, and rural homeless youth have been compared (Cauce et al., 2000; Thrane & Yoder, 2000). Studies investigating street youth have generally been based in large metropolitan areas on the east and west coasts (e.g., Los Angeles, San Francisco, Seattle, and New York City), in part because researchers have not found large numbers of homeless street youth under age 18 in most midwestern and southern cities (Robertson & Toro, 1999).

Greenblatt and Robertson (1993) found both episodic and chronic patterns of homelessness among the youth they studied. However, the number of homeless episodes youth have experienced and the length of time they have been homeless seem to depend on whether shelter youth or street youth have been studied. Many youth in shelter samples are homeless for the first time and have not been homeless for very long (McCaskill, Toro, & Wolfe, 1998), whereas street youth tend to experience longer and more frequent episodes of homelessness (Whitbeck, Hoyt, & Yoder, 1999; Witken et al., 2005).

## Age, Gender, Race/Ethnicity, Sexual Orientation, and Pregnancy

The vast majority of homeless youth are age 13 or older, although a few studies have identified small numbers of youth who are homeless on their own as young as 9 years old (Clark & Robertson, 1996; Robertson, 1991). Although at least one national survey of youth found that males were significantly more likely than females to report recent homelessness (Ringwalt et al. 1998), the distribution of males and females among homeless youth seems to vary depending on the source and age of the sample. Shelter samples tend to include either equal numbers of males and females or more females (e.g., Heinze, Toro, & Urberg, 2004). Samples of street youth or older homeless youth are disproportionately male (e.g., Cauce et al., 2000). There is also some evidence that during the transition from adolescence to young adulthood the risk of becoming homeless declines for females but rises for males (Boesky, Toro, & Bukowski, 1997).

There have been contradictory findings with respect to race/ethnicity. Neither Ringwalt et al. (1998) nor Hammer et al. (2002) found racial or ethnic differences in rates of homelessness among the youth they studied, and at least some research suggests that homeless youth tend to reflect the racial and ethnic make-up of the surrounding area. However, other studies indicate that racial and ethnic minority youth are over-represented (Cauce et al., 1994; McCaskill, Toro, & Wolfe, 1998; Owen et al., 1998).

Gay, lesbian, bisexual, and transgender (GLBT) youth comprise 6 percent of the homeless youth population according to the National Network of Runaway and Youth Services. However, other prevalence estimates range from 11 to 35 percent (Kruks, 1991; Tenner et al., 1998; Whitbeck et al., 2004). Compared to heterosexual homeless youth, GLBT homeless youth leave home more frequently and are exposed to greater victimization while on the streets (Cochran et al., 2002). In addition, these youth may experience more physical and sexual abuse from caretakers (Whitbeck et al., 2004). GLBT youth may be at particular risk for homelessness due to conflict with their family regarding their sexual orientation (Milburn, Ayala, Rice, Batterham, & Rotheram-Borus, 2006; Remafedi, 1987).

A significant percentage of homeless youth are pregnant or parenting. Greene and Ringwalt (1998) found that 48 percent of street youth and 33 percent of shelter youth had ever been pregnant or impregnated someone, compared to 10 percent of a nationally representative sample of housed youth. Research also suggests that approximately 10 percent of both street and shelter female youth are currently pregnant (Greene & Ringwalt, 1998; Solorio et al., 2006). The high rates of pregnancy in this population may reflect the fact that many homeless youth engage in risky behaviors, including sex at an early age, survival sex, and inconsistent use of birth control.

## Background Characteristics

Regardless of their pathways into homelessness, homeless youth share many background characteristics and experience many of the same psychosocial problems (MacLean, Embry, & Cauce, 1999). For example, they tend to come from low-income communities (McCaskill, Toro, & Wolfe, 1998) and their families are disproportionately poor or working class (Whitbeck et al., 1997). It is also not uncommon for homeless youth to report a history of family disruption. Many grew up in single-parent households or "blended" (i.e., stepparent) families (Boesky, Toro, & Wright, 1995; Greenblatt & Robertson, 1993), and a significant number of these youth have not had any contact with their non-custodial parent (Greenblatt & Robertson, 1993). The families of homeless youth also seem to have experienced far more residential moves than those of their housed peers (Cauce et al., 2000; Toro & Goldstein, 2000). In other words, their homelessness seems to be part of a longer pattern of residential instability.

## Difficulties with School

Homeless youth often have a history of academic and school behavior problems. Between 25 and 35 percent of homeless youth report that they had to repeat a grade (Clark & Robertson, 1996; Robertson, 1989; Upshur, 1986; Young et al., 1983), and many have been suspended or expelled (Toro & Goldstein, 2000). Drop-out rates are also high (Thompson, Kost, & Pollio, 2003). Research suggests that at least some of these academic and school behavior problems may be attributable to attention deficit disorder (Cauce et al., 2000) or learning disabilities (Barwick & Siegel, 1996), which may be why homeless youth often report being placed in special education or remedial classes (Clark & Robertson, 1996;

Robertson, 1989). Regardless of their cause, these academic and school behavior problems can be a source of family conflict and hence contribute to homelessness.


## Family Conflict and Child Maltreatment

Youth consistently identify conflict with their parents as the primary reason for their homelessness (Whitbeck et al., 2002; Robertson & Toro, 1999), and they tend to report more family conflict than their peers who are housed (Toro & Goldstein, 2000; Wolfe, Toro, & McCaskill, 1999). These conflicts tend to reflect longstanding patterns rather than problems that arise just before youth leave home (Smollar, 1999). Conflicts related to step-parent relationships, sexual activity, pregnancy, sexual orientation, school problems, and alcohol or drug use seem to be the most common (Owen et al., 1998; Robertson & Toro, 1999; Whitbeck & Hoyt, 1999).

In addition to family conflict, many homeless youth have experienced child abuse and/or neglect (Boesky, Toro, & Wright, 1995; Molnar et al., 1998; Powers, Eckenrode, & Jacklitsh, 1990; Robertson, 1989; Rotherman-Borus et al., 1996; Rothman & David, 1985; Ryan et al., 2000; Tyler et al., 2001; Unger et al., 1998; Yates et al., 1988). In fact, homeless youth often cite physical or sexual abuse as their reason for leaving home (Robertson, 1989). Although the percentage of homeless youth who report a history of maltreatment varies widely across studies, research using comparison groups has found that homeless youth are more likely to have been abused and/or neglected than their peers who are housed (Wolfe, Toro, & McCaskill, 1999). This may also explain why homeless youth are more likely to have been verbally and physically aggressive toward their parents compared to their housed peers (Toro & Goldstein, 2000).

That is, their aggression may be in response to parental aggression directed at them (Haber & Toro, 2003).


## Mental Health and Behavioral Disorders

Homeless youth seem to be at elevated risk for a variety of mental health problems, including mood disorders, suicide attempts, and posttraumatic stress disorder (Cauce et al., 2000; Clark & Robertson, 1996; Feitel et al., 1992; Fronczak & Toro, 2003; Greenblatt & Robertson, 1993; McCaskill, Toro, & Wolfe, 1998; Powers, Eckenrode, & Jaklitsch, 1990; Rew, Thomas, Horner, Resnick, & Beuhring, 2001; Rotheram-Borus, 1993; Robertson, 1989; Stewart et al., 2004; Toro & Goldstein, 2000, Yates et al., 1988). The risk of mental health problems may be particularly high among street youth, who tend to have experienced more stressful events and to exhibit more psychological symptoms than homeless youth who have not spent time on the streets (Robertson & Toro, 1999; Whitbeck & Hoyt, 1999).

Behavioral problems, such as conduct or oppositional defiant disorder, may be even more prevalent than mental health problems (Cauce et al., 2000; McCaskill, Toro, & Wolfe, 1998; Toro & Goldstein, 2000). Homeless youth also exhibit high rates of substance use disorders, including alcohol abuse or dependence and drug abuse or dependence (e.g., Baer, Ginzler, & Peterson, 2003; MacLean, Paradise, & Cauce, 1999; Robertson, 1989; Rotheram-Borus,

1993; Thompson, Sayfer, & Polio, 2001; Thompson, Kost, & Pollio, 2003; Van Leeuwen, 2002; Van Leeuwen et al., 2005; Yates et al., 1988).

Although the prevalence of some diagnoses (e.g., depression) has been consistent across studies, lower rates are found for other disorders (e.g., conduct disorder) when more rigorous assessments are used and when homeless youth are recruited from shelters rather than the streets (Robertson & Toro, 1999). Nevertheless, regardless of the sample or the assessment method used, mental health and behavioral disorders seem to be more prevalent among homeless youth than among matched housed peers or the general adolescent population (McCaskill, Toro, & Wolfe, 1998; Toro & Goldstein, 2000). Unfortunately, the reason for the high prevalence rates observed among homeless youth is far from clear (Robertson, 1992; Robertson & Toro, 1999; Toro, 1998). Mental health and behavioral disorders contribute to family conflict and thus to homelessness. However, causality could also be in the opposite direction (Cauce et al., 1994; MacLean, Embry, & Cauce, 1999). Alternatively, some other factor or combination of factors could be a cause of both.

## Risky Behaviors and Victimization

A number of studies have found not only that many homeless youth are sexually active, but also that they engage in sexual behaviors that put them at high risk for both sexually transmitted diseases and pregnancy (Cauce et al., 1994; Kipke et al., 1995; Lombardo & Toro, 2004; Rotheram-Borus, 1991; Rotheram-Borus et al., 1992a, 1992b; Staller & Kirk, 1997; Toro & Goldstein, 2000; Whitbeck & Hoyt, 1999).

Homeless youth also report engaging in delinquent or illegal activities, including stealing, forcibly entering a residence, prostitution, and dealing drugs (Whitbeck, Hoyt, & Ackley, 1997). Youth who engage in these "deviant" behaviors often report that they do so to obtain money, food or shelter (Van Leeuwen, 2002; Van Leeuwen et al., 2005). In other words, these behaviors may be part of a survival strategy (Robertson & Toro, 1999).

Being on their own without adult supervision means not only that homeless youth are likely to behave in ways that are unsafe, but also that they comprise an especially vulnerable group. This is reflected in the high rates of physical and sexual victimization they report (Greenblatt & Robertson, 1993; Tyler et al., 2004). Research has found not only that homeless youth are far more likely to be victimized than their peers who are housed (Stewart et al., 2004; Yates et al., 1988) but that many homeless youth are victimized repeatedly (Whitbeck, Hoyt, & Ackley, 1997).

## Service Utilization

Despite extensive demonstration of the needs of homeless adolescents, few studies have explicitly attempted to document the full range of service utilization among this needy group. In a recent study done in Detroit (described in more detail below), a majority of both homeless and matched housed youth failed to receive adequate services given their risks for disturbances in medical and psychosocial functioning (Toro & Goldstein, 2000). Only 2 percent of the homeless youth reported utilizing soup kitchen or outreach services, while 18 percent reported using inpatient or outpatient psychological services (Toro & Goldstein, 2000). Following youths for over two years showed that less than 1 percent reported using services after the initial interview.

# NEW AREAS OF RESEARCH SINCE 1998

Several new areas of research on homeless youth have emerged since Robertson and Toro completed their review for the 1998 National Symposium on Homelessness Research. These areas include longitudinal studies of homeless youth, research on youth leaving the foster care and juvenile justice systems, and intervention and prevention research. Also there has been some development and evaluation of theoretical models explaining youth homelessness.

## Longitudinal Studies

Tracking homeless youth over time can suggest both causes of and possible solutions to the problems they experience. Unfortunately, only a few such studies have been done to date (e.g., Cauce et al., 1994), and few of their findings have yet been published in peer reviewed journals. In part, this paucity of data reflects the fact that data in these longitudinal studies are still being collected. However, it also indicates a general lack of research on homeless youth (as compared to other homeless groups) and a particular lack of longitudinal research on this population.

In any event, we can draw some conclusions based on preliminary results from a study by Toro and his colleagues. A probability sample of 249 homeless youth from throughout the Detroit metropolitan area, plus a matched sample of 149 housed youth, were initially interviewed at ages 13 to 17 and have been followed since at six time-points over a seven-year period. The youth are now aged 20 to 24, and data collection is nearly complete. Most of the adolescents returned fairly quickly to their family of origin. Nearly all (93 percent) of the initially homeless adolescents in the sample were no longer homeless at the 4.5-year follow-up, with one-third living with their parents (33 percent), another third living on their own (34 percent), and still others living with friends or relatives (21 percent). At follow-up, the initially homeless adolescents also reported significantly less conflict with their family and fewer stressful events (Toro & Janisse, 2004). Such trends have also been observed in longitudinal studies of homeless adults (e.g., Toro et al., 1999). People who are sampled because they are currently homeless are often at a particularly low point in their lives. Over time, many exit homelessness and thus appear to function at least somewhat better at follow-up, even though they often are not fully part of "mainstream society" and are likely to be at risk for future homelessness and/or other poor life outcomes.

Ahmed and Toro (2004) used data from the same longitudinal study to examine the relationship between several dimensions of religiosity and substance abuse outcomes over an 18-month follow-up period. Both cross-sectional and longitudinal analyses found that religiosity "buffered" the potentially harmful impact of stress on the outcomes. At the 4.5-year follow-up, greater spirituality protected African American, but not European American, young adults exposed to high levels of community violence or alcohol and drug abuse (Fowler, Ahmed et al., 2006).

Roy and her colleagues in Montreal have been studying various samples of street youth (age 14 to 25) and have followed one sample to observe various health outcomes, including HIV infection (Roy et al., 2003). They have, for example, found high mortality, with an annual death rate of 1 percent (Roy et al., 2004). The most common cause of death, by far, was suicide. This research group is now conducting another longitudinal study with more general purposes. Longitudinal findings will begin to be available in late 2007.

Milburn and her colleagues have followed homeless youth, aged 12 to 20, in Los Angeles (*N*=498) and in Melbourne, Australia (*N*=398), over a 12-month period (see Milburn, Rotheram-Borus et al., 2006; Witken et al., 2005). The longitudinal findings are just beginning to be reported in the professional literature (e.g., Milburn, Ayala, et al., 2006; Rosenthal et al., 2007).

## Homelessness among Former Foster Youth

Many homeless youth report a history of out-of-home care placement. The percentage who report being placed in foster care or an institutional setting varies across studies, but estimates range between 21 and 53 percent (Cauce et al., 1998; Robertson, 1989, 1991; Toro & Goldstein, 2000). A similar pattern has been observed among homeless adults (Firdion, 2004; Toro, Wolfe et al., 1999).

Of particular concern in this regard is the experience of youth who "age out" of foster care when they turn 18 or, in some states, 21. Although these youth are expected to live independently and support themselves once they leave the child welfare system, they often lack the financial, social, and personal resources needed to do so (Lindblom, 1996). As a result, this population is at high risk of becoming homeless after they age out. In fact, studies conducted in both Hollywood and San Francisco found that more than one- quarter of the street youth who had been discharged from state care spent their first night in a shelter or on the streets (Clark & Robertson, 1996; Robertson, 1989). Findings from several recent studies of youth aging out of foster care also illustrate this link.

### *The Foster Youth Transitions to Adulthood Study*
Courtney et al. (2001) collected baseline survey data from 141 Wisconsin foster youth in 1995. The youth were 17 or 18 years old and had been in care for a minimum of 18 months. Eighty percent, or 113, of these foster youth were re-interviewed 12 to 18 months after they left care. These young adults were similar to the baseline sample with respect to gender, race/ethnicity, and placement region (Milwaukee vs. the balance of the state). Among the outcomes the researchers examined was homelessness. Twelve percent of the follow-up sample reported being homeless for at least one night within 12 months of aging out (Courtney et al., 2001).

### *Youth Aging Out of Foster Care in Metropolitan Detroit*
Fowler, Toro et al. (2006) surveyed 264 youth from the total population of the 867 youth who had aged out over a two-year period from the foster care system in the three largest counties

in the metropolitan Detroit area. The 264 youth were interviewed, on average, 3.6 years after exiting from foster care. At follow-up, the sample had an average age of 20.6 years; 52 percent were female; and 78 percent were African American. The follow-up sample of 264 was representative of the population of 867 in terms of demographic characteristics (e.g., gender, age, race/ethnicity) and foster care experiences (e.g., number of placements, age at entry, reason for placement). The purpose of the survey was to assess the functioning of these youth across various life domains since leaving foster care. The domains included housing, education, employment, emotional and behavioral well-being, substance abuse, risky sexual behavior, and victimization.

A total of 17 percent of the youth experienced literal homelessness during the follow-up period, including 3 percent who were literally homeless at the time they were interviewed. By comparison, the national five-year prevalence rate for literal homelessness among all adults in the United States was just 2 percent in 2001 (Tompsett et al., 2006). Those who experienced literal homelessness did so for an average of 61 days; the likelihood of experiencing literal homelessness did not vary by gender or race/ethnicity.

Just because youth were not literally homeless did not mean that they always had a stable place to live. On the contrary, one-third of the youth had spent time doubled up with other families or "couch surfing" among friends and relatives because they could not afford more permanent housing. This includes 12 percent who were precariously housed at the time of their interview. The mean number of times that these youth were precariously housed was 2.8 and the median duration of each episode was 13 months.

Most commonly, youth attributed their precarious housing or homelessness to economic factors such as a lack of employment, lack of affordable housing, termination of public assistance, or eviction. One-quarter of the youth who became homeless attributed their homelessness to problems with their families. In fact, this was the most common reason for becoming homeless immediately following exit from the foster care system.

Significant differences were found among the literally homeless, the precariously housed, and the continuously housed. Literally homeless youth reported significantly more personal victimization and deviant behavior than youth who were either continuously or precariously housed. However, both literally homeless and precariously housed youth experienced higher rates of psychological distress and alcohol or other drug abuse than continuously housed youth. In addition, literally homeless youth were more likely to report engaging in risky sexual behavior as compared to housed youth. Additional analyses suggested that both literal homelessness and precarious housing increased the risk of personal victimization, which in turn, increased the likelihood of other negative outcomes, such as psychological distress, deviant behavior, and marijuana use, even after controlling for age, gender, and race.

There was also some evidence that becoming homeless immediately post-discharge may have particularly negative effects. Youth who experienced homelessness right after they left care reported greater psychological distress, victimization, and deviant behavior than those who did not become homeless until later. The former were also less likely to have a high school diploma or GED and less likely to have received additional schooling since leaving care. What is not clear is whether the youth who became homeless immediately were already more vulnerable at the time they exited, or whether they became more vulnerable as a result of becoming homeless so quickly.

In many cases, the youth who experienced housing problems after exiting foster care did not receive services to address their needs. Less than one-third received services at homeless shelters and only 3 percent received help from outreach services. Although nearly two thirds reported going a whole day without food, just 15 percent received assistance from soup kitchens. Likewise, 70 percent of these youth had clinically significant mental health, substance abuse, or behavioral problems, but only 21 percent received psychological services. In contrast, 88 percent of these precariously housed and homeless youth received medical care since aging out of the system. Many of the youth were able to take advantage of Medicaid eligibility allowed under state foster care policy in order to get medical care.

### *The Midwest Evaluation of the Adult Functioning of Former Foster Youth*

The relationship between homelessness and out-of-home care placement is also being examined by an ongoing three-state longitudinal study that is following a sample of 732 foster youth from Iowa (63 youth), Wisconsin (195), and Illinois (474) as they age out of the child welfare system and transition into adulthood (Courtney et al., 2005). All of these youth had been victims of child maltreatment and entered foster care before age 16. The youth were initially interviewed at age 17 or 18, while they were still state wards, and then again at age 19. Just over half (321) of the 603 foster youth who completed a follow-up interview were no longer in care, and their mean time since leaving care was 14.5 months.

Although few of these youth were currently living on the streets, 14 percent (45) had been homeless for at least one night since they aged out. Homelessness was defined as sleeping "in a place where people weren't meant to sleep," sleeping "in a homeless shelter," or not having "a regular residence in which to sleep." Two-thirds of the ever-homeless group had become homeless within six months of exiting and more than half (54 percent) had experienced more than one homeless episode.

A multivariate analysis using logistic regression showed that the best predictor of becoming homeless after aging out was whether a youth had repeatedly run away from an out-of-home care placement. Running away more than once was associated with an almost ninefold increase in the odds of becoming homeless. There was also a positive relationship between the odds of becoming homeless and the number of delinquent behaviors in which the youth had engaged. By contrast, feeling very close to at least one family member reduced the odds of becoming homeless by nearly 80 percent.

## Homelessness among Youthful Offenders

Every year, approximately 200,000 juveniles and young adults ages 10 to 24 years are released from secure detention or correctional facilities and reenter their communities. Most of these individuals are not high school graduates and most have never held a job. Many have physical, mental health, or substance abuse problems. A recent study of 1,800 arrested and detained youth found that nearly two-thirds of males and nearly three-quarters of females met diagnostic criteria for one or more psychiatric disorders (Teplin, Abram, McClelland, Dulcan, & Mericle, 2002). Yet, few youth will have received high quality services while in custody. Moreover, as if their transition back into society were not difficult enough, they are often returning to neighborhoods with high rates of poverty, unemployment, and crime (Mears & Travis, 2004).

Although relatively little is known about the process of reentry among this population, Altschuler and Brash (2004) have identified a number of challenges they are likely to confront, including problems with family and living arrangements. Some youth return to supportive homes; others do not. Still others are precluded from doing so by policies that prohibit individuals who have been convicted of certain drug offenses and other crimes from living in public or Section 8 housing (Popkin & Cunningham, 2001). Without a positive support network or stable living arrangement to which they can return, these juvenile and young adult offenders are at high risk of becoming homeless after their release. Once homeless, they may find themselves engaging in prostitution, selling or using drugs, or participating in other activities that could lead to their re-arrest.

There are no good estimates of the number of juveniles or young adults who become homeless upon release from detention or incarceration. Covenant House, a shelter for homeless youth in New York City, reports that approximately 30 percent of the youth they serve have been detained or incarcerated (New York City Association, 2005). These data also indicate that 68 percent had been living with family or guardians before incarceration. Eighty percent of the youthful offenders they served had neither completed high school nor obtained a GED, and 41 percent had a history of substance use. Interestingly, 49 percent also had a history of out-of-home care placement. In some instances, their child welfare case had been closed when they were detained or incarcerated and they had nowhere else to go upon release. This is true even if they had not yet turned 18 years of age because child welfare agencies are reluctant to take these youth back into their custody, especially if they have frequently "gone AWOL" or exhibited violent behavior (Riley, 2003; Travis, 2002).

Although most studies of youthful offenders have not included homelessness as an outcome measure, at least some research suggests that they are more likely to be homeless or precariously housed than other youth. Specifically, Feldman and Patterson (2003) compared 209 court-involved youth who participated in Workforce Investment Act (WIA) programs in Seattle–King County, Washington to 419 non-involved youth who participated in the same programs between July 1, 2000 and June 30, 2002. At program entry, the court-involved youth were less likely to be living with their parents and more likely to have no permanent address. Research on homeless adults has also consistently found high rates of prior incarceration, including incarceration while the adults were juveniles (Toro, 1998).

## Intervention Research

Much progress has been made in providing services to homeless youth and families since 1987 when the Stuart B. McKinney Homeless Assistance Act (Public Law 100-77) was signed into law. There now exist a vast array of shelters and other emergency services to address the diverse needs of homeless individuals and families, including homeless youth (Toro & Warren, 1999). Increased funding from the federal government as well as other sources has also led to the development of new interventions. Although many of these interventions are designed to help homeless youth become and remain housed, some include other components such as mental health services, alcohol and other drug treatment, or HIV/AIDS risk reduction.

Unfortunately, few of these new interventions have been formally evaluated, and when evaluations have been done, rigorous experimental or quasi-experimental designs have generally not been used. In fact, we are aware of only one rigorous evaluation of a program for homeless youth (Cauce et al., 1998). Below, we describe some of the interventions that have been evaluated, discuss the results of those evaluations, and suggest directions for future research on promising interventions, even if those interventions have yet to be tested among homeless youth.

### Case Management

Recognizing the multiple and diverse needs of homeless youth, Robertson and Toro (1999) advocated for a comprehensive and intensive case management approach that would address the unique needs of each homeless youth. Such an approach could be implemented in existing shelters and drop-in centers, and the relationship that developed between homeless youth and their case managers could become an important resource for the homeless youth and their families.

Intensive case management has been used successfully with homeless families and adults (Homan et al., 1993; James, Smith, & Mann, 1991; Toro et al., 1997). At least some research suggests that it might also be effective with homeless youth (Paradise et al., 2001). For example, Cauce et al. (1994) evaluated an intensive case management program for homeless youth in King County (Seattle), Washington. Youth were randomly assigned to either intensive or regular case management. Both groups experienced improved psychological well-being and a reduction in problem behaviors after the first three months of the intervention. However, youth who received intensive case management exhibited less aggression, fewer externalizing behaviors, and more satisfaction with their quality of life than youth who received "treatment as usual."

Another promising service model is Urban Peak Denver, which provides overnight shelter as well as a variety of other services to homeless youth between the ages of 15 and 21 years. A case manager conducts a needs assessment and develops a case plan that includes educational and employment goals. Youth can receive shelter for as long as they are moving forward on their case plans, and those who have been discharged are followed for six months. According to Urban Peak's Client Database, which tracks the housing outcomes of youth who receive services, the percentage who experienced a positive housing outcome (e.g., moving into their own apartment, obtaining permanent supportive housing, or returning to their family of origin) ranged from a low of 48 percent in 2000 to a high of 65 percent in 2003 (Burt, Pearson, & Montgomery, 2005).

### Family-Focused Interventions

Although many programs work primarily, if not exclusively, with the youth who are homeless, others have targeted the family. This makes sense given that youth often cite family conflict as the cause of their homelessness (Whitbeck et al., 2002; Robertson & Toro, 1999) and they often end up returning to their families of origin anyway (Toro & Janisse, 2004). Moreover, at least one study found that youth who return home to live with their parents experience more positive outcomes than other youth (Thompson, Pollio, & Bitner, 2000). Of course, this could simply reflect the fact that the youth who are able to reunify are the youth with the fewest problems.

In any event, there is relatively little evidence as to the effectiveness of family-focused interventions. One example that is sometimes cited is a 1998 study by Coco and Courtney. They described a family systems approach for preventing recidivism among runaway females. Unfortunately, their evaluation of the intervention was weak, being based on a single-case design with a simple pre and post assessment of family satisfaction to assess the impact of the intervention.

It should be recognized that there are cases in which a family-focused intervention would not be in a homeless youth's best interest. The most obvious example is a youth who has been severely neglected or abused. Other examples would include youth who have irreconcilable differences with their families, youth who have lost contact with their families, and youth whose families are homeless or precariously housed. In these cases, efforts must be made to find alternatives such as placement in foster care or independent living. Unfortunately, placement options may be limited, and may not represent an improvement in living situation (e.g., Benedict et al., 1994; Rosenthal, et al., 1991).

### Social Skills Training

In addition to their various service needs, many homeless youth lack what might be considered basic life skills, including meal preparation, household cleaning, time management, and budgeting (Aviles & Helfrich, 2004). Such skills are essential if they are to successfully transition out of homelessness and into successful adult functioning. Teare, Authier, and Peterson (1994) evaluated an intervention that used role-playing and a token economy to teach social skills to homeless youth receiving emergency shelter services. The assumption was that youth with social skills would experience fewer conflicts both during and after their shelter stay. The researchers reported that youth satisfaction with the program was generally high, that only 13 percent of the youth engaged in or expressed an intention to engage in self-destructive behavior, and that 69 percent did not exhibit any behaviors that were considered "out of control" (e.g., verbal or physical aggression). However, the researchers did not examine whether these outcomes reflected a change in behavior and their design did not include a comparison group that would have allowed them to assess the relationship between outcomes and participation.

### School-based Interventions

School contexts provide an opportunity to assess and address the needs of homeless youth. Although there is some evidence that school-based interventions can benefit school age children who are homeless with their families, we are not aware of any school-based interventions that target unaccompanied homeless youth. However, we believe that such interventions could easily be adapted for homeless youth, most of whom do attend school (even if not consistently). For example, the Empowerment Zone provided a mental health treatment package for low-income and homeless elementary school age children during summer school (Nabors, Proescher, & DeSilva, 2001). Trained teachers and mental health providers administered classroom and small group interventions and individual counseling, and parents were offered parenting classes. Results showed that parents reported a significant decrease in child behavioral problems following the intervention. Another study found favorable results for a classroom behavioral management system in which trained teacher assistants used bracelets to reinforce positive behavior among homeless elementary school age children (Nabors, Hines, & Monnier, 2002). Although these initial findings are promising, the programs need to be expanded and more thoroughly evaluated.

### Other Intervention Research

A number of other studies have also examined the outcomes of homeless youth who received shelter services. Several of these studies have analyzed data from the Runaway and Homeless Youth Management Information System (RHYMIS). RHYMIS includes information about all of the runaway and homeless youth served by the Family and Youth Services Bureau's (FYSB) Basic Center and Transitional Living and Street Outreach programs. RHYMIS includes demographic characteristics, services provided, and status at program exit (Family and Youth Services Bureau, 2006).

For example, Thompson et al. (2002) examined the outcomes of 261 runaway and homeless youth in four Midwestern states who received emergency shelter and crisis services, and compared their outcomes to the outcomes of 47 at-risk youth who received services from longer-term day treatment programs. Demographic information about the runaway and homeless youth was obtained from RHYMIS. Baseline data were collected from both groups at program intake. Follow-up data were collected six weeks post-discharge from the runaway or homeless youth and six weeks after intake from the comparison youth. Both the shelter youth and the day treatment youth experienced positive changes across six domains (runaway behavior, family relationships, school behavior, employment, sexual behavior, and self-esteem) and there were no significant group differences in the amount of change they experienced. Whether these improved outcomes persisted beyond the six-week observation period was not addressed.

## Prevention Research

In addition to research on how to best address the needs of youth who are already homeless, other studies have focused on preventive interventions. This interest in the prevention of homelessness among youth is a relatively recent development (e.g., Lindblom, 1996; Shinn & Baumohl, 1999; Toro, Lombardo, & Yapchai, 2002), and many interventions designed to prevent youth from ever becoming homeless (primary prevention) could just as easily be used to prevent youth who are currently homeless from becoming homeless again (secondary prevention; see Dalton, Elias, & Wandersman, 2007). Below, we discuss a number of issues regarding the prevention of homelessness. We focus on two groups of youth for whom the risk of becoming homeless appears to be particularly high: youth aging out of foster care and juvenile offenders.

### Family-focused preventive programs

Given that the youth frequently cite family conflict as the main reason for their homelessness, it should not be surprising that some homelessness prevention programs have focused on family dynamics and their impact on youth development. These programs include support groups for parents, parenting skills classes, and teaching conflict resolution skills. The assumption is that these programs will lead to improved family relationships, and thus prevent youth from becoming homeless.

One example of this approach is Project SAFE, a program operated by Cocoon House in Snohomish County, Washington (National Alliance to End Homelessness, 2002). Project SAFE provides three services to parents and other caretakers who are concerned about a youth's behavior: phone consultation, groups or workshops, and a resource library. Parents or caretakers can call and speak with a master's level therapist who works with parents to develop a plan of action and decide what community resources will be needed to implement the plan. Plans can include steps to help parents deal with personal problems that may be contributing to the conflict with their youth. Parents receive a follow-up call, usually one week later, to check on their situation and provide any additional referrals. Parents can also participate in support groups that focus on cognitive behavioral skills or educational workshops that seek to raise awareness of parental risk factors that contribute to problem behaviors. In both cases, the goal is to promote healthier family functioning and to prevent teen homelessness. In FY 2005–2006, Project SAFE served 194 parents/caretakers. Outcome data showed a significant increase in parents' perceived ability to cope with their youth as well as a significant decrease in parental perception of the youth needing to leave the home (Gagliano, 2006).

Another family-focused intervention that has the potential to reduce youth homelessness is multisystemic therapy (MST). Families are provided with intensive, home-based services. Master's-level therapists empower parents to control their adolescent's behavior by enhancing supervisory and monitoring skills. They also coordinate service provision among parents, individual counselors, teachers, peers, and others with a stake in the youth's future.

Numerous randomized controlled trials have shown that MST can reduce antisocial behavior, even years following the treatment among chronic juvenile delinquents (Henggeler et al., 1997; Henggeler, Pickrel, & Brondino, 1999). MST clients have significantly fewer out-of-home placements and decreased recidivism (Henggeler et al., 1997; Henggeler, Pickrel, & Brondino, 1999). MST has also been successfully adapted for a wide range of other target groups of youth, including those with mental disorders and chronic health problems (Henggeler, 2006).

Homeless youth and delinquent youth have many similarities, including an absence of adult supervision, a lack of consistent discipline, and association with deviant peers (Whitbeck & Hoyt, 1999). Thus, future research should examine ways to tailor such programs to directly address the needs of youth at risk for homelessness as well as evaluate the efficacy of such programs.

### *School-based preventive programs*

School-based programs have the potential to prevent homelessness in adolescents at risk to run away by providing prosocial niches outside the home where they may be less vulnerable to influences of deviant peers (Johanson, Duffy, & Anthony, 1996). In addition, youth may have more opportunity to develop positive social bonds that discourage deviant behavior often associated with family conflict (Hirschi, 1969). However, programs that target youth at risk for homelessness have yet to be developed or evaluated. In-school and after-school prevention programs have shown to be effective in reducing the risk of youth delinquency and substance abuse (Crank, Crank, & Christensen, 2003; Pierce & Shields, 1998), and thus, may be extended to reductions of homelessness.

*Preventing homelessness among youth aging out of foster care*

Preventing homelessness among youth aging out of care has long been a goal of federal policy. In fact, it was partly in response to several studies indicating that young adults who had aged out of care were at high risk of becoming homeless that Congress created the Title IV-E Independent Living Program in 1986 (Citizens' Committee for Children of New York City, 1984; New York State Council on Children and Families, 1984; Shaffer & Caton, 1984). For more than a decade, this was the primary source of funding available to states to prepare their foster youth for the transition to young adulthood. States could use their Title IV-E funds to provide housing services such as helping youth find a place to live; however, the law prohibited those funds from being used for transitional housing or independent living subsidies (Allen, Bonner, & Greenan, 1988; Barth, 1990).

The Title IV-E program was replaced when Congress passed the Foster Care Independence Act of 1999 (FCIA). Title I of this legislation established the John H. Chafee Foster Care Independence Program and doubled the federal allotment for state independent living programs that prepare foster youth for the transition to adulthood. These funds can be used to provide youth with a wide range of services, including services to promote education and employment, life skills training, health education, case management, and mentoring (Ansell, 2001). Two provisions, in particular, are relevant to the prevention of homeless among youth aging out of foster care. One allows states to use up to 30 percent of their federal Chafee funds to pay for the room and board of former foster youth who are at least 18 years old but not yet 21. The other requires states to use at least some portion of their funds to provide follow-up services to foster youth after they age out. In the past, such services could be provided at state option, but seldom were.

States are currently using their Chafee funds as well as funding from other sources to assist foster youth with housing. For example, the Massachusetts Department of Social Services uses some of its Chafee money to fund its Discharge Support Program, which helps foster youth with their first month's rent, security deposits, and other assistance, but the youth must be employed and able to pay their own rent. Connecticut's Community Housing Assistance Program (CHAPS) provides foster youth, age 18 and older who are working and enrolled in school, with a subsidy for rent and other living expenses. In fact, CHAPS is part of a continuum of housing options for Connecticut foster youth that also includes group homes for 14- to 16-year-olds and transitional living apartments for 16- and 17-year-olds. Illinois's Youth Housing Assistance Program targets youth who have aged out or will soon age out and are at risk of becoming homeless. The program provides housing advocacy services to help youth between the ages of 17.5 and 21 to secure and maintain stable housing as well as cash assistance to help with deposits, emergency rental assistance, temporary rental subsidies, and furniture and appliances.

Partnering is another strategy that states have implemented to address the housing needs of foster youth. Some states are taking advantage of federal legislation that made youth aging out of foster care eligible for housing assistance under the Department of Housing and Urban Development's Family Unification Program (FUP). In these states, child welfare agencies collaborate with housing authorities and/or community-based organizations to provide foster youth with time-limited housing vouchers over 18 months as well as other services. States with FUP programs for foster youth include New York, Colorado, Ohio, and California. In addition, some localities, including New York City, give foster youth priority access to Section 8 vouchers.

Most recently, Toro, et al. (2006) have proposed a comprehensive program that would both prevent homelessness and other negative outcomes among youth aging out of foster care and improve their emotional, behavioral, and socioeconomic well-being. The intervention would target foster youth transitioning to adulthood beginning at age 17. The program would be based on an intensive case management model and MST approaches and would involve the assessment of service needs across a number of domains, advocacy for the provision of services, coordination of service provision, and monitoring of service delivery. Small caseloads and frequent contact between case managers and youth would be important to keep youth who lack support from family members or other adults from falling through the cracks and because the quality of the client-case manager relationship is a key predictor of successful outcomes (Casey Family Programs, 2005; Thompson et al., 2006).

Youth would generally be referred to community resources, but program staff could provide services that are not available as well as direct funds to support independence (e.g., rent money to avoid eviction). In addition to service provision, the program would focus on empowering youth to make responsible life decisions. Toward this end, case managers would use a person-centered approach that emphasizes youth's strengths and preferences as well as motivational interviewing (Miller & Rollnick, 2002), a therapeutic technique that seems to be effective in promoting positive change behaviors even among multi-problem populations such as low-income, African American substance abusing mothers (Ondersma et a., 2005). Toro et al. (2006) have also recommended that the intervention be evaluated using random assignment within a longitudinal design, with data collected at baseline and then again at 6-month intefvals for 18 months in total. It is hoped that this intervention will be implemented and evaluated starting in late 2007.

Although independent living programs have been described (e.g., Hoge & Idalski, 2001), there is very little in the way of empirical data regarding their effectiveness. Due to another provision in the FCIA, states will soon be required to track the outcomes of current and former foster youth at ages 17, 19, and 21 and report those outcomes to the National Youth in Transition Database. Homelessness is one of the six outcomes about which they will be required to report.

Several other issues related to research on the prevention of homelessness among youth aging out of care also merit attention. First, findings from the Midwest study indicate that some foster youth, including those who run away repeatedly, are at even greater risk. Targeting those youth for preventive interventions both before and after they leave care would seem to make sense, and the impacts of those interventions should be formally evaluated. Second, the Midwest study also found that feeling close to at least one family member reduced the likelihood of becoming homeless. This has important practice implications for child welfare agencies. Specifically, it suggests that more attention should be paid to maintaining relationships between foster youth and members of their biological family, including grandparents and siblings. Such attention may, perhaps, even be appropriate when the family is somewhat dysfunctional, because, if we wish to prevent homelessness, some (even imperfect) support from family may be better than no support at all. What is not yet clear, and merits further investigation, is why closeness to family has what appears to be a protective effect. One possibility is that family members are a resource to whom foster youth can turn if there is no other place for them to stay. Another is that strong family ties reflect underlying individual or environmental resources that function to protect youth. In any event, interventions aimed at promoting family ties, where doing so is in a youth's best interest, should be developed and their ability to reduce the risk of homelessness should be explored.

Third, one of the most striking findings to emerge from the Midwest study was that the foster youth who were still in care at age 19 seemed to be faring better than their peers who had left. There were statistically significant differences across a number of domains, including college enrollment, access to health care, and criminal justice system involvement, and they consistently favored the 19-year-olds who were still in care. It remains to be seen whether those differences will persist once the foster youth who were still in care at age 19 have also exited. A third wave of survey data being collected from the foster youth when they are 21 years old will begin to address this question. For now, at least, the results suggest that one way to reduce the percentage of youth who become homeless after aging out of care would be to extend their eligibility until age 21, as is already the case in a few states like Illinois.

Fourth, an often overlooked provision of the FCIA requires states to use some of their federal training funds to assist foster parents, group home workers, and case managers do a better job of preparing foster youth for the challenges they face during the transition to adulthood. With respect to preventing homelessness, this means educating foster parents, group home workers, and case managers about how to help their foster youth find housing and remain housed. To this end, Casey Family Programs (2005) has published *It's My Life*, a series of guides, including one focused on housing, that contain practical strategies and on-line resources for adults working with these youth. Researchers could examine whether educating foster parents, group home workers, or case managers about these or other strategies leads to more stable housing and lower rates of homelessness.

Finally, although the FCIA requires states to use a portion of their Chafee funds to provide supportive services to foster youth after they age out, at least some research suggests that young adults may not take advantage of such services even when they are available (Lindblom, 1996). Just why this is the case is not well understood. It may be that young adults are reluctant to participate in services that they associate with foster care or that they object to the conditions of participation. It is also possible that such services are perceived to be of little help.

### *Preventing homelessness among youthful offenders*

As explained above, youthful offenders can become trapped in a cycle of homelessness and incarceration. If they return to the streets after their release, there is a strong chance they will become involved in the same behaviors that initially led to their arrest (National Alliance to End Homelessness, 2001). Thus, programs that assist youthful offenders to find housing and stay housed have the potential not only to prevent homelessness but also to reduce recidivism in the criminal justice system.

Unfortunately, although a number of programs have been developed to help youthful offenders with the process of reentry, not much is known about their effects on homelessness prevention. One exception is the young adult component of the Going Home Reentry Grant in Polk County, Iowa. This program targets youthful offenders, aged 17.5 to 20 years, who are leaving state training schools. A Community Transition Team works with the youthful offender to create an individualized wrap-around plan that addresses housing and other service needs. In some cases, this plan involves reunification with parents or other family members. In other cases, housing is secured using project funds. Although there has been no formal evaluation of the program, there are outcome data for the 47 youthful offenders (32 males and 15 females) who were served during a three-year grant period. Seventy-nine percent of the females and 84 percent of the males were able to establish a stable residence.

The housing needs of youthful offenders have also been addressed by programs that target youth aging out of foster care. For example, Lighthouse Youth Services in Cincinnati, Ohio, runs an independent living program that focuses on foster youth between the ages of 16 and 19 as well as a transitional living program that targets homeless youth between the ages of 18 and 25 (Kroner, 2005). However, a number of youthful offenders are also served each year. Referrals come from child welfare agencies, homeless shelters, juvenile courts, and community-based organizations. Lighthouse's housing continuum includes several housing options for youth: scattered-site apartments, supervised apartments, shared homes (for four or five youth), host homes, and boarding homes. Youth move from more structured to less restrictive living arrangements, depending on the level of support and services they need. Unfortunately, no formal outcome data have been collected to date.

### Employment programs as a prevention strategy

Although preventing homelessness is usually not a primary goal of employment programs, it stands to reason that youth and young adults are less likely to become homeless if they are self-sufficient and stably employed. From this perspective, several programs funded by the U.S. Department of Labor (DOL) could be considered preventive interventions. One example of this approach involves programs funded under the Workforce Investment Act (WIA). Low- income youth between the ages of 14 and 21 are eligible to receive WIA-funded services if they face one or more recognized barriers to completing school and attaining economic self-sufficiency. These services allow youth to continue their education and pursue employment. Youth aging out of foster care, homeless youth, and youth who have been involved with the juvenile justice system are among WIA's target populations.

In addition to these WIA services, DOL also funds a number of other workforce development and support services that can help prevent homelessness among at-risk youth. Job Corps is the largest and most comprehensive residential vocational training and education program for at-risk youth between the ages of 16 and 24. Youth aging out of foster care and runaway or homeless youth are among the target populations of Job Corps. In a multi-year evaluation of the program, eligible youth were randomly assigned to a treatment group that received Job Corps services or a control group that did not. They were interviewed at the time of enrollment and then again at 12, 30, and 48 months after random assignment. The researchers did not look specifically at homelessness. However, Job Corps participation was related to independent living at the 48-month interview. A slightly smaller percentage of program group members were living with their parents, and a slightly larger percentage were living with a partner and reported being the head of the household (Burghart et al., 2001; Schochet, Burghardt, & Glazerman, 2001).

Likewise, DOL's Youth Offender Demonstration Program (YODP) is a labor-focused reentry program for youth ages 14 to 24 returning to their communities from detention or incarceration and who are already involved in the juvenile/criminal justice system, are gang members, or are at risk of gang or court involvement. Of particular relevance to homelessness prevention, some YODP sites are working with nonprofit housing programs. Unfortunately, no formal evaluation of the YODP has ever been completed.

## Theoretical Developments

Haber and Toro (2004) provide a thorough review of various theories that have been applied in recent research on homeless children and youth. The theories most relevant to homeless youth include variants based on social learning theory (Bandura, 1977; Patterson, 1982). The Risk Amplification Model (RAM), one of the most widely applied of these variants, posits that noxious early environments, including poor parenting practices in the home, put youth at risk for homelessness and that being homeless further "amplifies" the risk for poor outcomes among such youth (Paradise et al., 2001; Whitbeck & Hoyt, 1999). The RAM suggests that risk is amplified by homelessness through victimization on the streets, engagement in subsistence strategies (e.g., stealing food, prostitution), association with deviant peers and adults, and other negative experiences.

Cross-sectional studies provide some empirical support for the RAM. For example, homeless youth tend to come from more deleterious home environments and experience higher rates of victimization compared to matched housed youth (Robertson & Toro, 1999). In a more direct test of the RAM, Whitbeck, Hoyt, and Yoder (1999) found that affiliation with deviant peers, deviant subsistence strategies, risky sexual behaviors, and substance use amplified the effects of a negative family environment on victimization and depressive symptoms among homeless female youth (but not among homeless males).

There is also some support from longitudinal studies. Using the Detroit-based dataset described earlier, Lombardo and Toro (2005) found that family conflict was related to heightened self-reported symptomatology and deviant peer associations, and that both of these were associated with risky sexual behaviors and substance abuse six months later. Analyses testing the RAM over longer periods of time (up to 6.5 years) are currently being conducted by Toro and colleagues.

## CONCLUSION

Much has been learned since Robertson and Toro reviewed the literature on homeless youth for the 1998 National Symposium on Homelessness Research. Yet many important questions remain unanswered. Several areas, in particular, could be the focus of future research.

1. Many risk factors associated with youth homelessness have been identified. Examples include family conflict, aging out of foster care, and identifying as GLBT. What is not well understood is how these factors operate. That is, what are the pathways leading to homelessness among youth with these risk factors? Future research needs to explore these pathways and consider how other factors (e.g., access to and quality of services received during childhood or early adolescence, growing up in a family that experienced homelessness) either aggravate or mitigate those risks.

2. Although many interventions have been developed to address the diverse needs of homeless youth, the vast majority have not been evaluated. As a result, we know relatively little about what works. Closing this gap will require methodologically

sound studies that include control (or at least comparison) groups in experimental (or at least quasi-experimental) research designs.

3. Researchers should examine whether certain types of interventions are more effective with some homeless youth than others (e.g., runaway youth vs. throwaway youth vs. systems youth; street youth vs. shelter youth; rural youth vs. urban youth; youth homeless with their families vs. youth homeless on their own). Groups that are likely to have unique needs and hence for whom unique interventions may be merited include LGBT youth and youth who are pregnant or parenting.

4. Broadly speaking, there are two types of prevention strategies: universal approaches that seek to promote positive youth development, and more targeted approaches that focus on youth thought to be at greatest risk. Research is needed on both types of strategies to determine whether both can prevent homelessness and other negative outcomes among youth.

5. Because so many homeless youth cite family conflict as the reason for their homelessness, more attention should be paid to prevention and intervention strategies that focus on the family. Strategies might involve improving communication, developing conflict resolution skills, and increasing understanding of adolescent development. It is important for social workers and others assisting homeless youth and those at risk for homelessness (such as youth aging out of foster care) to help these youth connect with family members who might assist them in the future (often after the workers end their assistance). It is also important that "family" be broadly defined to include not only biological relatives but also others (e.g., fictive kin, close friends) who youth regard as part of their family.

6. Although interventions may benefit from tapping into familial resources, reunification may not be a good option for certain homeless youth. More research is needed to determine the individual and environmental circumstances that argue for and against familial reunification. Interventions should be developed using this information.

7. Not much is known about why so few homeless youth, whether in shelters or on the streets, use human services available to them (aside from short-term use of shelters for some). Similar to recent studies of homelessness among adults (e.g., Acosta & Toro, 2000), future research needs to ask the homeless youth themselves about their experiences and satisfaction with various services. Most likely, attention will be needed to alter approaches used by existing programs and services to make them more accessible and "user friendly."

8. Most existing research on homeless youth has focused on the "literally homeless," those who have spent at least some time in homeless shelters, on the streets, or living in other unconventional settings (Toro, 1998). Future research should also focus on youth who "couch surf" or who are otherwise precariously housed. This group may be larger than, and at equal risk as, those who are literally homeless.

9. Developing effective prevention and intervention strategies requires a clearer understanding of what youth experience before and after they become homeless. Toward that end, we need more quantitative and qualitative research to explore the outcomes of homeless youth, including the pathways through which they exit, or fail to exit, homelessness. More longitudinal studies are also needed to examine how environmental, family, and individual factors affect both their short- term and long-

term outcomes. Disentangling the effects of these different types of factors will also require multivariate data analytic techniques.

10. Preventive interventions with youth aging out of foster care and youthful offenders should be expanded. Although some programs exist, little firm empirical evidence exists on what works. Broader and better designed preventive interventions are needed.

11. It appears that few if any of the studies reviewed above directly involved homeless or other at- risk youth in the research process. We believe that such youth should, ideally, be consulted at every stage, including the design of the study, the development of survey instruments or interview protocols, the collection of data, the interpretation of results, and the dissemination of findings. Not only can involving homeless or other at-risk youth in the research process improve the quality of the research (Jason et al., 2004), but it may increase the likelihood that the research leads to better policy and practice. Similarly, there should be more collaboration between service providers and researchers, both to improve the quality of the research and the ability for the research to be applied to policy and intervention.

12. With regard to theoretical approaches, there is a need to move beyond the pervasive deficit orientation in much of the research toward more positive, resilience-based frameworks. There is also a need to more carefully consider the developmental contexts in which youth who are homeless or at risk for homelessness exist and to develop a better international understanding of homeless youth.

## REFERENCES

Acosta, O., & Toro, P. A. (2000). Let's ask the homeless people themselves: A needs assessment based on a probability sample of adults. *American Journal of Community Psychology, 28,* 343–366.

Ahmed, S., & Toro, P. A. (2004). *Religiosity and ethnicity as moderators of substance abuse in at-risk adolescents.* Unpublished manuscript, Department of Psychology, Wayne State University.

Allen, M., Bonner, K., & Greenan, L. (1988). Federal legislative support for independent living. *Child Welfare, 67,* 19–32.

Altschuler, D. M., & Brash, R. (2004). Adolescent and teenage offenders confronting the challenges and opportunities of reentry. *Youth Violence and Juvenile Justice, 2,* 72–87.

Ansell, D. (2001). Where are we going tomorrow: Independent living practice. In K. A. Nollan & A. C. Downs (Eds.), *Preparing youth for long-term success: Proceedings from the Casey Family Program National Independent Living Forum* (pp.35–44). Washington DC: Child Welfare League of America.

Aviles, A., & Helfrich, C. (2004). Life skills service needs: Perspectives of homeless youth. *Journal of Youth and Adolescence, 33,* 331–338.

Baer, J., Ginzler, J., & Peterson, P. (2003). DSM-IV alcohol and substance abuse and dependence in homeless youth. *Journal of Studies on Alcohol, 64,* 5–14.

Bandura, A. (1977). *Social learning theory.* Englewood Cliffs, NJ: Prentice-Hall.

Barth, R. (1990). On their own: The experiences of youth after foster care. *Child and Adolescent Social Work, 7,* 419–440.

Barwick, M. A., & Siegel, L. S. (1996). Learning difficulties in adolescent clients of a shelter for runaway and homeless street youths. *Journal of Research on Adolescence, 6,* 649–670.

Benedict, M. I., Zuravin, S., Brandt, D., & Abbey, H. (1994). Types and frequency of child maltreatment by family foster care providers in an urban population. *Child Abuse & Neglect, 18,* 577–585.

Boesky, L. M., Toro, P. A., & Bukowski, P. A. (1997). Differences in psychosocial factors among older and younger homeless adolescents found in youth shelters. *Journal of Prevention and Intervention in the Community, 15*(2), 19–36.

Boesky, L. M., Toro, P. A., & Wright, K. L. (1995, November). *Maltreatment in a probability sample of homeless adolescents: A subgroup comparison.* Presented at the Annual Meeting of the American Public Health Association, San Diego, CA.

Buckner, J. C., Bassuk, E. L., & Weinreb, L. E. (2001). Predictors of academic achievement among homeless and low-income housed children. *Journal of School Psychology, 39,* 45–69.

Buckner, J. C., Bassuk, E. L., Weinreb, L. E., & Brooks, M. (1999). Homelessness and its relation to the mental health and behavior of low-income school-age children. *Developmental Psychology, 35,* 246–257.

Burghardt, J, Schochet, P., McConnell, S., Johnson, T., Gritz, M. R.., Glazerman, S., Homrighausen, J., & Jackson, R. (2001). *Does Job Corps Work? Summary of the National Job Corps Study* (Report 8140-530). Princeton, NJ: Mathematica Policy Research, Inc.

Burt, M., Aron, L. Y., Lee, E., & Valente, J. (2001). *Helping America's homeless: Emergency shelter or affordable housing?* Washington, DC: The Urban Institute.

Burt, M., Pearson, C., & Montgomery, A. (2005). *Strategies for preventing homelessness.* Washington, DC: U.S. Department of Housing and Urban Development, Office of Policy Development and Research.

Casey Family Programs. (2005). *A guide for transition services from Casey Family Programs.* Seattle, WA: Casey Family Programs.

Cauce, A. M., Morgan, C. J., Wagner, V., Moore, E., Sy, J., Wurzbacher, K., et al. (1994). Effectiveness of intensive case management for homeless adolescents: Results of a 3-month follow-up. *Journal of Emotional and Behavioral Disorders, 2,* 219–227.

Cauce, A. M., Paradise, M., Embry, L., Morgan, C., Theofelis, J., Heger, J., & Wagner, V. (1998). Homeless youth in Seattle: Youth characteristics, mental health needs, and intensive case management. In M. Epstein, K. Kutash, & A. Duchnowski (Eds.), *Outcomes for children and youth with emotional and behavioral disorders and their families: Programs and evaluation best practices.* Austin, TX: PRO-ED.

Cauce, A. M., Paradise. M., Ginzler, J. A., Embry, L., Morgan, C. J., Lohr, Y., & Theofelis, J. (2000). The characteristics and mental health of homeless adolescents: Age and gender differences. *Journal of Emotional and Behavioral Disorders, 8*(4), 230–239.

Citizens' Committee for Children of New York. (1984). *Foster care exit: Ready or not.* New York: Author.

Clark, R., & Robertson, M. J. (1996). *Surviving for the moment: A report on homeless youth in San Francisco.* Berkeley: Alcohol Research Group.

Cochran, B. N., Stewart, A. J., Ginzler, J. A., & Cauce, A. M. (2002). Challenges faced by homeless sexual minorities: Comparison of gay, lesbian, and transgender homeless adolescents with their heterosexual counterparts. *American Journal of Public Health, 92,* 773–777.

Coco, E. L., & Courtney, L. J. (1998). A family systems approach for preventing adolescent runaway behavior. *Adolescence, 33*(130), 485–496.

Courtney, M. E., Piliavin, I., Grogan-Kaylor, A., & Nesmith, A. (2001). Foster youth transitions to adulthood: A longitudinal view of youth leaving care. *Child Welfare, 80,* 685–717.

Courtney, M., Dworsky, A., Ruth, G., Keller, T., Havlicek, J., & Bost, N. (2005). *Midwest evaluation of the adult functioning of former foster youth: Outcomes at age 19.* Unpublished report, Chapin Hall Center for Children, Chicago.

Crank, J., Crank, J., & Christensen, W. (2003). The Ada Sheriffs Youth Foundation: The development of a decentralized youth program. *Journal of Criminal Justice, 31,* 34 1–350.

Dalton, J. H., Elias, M. J., & Wandersman, A. (2007). *Community psychology: Linking individuals and communities* (2nd ed.). Stamford, CT: Wadsworth.

Family and Youth Services Bureau (2006). *Fact sheet: Runaway and Homeless Youth Management Information System.* Retrieved on November 29, 2006, from http://www.acf.hhs.gov/programs/fysb/content/youthdivision/resources/rhymsfactsheet.htm

Farrow, J. A., Deisher, R. W., Brown, R., Kulig, J. W., & Kipke, M. D. (1992). Health and health needs of homeless and runaway youth. A position paper of the Society for Adolescent Medicine. *Journal of Adolescent Health, 13,* 717–726.

Feitel, B., Margetson, N., Chamas, R., & Lipman, C. (1992). Psychosocial background and behavioral and emotional disorders of homeless and runaway youth. *Hospital and Community Psychiatry, 43,* 155–159.

Feldman, D., & Patterson, D. (2003). *Characteristics and program experiences of youthful offenders within Seattle-King County Workforce Investment Act (WIA) Programs.* Seattle, WA: Workforce Development Council of Seattle-King County Research & Development Committee.

Firdion, J. (2004). Foster care. In D. Levinson (Ed.), *Encyclopedia of homelessness* (pp. 167–171). Thousand Oaks, CA: Sage.

Fowler, P. J., Ahmed, S. A., Tompsett, C. J., Jozefowicz-Simbeni, D. M., & Toro, P. A. (2006). *Community violence, race, religiosity, and substance abuse from adolescence to emerging adulthood.* Unpublished manuscript, Department of Psychology, Wayne State University.

Fowler, P. J., Toro, P. A., Tompsett, C. J., & Hobden, K. (2006). *Youth aging out of foster care in Southeast Michigan: A follow-up study.* Report presented to the Michigan Department of Human Services.

Fronczak, E., & Toro, P. A. (2003). *Posttraumatic stress disorder in homeless and other high-risk urban adolescents.* Unpublished manuscript, Department of Psychology, Wayne State University.

Gagliano, N. (2006). *Cocoon House Prevention Program 2005–2006 year-end report.* Unpublished manuscript.

Greenblatt, M., & Robertson, M. J. (1993). Homeless adolescents: Lifestyle, survival strategies and sexual behaviors. *Hospital and Community Psychiatry, 44,* 1177–1180.

Greene, J. M. & Ringwalt, C. L. (1998). Pregnancy among three national samples of runaway and homeless youth. *Journal of Adolescent Health 23,* 370–377.

Haber, M. & Toro, P. A. (2003). *Parent-adolescent violence as a predictor of adolescent outcomes.* Poster session presented at the Biennial Conference on Community Research and Action, Las Vegas, NM.

Haber, M., & Toro, P. A. (2004). Homelessness among families, children and adolescents: An ecological-developmental perspective. *Clinical Child and Family Psychology Review, 7,* 123–164.

Hammer, H., Finkelhor, D. & Sedlak, A. (2002, October). Runaway/Thrownaway children: National estimates and characteristics. *National Incident Studies of Missing, Abducted, Runaway, and Thrownaway Children.* Washington, DC: U.S. Department of Justice, Office of Justice Programs, Office of Juvenile Justice and Delinquency Prevention.

Heinze, H., Toro, P. A., & Urberg, K. A. (2004). Delinquent behaviors and affiliation with male and female peers. *Journal of Clinical Child and Adolescent Psychology, 33,* 336–346.

Henggeler, S. W. (2006, September). *Multisystemic therapy approaches.* Presented at Wayne State University Children's Bridge and Children's Hospital of Michigan Children's Conference, Promoting the Well-Being of Children and Youth in Urban America: Best Practices to Next Practices, Detroit, MI.

Henggeler, S. W., Melton, G. B., Brondino, M. J., Scherer, D. G., & Hanley, J. H. (1997). Multisystemic therapy with violent and chronic juvenile offenders and their families: The role of treatment fidelity in successful dissemination. *Journal of Consulting and Clinical Psychology 65,* 821–833.

Henggeler, S. W., Pickrel, S. G., & Brondino, M. J. (1999). Multisystemic treatment of substance abusing and dependent delinquents: Outcomes, treatment fidelity, and transportability. *Mental Health Services Research. 1,* 17 1–184.

Hirschi, T. (1969). *Causes of delinquency.* Berkeley: University of California Press.

Hoge, J., & Idalski, A. (2001). How Boysville of Michigan specifies and evaluates its supervised independent living program. In K. A. Nollan & A. C. Downs (Eds.), *Preparing youth for longterm success: Proceedings from the Casey Family Program National Independent Living Forum* (pp. 83–93). Washington DC: Child Welfare League of America.

Homan, S. M., Flick, L. H., Heaton, T. M., & Mayer, M. (1993). Reaching beyond crisis management: Design and implementation of extended shelter based services for chemically dependent homeless women and their children: St. Louis. *Alcoholism Treatment Quarterly, 10,* 101–112.

James, W., Smith, A., & Mann, R. (1991). Educating homeless children: Interprofessional case management. *Childhood Education, 67(5),* 305–308.

Jason, L. A., Keys, C. B., Suarez-Balcazar, Y., Taylor, R. R., & Davis, M. I. (2004). *Participatory community research: Theories and methods in action,* Washington, DC: American Psychological Association.

Johanson, C., Duffy, F. F., & Anthony, J. C. (1996). Associations between drug use and behavioral repertoire in urban youths. *Addiction, 91,* 523–534.

Kipke, M. D., Montgomery, S., & MacKenzie, R. G. (1993). Substance use among youth seen at a community-based health clinic. *Journal of Adolescent Health, 14*(4), 289–294.

Kipke, M. D., O'Connor, S., Palmer, R., & MacKenzie, R. G. (1995). Street youth in Los Angeles: Profile of a group at high risk for human immunodeficiency virus infection. *Archives of Pediatrics & Adolescent Medicine, 149,* 513–519.

Kroner, M. (2005, June). *Housing options for youth aging out of foster care.* Paper presented at the Biennial Conference on Community Research and Action, Champaign, IL.

Kruks, G. (1991). Gay and lesbian homeless/street youth: Special issues and concerns. *Journal of Adolescent Health, 12,* 515–518.

Lindblom, E. N. (1996). Preventing homelessness. In J. Baumohl (Ed.), *Homelessness in America* (pp. 187–200). Phoenix: Oryx.

Lombardo, S., & Toro, P. A. (2004). *Risky sexual behaviors and substance abuse among homeless and other at-risk adolescents.* Unpublished manuscript, Department of Psychology, Wayne State University, Detroit, MI.

MacLean, M. G., Embry, L. E., & Cauce, A. M. (1999). Homeless adolescents' paths to separation from family: Comparison of family characteristics, psychological adjustment, and victimization. *Journal of Community Psychology, 27*(2), 179–187.

MacLean, M. G., Paradise, M. J., & Cauce, A. M. (1999). Substance use and psychological adjustment in homeless adolescents: A test of three models. *American Journal of Community Psychology, 27*(3), 405–427.

McCaskill, P. A., Toro, P. A., & Wolfe, S. M. (1998). Homeless and matched housed adolescents: A comparative study of psychopathology. *Journal of Clinical Child Psychology, 27,* 306–319.

Mears, D. P., & Travis, J. (2004). Youth development and reentry. *Youth Violence and Juvenile Justice, 2,* 3–20.

Milburn, N. G., Ayala, G., Rice, E., Batterham, P., & Rotheram-Borus, M. J. (2006). Discrimination and exiting homelessness among homeless adolescents. *Cultural Diversity & Ethnic Minority Psychology, 12,* 658–672.

Milburn, N. G., Rotheram-Borus, M. J., Rice, E., Mallet, S., & Rosenthal, D. (2006). Cross-national variations in behavioral profiles among homeless youth. *American Journal of Community Psychology, 37,* 63–76.

Miller, W. R., & Rollnick, S. (2002). *Motivational interviewing: Preparing people for change* (2nd ed.). New York: Guilford

Molnar, B. E., Shade, S. B., Kral, A. H., Booth, R. E., & Watters, J. K. (1998). Suicidal behavior and sexual/physical abuse among street youth. *Child Abuse and Neglect, 22*(3), 213–222.

Nabors, L. A., Hines, A., & Monnier, L. (2002). Evaluation of an incentive system at a summer camp for youth experiencing homelessness. *Journal of Prevention & Intervention in the Community Special Issue: Community interventions, 24,* 17–31.

Nabors, L., Proescher, E., & DeSilva, M. (2001). School based mental health prevention activities for homeless and at-risk youth. *Child & Youth Forum, 30,* 3–18.

National Alliance to End Homelessness. (2001). *North Dakota Department of Corrections and Rehabilitation.* Retrieved on November 29, 2006, from *http://www.endhome lessness.org/content/article/detail/1127*

National Alliance to End Homelessness. (2002). *Project SAFE, Everett, WA.* Retrieved on November 29, 2006, from http://www.endhomelessness.org/content/article/detail/1114

New York City Association of Homeless and Street-Involved Youth Organizations. (2005). *State of the city's homeless youth report.* New York: Author.

New York State Council on Children and Families. (1984). *Meeting needs of homeless youth.* Albany: Author.

Ondersma, S. J., Chase, S. K., Svikis, D. S., & Schuster, C. R. (2005). Computer-based brief motivational interviewing for perinatal drug use. *Journal of Substance Abuse Treatment, 28*(4), 305–312.

Owen, G., Heineman, J., Minton, C., Lloyd, B., Larsen, P., & Zierman, C. (1998). *Minnesota statewide survey of persons without permanent shelter: Vol. II, Unaccompanied youth.* St. Paul, MN: Wilder Foundation.

Paradise, M., Cauce, A. M., Ginzler, J., Wert, S., Wruck, K., Brooker, M. (2001). The role of relationships in developmental trajectories of homeless and runaway youth. In B. Sarason & S. Duck (Eds.), *Personal relationships: Implications for clinical and community psychology* (pp. 159–179). Chichester, UK: Wiley.

Patterson, G. R. (1982). *Coercive family process.* Eugene, OR: Castalia.

Pierce, L. H., & Shields, N. (1998). The Be a Star community-based after-school program: Developing resiliency factors in high-risk preadolescent youth. *Journal of Community Psychology, 26,* 175– 183.

Popkin, S. J., & Cunningham, M. K. (2001, July). *CHA relocation counseling assessment: Interim report.* Washington, DC: The Urban Institute.

Powers, J. L., Eckenrode, J., & Jaklitsch, B. (1990). Maltreatment among runaway and homeless youth. *Child Abuse and Neglect, 14*(1), 87–98.

Remafedi, G. (1987). Male homosexuality: The adolescent's perspective. *Pediatrics, 79,* 326– 330).

Rew, L., Thomas, N., Horner, S. D., Resnick, M. D., & Beuhring, T. (2001). Correlates of recent suicide attempts in a triethnic group of adolescents. *Journal of Nursing Scholarship, 33(4),* 36 1–367.

Riley, J. (2003, August 3). Freed into limbo: Laws, lack of preparation leave ex-cons struggling to stay straight. *Newsday,* p A03.

Ringwalt, C. L., Greene, J. M., & Iachan, R. (1994, November). *Prevalence and characteristics of youth in households with runaway and homeless experience.* Paper presented at Annual Meeting of the American Public Health Association, Washington, DC.

Ringwalt, C. L., Greene, J. M., Robertson, M., & McPheeters, M. (1998). The prevalence of homelessness among adolescents in the United States. *American Journal of Public Health, 88,* 1325–1329.

Robertson, M. J. (1989). *Homeless youth in Hollywood: Patterns of alcohol use.* Report to the National Institute on Alcohol Abuse and Alcoholism (No. C5 1). Berkeley, CA: Alcohol Research Group.

Robertson, M. J. (1991). Homeless youth: An overview of recent literature. In J. H. Kryder-Coe, L. M. Salamon, & J. M. Molnar (Eds.), *Homeless children and youth: A new American dilemma* (pp. 33–68). London: Transaction Publishers.

Robertson, M. J. (1992). The prevalence of mental disorder among homeless people. In R. I. Jahiel (Ed.), *Homelessness: A prevention oriented approach* (pp. 5 7–86). Baltimore: Johns Hopkins University Press.

Robertson, M. J., & Toro, P. A. (1999). Homeless youth: Research, intervention, and policy. In L. B. Fosburg & D. L. Dennis (Eds.), *Practical lessons: The 1998 National Symposium on Homelessness Research* (pp. 3-1–3-32). Washington DC: U.S. Department of Housing and Urban Development and U.S. Department of Health and Human Services.

Rosenthal, D., Mallett, S., Gurrin, L., Milburn, N. G., & Rotheram-Borus, M. J. (2007). Changes over time among homeless young people in drug dependency, mental illness and their co-morbidity. *Psychology, Health & Medicine, 12*, 70–80.

Rosenthal, J. A., Motz, J. K., Edmonson, D. A., & Groze, V. (1991). A descriptive study of abuse and neglect in out-of-home placement. *Child Abuse and Neglect, 15*, 249–260.

Rotheram-Borus, M. J. (1991). Homeless youths and HIV infection. *American Psychologist, 46*, 1188–1197.

Rotheram-Borus, M. J. (1993). Suicidal behavior and risk factors among runaway youths. *American Journal of Psychiatry, 150*(1), 103–107.

Rotheram-Borus, M. J., Mahler, K. A., Koopman, C., Langabeer, K. (1996). Sexual abuse history and associated multiple risk behavior in adolescent runaways. *American Journal of Orthopsychiatry, 66*(3), 390–400.

Rotheram-Borus, M. J., Meyer-Bahlberg, H. F. L., Koopman, C., Rosario, M., Exner, T. M., Henderson, et al. (1992a). Lifetime sexual behaviors among runaway males and females. *Journal of Sex Research, 29*, 15–29.

Rotheram-Borus, M. J., Meyer-Bahlberg, H. F. L., Koopman, C., Rosario, M., Exner, T. M., Henderson, R., et al. (1992b). Lifetime sexual behaviors among predominantly minority male runaways and gay/bisexual adolescents in New York City. *AIDS Education & Prevention, Supplement (Fall)*, 34–42.

Rothman, J., & David, T. (1985). *Status offenders in Los Angeles County: Focus on runaway and homeless youth.* Bush Program in Child and Family Policy. Los Angeles: University of California.

Roy, E., Haley, N., Leclerc, P., Cedras, L., Blais, L., & Boivin, J. F. (2003). Drug injection among street youths in Montreal: Predictors of initiation. *Journal of Urban Health, 80*, 92–105.

Roy, E., Haley, N., Leclerc, P., Sochanski, B., Boudreau, J., & Boivin, J. F. (2004). Mortality in a cohort of street youth in Montreal. *Journal of the American Medical Association, 292*, 569–575.

Roy, E., Lemire, N., Haley, N., Bolvin, J. F., Frappier, J.Y., & Claessens, C. (1998). Injection drug use among street youth: A dynamic process. *Canadian Journal of Public Health, 89*, 23 9–240.

Ryan, K. D., Kilmer, R. P., & Cauce, A. M., Watanabe, H., & Hoyt, D. R. (2000). Psychological consequences of child maltreatment in homeless adolescents: Untangling the unique effects of maltreatment and family environment. *Child Abuse & Neglect 24*(3): 333–3 52.

Schochet, P., Burghardt, J., & Glazerman, S. (2001). *National Job Corps Study: The impacts of Job Corps on participants' employment and related outcomes.* Princeton, N.J.: Mathematica Policy Research, Inc.

Shaffer, D., & Caton, C. (1984). *Runaway and homeless youth in New York City.* New York: New York State Psychiatric Institute and Columbia College of Physicians and Surgeons.

Shinn, M. (1992). Homelessness: What is a psychologist to do? *American Journal of Community Psychology, 20*, 1–24.

Shinn, M., & Baumohl, J. (1999). Rethinking the prevention of homelessness. In L. B. Fosburg & D. L. Dennis (Eds.), *Practical lessons: The 1998 National Symposium on Homelessness Research.* Washington DC: U.S. Department of Housing and Urban Development and U.S. Department of Health and Human Services.

Smollar, J. (1999). Homeless youth in the United States: Description and developmental issues. In Raffaelli, M. & Larson, R. W. (Eds.), *Homeless and working youth around the world: Exploring developmental issues. New directions for child and adolescent development, no. 85* (pp. 47–5 8). San Francisco: Jossey-Bass.

Solorio, M. R., Milburn, N. G., Weiss, R. E., & Batterham, P. J. (2006). Newly homeless youth STD testing patterns over time. *Journal of Adolescent Health, 39,* 443e9-443e16.

Staller, K. M., & Kirk, S. A. (1997). Unjust freedom: The ethics of client self-determination in runaway youth shelters. *Child & Adolescent Social Work Journal, 14*(3), 223–242.

Stewart, A. J., Steiman, M., Cauce, A. M., Cochron, B. N., Whitbeck, L. B., & Hoyt, D. R. (2004). Victimization and posttraumatic stress disorder among homeless adolescents. *Journal of the American Academy of Child and Adolescent Psychiatry 43,* 325–331.

Teare, J. F., Authier, K., & Peterson, R. (1994). Differential patterns of post-shelter placement as a function of problem type and severity. *Journal of Child & Family Studies, 3(1),* 7–22.

Tenner, A. D., Trevithick, L. A., Wagner, V., & Burch, R. (1998). Seattle YouthCare's prevention, intervention and education program: A model of care for HIV-positive, homeless, and at-risk youth. *Journal of Adolescent Health, 23,* 96–106.

Teplin, L. 'A., Abram, K. M., McClelland, G. M., Dulcan, M. K., & Mericle, A. A. (2002), Prevalence of psychiatric disorders in youth in juvenile detention. *Archives of General Psychiatry, 59,* 1133– 1143.

Thompson, S. J., Kost, K. A., & Pollio, D. E. (2003). Examining risk factors associated with family reunification for runaway youth: Does ethnicity matter? *Family Relations, 52,* 296–304.

Thompson, S. J., McManus, H., Lantry, J., Windsor, L., & Flynn, P. (2006). Insights from the street: Perceptions of services and providers by homeless young adults. *Evaluation and Program Planning, 29,* 34–43.

Thompson, S. J., Pollio, D. E., & Bitner, L. (2000). Outcomes for adolescents using runaway and homeless youth services. *Journal of Human Behavior in the Social Environment, 3*(1), 79–97.

Thompson, S. J., Pollio, D. E., Constantine, J., Reid, D., & Nebbitt, V. (2002). Short-term outcomes for youth receiving runaway and homeless shelter services. *Research on Social Work Practice, 12,* 589–603.

Thompson, S. J., Safyer, A. J., & Pollio, D. E. (2001). Differences and predictors of family reunification among subgroups of runaway youths using shelter services. *Social Work Research, 25*(3), 163– 172.

Thrane, L. E., & Yoder, K. A. (2000). Comparing rural and urban runaway and homeless adolescents: Age at first run, deviant subsistence strategies, and street victimization. Poster session presented at the Society for Research on Adolescence, Chicago, IL.

Tompsett, C. J., Toro, P. A., Guzicki, M., Manrique, M., & Zatakia, J. (2006). Homelessness in the United States: Assessing changes in prevalence and public opinion, 1993–2001. *American Journal of Community Psychology, 37*(1/2), 47–61.

Toro, P. A. (1998). Homelessness. In A. S. Bellack & M. Hersen (Eds.), *Comprehensive clinical psychology: Vol. 9. Applications in diverse populations* (pp. 119–135). New York: Pergamon.

Toro, P. A., Fowler, P. J., Miles, B. W., Jozefowicz-Simbeni, D. M. H., & Hobden, K. (2006). *Bridging Resilience through Intervention, Guidance, and Empowerment (BRIGE): An intervention for aging out foster youth in Southeast Michigan.* Unpublished manuscript, Department of Psychology, Wayne State University.

Toro, P. A., & Goldstein, M. S. (2000, August). *Outcomes among homeless and matched housed adolescents: A longitudinal comparison.* Presented at the 108th Annual Convention of the American Psychological Association, Washington, DC.

Toro, P. A., Goldstein, M. S., Rowland, L. L., Bellavia, C. W., Wolfe, S. M., Thomas, D. M., & Acosta, O. (1999). Severe mental illness among homeless adults and its association with longitudinal outcomes. *Behavior Therapy, 30,* 431–452.

Toro, P. A., & Janisse, H. C. (2004). Homelessness, patterns of. In D. Levinson (Ed.), *Encyclopedia of homelessness* (pp. 244–250). Thousand Oaks, CA: Sage.

Toro, P. A., Lombardo, S., & Yapchai, C. J. (2002). Homelessness, childhood. In T. Gullotta & M. Bloom (Eds.), *Encyclopedia of Prevention and Health Promotion.* New York: Kluwer/Plenum.

Toro, P. A., Rabideau, J. M. P., Bellavia, C. W., Daeschler, C. V., Wall, D. D., Thomas, D. M., & Smith, S. J. (1997). Evaluating an intervention for homeless persons: Results of a field experiment. *Journal of Consulting and Clinical Psychology, 65,* 476–484.

Toro, P. A., Trickett, E. J., Wall, D. D., & Salem, D. A. (1991). Homelessness in the United States: An ecological perspective. *American Psychologist, 46,* 1208–1218.

Toro, P. A., & Warren, M. G. (1999). Homelessness in the United States: Policy considerations, *Journal of Community Psychology, 27,* 119–136.

Toro, P. A., Wolfe, S. M., Bellavia, C. W., Thomas, D. M., Rowland, L. L., Daeschler, C. V., & McCaskill, P. A. (1999). Obtaining representative samples of homeless persons: A two-city study. *Journal of Community Psychology, 27,* 157–178.

Travis, J. (2002). Invisible punishment: An instrument of social exclusion. In M. Mauer & M. Chesney- Lind (Eds.), *Invisible punishment: The collateral consequences of mass imprisonment.* Washington, DC: The Urban Institute.

Tyler, K. A., Hoyt, D. R., Whitbeck, L. B., & Cauce, A. M. (2001). The impact of childhood sexual abuse on later sexual victimization among runaway youth. *Journal of Research on Adolescence, 11,15* 1–176.

Tyler, K., Whitbeck, L., Hoyt, D., & Cauce, A. (2004). Risk factors for sexual victimization among male and female homeless and runaway youth. *Journal of Interpersonal Violence, 19*(5), 503–520.

Unger, J. B., Simon, T. R., Newman, T. L., Montgomery, S. B., Kipke, M. D., & Albornoz, M. (1998). Early adolescent street youth: An overlooked population with unique problems and service needs. *Journal of Early Adolescence, 18,* 325–348.

Upshur, C. (1986). *Research report: The Bridge, Inc., independent living demonstration, Amendments to the foster care and adoption assistance program: Hearing before the subcommittee on public assistance and unemployment compensation of the Committee on Ways and Means, House of Representatives,* 99th Cong. Serial 99 54 (September 19, 1985) (testimony of C. C. Upshur). Washington, DC: Government Printing Office.

van Leeuwen, J. (2002, September). *Drug and alcohol survey results: Homeless and runaway youth.* Denver, CO: Urban Peak/ARTS Collaborative: Author.

van Leeuwen, J., Mendelson, B., Hopfer, C., Kelly, S., Green, J., & Petersen, J. (2005.) *Substance use and corresponding risk factors among homeless and runaway youth in Denver, Colorado.* (Manuscript submitted for publication.).

Whitbeck, L. B., Chen, X., Hoyt, D. R., Tyler, K. A., & Johnson, K. D. (2004). Mental disorder, subsistence strategies, and victimization among gay, lesbian, and bisexual homeless and runaway adolescents. *Journal of Sex Research, 41,* 329–342.

Whitbeck, L. B., & Hoyt, D. R. (1999). *Nowhere to grow: Homeless and runaway adolescents and their families.* New York: Aldine de Gruyter.

Whitbeck, L. B., Hoyt, D. R., & Ackley, K. A. (1997). Abusive family backgrounds and victimization among runaway and homeless adolescents. *Journal of Research on Adolescence, 7,* 375–392.

Whitbeck, L. B., Hoyt, D. R., Johnson, K. D., Berdahl, T. A., & Whiteford, S. W. (2002). *Midwest longitudinal study of homeless adolescents. Baseline report for all participating agencies.* Lincoln, NE: University of Nebraska, Department of Sociology.

Whitbeck, L. B., Hoyt, D. R., Tyler, K. A., Ackley, K. A., & Fields, S. C. (1997). *Midwest homeless and runaway adolescent project: Summary report to participating agencies.* Unpublished manuscript, Department of Sociology, Iowa State University.

Whitbeck, L. B., Hoyt, D. R., & Yoder, K. A. (1999). A risk-amplification model of victimization and depressive symptoms among runaway and homeless adolescents. *American Journal of Community Psychology, 27,* 273–296.

Whitbeck, L. B., Hoyt, D. R., Yoder, K. A., Cauce, A. M., & Paradise, M. (2001). Deviant behavior and victimization among homeless and runaway adolescents. *Journal of Interpersonal Violence, 16,* 1175–1204.

Windle, M. (1989). Substance use and abuse among adolescent runaways: A four-year follow-up study. *Journal of Youth and Adolescence, 18,* 331–344.

Witken, A. L., Milburn, N. G., Rotheram-Borus, M. J., Batterham, P., May, S., & Brooks, R. (2005). Finding homeless youth: Patterns based on geographical area and number of homeless episodes. *Youth & Society, 37,* 62–84.

Wolfe, S. M., Toro, P. A., & McCaskill, P. A. (1999). A comparison of homeless and matched housed adolescents on family environment variables. *Journal of Research on Adolescence, 9,* 53–66.

Yates, G. L., MacKenzie, R., Pennbridge, J., & Cohen, E. (1988). A risk profile comparison of runaway and non-runaway youth. *American Journal of Public Health, 78,* 820–821.

Young, R. L., Godfrey, W., Matthews, B., & Adams, G. R. (1983). Runaways: A review of negative consequences. *Family Relations, 32,* 275–281.

## End Note

[1] In the U.S. and other developed nations, relatively few homeless families (12 to 20 percent) include children age 12 or older (Buckner, Bassuk, Weinreb, & Brooks, 1999; Burt et al., 2001), and children under age 12 are rarely found homeless on their own (Robertson & Toro, 1999). In fact, many shelters for homeless families exclude children age 12 or older who shelter staff fear might prey upon the younger ones. As a result, homeless families with older children are often compelled to leave their older children with friends or relatives before entering a shelter.

Disclaimer: This paper was developed for the National Symposium on Homelessness Research held on March 1-2, 2007. The Symposium was conducted by Abt Associates Inc. and Policy Research Associates Inc. under contract for the Office of the Assistant Secretary for Planning and Evaluation, U.S. Department of Health and Human Services; and the Office of Policy, Development, and Research, U.S. Department of Housing and Urban Development. The paper presents the views and opinions of the respective author(s) and does not necessarily represent the views, positions, and policies of the federal government.

In: Runaway and Homeless Youth
Editors: Josiah Hughes and Isiah Wright

ISBN: 978-1-60741-521-3
© 2010 Nova Science Publishers, Inc.

*Chapter 2*

# PROMISING STRATEGIES TO END YOUTH HOMELESSNESS[*]

## *United States Deptment of Health and Human Services*

## I. INTRODUCTION

Youth homelessness has profound consequences reaching well beyond individual youth and their immediate families. Indeed, negative impacts from youth homelessness enter into the very fabric of our communities and the nation as a whole. Research suggests that as many as 1.6 million young people may be homeless at some point during the year. When youth leave their homes and enter the homeless population, they are in jeopardy of engaging in anti-social and risky behaviors as well as becoming one of the most severely victimized groups in our society.[1] Alarmingly, an increasing amount of research on the chronic homeless population notes a correspondence of homelessness experienced in youth to subsequent adult experiences of homelessness.

When the Runaway and Homeless Youth Act (RHYA, Title III of the Juvenile Justice and Delinquency Prevention Act of 1974, JJDPA, P.L. 93-415) was reauthorized in 2003 during the 108th Congress by the Runaway, Homeless, and Missing Children Protection Act, it included a provision for a Report on promising strategies to end youth homelessness. The Report provides Members of Congress information on the needs of the homeless youth population and the characteristics of homeless youth, theoretical perspectives, prevention and amelioration interventions, and implications for policy and program development. This Report also includes a review of the range of supports and services available to meet the population's needs, including those services funded in the Runaway and Homeless Youth Act.[2]

The two principle causes of youth homelessness are 1) a breakdown in family relationships and 2) inadequate interventions from systems that are charged with protecting,

---

[*] This is an edited, reformatted and augmented version of a Department of Health and Human Services publication dated 2007.

nurturing, and supervising youth when their families cannot. The primary reason youth consistently state for their homelessness is family conflict. [3] The second leading cause of youth homelessness links to the high proportion of homeless youth who have been in foster care. Additionally, there is growing evidence suggesting that many homeless youth have spent time in juvenile detention. [4] Finding effective ways to address these causes of homelessness is critical in the campaign to prevent and ameliorate youth homelessness.

Stable and nurturing families are the most potent barrier to the dangers of youth homelessness — and its consequences: anti-social behaviors, crime, and sexual exploitation. Increasing positive parenting skills, as well as connecting youth and their families to community resources, can help parents and caregivers manage issues that have the potential to unravel families. On their own, youth typically are disconnected from positive communities and social networks, and the systems — education, employment, and health care — that could help them to change their circumstances.

President Bush has initiated actions to address the leading causes of youth homelessness. The Administration's initiatives include strengthening families (the Responsible Fatherhood and Healthy Marriage initiative and the Promoting Safe and Stable Families program), providing role-models and mentors to youth in disadvantaged circumstances (Mentoring Children of Prisoners programs), and promoting effective coordination among Federal agencies, as well as with State and local governments that deliver services to homeless youth, youth-at-risk, and their families (FYSB State Collaboration Grants).

The Administration's actions offer homeless youth (and their families) both positive opportunities and crucial interventions as young people strive to successfully negotiate the transition from childhood to adolescence and ultimately into responsible adulthood. An important feature is promoting the benefits of collaborations by public and private non-profit and faith-based organizations in preventing youth homelessness. Partnerships enhance resources that lead to positive outcomes within the criminal justice, mental health, medical, and welfare systems.

In December 2002, the President established the White House Task Force for Disadvantaged Youth. Given a one-year term, it was charged with developing a framework for federal youth policy -- under existing authorities and programs -- that encompasses a comprehensive Federal response to the problems facing America's youth.

Its goal was to identify strategies to enhance agency accountability and effectiveness and submit action recommendations. The Report was presented to the President in October, 2003. A key recommendation was to target special populations for support — those who "carry disproportionately negative consequences for youth and their communities if not addressed." Youth in public care (in and aging-out of foster care) and youth in the juvenile justice system were identified as examples of this population of "disconnected" and "neediest" youth.[5]

In the fall of 2005, the President and First Lady convened a national policy conference focusing on the nation's at-risk youth population, "Helping America's Youth" (HAY). The conference served as the launch of the first interactive, comprehensive web-based tool, "The Community Guide to Helping America's Youth," which was developed under the First Lady's leadership. The Guide currently includes over 180 evidence-based programs located in communities throughout the nation that prevent and reduce delinquency and other negative youth behaviors. The listed programs have been evaluated using scientific techniques and have demonstrated a statistically significant decline in these negative outcomes. The Guide is intended to facilitate strategic, efficient and effective planning. It will assist community partnerships in their collaborative efforts to prioritize issues, identify existing resources, and fill gaps or unmet needs with effective programs. Through the Guide, communities will have an additional tool in meeting the challenge of preventing and ameliorating youth homelessness.

Based on results from regional forums, the Federal Partnership has focused on creating cross-agency teams to consult with state teams; providing a "crosswalk" of key Federal program definitions and program policies in order to better align programs and funds; providing States and Tribal governments with information on the funding from each of the Federal agencies that is available in their State to serve the neediest youth; and providing models of collaboration.

## The Runaway and Homeless Youth Act

The Runaway and Homeless Youth Act (RHYA) was enacted to provide the core services to stabilize and address the needs of runaway and homeless youth. The Act established and authorizes funding for programs that provide a range of supports and services for runaway and homeless youth, including pregnant and parenting teens.

The Family and Youth Services Bureau (FYSB) in the Administration for Children and Families (ACF), Department of Health Services (DHHS), administers the RHYA, awarding funds in the form of grants that support homeless youth through youth shelters, street outreach, and transitional living programs operated by faith-based and community organizations or local public or tribal agencies. These organizations and agencies also work in partnership with schools, mentoring programs, and other local, regional, tribal, or national organizations that serve youth. In the 30 years since RHYA was enacted, it has supported the efforts of local grantees targeting outreach efforts to homeless youth, assessing and responding to their needs, and stabilizing youth through reunification with their families or other permanent living options, where appropriate. [6]

Three programs receive funding under RHYA: the Basic Center Program, the Street Outreach Program and the Transitional Living Program.

**Basic Center Program (BCP)** — funds short-term (no more than 15 days) shelter services for youth under 18 years of age, as well as other supportive services, including counseling for youth and their family, to reunite youth and their families, or to connect youth to alternative supervised placements.

**Street Outreach Program (SOP)** — supports outreach activities designed to serve youth who have experienced or are at-risk of sexual abuse, prostitution or sexual exploitation. Services are available to youth under 21 years of age and can include identification and outreach, information and referral to housing and health care services as well as education and prevention services.

**Transitional Living Program (TLP)** — provides food and shelter, life skills, education and employment training, and other services to help youth who cannot be reunited with their families develop the knowledge and skills to live independently. Programs funded under the

TLP are available to youth 16 through 21 years of age for approximately 18 months. The recent reauthorization of RHYA also includes funding for transitional living programs targeted to young mothers and their children. These maternity group homes meet the unique needs of this population and provide pregnant youth and young mothers aged 16-21 with food and shelter, as well as parenting education and support programs.

The Runaway and Homeless Youth Management Information System (RHYMIS), instituted over three decades ago and modified over time, has been used by ACF as its primary data collection tool. In keeping with the President's direction to bring greater coordination and accountability to government, RHYMIS continues to be upgraded and streamlined by FYSB. As of 2005, the enhanced "NEO RHYMIS" is used by RHYA grantees to collect and record the characteristics on the young people they serve, their critical issues, and the services received under the RHYA.

## Background

When analyzing programs for homeless youth, it is important to note three factors: 1) Programs funded by RHYA have general standards and requirements that guide grantees but specific program approaches and models vary among grantees. 2) The multiple needs of homeless youth require targeted services from public systems outside the RHY network— child welfare, welfare, juvenile justice, mental and physical health care, education, housing, and labor. 3) State and local efforts to coordinate and deliver comprehensive services for homeless youth vary significantly in scope, approach, and effectiveness throughout the nation.

In order to compile and synthesize the most current information on promising strategies to end youth homelessness, a review was conducted of the literature on youth homelessness that included studies, articles, reports and publications from academic researchers, government and youth-serving agencies. The development of a rich research base on youth homelessness is still in its early stages. Nevertheless, existing studies and data, evaluations of interventions in related fields, and information drawn from practitioners provide a window into the world of homeless youth. Understanding this population's characteristics in the context of robust social theory can help to inform the development of effective policies and practices to address youth homelessness.

Other materials consulted were "The White House Task Force on Disadvantaged Youth Final Report to the President" and "Helping America's Youth" materials, as well as information and policy analyses published by national coalitions and organizations addressing youth homelessness. Additionally, practitioners and professionals in the field were contacted for knowledge based on their experiences. The current review by ACF focused primarily on information generated since 1998, when DHHS and the Department of Housing and Urban Development sponsored the National Symposium on Homelessness Research.

There is an emerging body of research and data from both qualitative and quantitative studies that provides significant information on who homeless youth are and how they experience homelessness. Researchers have examined the prevalence of the problem, the characteristics of homeless youth, and their experiences on the street. Several researchers also have developed theoretical constructs to understand the pathways to homelessness among adolescents and to improve interventions.

However, data on long-term outcomes evaluating the effectiveness of interventions specifically addressing youth homelessness are limited. While some homeless youth programs track data to measure the effectiveness of their work, often these are not based on rigorous experimental or quasi-experimental research design. Accordingly, the Report's literature review was expanded to include interventions in related fields designed for high-risk youth that are grounded in theory and have been rigorously evaluated.

Based upon the broad review of available information on homeless youth and interventions to address youth homelessness, this Report focuses on three critical issues:

- Who the homeless youth are;
- The extent of youth homelessness; and
- The strategies which hold the most promise for addressing and ending youth homelessness.

## Homeless Youth

Research conducted on homeless youth and their experiences on the street has been obtained from surveys with youth in local service agencies, including shelters, drop-in centers and transitional living programs, or in street locations in large urban cities or metropolitan areas. The Seattle Homeless Youth Project [7] surveyed youth drawn from a variety of service agencies in the Seattle metropolitan area [8] and examined adolescent substance abuse, anti-social behavior, and effects of early childhood experiences including the psychological effects of child maltreatment. Another often-cited work is that of Whitbeck [9] and colleagues[10] in four mid-sized cities in four midwestern States. In addition to examining the characteristics of homeless youth identified on the streets and in shelters in Missouri, Iowa, Nebraska and Kansas, the researchers examined the effects of street experiences (e.g., affiliation with problem peers, negative subsistence strategies, risky sexual behaviors and drug and/or alcohol use) and early family abuse on victimization and depression for street youth.

While researchers have developed a significant amount of descriptive information on homeless youth, the challenges related to tracking homeless youth over time has resulted in few longitudinal studies on this population. Consequently, there is little information on patterns of youth homelessness and factors that may be associated with more or less chronic experiences and repeat episodes of homelessness. The relationship between specific behaviors or experiences of homeless youth and long-term developmental outcomes has not been examined closely nor have the factors associated with an increased risk of homelessness or the long-term outcomes for homeless youth. Because researchers have been unable to develop studies of homeless adolescents and their prior experiences and match them rigorously with valid comparison groups, it is difficult to conclusively determine the factors associated with an increased risk of homelessness or determine which of the characteristics attributed to homeless youth are unique to this population.

## Extent of Youth Homelessness

The Substance Abuse and Mental Health Services Administration, Office of Applied Statistics, July 2, 2004, reported that in 2002, 1.6 million youths, or 7 percent of 12- to 17-year olds ran away from home and slept in exposed or poorly sheltered locations. This number corresponds to earlier credible survey estimates from 1998 (1.5 million) and 1999 (1.7 million). Estimates vary mainly because researchers use different age and definitional parameters in their measurements, and homeless youth are a transient and "mobile" population, therefore difficult to track. Youth are not easily accessible to researchers, and they often move in and out of homelessness, avoiding contact with service systems and adults.

**Strategies That Hold the Most Promise for Addressing Youth Homelessness** Few programs and interventions designed to prevent or end homelessness based on theoretical constructs were found. Studies of programs have not been based on rigorous experimental or quasi-experimental research designs. This is due in part because the needs of homeless youth are so urgent that assignment to a control group, an important methodological tool in research evaluation, raises significant ethical concerns. One exception is a study, undertaken in 1994 by Cauce and colleagues, which evaluated the effects of an intensive case management program for homeless adolescents compared to a matched comparison group. The authors found that youth receiving intensive case management services showed greater reductions in aggressive and problem behavior and improved satisfaction with quality of life. [11]

Beyond the ethical questions, valid comparison groups also are difficult to develop because homeless youth are a diverse population and homelessness is an episodic phenomenon. This makes it particularly difficult to conduct longitudinal studies of homeless youth. However, a longitudinal study of youth aging out of foster care helped to shed light on youth homelessness, as it revealed that many youth aging out of foster care became homeless. [12] In addition, two longitudinal studies with matched comparison groups currently underway will greatly contribute to the knowledge base about this population.

The Housing, Adolescence and Life Outcomes (HALO) Project funded by the National Institute on Alcohol Abuse and Alcoholism is following 251 homeless youth, and a matched housed sample of 150 adolescents over 1.5 years to document the longitudinal consequences of homelessness and to investigate risk and resilience factors associated with negative and positive outcomes.[13] Similarly, the National Institute on Mental Health has provided funding for *Project i,* a five-year study of homeless young people in Melbourne, Australia and Los Angeles, CA.[14] The study seeks to understand the life course of new homeless youth and the factors that influence youth's pathways in and out of homelessness as well as their risk of contracting HIV. In Los Angeles alone, *Project i* is following approximately 240 new homeless youth (youth who report having left home for no more than 180 days) and 200 more experienced youth (youth who report having left home for more than 180 days) over a three-year period. Results of these evaluations should benefit decision-makers in designing interventions for the homeless youth population.

# II. UNDERSTANDING THE PROBLEM

## Who Are Homeless Youth?

Despite the complexity and episodic nature of youth homelessness and the limited availability of longitudinal or comparative studies, emerging research on youth homelessness helps us to understand several important aspects of this population.

## Defining Youth Homelessness

Defining who is a "homeless youth" is neither easy nor straightforward. It involves an array of issues concerning age, length of time on the street or in arrangements without supervised adult care-givers, and the circumstances that led the youth to be on their own without a permanent residence.

Different terms are used to refer to homeless youth depending on how they came to be separated from their families. "Homeless youth" typically refer to youth who are on their own or "unaccompanied" by their caregivers. Adolescents who are homeless with their families and served by interventions targeted to homeless families are generally not included in studies focused on homeless youth. "Runaway youth" are youth who have left their home without the consent of their parents or legal guardians, while the term *throwaway* (or thrown-away) is frequently used to refer to youth who have been asked or told to leave by their parents or caregivers.

In general, when defining homeless youth, researchers have placed less emphasis on the setting or place where youth reside and have focused on the presence or absence of an adult caregiver.[15] Federal guidelines define homeless youth as "unaccompanied youth" or adolescents "on their own" living in a shelter, public place or with a stranger because they needed a place to stay.

While the majority of homeless youth reside in shelters or "sofa surf" with multiple acquaintances, a subpopulation of youth referred to as street youth spend a significant amount of time living on the streets or in inappropriate locations, such as abandoned buildings, cars, or under bridges. Street youth tend to have the most chronic experience of homelessness, and face the highest level of risk.

As theory and research regarding adolescent development have expanded over the last 20 years, scholars and practitioners generally have come to accept that 18, the legal age of adulthood, is not the age at which individuals reach adulthood developmentally. Accordingly, many interventions targeted to homeless youth serve individuals through age 21, and in some cases, through age 24. Likewise, researchers examining the problem of youth homelessness and interventions to address it, frequently include "youth" older than age 18 in their studies.

The Runaway and Homeless Youth Act defines homeless youth as individuals not more than 21 years of age and restricts programming provided with RHYA funds to this age range. For purposes of this report, the literature review focused on unaccompanied youth and has included research focused on homeless youth, regardless of the upper age defined by researchers.[16]

As with Federal guidelines related to domicile, researchers typically include youth who have spent at least one night in a homeless setting (e.g., shelter, street or other public place or with a stranger) in their count when determining the number of youth who experience homelessness. Youth's homeless episodes vary greatly across studies: some youth report being homeless for the first time; some have experienced multiple (although short-term) homelessness episodes; and others report being homeless for a period of several months. Although researchers have identified youth with more chronic homeless episodes (i.e., one year or longer), research into chronic homelessness among youth is relatively sparse.[17]

Given these issues, a research-based substantiated estimate of homeless youth remains elusive.

## Characteristics of Homeless Youth

Numerous studies indicate that certain characteristics are more prevalent among runaway and homeless youth than their peers. Among these trends are alcohol and other drug abuse, poverty/economic instability, and mental health disorders.

## Alcohol and Other Drug Abuse

Studies indicate that homeless adolescents report higher frequencies of alcohol and other drug use and abuse than housed adolescents.[18] Analysis of 2003 FYSB data indicate that alcohol and other drug abuse was a critical issue for 23.5 percent of youth in Basic Center Programs and 42.3 percent of youth in TLPs.

## Poverty/Economic Instability

Research is somewhat mixed regarding the extent to which family poverty is a common factor among homeless youth. This is likely because family conflict and related issues, which appear to be the primary factor associated with youth homelessness, occur across the spectrum of socioeconomic backgrounds. In addition, Cauce and colleagues note that although most homeless youth come from difficult backgrounds, those difficulties cannot be assumed to include poverty or economic disadvantage.[19]

## Mental Health Disorders

Researchers have found high rates of a number of psychiatric disorders among homeless youth, including depression, anxiety, ideas of suicide, and conduct disorders. MacLean and colleagues found that of 354 homeless youth, 76.9 percent met the American Psychiatric Association's DSM-III-R criteria for at least one disorder — about eighteen percent were depressed and forty-three percent reported having attempted suicide.[20] Mental health was the third most commonly cited critical issue for youth in Federally-funded Basic Center

Programs — identified by 30.9 percent of shelter youth in 2003. The issue was also identified by 41.3 percent of TLP youth.

It remains difficult to determine whether psychological and emotional disturbance is associated solely with homelessness, family violence or parental abuse, youth's use of alcohol or drugs, or a combination of these.[21]

Despite the high rates of mental health disorders among this population, preliminary research notes that homeless adolescents often lack access to health and mental health care. In addition, it is possible that homeless youth do not seek health care because they distrust authority and are likely to be asked for a permanent address, health insurance information or parental permission for treatment.

## Pathways to Homelessness

Self-reported data from youth and research on the characteristics of homeless youth suggest common pathways to youth homelessness. Specifically 1) the presence of family conflict and violence, 2) foster care placement and 3) involvement in the juvenile justice system appear to place youth at greater risk of experiencing homelessness.

## Family Conflict and Violence

Homeless youth report experiencing many types of family conflict in their homes, including fights with parents or caregivers, parental rejection, as well as neglect and/or abuse by a parent, caregiver, or other individual with access to the home.

- Youth who have been "thrown out" of their homes were more likely than other homeless youth to report spending a night away from home because of family conflict.[22]
- Whitbeck and colleagues found that parents of runaways reported high rates of serious violence between parents and their children.[23]
- RHYMIS data (2003) from FYSB-funded shelters and residential programs indicates that 89.7 percent of runaway youth entering shelters and 75.5 percent of homeless youth joining residential programs rate family dynamics as a critical issue leading to their homelessness.
- Approximately 28 percent of runaway youth who entered the shelters cited abuse and/or neglect as a critical issue.
- High rates of physical and sexual abuse occur among this population. In their analysis of antecedents to homelessness, Yoder and Whitbeck report that neglected and sexually abused youth (regardless of their ages) were approximately three times more likely to run away than were non-neglected youth.[24] Among the most rigorous studies, rates of sexual abuse tend to cluster in a range from 21 to 42 percent.[25]
- While both boys and girls experience parental or caregiver abuse, girls are more likely than boys to experience sexual abuse.[26] Available research shows that many

youth who have been sexually abused have been abused by more than one person.[27]

- Research on the negative consequences of physical and sexual abuse points to a connection between sexual abuse and suicidal notions among homeless youth.
- Rejection is likely to lead to homelessness for subpopulations of youth. In their comparative study of heterosexual and gay, lesbian, bi-sexual, and transgender (GLBT) youth, Cochran and colleagues found that GLBT youth indicated leaving their homes because of conflicts with parents over their sexual orientation.[28]
- Family conflict resulting from teen pregnancy may lead to adolescent homelessness.[29]
- Teen mothers have a higher risk of becoming homeless than their peers and compared to adult mothers, teen mothers are more likely to be homeless at a younger age and homeless more often than adult mothers.[30]
- Homeless parenting teens are often served by interventions targeted to families rather than youth. As a result, homeless youth with children often are not included in estimates and studies of homeless youth, which could impact policy decisions.

## Foster Care Placement

One population particularly prone to homelessness is adolescents who have had experiences with the child welfare system.

- Courtney and colleagues interviewed 474 foster care youth in Illinois in out-of-home care and found that over 52 percent had run away at least once; of these, two-thirds reported more than one run.[31]
- In a study of 364 homeless youth in Washington, Cauce et al., found that 33 percent of the youth in the study reported a foster home placement -- the average number of placements was 3.3 with 14 percent reporting four or more placements. In addition, 18 percent of the time, homelessness resulted from a youth being removed from their parents by a public official. [32]
- Youth may run away due to reluctance to enter foster care, or unhappiness with foster care placements. Youth who have emancipated or who "age out" of the foster care system upon their 18th birthday are at particularly high risk of becoming homeless.
- Emancipated youth often lack "permanency" and do not have the independent living skills necessary to make a successful transition to self-sufficiency. They are disconnected from families and caring adults and lack the education and employment skills needed to obtain employment and maintain a household.
- Youth who age out of the foster care system are more likely to abuse drugs and alcohol and are more likely to be involved with the criminal justice system.[33] In their longitudinal study of youth leaving foster care, Courtney and colleagues found that of the 141 youth who left foster care, approximately 12 percent reported being homeless at least once since discharge and a significant number (22 percent) had lived in four or more separate places since discharge.[34]

- A study of foster care alumni found that 22 percent were homeless for one or more nights at any time within a year after being discharged from foster care and almost one out of five were homeless for the first time ever for a week or more after leaving foster care.[35]

## Juvenile Detention

Though limited, the existing body of research documents high rates of involvement with the juvenile justice system among homeless youth (statistics on the number of youth that become homeless upon release from incarceration are not available).

- Data from a homeless youth shelter in New York City indicate that approximately 30 percent of the youth who entered the shelter had a history of incarceration.[36]
- Analysis of data from nine Federally-funded shelters in Northern Washington State found that out of 940 surveyed youth, 28 percent were involved with the juvenile justice system.[37]
- Results from a statewide survey in Minnesota revealed similar rates of juvenile justice involvement among younger and older homeless youth. Among 209 homeless youth ages 17 and younger, close to half (46 percent) had spent at least one night in a detention center, while approximately two-fifths (38 percent) of the 285 homeless young adults (ages 18-20) surveyed also reported spending at least one night in a detention center.[38]
- Both age groups from the study reported that having a criminal background interfered with getting or keeping housing.[39]

## Prevalence of the Problem

Homelessness among youth is a problem defined by a constellation of constantly changing variables in the lives of youth — where they live, the status of their relationship with caregivers, and their age. In the course of a year, a single youth might be asked to leave home by a parent, spend time in a shelter, return home, runaway from home, and end up on the street. Depending on when a researcher interacted with this young person, he or she might be classified as homeless or housed, runaway or "thrown-away", or a street youth. If he or she were age 21 and turned 22 during the course of the year, some researchers might include this person within the population of homeless youth, while others would not. Classifying youth within these categories is necessary for researchers to capture the prevalence and severity of youth homelessness, the reason it occurs, and how it may be changing over time.

- Estimates of the prevalence of youth homelessness range from 500,000 to 2.8 million youth, depending on the sampling methodology and definitions of youth homelessness used.

- The DHHS Substance Abuse and Mental Health Services Administration reported that in 2002, 1.6 million youths, or 7 percent of 12- to 17-year olds, ran away from home and slept on the street during the study year.
- Analysis of survey data from a national probability sample of households and juvenile facilities indicates that in 1999, 1.7 million youth had a runaway/throwaway episode. The authors report that youth ages 15-17 years accounted for two thirds of youth with runaway/throwaway episodes during the study year.[40]
- These and other studies of the prevalence of youth homelessness do not typically include individuals 18 and older, making it difficult to determine how many youth between the ages of 18-24 experience homelessness annually.[41]

## Duration of Homelessness

Research findings suggest that youth homelessness typically is an episodic phenomenon, although it appears that street youth tend to have more chronic homeless experiences.

- Because youth typically transition in and out of homelessness, the total accumulated time they spend on their own may be a better indicator of their homeless experience than the length of any single episode. Whitbeck and colleagues found that adolescents in the homeless population reported an average of 123 days on the street in their lifetimes.[42]
- Halcón and Lifson report that estimates of long-term (up to one year) homelessness among youth vary from 25 to 80 percent.[43]
- A study of·631 shelter youth residing in Federal and non-federally funded shelters and 528 street youth, found that while almost half the street youth had currently been away from home for more than a year, the majority of the shelter youth had been away less than one month.[44]
- Because older youth have had longer time to accumulate homeless experience, studies that include adolescents over the age of 18 are likely to document more chronic patterns of homelessness.[45]
- To date, few studies have examined the factors that lead youth to have chronic compared to single episodes of homeless experiences.

## Street Life and Homeless Youth

The homeless subpopulation of street youth is most at-risk of negative outcomes. [46] While there is no data clearly indicating the long-term effects of living on the street as a youth, it is clear that the realities of street life lead many young people to engage in a range of high-risk behaviors, both in order to meet basic survival needs, and as a result of engaging with other troubled peers. Though peers on the street provide friendship, support and a sense of community, they also may introduce youth to and/or reinforce negative and risk-taking behaviors. In addition, street youth are particularly vulnerable to victimization, including assault and sexual exploitation.

Studies have shown that street youth engage in a multitude of risky behaviors that include 1) alcohol and other drug abuse, and 2) sexual and criminal activities. Research finds that youth are likely to engage in negative activities as a result of peer dynamics involved in engaging with other troubled peers and/or in order to survive street life.

## Substance Use and Abuse

- In a study of street youth in the Midwest, almost one half of the males and one third of the females sold drugs.[47]
- High rates of affiliation with troubled peers were associated with substance abuse and dependence.[48]

## Sexual and Criminal Activity

- Many homeless youth engage in "survival sex" (exchanging sex for shelter, money, drugs, food or clothing). In their nationally representative sample, Greene, Ennet and Ringwalt noted that 27.5 percent of street youth and 9.5 percent of shelter youth reported participating in survival sex (1999). In a study of 203 homeless and street youth in Minneapolis, HalcOn and Lifson found that more than one in five youth reported a history of exchanging sex for money, drugs or other goods.[49]
- In a study of 272 homeless youth in Seattle, Wagner and colleagues determined that almost 80 percent of those interviewed engaged in sexual activity in the three months prior to the study. Sexually active youth reported having had at least one sexually transmitted disease, and of the sexually active women, a large number had been pregnant at least once.[50]
- Gay, bisexual, and transgender males report high rates of unprotected intercourse, sex with persons known to be HIV-positive, sex while high on drugs and sex with an injection drug user.[51]
- Whitbeck and colleagues found that adolescent females were more likely to engage in survival sex than adolescent males. In addition, Moon found that compared to their heterosexual counterparts, male and female GLBT participants were more likely to report exchanging sex for money.[52]

## Homeless Youth as Victims of Crime

Recognizing that a large proportion of homeless youth come from violent and abusive family backgrounds, researchers have explored the consequences of a family abuse history on the likelihood of homeless youth being victimized. Because homeless youth who have been victims are at risk of engaging in negative behaviors, lack adult supervision or connection and live in dangerous environments, they are particularly vulnerable to physical and sexual assault.

- Whitbeck and colleagues traced the process through which early abuse by caregivers increases the likelihood of anti-social behaviors among homeless adolescents. Their study revealed that family abuse was correlated with physical and sexual abuse/exploitation on the street – 25 percent of the females and 9.2 percent of the males reported that they had been forced to engage in some form of sexual activity while at home, while a smaller percentage reported that they had been sexually assaulted or raped. [53]
- Severity and occurrence of abuse vary by gender. [54] In their study, Cauce and colleagues found that males reported higher rates of physical assaults than females while more females than males reported instances of rape. [55]
- Street youth have fewer resources with which to respond to physical and sexual assaults, due in part to their fear that authorities may have them returned to their families or placed back in the public system from which they have run away. [56]

Given what is known about the characteristics of homeless youth and their experiences on the street — high levels of victimization and engagement in risky behaviors and subsistence activities (sexual and criminal) — it is clear these youth are particularly vulnerable to experience further instability, injury, compromised mental and physical health, and chronic homelessness.

# III. THEORETICAL PERSPECTIVES

Several theoretical perspectives focused on youth homelessness illuminate the social development of youth and the dynamics of interaction between homeless youth and their families, peers, and environments. These perspectives integrate research on the characteristics of homeless youth with research on adolescent development, juvenile risk and anti-social behaviors, and the impact of family dynamics and poverty.

Two general frameworks that can inform work with homeless youth are youth development (personal and social assets) and ecological-developmental perspectives. Additionally, there are two models researchers use to explain the trajectory of youth homelessness — the Risk Amplification Model (RAM) and the Life Cycle Model.

## Youth Development Perspectives

Programs for homeless youth need an environment in which youth are given opportunities to participate in decision-making, as well as necessary resources and supports to help them avoid or overcome difficult situations and risky behaviors. A key tenet of the youth development perspective is that remediating and preventing negative behaviors is not enough. Interventions are needed that focus on preparing youth for successful adulthood by fostering development of positive traits.[57] ACF's Positive Youth Development (PYD) approach to working with homeless youth includes prevention and resiliency. Prevention research identifies risk factors that lead to specific problem behaviors, as well as protective factors that help children and youth avoid negative behaviors. Resiliency research shows that children who are able to overcome situations of disadvantage typically possess strong social skills, pleasing personalities, strong intellects[58], and possess a sense of independence and purpose.[59] They also have connections to caring adults who encourage them to aim high and opportunities to contribute through participation in meaningful activities.[60]

The very factors that place homeless youth at risk — the inability of youth and their families to maintain supportive relationships — make the task of preparation for adulthood all the more urgent. In the United States young people often have maintained a level of dependence on family into their early to mid-twenties, while experimenting with roles, gaining education, and developing more intimate and lasting relationships. Young people who experience homelessness do not have the security of family guidance and resources as they negotiate the challenges of adolescence and the transition to adulthood (often at an earlier age than other young people).

**Personal and Social Assets that Facilitate Positive Youth Development**
From Community Programs that Promote Youth Development

**Physical Development**
✓ Good health habits
✓ Good health management skills

**Intellectual Development**
✓ Knowledge of essential life skills
✓ Knowledge of essential vocational skills
✓ School Success
✓ Rational habits of mind
✓ In-depth knowledge of more than one culture
✓ Good decision-making skills
✓ Knowledge of skills needed to navigate through multiple cultural contexts

**Psychological and Emotional Development**
✓ Good mental health including positive self-report
✓ Good emotional self-regulation skills
✓ Good coping skills
✓ Good conflict resolution skills
✓ Mastery motivation and positive achievement motivation
✓ Confidence in one's personal efficacy
✓ "Planfulness" – planning for the future and future life events
✓ Sense of personal autonomy/responsibility for self
✓ Optimism coupled with realism
✓ Coherent personal and social identity
✓ Prosocial and culturally sensitive values
✓ Spirituality or a sense of a "larger" purpose in life
✓ Strong moral character
✓ A commitment to good use of time

**Social Development**
✓ Connectedness – perceived good relationships and trust with parents, peers, and some other adults.
✓ Sense of social place/integration – being connected and valued by larger social networks
✓ Attachment to prosocial/conventional institutions, such as school, church, nonschool youth programs
✓ Ability to navigate multiple cultural contexts
✓ Commitment to civic engagement.

In recent years, youth development researchers and theorists have synthesized findings from these areas — adolescent development, prevention, and resiliency research — and have developed comprehensive lists of developmental assets. Assets are positive traits that indicate successful development in adolescence and greater preparation for successful transition to adulthood. Generally speaking, the more assets that young people possess, the better prepared they are for a healthy and successful adulthood. [61]

The National Research Council synthesized many separately identified sets of assets into one comprehensive list of developmental assets. The assets are organized around four developmental areas: physical development, intellectual development, psychological and emotional development, and social development.

Among other research, Catalano and associates conducted a comprehensive review of evaluations of positive youth development programs, and found that successful programs included strategies that focused on:

- Strengthening social, emotional, behavioral, cognitive, and moral competencies;
- Building self-efficacy;
- Sharing messages from family and community about clear standards for youth behavior;
- Increasing healthy bonding with adults, peers, and younger children; and
- Expanding opportunities and recognition for youth.

They also found that successful programs strive to provide structure and consistency in program delivery, typically through the development of curriculum that guides interaction between workers and youth. Successful interventions usually were longer- term, with involvement by youth for at least nine months.[62]

Finally, reviews of evaluations and theoretical research were conducted by the National Research Council. The review identified these features of positive developmental settings:

- Appropriate structure
- Integration of family, school, and community efforts
- Supportive relationships
- Opportunities to belong
- Positive social norms
- Support for efficacy and mattering
- Opportunities for skill building
- Physical and psychological safety

Youth development theorists emphasize that individuals do not develop assets solely by understanding and avoiding risk. They also must have a whole range of positive opportunities: for nurturing and mutual relationships with adults and peers; to explore talents and interests and develop a sense of competence and personal identity; to engage in leadership and decision making and develop a sense of self-efficacy and control over their future. In the case of youth aging out of foster care, the PYD approach offers opportunities for young people to select services they believe will help them in their future. The Federal Interagency Council on Homelessness, noting that "consumer preference" should be included in homeless youth program design, has found employment and housing are key "consumer choices" by youth aging out of foster care.

Naturally, interventions targeted to homeless youth must address urgent basic needs for safety, nutrition, supervision and shelter, and pressing physical and mental health problems. However, practitioners recognize that prevention and remediation provide youth with positive developmental opportunities and are not mutually exclusive or competitive. Implicit in youth development theory is the belief that interventions are most effective when staff engage youth as partners in planning and decision-making. Each youth should be seen as an individual and an adult-in-progress, with unique strengths and assets. Creativity, mutual respectfulness and the quality of person-to-person relationships between program staff and youth can make a significant difference in fostering trust, motivation to grow, willingness to listen as well as speak out, and other factors needed by youth to learn from and work with adults.

For instance, a substance abuse program might incorporate the dramatic arts in order to provide for self-expression and an opportunity to tap into latent talents, not only in performing, but in organizational and technical skill areas such as event management, stage direction, sound and lighting. In place of short-term basic budgeting courses for foster care youth that focus on the dangers of financial irresponsibility, a program could offer opportunities to set financial goals and accumulate assets through matched savings accounts (individual Development Accounts) and/or entrepreneurial training.

The PYD perspective is gaining greater recognition as a way to view juveniles — regardless of their circumstances — as individuals who possess positive as well as negative attributes. In order to promote the tenets of PYD and enhance youth worker competencies, FYSB's regional technical assistance providers offer PYD and other training to program administrators and youth workers throughout the country. Other efforts to establish youth worker competencies and offer training in youth development principles occur at the national and local levels, including the Department of Labor's 2002 National Youth Worker Apprenticeship Initiative. These training projects enhance staff understanding of the most effective means for placing youth development at the core of programs for youth who are already homeless or at risk.

Finally, it is important that programs serving homeless youth develop partnerships with a variety of organizations and agencies in their communities in order to support positive youth development. While individual programs may not have the resources to offer a full array of developmental opportunities to meet youth's varied interests — programs can link youth to a variety of available resources through partnerships and collaborations.

## Ecological-Developmental Perspective on Youth Homelessness

In general, the ecological perspective encourages researchers, program designers and practitioners to consider the extent to which community factors and characteristics of individuals interact to lead to homelessness, rather than focusing exclusively on individual traits.[63] Haber and Toro emphasize that youth homelessness should not be conceptualized as either the result of failure or poor adaptation on the part of adolescents or their parents, but rather as a breakdown of the parent-adolescent relationship, which takes place within and is influenced by a whole constellation of social factors, such as economic stress, peer associations, and levels of community violence. They further suggest that youth experiences within their families and in the larger social environment will have different effects on young people depending on their stage of development. Thus, effective interventions must be tailored to address the individuals' developmental stage as well as the context of their relationships and their environment.

Applying an ecological-developmental perspective to youth homelessness has a number of implications for intervention. Perhaps most compelling is the importance of understanding and attempting to address social trends contributing to homelessness as well as individual traits. The ecological perspective suggests that interventions to prevent and ameliorate youth homelessness should place more emphasis on youth in the context of their families and communities. For example, several studies on homeless families, suggest that the availability of subsidized housing is as important in predicting future residential stability as individual characteristics of parents. [64] While the trajectories of homelessness are different for youth and families, the need for affordable housing is shared by both. Indeed, since some youth cannot reunite safely with their families, they need resources to transition into living independently in their communities.

## Risk Amplification Model (RAM)

According to the RAM model, youth homelessness involves a pattern of exposure to increasing risks related to negative social interactions and environmental disruptions. Critical factors integrated in this theory include the influence of family environments and peer networks on youth. Essentially, the theory proposes that risks associated with family conflict and negative peer networks lead to and are then compounded by the experience of homelessness.[65] The theory integrates research on the high degree of family conflict reported by homeless youth, as well as research indicating the critical role that both early family influences and peer influences have on negative behavior in adolescents.[66,67] Building on this research, RAM suggests that youth who experience family conflict and violence at home, and those who associate with anti-social peers are more likely to end up homeless. Once homeless, these youth are more likely to continue to associate with anti-social peers, engage in high-risk activities such as drug abuse and survival sex, and be victimized. These experiences amplify the risks experienced prior to homelessness and compound the negative outcomes, such as antisocial behavior, depression, and addiction. As the problems youth experience are multiplied, it becomes increasingly difficult for them to successfully transition to more stable living arrangements and develop healthy relationships with family or other caregivers as well as positive peers.

RAM underlines the importance of early intervention and the need to quickly stabilize homeless youth through reunification with their families or placement in other settings. The first experience of homelessness often is a critical intervention point since the greater number and length of homeless episodes youth experience, the greater the risk amplification. It also is essential to maintain contact with the young people to prevent additional episodes of homelessness. However, emergency shelters which frequently have contact with youth early in their experience of homelessness, are primarily focused on short-term stabilization. While some emergency shelters put strong emphasis on continuing support, many have very little in the way of resources to support follow-up services. This is particularly problematic for youth who return home. In all likelihood, many of them are returning to troubled home environments, and their experiences while homeless may have increased the challenges they face in successfully readapting to their families or households of origin. Runaway and Homeless Youth Act-funded shelters are required by statute and the program standards to provide after-care and to conduct follow-up contacts when runaways are returned to their parents or guardians. However, they are rarely in a position to investigate and confirm that all is well.

Research on adolescent development emphasizes the importance of youth establishing strong connections with their peers and the strong influence that peers can have on social development and behavior. Homeless youth often depend on peers for emotional support and for meeting their basic needs, which can have both positive and negative outcomes. Drawing upon such studies, RAM also hypothesizes that association with anti-social peers can significantly amplify the risks associated with youth homelessness. The influence of peers also has implications for practice.

## Life Cycle Model of Youth Homelessness

Similar to RAM, the Life Cycle Model of youth homelessness focuses on the trajectory of homelessness for street youth. The Life Cycle Model, developed by researchers at the University of California at San Francisco, is based on a small, exploratory ethnographic study of street youth in that city. Though the study involves a small number of youth in a specific setting, it nevertheless provides a useful framework for conceptualizing cycles of homelessness for street youth.

Based on youth observations gleaned from exploratory and semi-structured interviews, researchers developed a proposed model of life on the street that includes seven stages. (1) In the "first on the street phase," youth struggle with intense feelings of "outsiderness" and the burden of meeting basic needs. (2) The difficulties of life on the street may lead youth to seek help from systems or return home and potentially escape street life. (3) Youth who remain on the street are initiated into the culture of street life by "street mentors", typically their peers. (4) They learn necessary survival skills, are acculturated into belief systems rejecting mainstream society and validating life on the street, and frequently begin using and/or selling drugs. (5) As youth become more accustomed to living on the street they enter a stage of "stasis" in which they are generally able to meet basic needs, may have strong, though often ambivalent, relationships with other street youth, and have a strong mistrust and rejection of mainstream society. (6) The "stasis" stage is interrupted by frequent periods of "disequilibrium", when their ability to continue to survive on the street is threatened by a variety of experiences, such as victimization, conflicts with peers, and arrests. (7) When youth are in disequilibrium, they may question their way of life, or come into contact with mainstream institutions that help them to escape street life. Disequilibrium may also reinforce street youths' perception of themselves as outsiders and their distrust of mainstream institutions. Depending on these experiences, youth may extricate themselves from street life, remain on the street, or experience cycles of return to mainstream life followed by recidivism.[68]

Though the Life Cycle Model is still preliminary and based on a small sample, findings suggest that the openness of youth to effects from interventions will vary depending on what stage they are in. Youth who are just entering the street and youth who are experiencing disequilibrium are likely to be the most responsive to outreach and intervention. Street outreach programs could place more emphasis on targeting youth who are new to the streets and actively work to engage these young people in supportive environments before they are initiated fully into street life. Street outreach programs also could focus activities on a few "non-street" settings and develop partnerships where youth experiencing disequilibrium are most likely to be found, such as in emergency rooms or jails. In addition, the model's emphasis on the influential role of initiation into the culture of street life suggests that mentoring homeless youth at this stage of their experience may be an effective strategy for discouraging homelessness. Auerswald and Eyre further suggest that just as youth have to learn "street smarts" in order to survive on the street, to successfully escape the street they need to learn "mainstream smarts." This involves modifying belief systems that reject mainstream society, establishing a means of supporting oneself, and developing relationships with healthy peers and connecting with adult mentors from faith-based and community programs, youth sports organizations, education and youth service programs in the community.

## IV. INTERVENTIONS TO PREVENT YOUTH HOMELESSNESS

Pathways leading young people to homelessness are largely related to family dynamics. Family conflict is the most common factor reported by youth for being on their own (RHYMIS data).[69] In addition to negative family dynamics, when families are either unable or unwilling to care for and/or control their children, out-of-home placements in foster care and juvenile detention settings have been identified as antecedents of youth homelessness.

Preventing youth homelessness requires strengthening families, a consistent domestic policy theme of the Bush Administration. By helping parents develop the capacity to care and nurture their children, the risk of youth homelessness is greatly reduced. Risk factors that lead to family conflict and residential placements must be addressed and protective factors at the individual, family and community levels must be supported.

Interventions most directly relevant to youth who are at high risk of homelessness, and supported by theory and evaluative research include: family interventions to prevent child abuse and neglect; interventions to reduce juvenile violence; and, interventions that support successful transitions.

### Preventing Child Abuse and Neglect

As data have revealed, a high portion of homeless youth experience abuse and/or neglect in their homes. Therefore, it is crucial that interventions take place as early as possible to create violence-free and stable families. Within nurturing families, children can grow and move safely through adolescence and into adulthood. At ACF, several initiatives to support families have been advanced, including responsible fatherhood, and healthy marriage activities, as well as programs in the Promoting Safe and Stable Families statute.

Parent support and education strategies, often provided as components of comprehensive, community-based family supports, can strengthen families, connect families to community resources, promote positive parenting and increase parents' capacity to care for their own children.

Currently, approximately 500,000 children are in Foster Care as a result of being removed from their homes as a result of a child abuse investigation or assessment. These children are at greater risk of brain damage, developmental delays, learning disorders and problems forming relationships; further, they have a greater risk of engaging in antisocial and criminal behavior later in life.[70] Children who are removed from their homes and enter foster care are particularly at risk for homelessness.

Changing negative family dynamics is essential to eliminating the primary reason adolescents leave home -- family conflict. To date, most of the intervention research on preventing child maltreatment has focused on parent education and home visitation programs. Although not conclusive, evaluation findings suggest that these intervention approaches hold promise for preventing child abuse.

## Parent Education

RHYMIS data reveals that family conflict is the most often cited reason youth give for leaving their homes. The goal of parent education is to help parents (or caregivers) gain the knowledge and skills to be effective parents/caregivers and to facilitate the development of healthy children. Parent education programs that focus on improving parenting and life skills can be delivered in a variety of settings, and often target at-risk families (pregnant and parenting teens, single-parents and low-income families). Programs range in their approach, with some grounded in behavioral principles, such as parent nurturing, and others grounded in psychological principles, such as parent effectiveness training.[71]

Research findings demonstrate that some parent education programs lead to reductions in risk factors for child abuse and neglect as well as improvements in parenting skills. Studies have found decreased levels of stress and unhappiness among program participants as well as increased knowledge of child development and attitudes toward parenting and discipline.[72] Unfortunately, most studies have focused on short-term gains of knowledge, skills or behaviors, and little is known about the long-term impact of these programs.[73]

## HOME VISITING

Home visiting programs are predicated on the view that one of the best ways to reach families with young children is to bring services to them, rather than expecting them to seek assistance in their communities. A person trained in child development (e.g., a nurse or other professional, a certified parent educator or other paraprofessional) visits the home of new or expectant families to deliver information, coach effective parenting behavior, conduct outreach and needs assessments, and other case-finding activities.[74]

Although home visiting programs vary, researchers have identified key factors that are likely to maximize program effectiveness: 1) comprehensive, frequent visits;[75] 2) flexible core educational program; 3) staffing by well-trained professionals; and, 4) connecting families to needed services.[76] However, because studies of home visiting programs have not tested the same intervention, it is not possible to know which service delivery component or combination of components is most effective in achieving positive outcomes for children and families.

## Reducing Violence and Delinquency Among Juveniles

Two family-based prevention/intervention approaches, Functional Family Therapy and Multi-Systemic Therapy, have strong evidence documenting their effectiveness in reducing juvenile violence and delinquency. Both service delivery models aim to strengthen and stabilize youth and their families, prevent antisocial behaviors and address the environmental factors associated with delinquency.

Homeless youth have high levels of involvement with the juvenile justice system.[77] Interventions to stabilize troubled juveniles, prevent antisocial behavior problems and disruption, or removal from home may help youth to avoid trajectories of amplified risk and eventual homelessness. The body of research evaluating violence and juvenile delinquency prevention programs is much better developed than the body of research focused on homeless youth. Interventions that have been studied and evaluated include programs designed to promote a resilient family environment that supports healthy family relationships and positive connections for youth.[78] Functional Family Therapy and Multi-Systemic Therapy both have a sound base of scientific research supporting their effectiveness in reducing violence and delinquency among youth.

## FUNCTIONAL FAMILY THERAPY

Functional Family Therapy (FFT), an outcome-driven approach used and tested for over 30 years, is a family-based prevention/intervention program for youth, ages 11 to 18, at risk for, or presenting, problem behaviors. The primary goal of FFT is to produce positive outcomes by preventing the continuation of targeted activities in identified youth — for example, delinquency, violence and substance use.[79] The program seeks to address adolescents' issues within their families, their communities and the systems that youth and families rely upon — schools, health care, child welfare and juvenile justice. The FFT model also places emphasis on respecting the manner in which all family members experience the intervention process. The program can be home-based, clinic-based or school-based. A major goal is to meet with families in settings where they are most comfortable and receptive.

FFT programs aim to motivate families to change by identifying and building on the family's strengths and providing specific ways to overcome difficulties.[80] The therapy model uses a multiphase intervention map that outlines specific goals. Each of the model's three phases includes an assessment process that focuses on understanding the ways in which behavioral problems develop within family relationship systems.

- **Engagement and motivation** — The initial phase is designed to engage, motivate and retain families and targeted youth in prevention/intervention activities by developing credibility in the intervention process and enhancing families' perception that positive change is possible. During this phase, such risk factors as negativity, blaming, hopelessness and lack of motivation are addressed, while at the same time nurturing such protective factors as trust, credibility, alliance and treatment availability (i.e., minimizing those factors that might signify insensitivity and/or inappropriate resources).
- **Behavior change** — During the next phase, families and FFT clinicians develop and implement intermediate and long-term behavior change plans that are culturally appropriate and specifically tailored to the unique characteristics of each family member. The assessment focus includes attribution-processes and coping strategies, reciprocity of positive behaviors and competent parenting. To help families achieve the desired behavior change, within the family's relational system, clinicians guide and model specific behavior changes (e.g., parenting, communication and conflict management).
- **Generalization** — The final phase of the intervention focuses on applying positive behavior change to other issues, problems or situations affecting the family. The focus is on enhancing the family's ability to maintain change and prevent relapse by linking families to available community resources and mobilizing the community supports and services necessary to maintain the intervention's positive impact.

Studies have shown that when compared with no treatment, other family therapy interventions and traditional juvenile court services, such as probation, FFT can reduce adolescent re-arrests by 20 to 60 percent.[81] Significantly, in addition to its effectiveness in reducing adolescents' re-offense rates, the model also has been shown to successfully reduce the onset of delinquency among the siblings of treated adolescents[82]

Studies also indicate that FFT reduces treatment costs to levels well below those of traditional services and other interventions. Total "crime-cost" (system cost plus crime victim cost) savings using FFT are significantly greater than the potential savings achieved as the result of all other residential and probation-based services.[83]

## MULTI-SYSTEMIC THERAPY

Multi-Systemic Therapy (MST) is an intensive family- and community-based clinical intervention approach targeted to chronic, violent or substance-abusing juvenile offenders, ages 12 to 17, at risk of institutional placement. MST posits that youth antisocial behavior is rooted in a variety of environmental factors and innate characteristics of the individual youth and his or her family.[84] Consequently, the treatment model aims to target those factors associated with delinquency in all aspects of young people's lives (e.g., family, peers, school and neighborhood). MST uses the strengths of each system to facilitate and promote behavior change in the youth's natural environment.

The treatment approach focuses on a home-based model of service delivery, which helps to overcome barriers to service access, increases family retention and enhances the maintenance of treatment goals. MST services also can be delivered in schools and other community settings. Initial therapy sessions identify the strengths of the adolescent and family, and the positive aspects of their transactions with peers, friends, school, parental workplace, and other relevant systems. Problems are targeted for change and the resources (i.e., strengths) of each system identified to facilitate such change. A major goal of the intervention is to empower parents by providing them with the skills and resources necessary to address the challenges of raising teenagers and to empower youth to cope with family, peer, school and neighborhood problems. Through this process, a treatment plan is developed that is both family-focused and family-driven, identifies treatment goals at the family, peer and school level and takes into account extended family, community and informal support networks for the family.

Since 1986, MST has been evaluated in over 20 randomized clinical trials with a variety of youth and their families. Results of controlled studies with violent and chronic juvenile offenders have shown MST's effectiveness in reducing youth criminal activity and violent offenses. Evaluations of MST for serious juvenile offenders have demonstrated reductions of 25 to 70 percent in long-term rates of re-arrest.[85] These outcomes signify the potential cost savings associated with MST in comparison to traditional services (e.g., incarceration, hospitalization).

By reducing juvenile offense rates and stabilizing youth involved with the juvenile justice system, both Functional Family Therapy and Multi-Systemic Therapy hold promise for reducing the onset of homelessness among this high-risk population. Furthermore, because of their documented success in intervening and stabilizing very high-risk youth within the context of their families, these strategies are a useful resource for program developers and service providers working with homeless youth in emergency shelters and street outreach programs. These models could be adapted and implemented as a means of providing support to homeless youth who are returned to their families.

## Supporting Successful Transitions to Independent Living

Providing transition plans in Independent Living Programs for foster youth and Intensive Aftercare Programs for youth leaving juvenile detention is extremely important. Transition interventions help youth who are expected to live on their own acquire the knowledge and skills, economic resources, supportive services, and connections to community networks and caring adults.

Although research findings demonstrate that the interventions described earlier can positively impact and strengthen family-youth relationships, some children and youth are not able to benefit from them. This is particularly the case for children and youth in the foster care and juvenile justice systems when family reunification is not possible. When youth leave these systems the expectation is that they will be able to live on their own. This often is not the case. Given the large number of homeless adolescents with a history of foster care placements and juvenile justice involvement, targeted strategies are needed to support healthy transitions and prevent the onset of homelessness among these high-risk populations. Two promising interventions are the Independent Living Program (ILP) for foster youth and reintegration and aftercare services for youth in the juvenile justice system.

Research findings demonstrate that compared to the general youth population, youth in foster care exhibit lower functioning levels in the areas of physical and emotional wellbeing, education, employment and economic status.[86] Youth who spend a significant amount of time in foster care often are unprepared to live independently, and lack the adult support that most individuals depend on well into young adulthood. It is not surprising, therefore, that a large proportion of homeless youth also have a history of foster care placements. To address this growing problem, Congress enacted the Independent Living Program in 1986 and Title I of the Foster Care Independence Act of 1999 (the John H. Chafee Foster Care Independence Program) to help older adolescents, who will leave foster care at the age of 18, successfully develop the knowledge, skills and habits to live independently. These policy initiatives have led to the widespread implementation of independent living programs across the country.[87]

Few studies have rigorously evaluated the effectiveness of Independent Living Programs (ILP) in achieving positive outcomes for transitioning youth. Those studies that have been conducted indicate that when implemented comprehensively, these programs hold promise for helping youth successfully move to independence. [88] Additional studies have examined the characteristics of youth leaving care, and the range of supports and services that need to be in place to most effectively prepare them for the transition to independence and support them after they leave care. These research efforts provide information on the characteristics and needs of foster youth and what works in preparing them to live on their own. Critical components of intervention strategies are described below.

- **Assessments** — To develop individualized and youth-focused ILP plans, programs must assess the strengths (i.e., skills and knowledge) and needs of foster youth. These assessments can be conducted formally through the use of standardized assessment tools and protocols and informally through observations and discussions with youth. Areas to be assessed include adolescents' academic/educational level, employment/vocational skills, personal and social skills (relationships with peers and adults; communication skills), health, residential living/home management skills, personal hygiene and safety, purchasing habits, budgeting and banking. Based on these assessments, ILP staff can actively work with and engage youth, foster parents and other supportive adults in the development of targeted ILP plans that build on each youth's unique strengths and address his or her needs.
- **Life skills preparation and training** — Youth transitioning out of care need to develop basic life skills and must be prepared for the realities and responsibilities of living on their own. Specific ILP intervention components should include education and job training, career development, assistance securing stable and affordable housing, education and training on maintaining a residence, planning for health care needs, accessing community resources, financial planning and decision-making and leadership skill development opportunities. Some independent living programs also pay for work-related expenses and transportation costs to help youth maintain their employment.[89] While few studies have rigorously evaluated the impact of life skills preparation and training, results from the most comprehensive study of the outcomes for youth formerly in foster care demonstrate that consistent training in a few skill areas (e.g., health care, education and employment training opportunities) was associated with positive outcomes for youth.[90] Cook and colleagues found that youth who received an increasing number of skills training in the areas of money,

consumer skills, credit, education and employment were more likely to maintain a job for at least a year and access health care if they needed it. Similarly, youth who received health training were significantly more likely to access health care services after discharge than those who did not receive such training.

To be effective, however, ILP training and preparation needs to go beyond classroom instruction and provide youth with opportunities for experiential learning and practice.[91] For example, programs can be designed to allow youth to live in unsupervised or semi-supervised settings, such as scattered-site and supervised apartments, where youth take ownership and responsibility for buying groceries, cooking and cleaning and maintaining their apartments. These experiences will give youth the opportunity to experience the realities of living on their own, make mistakes and learn by doing while at the same time developing the skills necessary for successful independent living.[92]

In addition, while ILP services and supports have traditionally focused on helping youth develop life skills through short-tenn training and preparation, there is growing recognition that youth need more intensive and sustained help focused on preparing them for the economic realities of self-support.[93] Youth need to learn about budgeting and they also need opportunities to develop effective financial management skills and the resources that will enable them to save and accumulate material assets. A number of innovative programs have begun to utilize Individual Development Accounts (IDA) in combination with financial literacy education, to help youth develop savings habits and accumulate critical assets, including post-secondary education or their first house or apartment. Some ILPs also are developing enhanced job training, internship, and entrepreneurial training and opportunities, as well as linking youth with professional mentors from fields of interest.

---

**SUPPORTING THE ECONOMIC SUCCESS OF TRANSITIONING YOUTH**

With support from several national foundations, a number of community-based initiatives currently are testing and evaluating comprehensive approaches to provide transitioning youth opportunities to acquire the means to achieve economic success. Several communities provide current and former foster care youth with opportunities to learn financial management; obtain experience with the banking system; save money for education, housing, and health care through a matched IDA programs, and gain streamlined access to educational, training, and vocational opportunities. Evaluation of these efforts will provide the child welfare field information on what strategies assist successful transitions to adulthood.

---

- **Affordable housing** — Affordable housing is a critical need for youth aging out of foster care. Researchers and practitioners encourage youth service providers to help youth find housing in communities where they will have access to employment opportunities, social services, transportation and social support systems that will help increase the odds for success.[94] Providing transitioning youth access to appropriate housing options requires child welfare agencies to carefully assess youth's readiness to live in semi-supervised or unsupervised settings as well as the creation of partnerships and collaborative relationships with landlords and public housing authorities to increase the supply and availability of apartments and other housing options for foster youth. Although the John H. Chafee Foster Care Independence Program (CFCIP) requires that child welfare agencies coordinate with Federal and State housing programs that provide services to youth, the General Accounting Office reports that few States are using housing services provided by HUD and State housing authorities for emancipated foster youth.[95]

- **Connections to caring adults** — Promising intervention strategies for youth aging out of care also focus on ensuring that young people are connected to caring adults. Studies have shown that biological, extended and foster families play an important role in the lives of many youth who exit care; they often are the only source of emotional, social and financial support available to this population.[96] Therefore, important components of ILPs preparing youth to exit care include:
  - Exploring resources of families (biological, foster and adoptive) and relatives;
  - Facilitating visitation between youth and family members;
  - Engaging family members in the development of youth ILP plans; and
  - Developing alternative support systems through relationships with mentors and other supportive adults to connect youth to a wide range of community resources.

Promoting these relationships also is important because in many instances, successfully engaging youth in 1LP activities requires the active engagement of foster parents, mentors and other caring adults who can recruit, advocate for, encourage and motivate young people to participate in these activities and teach youth by modeling positive skills and behaviors.

Finally, to sustain the transition and ensure positive long-term outcomes for this vulnerable population, ILPs also must provide youth with aftercare services upon exit from care that may include counseling, case management, limited financial assistance to meet emergency needs and information on available community resources.[97]

Additionally, given the similarities between ILPs for foster care youth and Transitional Living Programs (TLP) for homeless youth, significant opportunities for coordination and service integration exists. ACF annually holds joint conferences for both ILP and TLP program grantees ("Pathways to Independence").

# RE-INTEGRATION AND AFTERCARE
# SERVICES FOR OFFENDING YOUTH

Aftercare interventions have been advanced as an effective strategy to reduce recidivism, increase public safety and provide juvenile parolees with the treatment and support to enable them to be successfully reintegrated.

Available research indicates that recidivism rates among juvenile offenders are high and the current juvenile corrections systems are not equipped to adequately prepare youth to return to their communities.[98] One specific approach that has promise is the Intensive Aftercare Program (TAP), a theory-driven model that seeks to reduce recidivism by providing a continuum of supervision and services to high-risk juvenile offenders during institutionalization and after release.[99] The IAP premise is that a continuum of services must include pre-release preparation and planning, supportive services by institutional and aftercare staff, and long-term re-integrative activities to ensure that youth have access to service delivery and are monitored post-release.

Like other models, IAP examines youth problems in the context of their families, peer relationships, schools and communities. Interventions are not simply focused on addressing "youth problems" but are designed to holistically address risk factors and strengthen protective factors present in the settings and contexts in which youth live. Five principles guide the implementation of IAP interventions:[100]

- Preparing youth for progressively increased responsibility and freedom in the community;
- Facilitating youth-community interaction and involvement;
- Working with the youth and targeted community support systems on traits needed for constructive interaction and the youth's successful community adjustment;
- Developing new resources and supports; and
- Monitoring and testing the youth and the community on their ability to deal with the other productively.

These goals are effectuated through a comprehensive case management approach focused on identifying and assessing high-risk youth by the use of validated screening instruments and then developing individualized case plans. Plans are intended to engage and incorporate family and community perspectives, identify youths' service needs, and practical approaches for meeting them from incarceration to discharge. Staff members are assigned small caseloads that enable them to closely supervise youth and provide intensive services 24 hours a day, 7 days a week (IAP case managers may carry approximately one-half to one-third the amount of cases handled by non-IAP case managers as cited by Wiebush). [101] The supervision and monitoring of offending youth is based on a system of graduated sanctions and rewards that holds youth accountable and provides youth with incentives that encourage positive behavior and behavior modification.

To provide juvenile offenders with the necessary resources to transition successfully into the community, the IAP model requires the establishment of linkages with community resources and social networks. This cross-agency or cross-systems coordination is established early in the intervention through the use of a team-oriented approach to case planning and management. Through this collaboration, youth gain access to education, employment/vocational training, mental health counseling, drug and alcohol treatment, housing, mentoring and other supportive services available in the community. [102]

Working with youth during and after incarceration and providing them access to a comprehensive array of aftercare services, IAP interventions not only reduce juvenile recidivism rates but also lead to successful transition from the justice system and youth's reintegration into the community.[103] In so doing, the model has the potential to reduce homeless episodes among this high-risk population.

# V. INTERVENTIONS TO AMELIORATE HOMELESSNESS

Ending youth homelessness requires effective interventions that engage youth as early in the cycle of homelessness as possible and helps to stabilize them in appropriate, supportive environments.

Four categories of interventions are: Gateway Services, Shelter and Stabilizing Services, Targeted Supportive Services, and Programs Supporting Youth Transitions to Independence.

1. **Gateway Services** meet the urgent and basic needs of youth in an effort to gain their trust and eventually help them access a broader range of services. Gateway services are less structured and formalized than services to shelter and stabilize youth, and include drop-in centers and street outreach programs.

2. **Services to Shelter and Stabilize Youth** focus on sheltering and stabilizing homeless youth, through reunification with their family or appropriate transitional placement outside their families.

3. **Targeted Supportive Services** are intentional and intensive services to specific populations with special needs, including youth with drug and alcohol abuse and mental health problems, youth living with HIV/AIDS, and pregnant and parenting teens.

4. **Programs Supporting Youth Transitions to Independence** encompasses longer-term housing options and services that help young people who will not be returning to their families with their transition to independence.

## Principles for Effective Intervention Practice

Theoretical research and practitioners emphasize that a core set of principles for relating effectively to homeless youth should infuse all interventions. Most of the promising interventions coordinate and integrate services in an effort to provide seamless support.

- **Strengthening and supporting families** — To address the risk factors that lead to youth leaving and staying away from their homes, intervention approaches must emphasize strategies to strengthen and support families. Families, whether immediate or extended, are resources for homeless youth and should be actively involved in adolescents' transition to independence and adulthood. Service delivery should include: 1) coordination of supports and resources for youth and families in crises, 2) access and referrals to an array of services and strategies to reduce family conflict, and 3) development of parenting skills to understand adolescents' developmental transitions.
- **Supporting positive youth development** — Recognizing the strengths and needs of each individual youth, empowering youth to set goals and encouraging their involvement in making decisions that affect them are essential to all interventions.

- Programs for homeless youth need to provide opportunities to develop leadership skills by engaging youth in program design, planning and implementation. In many instances, youth are able to serve as peer mentors and role models to other young people, assist professional staff in recruiting, and increasing participation in program services and activities. These opportunities help young people develop confidence in their abilities, a sense of empowerment and self-efficacy, as well as a greater sense of ownership in program goals and activities.
- **Developing cultural competency** — To address the needs of homeless youth and maintain their participation and engagement in program activities, services must be provided in a safe and comfortable environment. Services must be culturally appropriate and non-judgmental and take into account and respect individual differences across race, ethnicity, gender, sexual orientation or lifestyle, and age. To ensure the provision of non-judgmental services, providers must train and develop culturally proficient workers, hire workers who are representative of the youth served and design interventions with knowledge of and respect for the differences in young people's life experiences and cultural beliefs. In addition, interventions should build upon youth's strengths and recognize their uniqueness. The provision of non-judgmental services is particularly important as youth's perception of workers and other professional staff greatly affects their willingness to seek services and participate in support programs.
- **Creating a continuum of integrated services** — Homeless youth are a diverse population and are vulnerable to a range of problems. Accordingly, to effectively address their needs, programs and services need to be integrated. Strategies should include the development of coordinated service plans involving a number of providers and programs to meet young people's multiple needs, establish linkages and referral systems across agencies, and provide cross-agency training to ensure that services are consistent and coherent. Developing comprehensive and integrated service strategies is particularly important because many service providers have limited resources to serve homeless youth, and the available funding streams are restricted to specific categories of services or eligible populations.
- **Tailoring services to individualized needs** — Given the particular challenges of the homeless youth population (e.g., multiple placements, precarious living situations, and co-occurring disorders), most homeless youth need access to individualized and tailored services that are integrated into a continuum of care. Intensive case management is one approach to achieve this goal. Case managers develop trusting and caring relationships with homeless clients, respond quickly to client needs and priorities, are dependable but flexible, and have the capacity to assess clients' often changing needs for intensive services or personal space.[104] Importantly, effective case managers provide active assistance to help clients access needed resources, follow clients' priorities and timing for services, respect client autonomy and focus on realistic goals. Small caseloads enable case managers to develop therapeutic relationships with youth, provide crisis intervention and serve as the unifying factor in service delivery by helping youth navigate the various service systems and act to facilitate communication between different service-providers involved with the youth. Because intensive case management can be implemented across a variety of program models, the approach can be easily adapted to meet the needs of individual

youth in a variety of settings, including emergency shelters, transitional living and supportive housing programs.

## RHYA Outreach and Gateway Services

Homeless youth are a difficult population to serve as they are often fearful of being forced to return to negative situations — whether in families or institutions — and they tend to be distrustful of adults. RHYA street outreach programs and drop-in centers, administered by ACF, strive to engage youth by providing services that meet their most urgent needs with relatively little structure and few demands. These services are intended to reduce the level of risk youth on the street face and provide a gateway through which hard-to-reach youth can eventually move into more intensive, transitional services.

## STREET OUTREACH

A significant number of homeless adolescents spend time living on the street at some point during their homeless experience. Time spent on the street is often associated with exposure to victimization and risky behavior. Street outreach is designed to minimize the negative impact of life on the street for homeless youth.

Generally, street outreach programs target homeless youth who might not otherwise take advantage of needed services because they lack trust in adults and service systems or they do not know how to find services they need.[105] The program goal is to prevent adolescents' exposure to sexual abuse and victimization, as well as prolonged episodes of homelessness. To achieve this goal, street outreach workers go to where homeless youth are likely to congregate, including abandoned buildings, bus stops and other street locations, and work directly with the young people to assess and respond to their needs. Outreach programs offer a variety of services including street-based education, access to emergency shelter, survival supplies such as blankets and food, individual assessments, treatment and counseling, prevention and education activities, information and referrals, crisis intervention, transportation and follow-up support. Practitioners contend that the most effective street outreach programs are those that provide homeless adolescents with access to caring adults who can show them how to maneuver myriad systems through which services and help are provided.

Successful outreach workers are trained in youth development principles, know how to communicate with young people, and are able to respect their personal space. Outreach workers understand the importance of relationship-building, have in-depth knowledge of the operations and services of youth-serving systems (such as social services, juvenile justice, health and education), and are able connect youth to critical supports and services.[106] Finally, workers know the street culture and can help vulnerable young people develop trusting, positive relationships. When youth are ready, outreach workers help them identify the services they need and link them to those services.

A promising outreach strategy is training peers, or formerly homeless youth, to serve as outreach workers. A peer-to-peer outreach approach is considered particularly effective in finding and identifying homeless adolescents since peer outreach workers typically know the places where street youth gather and can more easily connect and build a rapport with them. Peer models also help foster partnerships between youth and adults, increase self-esteem among peer outreach workers, and provide youth opportunities to participate in service design and delivery.[107]

To most successfully connect street youth to the help they need, outreach workers often travel in a van loaded with supplies to the areas where street youth typically congregate. Mobile outreach activities give outreach workers the flexibility to offer critically needed preventive and urgent health care services, distribute nutritious food and snacks, help youth complete applications for benefits, provide referrals to emergency shelter services, and assist with transportation. In addition to providing services, many street outreach programs are connected to, or coordinate with, drop-in centers, emergency shelters and other youth-serving agencies that further stabilize youth by providing case management, short-term shelter and long-term housing.

---

### COLLABORATIVE APPROACHES TO STREET OUTREACH

Understanding that one program alone cannot identify all street youth or meet all of their needs, innovative programs have organized collaboratives of agencies conducting street outreach. The goal is to have more trained counselors covering the streets at all hours and to provide appropriate linkages and referrals to homeless youth. Members of the collaborative share current information, conduct joint outreach activities, make appropriate service referrals, and enroll eligible participants in entitlement programs.

---

Successful outreach programs also engage service providers, neighborhood business owners who have frequent contact with street youth, community leaders, and local police to coordinate services and build cooperation in serving this population.

## DROP-IN CENTERS

Outreach and engagement also take place in drop-in centers. Drop-in centers provide homeless youth with an initial point of contact for a broad range of services and referrals. Drop-in centers meet immediate subsistence needs by providing free meals, showers, laundry facilities, toiletries and new and used clothing. Centers also may provide comprehensive programming and supportive services such as individual assessment, case management, crisis intervention, information and referrals. In addif on, in coordination with shelters and other youth-serving programs, drop-in centers provide youth access to housing, legal counsel, and health services. For many vulnerable youth, this approach enables them to control decisions concerning when and how they seek help, including when and how they transition from street life to other residential arrangements.

## PEER-TO-PEER MODELS TO REACH HOMELESS YOUTH

A street outreach program in the Northeast developed a peer outreach component to target youth at risk of becoming homeless. The agency trains youth who have successfully completed one of its programs to do street outreach that specifically targets youth who are in need of services but who might not relate to the agency's professional staff. To ensure continuity of services and further develop peer workers' skills, peer outreach workers have the opportunity to work in the agency's resource center where they assist with a variety of activities targeted to youth and their families (access to crisis intervention, education, legal and medical services).

## STRATEGIES TO ENGAGE HOMELESS YOUTH

Recognizing the importance of providing youth with a safe and non-threatening space, some drop-in centers encourage youth participation by providing a game room or drop-in room where youth can "hang out" and find some privacy. Others seek to foster a sense of community and connectedness among homeless youth by holding group sessions that allow youth to discuss issues in their lives, as well as conducting activities that allow youth to form friendships and develop trusting relationships with peers and professional staff.

## Sheltering and Stabilizing Homeless Youth

Youth shelters that place a strong emphasis on stabilizing youth and reunification with families or other appropriate long-term placements are critical in preventing prolonged episodes of homelessness among this population. Providers report that younger youth and those experiencing their first episode of homelessness are more likely to reconcile with families, if early intervention is available.[108]

Through the Basic Center Program, ACF provides core funding for many emergency shelters throughout the country. Emergency shelters are essential for stabilizing homeless youth, providing a temporary safe haven from victimization and the risks of life on the streets, and intervening quickly to ameliorate the short- and long-term effects of homelessness. Emergency shelters provide youth a safe place to spend the night away from the potentially dangerous environment of adult shelters and street life and serve as an entry point from which youth can access a variety of programs and services. Community-based emergency shelters represent the primary method of intervention for runaway youth and are required to reunify youth with their families.[109]

Shelter programs receiving Basic Center funding serve youth up to age 18, for a maximum of 15 days, and are required to provide room and board, clothing, medical services, individual, group, and family counseling, outreach, and aftercare services and referrals, as appropriate, for youth after they leave shelter. In addition to Basic Center funds, many shelters use other resources, such as local faith-based and community social service support, to provide additional services to homeless youth. Shelters also can provide crisis intervention through assessments, counseling, and case management services. Through crisis intervention, shelters meet young people's immediate needs, stabilize youth, assist them in making decisions about their lives, and reunify youth at- risk of homelessness with their families. When family reunification is not possible, however, shelters help youth transition to other appropriate and stable placements.

Research suggests that the first episode of homelessness is a critical time for intervention. Therefore, strong family-centered follow up services to support youth upon reunification with their families is critically important. Addressing issues that led to initial departure can prevent future homeless episodes. Shelters that successfully reunify youth and their families are more likely to develop strategies to engage families in the youth's treatment plan, provide adjunct youth-family mediation, counseling and other support services to reduce family conflict, address behavioral issues and reduce the risk factors that lead to youth leaving home.[110]

---

## FAMILY SUPPORT SERVICES TO REUNIFY YOUTH AND THEIR FAMILIES

Shelters can provide youth and families with group and individual-level counseling by trained professionals (i.e., family therapist) and a peer mentor assigned to the youth upon entry into the program. Through this triage approach, the program seeks to immediately engage youth and families in order to assess specific issues and determine how best to reunify youth with their families. The family therapist is available during the day and evening hours and the peer mentor works with the teen to promote positive decision-making, serve as a role model and engage the youth in experiential learning activities. These services are available to youth and their families during periods of crisis and throughout their engagement with the program.

---

In addition to short-term crisis interventions and family follow-up and support, promising programs also work with youth to ensure their transition and access to a continuum of supports and services. In some instances, youth work with case managers who link them to housing, jobs, school placements, public benefits, health care, legal assistance and other services as needed.

While some shelters coordinate with social service providers to facilitate homeless adolescents' access to supportive services, others have the capacity to provide these services on-site. The availability of on-site services not only ensures that youth have access to a continuum of care but also can facilitate tracking and monitoring.

Research has found a number of youth identified barriers which may prevent them from accessing assistance at emergency shelters. Boyer and colleagues found that youth may not seek shelter services because they do not want to comply with program rules (e.g., wake up time, curfew, and drug, alcohol or smoking restrictions), they fear for their safety (i.e., believe they will be victimized) or believe they will be treated badly by program staff [111] Then, too, some shelters will not serve homeless youth with presenting or severe problems that may place other youth and shelter staff at-risk.

## A Continuum of Care for Homeless Youth

To provide youth with the education, employment, and training skills necessary to become self-sufficient, one particularly innovative program developed a comprehensive workforce development initiative available to minors and young adults at its drop-in center, emergency shelter, or transitional living program. Components include:

- Education and employment assessment;
- Employment skill building and career exploration;
- Day labor program;
- Employability skills development through job readiness classes;
- Computer skills training;
- Individualized job placement;
- Pre and post-placement counseling and retention services; and
- Educational advocacy and post-secondary education advising.

The program's separate but integrated components can be accessed individually, enabling participants to utilize those services they need to achieve their employment or educational goals. Participants also may access the components consecutively to progressively develop marketable skills, clear career goals, and a positive attitude and behavioral outlook that will increase their chances of identifying career interests and setting a plan to achieve them. This flexibility allows the program to "meet youth where they are."

Although underage youth can stay at a shelter without a parent or guardian, Federal law requires that shelter programs contact a youth's family within 72 hours of a youth's entry into the shelter. This familial contact is a critical step in the reunification process, a primary goal of the Runaway and Homeless Youth program. State laws may also require that programs, particularly licensed shelters, contact a parent or guardian sooner or obtain a parent's consent for a youth to enter the program. Consequently, many shelters require that youth provide proper identification and/or parental contact information upon entry. Studies have found that these eligibility requirements can prevent youth from seeking shelter servi ces. [112]

## PROGRAMS AND SERVICES TO SUPPORT
## YOUTH TRANSITIONS TO INDEPENDENCE

There are two general strategies to help homeless youth make a successful transition to independence: TLPs and longer-term affordable housing. TLPs provide youth who cannot return home with prescribed, stable, living situation, as well as supports and services that help them prepare for independent living. Due to the growing recognition of the need, the Department of Housing and Urban Development is actively pursuing development of longer-term affordable housing options to help homeless youth successfully transition to independence.

## Transitional Living Programs

TLPs provide shelter, life skills and other services to help youth who cannot be reunited with their families move toward independence and self-sufficiency. These programs are very similar to the ILPs targeted to youth aging out of foster care, and in some instances providers integrate these programs. TLPs are primarily funded through RHYA and are available to youth 16 through 21 years of age for a period of approximately 18 months. These programs are intended to help homeless youth, including those who have been in foster care, avoid long-term dependency on social services and make a successful transition to independent living by providing temporary housing and mandatory services.[113] Living accommodations may include host family homes, group homes and supervised apartments. Supervised apartments are either agency-owned apartment buildings or scattered-site apartments which are rented directly by young people with support from the agency.

In addition to temporary or transitional housing, TLPs offer life-skills building, education and employment training, mental and physical health care, housing placement, benefits assistance, and case management services. The role of the case manager is to assess young people's needs, collaborate with youth in developing service and transition plans with clearly outlined goals and steps to achieve them, link youth to supportive services, monitor use of services and act as an advocate for youth to help them successfully achieve independence.

TLPs help homeless youth by providing them with real life experiences in a quasi-supervised setting. In this environment, young people make independent choices and have the opportunity to learn from any mistakes. Researchers contend that to be most effective, TLP services should recognize the adult-like status of homeless adolescents by teaching them life skills they may not have learned earlier.[114]

To enter a TLP program, youth may be required to meet the following conditions:

- Demonstrate homelessness status
- Agree to a criminal background check
- Undergo assessments (life-skills, parenting/pregnancy prevention); substance abuse evaluation/drug screening; and a physical examination
- Provide references
- Secure employment and/or attend school/educational program

To remain in a TLP program, youth may be required to meet the following conditions:

- Pay rent, based on their ability to pay
- Contribute a percentage of income towards household expenses and/or a savings account
- Attend school or an educational program and/or remain continuously employed
- Remain drug- and alcohol-free and meet other "house rules" including curfews
- Participate in program activities including weekly house meetings
- Meet housekeeping responsibilities
- Assist staff in making decisions about new youth entering the program by interviewing youth and providing feedback to staff

# PROVIDING COMPREHENSIVE AND INTEGRATED TRANSITIONAL SERVICES

A transitional living program on the West Coast provides transitional living services in a group home setting for homeless youth ages 15-17. The program is designed to provide youth with developmentally appropriate services necessary to assist them in making a successful transition to permanent housing and productive adulthood. Key components of this integrated service approach include:

- Stable housing in a safe and supporting residential environment that enables youth to focus their attention on their educational and life skills goals;
- Case management services to help youth develop individualized plans that reflect youth's assets, needs future goals and an action plan by which youth will meet identified goals;
- Educational services available in collaboration with the local school district or at the program's fully accredited school;
- Life skills training that includes budgeting and money management, conflict resolution, cooking and cleaning and other practical skills;
- Job readiness training including employment assessment, skill building, job placement and retention services;
- Medical care; and
- Substance abuse and mental health services, including assessments, wrap-around case management, medication service, counseling, aftercare and coordinated referrals to emergency and long-term care.

# INDIVIDUALIZED TRANSITIONAL LIVING SERVICES

A transitional living program for young adults, ages 18 to 24, fosters independence in a minimally restrictive environment by emphasizing a highly individualized approach and the opportunity for each resident to develop, with staff support, a customized action plan for economic self-sufficiency and long-term permanent housing. To assist youth obtain and maintain permanent housing, the program provides intensive case management services, life skills training, employment services and follow-up services. Youth work with a case manager and transition specialist to develop a plan for permanent housing that includes decisions about where the youth wants to live, anticipated rent expenses employment development for economic self-sufficiency. Through their participation in life skills training, youth not only learn about money management, food preparation, and housecleaning, but also about tenancy laws, and receive information on how to select roommates and neighborhoods. Finally, because youth must budget their own finances in preparation for their transition to permanent housing, they most obtain and retain full-time employment status and pay 30 percent of their income as "rent" while participating in the program. These rental "savings" are returned to the youth upon leaving the program and the money is most commonly used to cover move-in costs. including security deposits and furniture.

Compared to other interventions, TLPs provide more privacy, services that are more intensive and have more requirements, and greater expectations for youth participation. TLPs eligibility requirements vary. Some TLPs do not admit "hard-to-serve" homeless adolescents, such as youth with substance abuse, mental health issues or developmental disabilities, while these issues may not disqualify a youth for admission into other TLPs.[115] Programs that lack the resources to provide intensive support and specialized services often are unwilling to admit a more difficult-to-serve client population. Though they are sometimes criticized for "creaming," providers argue that they lack the capacity to both help large numbers of homeless youth make successful transitions and adequately address the serious problems of the most troubled young people.

## Affordable Housing

While historically there has been relatively little work in this area, there are promising models of affordable housing options targeted to the needs of youth developed by the Department of Housing and Urban Development as well as State and local agencies. Strategies include the provision of supportive housing as well as access to subsidized housing and voucher programs that will help youth find safe, affordable housing and live on their own.

To be effective, supportive housing strategies should include access to safe, decent and affordable rental housing as well as access and connections to relevant supports and services that give young people access to services they need. This approach is premised on the assumption that homeless youth need help with more than housing alone to successfully achieve independence.

What distinguishes supportive housing models from transitional and independent living programs is that they tend to be more flexible, longer-term and have fewer admission criteria. Supportive housing programs help youth and young adults develop independent living skills by combining housing and services while affording residents the rights and responsibilities of tenancy. Supportive housing programs typically target homeless youth and young adults from 18-25 years of age, including those who have aged out of the foster care system, transitioned from the juvenile justice system or children's mental health system, and/or are pregnant and parenting, and who would thrive in a more independent setting. Youth service providers have developed innovative congregate supportive housing programs for older homeless and precariously housed youth:[116]

## THE FOYER MODEL OF SUPPORTIVE HOUSING

Foyer is a supportive housing model developed in Europe to provide young adults who cannot live at home with a continuum of services to facilitate their transition to independent living and successful adulthood. In addition to stable housing, participants receive intensive case management services and linkages to job training, education and life skills development resources. The Foyer model is currently being adapted to serve homeless and aging-out youth in New York City.

Supportive housing may be organized in several ways: 1) housing dispersed throughout a community and usually rented from a private landlord (i.e., scattered site); 2) single, multi-unit buildings dedicated to youth and young adults (i.e., single site or congregate); and 3) units or entire floors set-aside especially for youth and young adults in affordable housing developments (i.e., set-aside units).

Two distinct program designs have emerged. In one approach, a youth or young adult signs a lease or occupancy agreement with a private landlord and has overall responsibility for meeting the stipulations of the lease. In this approach, there are no responsive to client needs, establish good relationships with landlords, ring housing in communities that are safe, affordable, with access to transportation, employment and other services that are familiar and/or comfortable to young people. In addition, given the limited resources available to serve this population, programs must have the capacity to access and coordinate funding from a variety of programs to develop supportive housing for homeless and at-risk youth. They also need to form positive partnerships with housing authorities and community development entities.

## SCATTERED SITE HOUSING FOR TRANSITIONING YOUTH

An agency on the West Coast operates a scattered site housing program through a master lease for youth ages 18-21, who have been discharged from foster care, homeless or at risk of homelessness. The agency master leases individual rental units throughout the community and subleases them to program participants. To qualify for the housing program, participants must complete an economic literacy curriculum and a rigorous certification program that makes them eligible for a housing micro-loan which pays their first month's rent and security deposit. Participants live in a two-bedroom shared apartment, accessible to public transportation and community amenities, and pay a portion of their rent (30 percent at entry into the program and a greater percentage as their participation in the program continues).

In addition to the micro-loan, participants receive a comprehensive array of supportive services that includes life skills training, assistance with rent payments, move-in, transportation, food stipends, and opportunities to interact with peers and adults in the community through participation in community events. Program participants also receive individualized services related to meeting their employment, health, education, financial management, and other goals.

In addition to supportive housing programs targeted to youth, young people can also benefit from access to traditional, affordable housing vouchers and subsidized housing available to low-income adults. To ensure that homeless youth access these resources, the Family Unification Program (FUP) was created at the Department of Housing and Urban Development in 1990 to meet the housing needs of children at risk of placement in foster care due to homelessness or other housing problems. In 2000, Congress expanded FUP eligibility to youth aging out of foster care. FUP provides housing assistance, through Section 8 vouchers, to families whose children are at risk of placement in foster care and to young adults transitioning out of foster care.[117]

---

### HUD GRANT FUNDS SERVICE TO HOMELESS YOUTH

To house homeless youth with mental health problems and substance dependence, one service provider accesses a Shelter Plus Care Federal housing grant from HUD to operate a 17-unit apartment complex. The HUD grant provides a housing subsidy for youth at 30 percent of their income while the service provider provides a dollar-for-dollar match with supportive case management services. Through partnership with a national homeless advocacy coalition and a mental health care provider, youth also have access to mental health screening, assessments, treatment, and psychotropic medications.

---

Youth ages 18-21, who have left foster care at age 16 or older, are eligible for FLIP housing assistance for up to 18 months. In order to receive these services, however, youth must be referred and certified as eligible by a local child welfare agency, and the agency must be willing to provide aftercare services to them. Service providers can help homeless youth access these resources by working with local child welfare agencies to verify young people's eligibility and to ensure that they receive aftercare services.

## Providing Targeted Supportive Services to Homeless Youth

While shelter, transitional living, and supportive housing programs frequently incorporate a range of services, they often do not have the capacity to effectively work with the most difficult-to-serve populations. Some homeless youth require intensive supports targeted to their special needs, in particular, pregnant and parenting teens as well as youth with extreme alcohol and other drug abuse problems, youth with severe mental health problems, and youth with HIV/AIDS.

# PREGNANT AND PARENTING TEENS

Homeless youth who are parents face the dual hardships of street life and responsibility for their children's safety and well-being. Their lack of social support networks, histories of family conflict and precarious living situation are risk factors that can lead to interactions with the child welfare system and separation from their children. Homeless teen parents are able to receive supportive services through youth shelters and through programs designed for homeless families.

Youth who are homeless and are parents require services tailored to their particular life circumstances and developmental needs. They require access to transitional living and supportive housing programs, specialized training and education programs to develop their parenting skills and access to services including child care, educational assistance and employment preparation and training. Recognizing the special needs of pregnant and parenting teens, the recent reauthorization of RHYA includes funding for TLPs targeted to young mothers and their children. These maternity group homes provide pregnant youth and young mothers aged 16-21 with food and shelter, as well as parenting education and support programs to promote their long-term economic independence and their ability to support their children.

## Substance Abusers

Studies suggest that homeless adolescents have higher rates of substance use disorders than housed youth.[118] The substance abuse rate of homeless youth has been estimated to range from 70 to 85 percent.[119] The use of dangerous and illicit substances can impair judgment and decision-making and lead youth to engage in violent behavior. Confounding this challenge is the fact that many homeless youth have co-occurring problems with alcohol and other drug use and mental health disorders.[120] These disorders hinder providers' ability to serve the population and limit youth's capacity to develop employability skills, find and keep a job and secure housing. Serving this population requires access to drug abuse assessments and evaluations, detoxification and treatment services, as well as ongoing counseling and education.

## Youth with Mental Health Problems

Although it is difficult to assess accurately the mental health status of homeless adolescents, research shows that prevalence rates of depression, suicidal initiations, and other mental health disorders among this population are higher than those found in housed matched groups or the general population.[121] While many homeless youth struggle with mental health issues, some have severe mental health needs that require intensive supervision and intervention. Frequently, runaway and homeless youth program staff find that they are faced with youth who have more intensive needs than they have the capacity to address. Homeless youth with mental health problems need access to intensive and structured services tailored to their specific needs. Services for this vulnerable population include daily living skills, supportive housing, transportation, education, vocational training, access to counseling and medical services and skills to develop their self-esteem and empowerment. Children and youth with serious mental and emotional disorders frequently get lost between the child and adult mental health systems.[122] Therefore, homeless youth service providers need to create linkages with both the child and adult mental health systems to effectively reach this population.

## HIV/AIDS

Homeless youth engage in risky behaviors, such as unprotected sex, sex with multiple partners, intravenous drug use and needle-sharing, that place them at high-risk for contracting HIV/AIDS.[123] To reduce the incidence of HIV/AIDS among homeless youth, prevention programs and services to educate young people about risky behaviors, their consequences, and how to avoid them, including abstinence education are needed. Prevention education is most effective when it is offered by trained professionals in conjunction with street outreach activities that engage youth and encourage them to seek supports and services. Results from an evaluation of HIV/AIDS street outreach projects indicate that youth in contact with street outreach were more likely to have sought health care and HIV counseling and testing than youth who did not come in contact with street outreach.[124]

In addition to prevention education, this high-risk population needs access to HIV/AIDS support groups and case management services that connect them to specialty clinics and treatment services. These services should be coordinated and integrated with transitional living, housing and other programmatic strategies to support homeless adolescents' successful transition to adulthood. Supportive services require positive partnerships between service providers, clinics, HIV/AIDS service organizations, and State and local health departments.

An effective service delivery system for this diverse population is multi-disciplinary and offers comprehensive, developmentally appropriate and coordinated services to promote healthy youth development and reduce delinquency and victimization.[125] In order to meet the needs of the homeless youth population, providers must develop relationships with other youth-serving agencies, share information, provide education, and develop coordinated approaches to service delivery. Outreach programs cannot be designed in isolation from other service programs. The effectiveness and success of any outreach effort hinges on the broader service system of which it is part, community linkages, resource sharing, and service availability.[126]

## VI. IMPLICATIONS FOR POLICY AND PROGRAM DEVELOPMENT

Youth homelessness is an issue of national concern that requires urgent public and private sector attention. The causes and antecedents are varied and complex. Negative consequences appear to multiply with successive episodes of homelessness and the greater the cumulative amount of time young people remain homeless. Service providers report that the population of homeless youth appears to be growing, and that clients have multiple problems and are generally more troubled than in the past.[127]

Youth who have runaway or have been thrown out of their homes and families, as well as those who become homeless after leaving foster care, incarceration and other residential settings, are at high risk for medical problems and other health compromising behaviors. This includes HIV/AIDS, and other sexually transmitted and infectious diseases; substance abuse; psychotic behavior, depression and suicide attempts; prostitution and other forms of trauma.[128]

Solutions to prevent and ameliorate youth homelessness will not be easily or rapidly accomplished. No single approach or quick fix exists to solve problems associated with youth homelessness. While more information is needed on the homeless youth population itself; and the costs, effects and effectiveness of interventions, several important points have emerged to provide guidance to decision-makers.

- Preventing young people from becoming homeless in the first place, or to prevent them from repeat episodes (with compounded problems), is a critical public policy issue. Negative behaviors and experiences that are likely to result from youth homelessness have devastating consequences which are difficult to remedy.
- Family conflict and violence is the most common underlying antecedent of youth homelessness. It is of utmost importance that public policies affirm the role and responsibility of families to care for their children as they transition into adolescence and successful, independent adulthood. Government and community institutions support the families' role.

- All young people do not experience stress and conflict the same way. Nor do they experience homelessness and life on the street the same way. A comprehensive array of policies and programs targeted to the special characteristics of youth, their families and their communities, takes into account the circumstances of teenagers and young adults from different social, cultural, and economic backgrounds and their accumulated experiences. Very young adolescents, pregnant and parenting teens, young people leaving foster care, juvenile detention and other residential facilities, and those with significant health and mental health problems require specialized support. Similarly, effective family programs respond to the needs and vulnerabilities of families in different circumstances, for instance: low-income, single-parent, teen-parent, immigrant, and others with special needs.

- Because homeless youth have multiple needs that cut-across categorical programs and service delivery systems, policies encouraging and facilitating the coordination of funding and services from a variety of agencies and programs at all levels of government (Federal, State and local) is important in providing services. In the process, it also is necessary to create broad-based accountability for achieving positive outcomes for youth, their families, and their communities, not just for enrolling vulnerable young people in programs.

## Programs and Policy Goals and Options

The following approaches address overarching issues of youth homelessness from a policy perspective and build on existing resources and initiatives.

### 1) Provide Targeted Education and Support Services to High-Risk Families to Reduce the Incidence and Prevalence of Youth Homelessness

The majority of youth grow up in families that provide support, structure and guidance throughout childhood until they are ready and able to meet the challenges of living on their own. They will reach adulthood healthy, prepared for work and able to contribute to the well-being of their families and communities. However, for youth who live in families that are plagued by stress, conflict and violence, and especially for adolescents who leave home before they reach adulthood, the future is often problematic.

Several general strategies have been identified that have potential for reducing the incidence of youth running away or being thrown out of their homes. Central to all of them is the need to strengthen families and to mitigate the conflict and violence that often lead to significant psychological and emotional problems, child physical and sexual abuse, neglect and abandonment. This entails helping parents acquire the knowledge and skills to raise their children responsibly and effectively, providing at-risk families the special resources they need to continue to care for their children and keep their families together, and intervening to help solve problems when parents and youth experience conflicts that threaten their relationships and their ability to continue to live together.

Research identifies two effective program approaches specifically targeted to supporting healthy relationships between youth and their families.

- **Parent Education Programs** — Parent education programs can be effective in reducing rates of child abuse and neglect among high risk families.[129] Because of the high rates of child abuse and neglect among homeless youth, this primary prevention strategy shows promise for preventing youth homelessness. Currently, there is an array of parent education efforts underway in States -- supported with Federal, State, local and private dollars. Typically, parent education efforts focus on the parents of young children, however for many parents and children, adolescence is when parent-child relationships break down. Many parents are in desperate need of good information on appropriate parenting practices to address the developmental needs of adolescents, to identify signs of problems, to communicate effectively about sensitive issues such as sexuality and drugs, and to set appropriate limits. In its *Final Report,* the White House Task Force for Disadvantaged Youth noted the importance of parents in the lives of youth and recommended the development of a continuum of parental involvement components in youth programs, including parent support groups and education.[130]

- Because of its access to parents and youth, a potential delivery system for parent education efforts targeted to teenagers is the school system. Community-based youth groups and faith-based organizations also can effectively reach parents and youth in an environment that may be perceived as more informal and supportive than schools. Generally speaking, engaging parents in programs is difficult for parents of children of all ages, but is notoriously difficult for parents of teenagers. Any effort to expand parent education to parents of teens should assess and build on knowledge garnered from the small base of research and education efforts targeted to the parents of teens.

- **Intensive Therapeutic Support for Families Near or in Crisis** — While parent education can provide broad scale support for effective parent-child relationships, some families need more intensive supports. These include families in which there are high levels of violence and conflict; families in which youth are acting out and parents feel they are helpless to intervene or control them; families in which there is parental substance abuse or mental health problems; and families in which parent-youth relationships have broken down to the point that youth run away, or parents throw them out. In these crisis situations, one of three systems becomes the entry point for support and services for youth and their families: 1) the child welfare system; 2) the juvenile justice system; or 3) the runaway and homeless youth system. Unfortunately, involvement with these systems typically occurs when families have been in crisis for some time and a significant and traumatic event occurs, such as a young person committing a crime, or ending up on the street, or a parent abusing or neglecting a child severely enough that it attracts attention and is reported. At this point, interventions are often punitive in nature, and typically do not place enough emphasis on working with the whole family to support healthier and more adaptive relationships.

There are, however, a number of "early warning signs" that existing programs and systems could respond to in more effective ways. These include actions on the part of youth such as truancy, minor criminal offenses and fighting, and excessive acting out in school, as well as actions on the part of parents or other adults in the household, such as domestic disturbances. Currently, many jurisdictions treat issues such as truancy as "status offenses" which are handled by the juvenile justice system.[131] The juvenile justice system also handles minor offenses, such as fighting or vandalism. Most typically, youth receive a "slap on the wrist" for these types of offenses with warnings of more severe punishment for future misbehavior. Likewise, in some jurisdictions, running away is also treated as a status offense. If runaway youth are picked up by the police, they often are simply returned home with little investigation into the problems that led them to run in the first place. If runaway youth end up in an emergency shelter, workers there make an effort to assess the appropriateness of the home environment before returning youth home, but often do not provide intensive follow-up support to youth and their families.

Violence reduction research provides evidence that it is indeed possible to effectively help very high-risk youth and their families to establish more supportive relationships. In the section "Reducing Violence and Delinquency Among Juveniles" two evidence-based, family-focused interventions for high-risk youth -- Multi-Systemic Therapy and Functional Family Therapy are described. While these interventions were designed specifically for violent youth, research on their effectiveness can inform the development of more effective family-focused interventions for a broader sub-population of high-risk youth and families. Support for the development of more intensive family therapy options, as well as more coordinated and concerted community-level efforts to detect early signs of trouble among youth and families could prevent the escalation of problems that lead to eventual homelessness.

## Options for Improving Supports for Families in Crisis

- Gather existing best practices aimed at early identification and coordinated response to youth risk behaviors by the juvenile justice, substance abuse and mental health, runaway and homeless youth, education, and child welfare systems;
- Identify challenges to implementation of more intensive and coordinated therapeutic supports for families in or near crisis; and
- Explore opportunities for increasing the flexibility of resources within existing programs that are well-positioned to respond to early warning signs with intensive therapeutic supports for families, such as the Basic Centers Program, and the Safe Schools/Healthy Students Initiative.

## *2) Provide Enhanced Preparation, Transitional Living, and Support Services for Youth in the Foster Care and Juvenile Justice Systems*

Youth aging out of foster care and those leaving juvenile detention appear to be at increased risk of homelessness. A natural target for prevention of youth homelessness is to improve the level of preparation, transitional living, and support services provided to youth by these systems. In recent years, new initiatives have focused increased attention and resources on the fate of youth leaving both of these systems. The *Final Report* of the White House Task Force on Disadvantaged Youth also emphasized the importance of targeting public investments in youth programs toward youth in public care, recognizing the high-risks and poor outcomes these populations face.

## Foster Care Youth

When youth in foster care turn 18 they are "emancipated" from the State system that has served as their custodian. Their connection to the child welfare system terminates, and they are on their own, usually without any safety net. Many of these young people suffer emotional disturbances and the behavioral problems that often accompany them, and many experience homelessness.[132] Research has shown that these young people are far less likely to become homeless if they have access to stable, affordable housing.[133] Research also has shown that youth who receive skill training in five key areas — education, employment, money management, credit management, and consumer skills — fare significantly better in their ability to live independently than those who do not receive training and support. Results from a national study suggest that youth who receive these services are better able to get and hold a job for at least a year, better able to obtain health care if they need it, less likely to go on welfare or to prison, and more likely to build a supportive social network.[134]

Historically, support and preparation for independent living for youth aging out of foster care has been marginal and uneven across States. Typically, States have provided a few weeks of voluntary independent living training that did little to prepare youth for the reality of life on their own. In recent years, public and private sector initiatives have placed increased focus and resources on addressing the needs of youth aging out of foster care. The John H. Chafee Foster Care Independence Program (CFCIP), established as part of the Foster Care Independence Act of 1999, extended eligibility for transition assistance to former foster care children up to age 21, increased funding for independent living activities and provided States increased flexibility in use of funds, increased State accountability for outcomes for young people transitioning from foster care, and gave States the option to provide Medicaid coverage to youth transitioning out of foster care between the ages of 18 and 21. Education and training vouchers, a component of the Bush Administration's initiatives to assist foster care youth in transitioning to independence, were made available through amendments to CFCIP passed in 2001. The vouchers provide youth with a maximum of $5,000 annually to support postsecondary training and education. Importantly, in 2000, Congress extended eligibility for the Family Unification Program (FUP), located at the Department of Housing and Urban Development, to youth aging out of foster care. FUP sets aside Section 8 vouchers for families at risk of losing their children because of housing problems, and for youth aging out of foster care. In addition to public sector efforts to better support youth aging out of foster care, private funders and faith-based groups have developed national demonstration initiatives to help prepare foster youth to become successful adults.[135]

"Supporting Successful Transitions to Independent Living" describes approaches that are helping youth to develop a community-wide network of connections and to develop a focus on the future and pathways to lifelong economic well-being and financial success. Innovative strategies, such as linking youth with intensive financial literacy training, individual development accounts (IDAs), as well as entrepreneurial training and opportunities are among these efforts.

The current trends aimed at supporting the needs of youth aging out of foster care are promising. CFCIP has led to the expansion and improvement of State efforts to prepare these youth for a successful adulthood. While many provisions of CFCIP are voluntary for States, and the level and quality of independent living preparation remains uneven across States, much is being learned. Many States are able to aid the efforts by policymakers to strengthen and expand supports for youth aging out of foster care, with a dual focus on meeting basic needs and preparation for successful adulthood.

## Options for supporting youth aging out of foster care

- Explore aspects of independent living programs that support youth becoming economically successful as well as helping them gain other skills to live successfully on their own.
- Explore effective methods of promoting Individual Development Accounts.
- Explore opportunities for providing financial literacy training for all foster youth aged 15 and older.

## Juvenile Justice Youth

Existing initiatives also focus on preparing youth being released from juvenile detention for successful reintegration into society. Homeless youth report in large numbers that they have been or currently are involved in the juvenile justice system. Youth who have spent time in juvenile detention face challenges gaining employment, may not be welcomed back into their families of origin, and/or may struggle to get along with their families and reconnect with their communities. The frequent result is recidivism. The U.S. Department of Justice estimates that reducing recidivism among juvenile offenders by just four percent would save $35 million in public funding for law enforcement, courts, and juvenile corrections system and $30 million in victim costs.[136]

The intensive Aftercare Program (IAP) is a theory-based model of reintegration for juveniles. (See "Supporting Successful Transitions to Independent Living") The Office of Juvenile Justice and Delinquency Prevention administers a number of funding streams that States can use to prevent and address juvenile delinquency, and support reintegration programs, such as IAP. Because the bulk of funding is administered through block grants, the degree to which States invest in reentry initiatives for juveniles varies widely nationwide. [137]

One Department of Justice initiative that is specifically targeted to supporting reentry efforts is the Serious and Violent Offenders Reentry Initiative.[138] This initiative is an interagency effort that provides funding to State criminal and juvenile justice agencies to develop, implement, enhance, and evaluate reentry strategies. The initiative has three distinct phases: institution-based programs to prepare incarcerated offenders to reenter society; community-based transition programs that work with offenders' pre and post- release; and community-based long-term support programs to provide ex-offenders with a network of social services agencies, faith-based and community organizations.[139] The initiative targets 160,000 offenders; however, only 10 percent of the target population is youth. Finally, OJJDP's Performance-Based Standards for Youth Correction and Detention Facilities (PBS) is a system to improve and track conditions and services for incarcerated youth that includes standards related to preparing youth for reintegration into the community. Seventeen States have voluntarily adopted these standards.

**Program Options to Help Youth in the Juvenile Justice System**

- Gather information on how and to what extent States are supporting reentry services for juvenile offenders;
- Analyze the cost of providing reentry services to offenders and the adequacy of current resources to address enforcement and detention costs, as well as costs associated with comprehensive reentry efforts;
- Identify where existing investments in other systems, such as education, workforce development, and substance abuse and mental health services, could be better targeted and coordinated to support youth reentry, and identify gaps in existing resources that warrant additional investments.

Another new and promising, small-scale initiative is the Department of Labor Responsible Reintegration of Youthful Offender grant to address the specific workforce challenges of youth offenders. This initiative is supporting demonstration grants in 15 States that support efforts to link youth offenders with jobs in high-growth industries.

Youth who commit crimes, serve time in juvenile detention and then are released back into communities without preparation and support appear to be at risk for a number of negative outcomes, including eventual homelessness. Targeting investments in prevention and reentry efforts could help some youth to avoid homelessness, as well as preventing a host of other negative outcomes with costly implications for society and public systems. Targeting investments requires an understanding of the current level of services and capacity that exist in States.

*3) Increase the Quality, Comprehensiveness and Capacity of Supports and Services for Homeless Youth*

Homeless youth in the United States tend to come from severely dysfunctional families, and they are at risk for negative developmental outcomes before they run away or are thrown out of their homes. Although leaving home may be an adaptive response to a threatening situation, young people who leave to escape serious family problems often face equally threatening problems on the street — troubled peers, substance abuse, unprotected and unwelcome sexual activity, criminal activity, violence and victimization. Altering the developmental pathways and outcomes for homeless youth is not easy. Often those in greatest need are those who are most difficult to locate and serve. Generally, they also have most "successfully" adapted to street life. Accordingly, aggressive outreach and efforts are needed to help homeless youth find their way to shelters and other programs that can meet their immediate needs for shelter, food and protection, and link them to longer-term support and services to address their health, mental health, educational, social and economic needs in stable settings. In the section "Interventions to Ameliorate Homelessness" interventions are described that address the needs of homeless youth, from gateway services to long-term supportive housing programs.

Practitioners and researchers identify comprehensive and integrated service delivery models that link youth to a continuum of services tailored to their unique needs as a promising practice. The foundation of comprehensive approaches is intensive case management services that enable youth-workers to create a strong relationship with youth.

The success of this model is dependent on the availability of a range of supports and services to which case managers can refer youth. Many programs that have a strong reputation in the field administer and co-locate the full range of services for homeless youth, from outreach to transitional living and affordable housing options.

Theoretical research summarized under section on "Comprehensive Independent Living and Life Skills Training," notes that it is not only comprehensiveness of services that matters, but also the quality of those services. In particular, the youth development perspective helps us to understand the importance of positive opportunities and preparation for successful adulthood. Research into human resiliency has shown that overcoming challenges and difficult circumstances is an innate human quality that can be nurtured.[140] Three general approaches often serve as protective factors for vulnerable youth, including:

- Caring and supportive relationships with adults and peers
- High expectations for success and achievement
- Opportunities for participation and leadership

These three factors are often missing in the lives of young people who become homeless and enter life on the street. One important implication for social policies and services is that homeless youth need opportunities to engage in interactions with adults and peers that are healthy, supportive, and can lead to positive developmental pathways. Young people who do not have parents and other family members on whom they can rely for support, encouragement and guidance, will look for it elsewhere. Once on the street, they likely will find it from adults and peers who may provide a sense of connectedness, but generally do not offer the assistance and support necessary to foster positive developmental pathways. Therefore, in the absence of nurturing families, youth need to form close trusting relationships with other caring adults — coaches, counselors, foster parents, youth leaders, faith members, and mentors — who can serve as advisors, gatekeepers, cheerleaders and comforters.

Viewing vulnerable youth as a "set of problems" may lead adults in their lives to have lowered expectations for them. But all youth need adults in their lives who have high expectations for their success, who will encourage them to set ambitious educational, career and personal goals, and maintain high expectations for themselves. Often expectations — whether low or high — become reality. Finally, young people need to be involved in decisions and choices that concern them — such as their participation in treatments and interventions. They are far more likely to feel an investment in the outcome, if they have a voice in the decision and a sense of control in their lives.

Opportunities to be contributing members of schools, neighborhoods and faith-based organizations which promote strong values can help vulnerable young people envision pathways out of the adversity that has scarred their early lives.

Many of the elements of a comprehensive continuum of services for homeless youth are already in place in communities, as are examples of quality practice built on youth development principles. However, in many communities the linkages do not exist between programs. An important starting point for addressing youth homelessness more effectively is to better understand how to link services, improve their quality, and target resources toward the most pressing capacity needs. The First Lady's Helping America's Youth Initiative and its "Community Resource Guide" is a new tool that addresses this need.

*4) Support Coordination of Programs and Services for Youth who are Homeless or At-Risk of Becoming Homeless*

Below are some examples of relevant Federal laws that play a critical role in funding and administering supports and services to youth at-risk of homelessness and those who are homeless. Congress established the Interagency Council on Homelessness in 1987 with the passage of the Stewart B. McKinney Homeless Assistance Act. The Council is responsible for providing Federal leadership for activities to assist homeless families and individuals. Its major activities include: planning and coordinating the Federal government's activities and programs to assist homeless people, and making or recommending policy changes to improve such assistance; monitoring and evaluating assistance to homeless persons provided by all levels of government and the private sector; ensuring that technical assistance is provided to help community and other organizations effectively assist homeless persons; and disseminating information on Federal resources available to assist the homeless population. Relevant Federal laws supporting programs and services for vulnerable youth include: the Runaway and Homeless Youth Act, the John H. Chafee Foster Care Independence Act, the McKinneyVento Act, the Mentoring Children of Prisoners Program, the Promoting Safe and Stable Families Program, the Juvenile Accountability Block Grant and the Title V Community Prevention Grants Program under the Juvenile Justice and Delinquency Prevention Act, and the Hope VI housing program. Each of these statutes places high priority on efforts to help vulnerable youth through difficult transitions and promote successful independent living, contains targeted funding to defined populations, and imposes specific administrative limits on the use of funds.

# VII. CONCLUSION

Adolescence is a time when young people explore talents and interests and choose paths that determine the direction of their adulthood. It is also a time when youth can become disconnected from adults as a result of family stress, tough communities and environments, and their own personal behavior. Teens and families with particular vulnerabilities do not always make it through this difficult transition with relationships intact. For a variety of reasons related to the characteristics of youth, the characteristics of their parents, the dynamics of their relationships, and the realities of their communities — youth may end up on their own. In other cases, they are running from or told to leave their home. In some cases, they have been separated from families and are running from foster homes or group homes. Or, when they reach age 18, those responsible for their care — parents or systems — expect them to fend for themselves.

While the population of homeless youth is extremely diverse, their common trait is that they are disconnected from adults they can depend upon to care for them. For over 30 years, the Federal government has supported the core of a safety net for these youth through runaway and homeless youth programs administered by the Administration for Children and Families. The child welfare and juvenile justice systems, too, play critical roles in the lives of this vulnerable population, as youth in public care tend to be at high risk for homelessness.

Drawing from existing research and informed discussions with practitioners in the field, policy experts and program administrators, conclusions about prevention and intervention reveal:

1. As youth homelessness primarily is related to the disconnection of youth from adults, ending it requires fostering supportive relationships between youth and adults - first and foremost between youth and families, and secondarily between youth and adults who become their support system when families are unable or unwilling to do so.
2. Youth who cannot depend on their family's support, need programs and services to meet their basic needs, as well as to help prepare them to transition successfully to independence.
3. Problems experienced by youth who are homeless cut across many systems thereby requiring effective coordination of targeted supports and services. This task involves interagency planning at the Federal, State, and local levels.

In recent years there has been an increased interest among policymakers, researchers, and faith-based and community groups in the issue of youth homelessness and the problems facing populations at particular risk of homelessness. The Bush Administration has directed considerable attention to addressing the needs of high-risk youth through its White House Task Force on Disadvantaged Youth, the First Lady's "Helping America's Youth" initiative, successful passage of it's legislative proposals including the creation of "Mentoring Children of Prisoners" and improvements to "Promoting Safe and Stable Families" programs, among others. This growing focus on youth presents an excellent opportunity to move the nation closer to the goal of ending youth homelessness with enhanced coordination by public agencies, private entities, practitioners, researchers, technical assistance providers, young people, and advocates, and the continued strong leadership by key Federal agencies and national policy makers.

## APPENDIX A

### FEDERAL PROGRAMS RELEVANT TO YOUTH HOMELESSNESS

| Funding Stream | Program Name | Administering Organization | Eligibility Requirements | Services Funded |
|---|---|---|---|---|
| Runaway and Homeless Youth Act (RHYA) | BASIC CENTER | Department of Health and Human Services, Administration for Children and Families | Youth under 18 years of age | Meets basic needs of youth as well as crisis intervention and family reunification |
| | STREET OUTREACH | Department of Health and Human Services, Administration for Children and Families | All youth | Provides youth with basic needs and provides information for accessing other services |
| | TRANSITIONAL LIVING PROGRAM (TLP) | Department of Health and Human Services, Administration for Children and Families | Youth ages 16-21 who are homeless, aging out of the foster care system, transitioning from the juvenile justice or mental health system, and are pregnant and/or parenting | Provides longer-term housing, often group-living or supervised apartments, from which youth can finish their education, learn independent living skills, and gain employment |

| Title IV-E | TITLE IV-E FOSTER CARE FUNDING | Department of Health and Human Services, Administration for Children & Families | Families and youth involved in the child welfare system | Foster care maintenance for eligible children, administrative costs to manage the program, training for staff, for foster parents, and for certain private agency staff |
|---|---|---|---|---|
| Workforce Investment Act (WIA), Youth Activities | WIA YOUTH ACTIVITIES | Department of Labor, Employment and Training Administration | Low income youth between the ages of 14 and 21 | The Act authorizes the use of funds for youth employment and training activities that will provide eligible youth assistance in achieving careers and academic and employment success; ensures ongoing mentoring opportunities; provides opportunities for training; provides continued supportive services; provides incentives for recognition and achievement; and provides opportunities for leadership, development, decision making, citizenship, and community service |

| Temporary Assistance for Needy Families (TANF) | TANF | Department of Health and Human Services, Administration for Children and Families | Families with children under the age of 18, that are deprived of financial support from a parent by reason of death, absence from the home, unemployment, or physical or mental incapacity | Provides cash assistance and supportive services to assist the family, helping them achieve economic self-sufficiency |
|---|---|---|---|---|
| Medicaid | MEDICAID | Department of Health and Human Services, Centers for Medicare and Medicaid | A parent or guardian with a low income may apply to receive Medicaid for a child who is 18 years old or younger, if your child is sick enough to need nursing home care, but could stay home with good quality care at home. Teenagers living on their own may be allowed by their State to apply for Medicaid on their own behalf or any adult may apply for them. Many States also cover children up to age 21 | Pays for medical assistance for certain individuals and families with low incomes and resources |

| | | | Department of Health and Human Services, Health Resources and Services Administration | Patients must be homeless | Primary health care and substance abuse services at locations accessible to people who are homeless; emergency care with referrals to hospitals for in-patient care services and/or other needed services, and outreach services to assist difficult-to-reach homeless persons in accessing care, and provide assistance in establishing eligibility for entitlement programs and housing. |
|---|---|---|---|---|---|
| **Public Health Service Act** | HEALTH CARE for the HOMELESS | | | | |
| **McKinney-Vento Homeless Assistance Act** | Title IV Housing Assistance Act | Emergency Shelter Grants | Department of Housing and Urban Development | Homeless persons Short-term homeless prevention assistance may aid persons at imminent risk of losing their own housing due to eviction, foreclosure, or utility shutoffs | Provides basic shelter and essential supportive services as well as short-term homeless prevention assistance to persons at imminent risk of losing their own housing |
| | | Supportive Housing Program | Department of Housing and Urban Development | Homeless persons | Provides rental assistance payments that cover the difference between a portion of the tenant's income (normally 30%) and the unit's rent, which must be within the fair market rent (FMR) |

| | | | | | established by HUD |
|---|---|---|---|---|---|
| **McKinney-Vento Homeless Assistance Act (cont)** | | Section 8 Assistance for Single Room Occupancy Dwellings | Department of Housing and Urban Development | Homeless persons | Develops supportive housing and services that will allow homeless persons to live as independently as possible |
| | | Shelter Plus Care | Department of Housing and Urban Development | Hard-to-serve homeless persons, (primarily those with serious mental illness, chronic problems with alcohol and/or drugs, and acquired immune deficiency syndrome (AIDS) or related diseases) and their families who are living in places not intended for humans habitation (e.g. the streets) or in emergency shelters | Provides housing and supportive services on a long-term basis |

| | | | Department | Target Population | Description |
|---|---|---|---|---|---|
| **McKinney-Vento Homeless Assistance Act (cont)** | Title VII | Education for Homeless Children and Youth | Department of Education | Children and youth who lack a fixed, regular, and adequate nighttime residence | Provides an array of supports including but not limited to tutoring, transportation, and cash assistance to ensure the participation of homeless children and youth in elementary and secondary school. The act guarantees access to school and a meaningful opportunity for educational success |
| **Section 8 Housing Choice Voucher Program** | FAMILY UNIFICATION PROGRAM (FUP) | | Department of Housing and Urban Development | Youth aging out of foster care and families at risk of losing their child to care or that are trying to reunite with child already in care | Provides housing assistance vouchers |
| **John H. Chafee Foster Care Independent Program** | EDUCATION & TRAINING VOUCHERS (ETV) | | Department of Health and Human Services, Administration for Children & Families | Youth aging out of foster care | Activities may include but are not limited to: tuition, fees, books, equipment (computer), supplies, uniforms, housing, internship and school related travel |
| | INDEPENDENT LIVING PROGRAM (ILP) | | Department of Health and Human Services, Administration for | Youth ages 18-21 who are parenting, preparing to emancipate from the | Enables youth to live on their own in the community with a range of |

| | | | Children & Families | foster care system, and those diagnosed with serious emotional disturbances | support services until they are fully stable |
|---|---|---|---|---|---|
| **Juvenile Justice and Delinquency Prevention Act (JJDPA)** | TITLE V INCENTIVE GRANTS FOR LOCAL DELINQUENCY PREVENTION | | Department of Justice, Office of Juvenile Justice and Delinquency Prevention | All youth | The program provides communities with funding and a guiding framework for developing and implementing comprehensive juvenile delinquency prevention plans. The 3-year prevention plans are designed to reduce risk factors associated with juvenile delinquency and decrease the incidence of juvenile problem behavior |
| | JUVENILE ACCOUNTABILITY BLOCK GRANTS (JABG) PROGRAM | | Department of Justice, Office of Juvenile Justice and Delinquency Prevention | Youth involved in the juvenile justice system | Rehabilitation of adjudicated youth. Reducing juvenile recidivism rates |

| | | | Department of Justice, Office of Juvenile Justice and Delinquency Prevention | Incarcerated youth offenders | Encompasses three phases: 1.) institution-based programs to prepare incarcerated offenders to reenter society, 2.) community-based transition programs to work with offenders before and following release from correctional institutions, 3.) community-based long-term support programs |
|---|---|---|---|---|---|
| **Juvenile Justice and Delinquency Prevention Act (JJDPA)** | SERIOUS AND VIOLENT OFFENDERS REENTRY INITIATIVE | | | | |

# REFERENCES

[1]    Whitbeck, L. B., Hoyt, D. R., Yoder, K. A., Cauce, A. M. & Paradise, M. (2001). Deviant behavior and victimization among homeless and runaway adolescents. *Journal of Interpersonal Violence, 16(11),* 1175-1204.

[2]    (2003). Runaway, Homeless, and Missing Children Protection Act of 2003, P.L. 108-96

[3]    Robertson, M. J., & Toro, P. A. (1998). Homeless youth: Research, intervention, and policy. In L. B, Fosburg & D. L. Dennis (Vol Eds.), *Practical lessons: The 1998 national symposium on homelessness research.* U.S. Department of Housing and Urban Development and the U.S. Department of Health and Human Services, August 1999. Available: http://aspe.hhs.gov/progsys/homeless/symposium/3-youth.htm.

[4]    Owen, G., & Nelson-Christinedaughter, J. (2001, September). *Homeless Youth in Minnesota: Statewide Survey of People without Permanent Shelter.* St. Paul, MN: Wilder Research Center. Available: http://www.wilder.org/ homelessness.o.html.

[5]    White House Task Force for Disadvantaged Youth. (October 2003). *The White House Task Force For Disadvantaged Youth: Final Report.* Washington, DC.

[6]    Runaway, Homeless, and Missing Children Protection Act of 2003, P.L. 108-96.

[7]    This project is also known as the Seattle Homeless Research Adolescent Project and Seattle Homeless Adolescent Research and Education Study.

[8]    Ryan, K. D., Kilmer, R. P., Cauce, A. M., Watanabe, H. & Hoyt, D. R. (2000). Psychological consequences of child maltreatment in homeless adolescents: Untangling the unique effects of maltreatment and family environment. *Child Abuse and Neglect, 24(3),* 333-352.

[9]    Whitbeck (2001). *op. cit.*

[10]   Whitbeck, L. B. & Hoyt, D. R. (1999). *Nowhere to Grow: Homeless and Runaway Adolescents and Their Families,* New York: NY, Aldine De Gruyter.

[11]   Cauce, A. M. & Morgan, C. J. (1994). Effectiveness of intensive case management for homeless adolescents: Results of a 3-month follow-up. *Journal of Emotional and behavioral Disorders, 2(4).*

[12]   Courtney, M.E., Skyles, A., Miranda, G., Zinn, A., Howard, E. & Goerge, R. (2005). Youth who runaway from substitute care. Chapin Hall Working Paper, Chapin Hall Center for Children. Chicago, IL: University of Chicago.

[13]   For information on the *HALO* project please see: http://sun.science.wayne.edu/—ptoro/halo.htm

[14]   For information on *Project i* please see: *http://www.npi.ucla.edu/center/communityks_projecti.html*

[15]   Haber, M. G., & Toro, P. A. (2004). Homelessness among children, families, adolescents: An ecological- developmental perspective. *Clinical Child and Psychology Review,* 7(3), 123-164.

[16]   Generally, interventions and research on the homeless are targeted to three categories of individuals: homeless adults without children, homeless families — parents and their children — and adolescents on their own

[17]   Haber (2004), *op.cit.*

[18]   Robertson (1998), *op. cit.*

[19]   Cauce, A. M. Paradise, M., Ginzler, J. A., Embry, L., Morgan, C. J., Lohr, Y. &

Theofelis, J. (2000). The characteristics and mental health of homeless adolescents: Age and gender differences. *Journal of Emotional and Behavioral Disorders, 8(4),* 230-239.

[20] MacLean, M.G., L.E. Embry, & A.M. Cauce. (1999). Homeless adolescents' paths to separation from family: Comparison of family characteristics, psychological adjustment, and victimization. *Journal of Community Psychology 27(2),* 179-187.

[21] Haber (2004), *op. cit.*

[22] Ringwalt, C. L., Greene, J. M., & Robertson, M. (1998). Familial backgrounds and risk behaviors of youth with thrownaway experiences. *Journal of Adolescence, 21,* 241-252.

[23] Whitbeck (2001), *op. cit.*

[24] *Ibid.*

[25] Greene, J. M., Sanchez, R., Manlove, J., Terry-Humen, E., Vandivere, S., Wertheimer, R., Williams, S., Zaff, J., & Ringwalt, C. (2002). *Sexual Abuse among Homeless Adolescents: Prevalence, Correlates and Sequalae* (Final report under Contract No. HHS-100-99-0006, Delivery Order No. 3 from the Administration on Children, Youth and Families). Research Triangle Park, NC: Research Triangle Institute.

[26] Owen, G., Heineman, J., Shelton, E. & Gerrard, M.D. (2004). *Homeless in Minnesota 2003.* St. Paul, MN: Wilder Research Center. Available: *http://www.wilder.org/ research/reports/pdf/Homeless2003.pdf*

[27] Greene (2002), *op. cit.*

[28] Cochran, B. N., Stewart, A. J., Ginzler, J. A. & Cauce, A. M. (2002). Challenges faced by homeless sexual minorities: Comparison of gay, lesbian, bisexual, and transgender homeless adolescents and their heterosexual counterparts. *American Journal of Public Health, 92(5),* 773-777.

[29] Robertson (1998), *op. cit.*

[30] Greene, J. M. & Ringwalt, C. (1998). Pregnancy among three national samples of runaway and homeless youth. *Journal of Adolescent Health, 23,* 370-377.

[31] Courtney, M. E., Terao, S. & Bost, N. (2004). Midwest evaluation of the adult functioning of former foster youth: Conditions of youth preparing to leave state care. Chapin Hall Center for Children at the University of Chicago.

[32] Cauce (2000), *op. cit.*

[33] Wertheimer, R. (2002). Youth who "age out" of foster care: Troubled lives, troubling perspectives (Child Trends Research Brief. Publication #2002-59). Washington, DC: Child Trends.

[34] Courtney (2005), *op. cit.*

[35] Pecora, P. J., Williams, J., Kessler, R. C., Downs, A. C., O'Brien, K., Hiripi, E. & Morello, S. (2003). *Assessing the Effects of Foster Care: Early Results from the Casey National Alumni Study.* Available: http://www. casey.org/NR/rdonlyres/CEFBB1B6-7ED1-440D-925AE5BAF602294D/ 148/casey_alumni studies reportl .pdf.

[36] New York City Association of Homeless and Street-Involved Youth Organizations (2003). *State of the city's homeless youth report 2003.* New York, NY: Empire State Coalition of Youth and Family Services. Available: http://www.empirestatecoalition. org/report.html.

[37] Estes, R. J. & Weiner, N. A. (2001). The commercial sexual exploitation of children in the U.S., Canada and Mexico. Full report of the U.S. National Study. University of Pennsylvania, School of Social Work, Center for the Study of Youth Policy. Available

at: http://www.sp2.upenn.edu/—restes/CSEC.htm Revised February 20, 2002.

[38] Owen (September 2001), *op. cit.*

[39] *Ibid.*

[40] Hammer, H., Finkelhor, D. & Sedlak, A. J. (2002). NISMART Bulletin: Runaway/thrownaway children: National estimates and characteristic (Prepared under grant number 95—MC—CX—K004 from the Office of Juvenile Justice and Delinquency Prevention, U.S. Department of Justice, to Temple University). Available: http://www.ncjrs.org/html/ojjdp/nismart/04/.

[41] Reeg, B. (2003). The Runaway and Homeless Youth Act. In J. Levin-Epstein & M.H. Greenberg (Vol. Eds.), *Leave No Youth Behind: Opportunities for Congress to Reach Disconnected Youth.* Washington, DC: Center for Law and Social Policy.

[42] Whitbeck (1999), *op. cit.*

[43] HalcOn, L. L. & Lifson, A. R. (2004). Prevalence and predictors of sexual risk among homeless youth. *Journal of Youth and Adolescence, 33(1),* 71-80.

[44] Greene, J. M. Ennett, S. T. & Ringwalt, C. L. (1997). Substance use among runaway and homeless youth in three national samples. *American Journal of Public Health, 87(2),* 229-235.

[45] Haber (2004), *op. cit.*

[46] Whitbeck, L. B. Hoyt, D. R. & Yoder, K. A. (1999). A risk-amplification model of victimization and depressive symptoms among runaway and homeless adolescents. *American Journal of Community Psychology, 27(2),* 273-296.

[47] Whitbeck, (1999), *op. cit.*

[48] Heinze, H. J., Toro, P. A., & Urberg, K. A. (2004). Antisocial behavior and affiliation with deviant peers. *Journal of Clinical Child and Adolescent Psychology 33(2),* 336-346.

[49] Halcón (2004), *op. cit.*

[50] Wagner, L. S., Carlin, L., Cauce, A. M., & Tenner, A. (2001). A snapshot of homeless youth in Seattle: Their characteristics, behaviors, and beliefs about HIV protective strategies. *Journal of Community Health, 26(3),* 219-232.

[51] Moon, M. W., McFarland, W., Kellogg, T., Baxter, M., Katz, M. H., MacKellar, D. & Valleroy, L.A. (2000). HIV risk behavior of runaway youth in San Francisco: Age of onset and relation to sexual orientation. *Youth & Society, 32(2),* 184-201.

[52] *Ibid.*

[53] Whitbeck (2001) *op. cit.*

[54] Whitbeck (2001) *op. cit.*

[55] Cauce (2000), *op. cit.*

[56] Hoyt, D., Ryan, K. D. & Cauce, A.M. (1999). Personal victimization in a high-risk environment: Homeless and runaway adolescents. *Journal of Research in Crime and Delinquency, 36(4),* 371392.

[57] Pittman, K., Irby, M., Tolman, J., Yohalem, N. & Ferber, T. (2003). Preventing Problems, Promoting Development, Encouraging Engagement: Competing Priorities or Inseparable Goals? Based upon Pittman, K. & Irby, M. (1996). Preventing Problems or Promoting Development? Washington, D.C.: The Forum for Youth Investment, Impact Strategies, Inc.

[58] Werner, E. E. (1995). Resilience in Development. *Current Directions in Psychological Science 4 (3),* 81-85.

[59]  Werner, E. E. and Smith, R. S. (1982). *Vulnerable but Invincible: A Study of Resilient Children.* New York: McGraw Hill.

[60]  Werner, E. E. & Smith, R. S. (1992). *Overcoming The Odds.* Ithaca, NY: Cornell University Press.

[61]  National Research Council and Institute of Medicine (2002). *Community Programs to Promote Youth Development.* Committee on Community-Level Programs for Youth. Jacquelynn Eccles and Jennifer A. Gootman, eds. Board on Children, Youth, and Families, Division of Behavioral and Social Sciences and Education. Washington, DC: National Academy Press.

[62]  Catalano, R. F., Berglund, L., Ryan. Jeanne A. M., Lonczak, S., and Hawkins, D. J (2002). Positive Youth Development in the United States: Research Findings on Evaluations of Positive Youth Development Programs. *Prevention and Treatment, 5, 15.*

[63]  Haber (2004), *op. cit.*

[64]  Shinn, M., Weitzman, B. C., Stojanoic, D. Knickman, J. R., Jimenez, L., Duchon, L., et al. (1998). Predictors of homelessness among families in New York City: From shelter request to housing stability. *American Journal of Public Health, 88,* 1651 — 1656.

[65]  Whitbeck (1999) *op. cit.*

[66]  Haber (2004), *op. cit.*

[67]  Dishion, T. J., McCord, J. & Poulin, F. (1999). When Interventions Harm: Peer Groups and Problem Behavior. *American Psychologist, 54 (9),* 755-764.

[68]  Auerswald (2002), *op. cit.*

[69]  Robertson (1998), *op. cit.*

[70]  Wiebush, R. G., McNulty, B. & Le, T. (2000). Implementation of the intensive community-based aftercare program. U.S. Department of Justice, Office of Justice Programs, Office of Juvenile Justice and Delinquency Prevention, Juvenile Justice Bulletin. Washington, DC.

[71]  Whipple, E. E. & Wilson, S. R. (1996). Evaluation of a parent education and support program for families at risk of physical child abuse. *Families in Society, 77(4),* 227-239.

[72]  Thomas, D., Leicht, C., Hughes, C., Madigan, A. & Dowell, K. (2003). Emerging practices in the prevention of child abuse and neglect. U.S. Department of Health and Human Services, Administration for Children and Families, Children's Bureau, Office of Child Abuse and Neglect. Washington, DC.

[73]  *Ibid.*

[74]  Gomby, D. S., Culross, P. L. & Behrman, R. E. (1999). Home visiting: Recent program evaluations— analysis and recommendations. *The Future of Children, 9 (1),* 4-26.

[75]  Weiss, H. B. (1993). Home visits: Necessary but not sufficient. *The Future of Children, 3(3),* 113-128.

[76]  Olds, D. L. & Kitzman, H. (1993). Review of research on home visiting for pregnant women and parents of young children. *The Future of Children, 3(3),* 53-92.

[77]  Owen (September 2001), *op. cit.*

[78]  Liddle, H. A., & Hogue, A. (2000). A family-based, developmental-ecological preventive intervention for high-risk adolescents. *Journal of Marital & Family Therapy, 26(3),* 265-279.

[79]  Alexander, J., Pugh, C., Parsons, B. & Sexton, T. (2002). *Functional family therapy. In*

*Blueprints for violence prevention* (Book 3), 3rd ed., D.S. Elliott (Ed). Boulder, CO: Center for the Study and Prevention of Violence, Institute of Behavioral Science, University of Colorado.

[80] Sexton, T.L. & Alexander, J.F. (2000). Functional family therapy. U.S. Department of Justice, Office of Justice Programs, Office of Juvenile Justice and Delinquency Prevention, Juvenile Justice Bulletin. Washington, DC.

[81] Sexton (2000), *op. cit.*

[82] Aos, S., Barnoski, R. and Lieb, R. (1998). Watching the bottom line: Cost-effective interventions for reducing crime in Washington. Olympia, WA: Washington State Institute for Public Policy. Available: *http://www.wsipp.wa.gov/default.asp?page=a uth.asp?authid=2.*

[83] Alexander (2002), *op. cit.*

[84] Henggeler, S. W., Mihalic, S. F., Rone, L., Thomas, C. & Timmons-Mitchell, J. (2001). Multisystemic therapy. In *Blueprints for violence prevention* (Book 6), 2nd ed., D.S. Elliott (Ed). Boulder, CO: Center for the Study and Prevention of Violence, Institute of Behavioral Science, University of Colorado.

[85] *Ibid.*

[86] Courtney (2004), *op. cit.*

[87] Chafee Foster Care Independence Act of 1999, P.L. 106-169, H.R. 3433, 106th Cong. (1999).

[88] The U.S. Department of Health and Human Services' (DHHS) Children's Bureau and its contractors are currently conducting an initial availability assessment and a five-year evaluation of selected programs funded through the John Chafee Foster Care Independence Program (CFCIP). The Evaluation will determine the effects of Independent Living Programs funded under CFCIP in achieving key outcomes for participating youth including increased educational attainment, higher employment rates and stability, greater interpersonal and relationship skills, reduced non-marital pregnancy and births, and reduced delinquency and crime rates.

[89] Lindsey, E. W. & Ahmed, F. U. (1999). The North Carolina independent living program: A comparison of outcomes for participants and nonparticipants. *Children and Youth Services Review, 21(5),* 389-412.

[90] Cook, R., Fleishman, E. & Grimes, V. (1991). *A national evaluation of Title IV-E foster care independent living programs for youth,* phase 2 final report, volume 1. (Developed by Westat, Inc., for the Department of Health and Human Services, Administration for Children and Families, Administration for Children, Youth and Families, under Contract No.: 105-87-1608).

[91] Courtney (2005), *op. cit.*

[92] Kroner, M. J. (2001). Developing housing options for independent living preparation. In K. A. Nollan & A. C. Downs (Eds), Preparing youth for long-term success. Proceedings from the Casey Family Program national independent living forum. Washington, DC: Child Welfare League of America Press.

[93] Foster Care Work Group and The Finance Project, 2004

[94] Choca, M. J., Minoff, J., Angene, L., Byrnes, M., Kenneally, L., Norris, D., Pearn, D. & Rivers, M. M. (2004). Can't do it alone: Housing collaborations to improve foster youth outcomes. *Child Welfare, 83(5), 469-492.*

[95] Chafee Foster Care Independence Act of 1999, P.L. 106-169, H.R. 3433, 106th Cong.

(1999).

[96]  Courtney, M. E., Piliavin, I. P. Grogran-Kaylor, A., & Nast, A. (2001). Foster youth transitions to adulthood: A longitudinal view of youth leaving foster care. *Child Welfare, 70(6),* 685-718.

[97]  *Ibid.*

[98]  Altschuler, D. M. & Armstrong, T. L. (1994). Intensive aftercare for high-risk juveniles: A community care model. Summary. U.S. Department of Justice, Office of Justice Programs, Office of Juvenile Justice and Delinquency Prevention. Washington, DC.

[99]  *Ibid.*

[100] *Ibid.*

[101] Wiebush (2000), *op. cit.*

[102] Gies, 2003

[103] Geis, S.V. (2003). Aftercare services. U.S. Department of Justice, Office of Justice Programs, Office of Juvenile Justice and. Delinquency Prevention, Juvenile Justice Bulletin. Washington, DC

[104] Morse, G. (1998). A review of case management for people who are homeless: Implications for practice, policy and research, in the 1998 National Symposium on Homelessness Research.

[105] Erickson, S. and Page, J. (1998). To dance with grace: Outreach and engagement to persons on the street, in the 1998 National Symposium on Homelessness Research.

[106] *Ibid.*

[107] *Ibid.*

[108] Robertson (1998), *op. cit.*

[109] Thompson, S. J., Safyer, A. W. & Pollio, D. E. (2001). Differences and predictors of family reunification among subgroups of runaway youths using shelter services. Social Work Research, 25(3).

[110] *Ibid.*

[111] Boyer, D., Hammons, G., Shaw, M., Coram, T., & Myers, R. (2002). Barriers to shelter study pilot project needs assessment. Final recommendations report. Available: http://www.cityofseattle.net/ humanservices/ homeless.htm#youth.

[112] *Ibid*

[113] Durham, K.(2003). Housing youth: Key issues in supportive housing. New York, NY: Corporation for Supportive Housing.

[114] Whitbeck And Hoyt (1999), *op. cit.*

[115] Bartlett, M., Copeman, A., Golin, J., Miller, D. & Needle, E. (2004). *Unlocking the potential of homeless older adolescents: Factors influencing client success in, four New England transitional living programs.* M. Wilson and D. Tanner (Eds.). New England Network for Child, Youth & Family Services.

[116] Straka, D., Tempel, D. & Epstein, E. (2003). *Supportive housing for youth: A background of the issues in the design and development of supportive housing for homeless youth.* Corporation for Supportive Housing, New York, NY: Corporation for Supportive Housing. Available: *http://documents.csh.org/documents/Communications/ familySH/supp* hsng youth.pdf.

[117] Family Unification Program, National Affordable Housing Act of 1990, P.L. 101-625, 101st Cong. (1990).

[118] Haber (2004), *op. cit.*

[119] Slesnick, N., Meyers, R. J., Meade, M. & Segelken, D. H. (2000). Bleak and hopeless no more: Engagement of reluctant substance-abusing runaway youth and their families. *Journal of Substance Abuse Treatment, 19,* 215-222.

[120] MacClean, Paradise and Cauce (1999)

[121] Haber (2004), *op. cit.*

[122] Straka (2003), *op. cit.*

[123] Wagner (2001), *op. cit*

[124] Greenberg, J. B. and Neumann, M. S. (1998). What we have learned from the AIDS evaluation of street outreach projects. Department of Health and Human Services, Centers for Disease Control and Prevention.

[125] Morely, Rossman, Kopczynski, Buck and Gouvis (2000)

[126] Erickson, S. and Page, J. (1998).

[127] Slesnick (2000), *op. cit.*

[128] Whitbeck (1999), *op. cit.*

[129] Thomas (2003), *op. cit.*

[130] White House Task Force for Disadvantaged Youth. (October 2003). *The White House Task Force For Disadvantaged Youth: Final Report.* Washington, DC.

[131] National Law Center on Homelessness and Poverty and National Network for Youth. (2004). Legal tools to end youth homelessness. Washington, DC.

[132] Slesnick (2000), *op. cit.*

[133] Kroner (2001), *op. cit.*

[134] Cook(1991), *op. cit.*

[135] Family Unification Program, National Affordable Housing Act of 1990, P.L. 101-625, 101st Cong. (1990).

[136] National Partnership to End Youth Homelessness. (no date available). *Reentry Housing for Youthful Offenders* (Issue Brief). Washington, DC: National Partnership to End Youth Homelessness.

[137] Office of Juvenile Justice and Delinquency Prevention. (2005). *Program Summary: Serious and Violent Offender Reentry Initiative.* Washington, DC: OJJDP.

[138] Second Chance Act

[139] *Ibid.*

[140] Fest, 1995

In: Runaway and Homeless Youth
Editors: Josiah Hughes and Isiah Wright

ISBN: 978-1-60741-5213
© 2010 Nova Science Publishers, Inc.

*Chapter 3*

# RUNAWAY AND HOMELESS YOUTH: DEMOGRAPHICS AND PROGRAMS[*]

### *Adrienne L. Fernandes*

## SUMMARY

There is no single definition of the term "runaway youth" or "homeless youth." However, both groups of youth share the risk of not having adequate shelter and other provisions, and may engage in harmful behaviors while away from a permanent home. These two groups also include "thrownaway" youth who are asked to leave their homes, and may include other vulnerable youth populations, such as current and former foster youth and youth with mental health or other issues.

The precise number of homeless and runaway youth is unknown due to their residential mobility and overlap among the populations. Determining the number of these youth is further complicated by the lack of a standardized methodology for counting the population and inconsistent definitions of what it means to be homeless or a runaway. Estimates of the homeless youth exceed one million. Estimates of runaway youth — including "thrownaway" youth (youth asked to leave their homes) — are between one million and 1.7 million.

From the early 20$^{th}$ century through the 1960s, the needs of a generally unspecified problem of runaway and homeless youth were handled locally through the child welfare agency, juvenile justice courts, or both. The 1970s marked a shift toward federal oversight of programs that help youth who had run afoul of the law, including those who committed status offenses (i.e., running away). In 1974, Congress passed the Runaway Youth Act of 1974 as Title III of the Juvenile Justice and Delinquency Prevention Act (P.L. 93-415) to assist runaways outside of the juvenile justice and child welfare systems. The scope of the act was expanded in 1977 to include homeless youth through the Runaway and Homeless Youth Act (P.L. 93-415). The Runaway and Homeless Youth Program (RHYP) has since been

---

[*] This is an edited, reformatted and augmented version of a CRS Report for Congress publication dated October 2008.

reauthorized approximately every five years since the 1970s, most recently by the Reconnecting Homeless Youth Act (P.L. 110-378). The law currently authorizes federal funding for three programs — the Basic Center Program, Transitional Living Program, and Street Outreach Program.

The Basic Center Program provides temporary shelter, counseling, and after care services to runaway and homeless youth under age 18 and their families, while the Transitional Living Program is targeted to older youth ages 16 to 21. Youth who use the TLP receive longer-term housing with supportive services. The Street Outreach Program provides education, treatment, counseling, and referrals for runaway, homeless, and street youth who have been subjected to or are at risk of being subjected to sexual abuse and exploitation. Related services authorized by the Runaway and Homeless Youth Act include a national communication system to facilitate communication between service providers, runaway youth, and their families; training and technical support for grantees; and evaluations of the programs; among other activities.

## INTRODUCTION

Running away from home is not a recent phenomenon. Folkloric heroes Huckleberry Finn and Davey Crockett fled their abusive fathers to find adventure and employment. Although some youth today also leave home due to abuse and neglect, they often endure far more negative outcomes than their romanticized counterparts from an earlier era. Without adequate and safe shelter, runaway and homeless youth are vulnerable to engaging in high-risk behaviors and further victimization. Youth who live away from home for extended periods may become removed from school and systems of support that promote positive development. They might also resort to illicit activities, including selling drugs and prostitution, for survival.

Congress began to hear concerns about the vulnerabilities of the runaway population in the 1970s due to increased awareness about these youth and the establishment of runaway shelters to assist them in returning home. Since that time, Congress has authorized services to provide support for runaway and homeless youth outside of the juvenile justice, mental health, and child welfare systems. The Runaway and Homeless Youth Act (RHYA), as currently amended, authorizes federal funding for three programs to assist runaway and homeless youth — the Basic Center Program (BCP), Transitional Living Program (TLP), and Street Outreach Program (SOP) — through FY2013.[1] These programs make up the Runaway and Homeless Youth Program, administered by the U.S. Department of Health and Human Services (HHS).

- *Basic Center Program:* To provide outreach, crisis intervention, temporary shelter, counseling, family unification, and after care services to runaway and homeless youth under age 18 and their families. In some cases, BCP-funded programs may serve older youth.
- *Transitional Living Program:* To support projects that provide homeless youth ages 16 through 22 with stable, safe longer-term residential services up to 18 months (or longer under certain circumstances), including counseling in basic life skills,

interpersonal skills building, educational advancement, job attainment skills, and physical and mental health care.

- *Street Outreach Program:* To provide street-based outreach and education, including treatment, counseling, provision of information, and referrals for runaway, homeless, and street youth who have been subjected to or are at risk of being subjected to sexual abuse and exploitation.[2]

This report begins with a brief discussion of the reauthorization of and appropriations for the Runaway and Homeless Youth Program, followed by an overview of the runaway and homeless youth population. The report describes the challenges in defining and counting the runaway and homeless youth population, as well as the factors that influence homelessness and leaving home. In particular, youth who experience foster care are vulnerable to running away or becoming homeless while in care or after having been emancipated from the system. The report also provides background on the evolution of the Runaway and Homeless Youth Act from the 1970s until it was last amended in 2008. Finally, it describes the administration and funding of the Basic Center, Transitional Living, and Street Outreach programs that were created from the act, as well as the functions of their ancillary components. (**Table A-1** in the **Appendix** provides BCP funding by state for FY2007 and FY2008.)

## REAUTHORIZATION ACTIVITIES

The Runaway and Homeless Youth Protection Act of 2008 (P.L. 110-378) reauthorized funding for the Runaway and Homeless Youth Program, established new requirements for grantees, and expanded oversight of the program.

- *Funding:* P.L. 110-378 authorized FY2009 appropriation levels for the BCP, TLP, and related activities that exceed the levels authorized for FY2004 by $35 million (these are the only recent years for which Congress has specified authorized appropriation levels). The law also increased the authorized annual minimum levels of BCP funding available for states and territories. The law requires HHS to reallocate unused BCP funds from one state to another and specified that the amount allocated to states for FY2009 and FY20 10 may not be lower than the amount appropriated to the states in FY2008.
- *Requirements:* P.L. 110-378 allows youth to remain in a program funded under the BCP and TLP longer they were able to under the prior law, although the law imposes additional criteria for youth who stay longer at TLP-funded programs. Further, the law changed the definition of "homeless youth" to permit youth older than age 18 and 22 to stay at BCP- and TLP-funded programs, respectively, but only under certain circumstances. Another change made by the law specifies that in funding grants for research and other projects related to runaway and homeless youth, HHS is to give priority to applicants that serve diverse youth and represent diverse geographic regions of the U.S. (The term "diverse" is not defined.) Other requirements pertain to BCP and TLP plans submitted by grant applicants.

- *Accountability:* P.L. 110-378 requires HHS to promulgate regulations that specify performance standards for public and nonprofit entities that receive BCP, TLP, and SOP grants. The law further requires HHS to periodically submit to Congress an incidence and prevalence study of runaway and homeless youth ages 13 to 26, as well as the characteristics of a representative sample of these youth. HHS must consult with the U.S. Interagency Council on Homelessness in developing the study. The law also directs the Government Accountability Office (GAO) to evaluate the process by which organizations apply for BCP, TLP, and SOP, including HHS 's response to these applicants. GAO is to submit a report on its findings to Congress.

## APPROPRIATIONS

### FY2009 Budget Request and Appropriations

The FY2009 budget request for the Runaway and Homeless Youth Program is identical to the level of funding appropriated for the program in FY2008.[3] Funding for FY2009 is not yet final. Congress has passed, and the President has signed into law, a continuing resolution for FY2009 (P.L. 110-329), which provides the same level of funding as in FY2008 for many federal programs. The resolution extends until March 9, 2009, and does not reflect final funding decisions.

### FY2008 Appropriations Finalized

On June 21, 2007, the Senate Committee on Appropriations reported the FY2008 appropriations bill (S. 1710) for the Departments of Labor, Health and Human Services, and Education, and related agencies (LHE).[4] The committee recommended $102.9 million for the BCP and TLP, an increase of $15 million over the current level. It also recommended $20 million for the SOP, an increase of $5 million over the current level. The House Committee on Appropriations reported its version of the bill (H.R. 3043) on July 13.[5] The committee recommended $97.8 million for the BCP and TLP, an increase of $10 million, and no change in funding for the SOP from its FY2007 level.

The House and Senate Labor-Health and Human Services-Education FY2008 appropriations bill (H.R. 3043), was consolidated with other appropriation bills into H.R. 2764 (the original State-Foreign Operations Appropriations Act for FY2008) as the vehicle for omnibus appropriations for FY2008. H.R. 2764 was signed into law as P.L. 110-161 and provides $52.9 million for the BCP, $43.3 million for the TLP, and $17.2 million for the SOP. The total FY2008 appropriation for the RHY program is $113.3 million, an increase of $10.5 million from the FY2007 level and the largest appropriation for the program to date.

**Table 1** shows funding levels for the Runaway and Homeless Youth Program from FY2001 to FY2008. Since FY2002, funding has generally remained stable for the Basic Center and Street Outreach Programs. Funding for the Transitional Living Program nearly doubled from FY2001 to FY2002 (as shown below), but remained at about $40 million from FY2002 to FY2007. Although the TLP authorized services for pregnant and parenting teens, the Administration sought funds specifically to serve this population and Congress provided the increased funds to enable these youth to access TLP services. In FY2003, amendments to the Runaway and Homeless Youth Act (P.L. 108-96) specifically authorized TLP funds to be used for services targeted at pregnant and parenting teens at TLP centers known as Maternity Group Homes. The FY2004 through FY2008 appropriations reflect funding for the Maternity Group Homes as part of the TLP.

# WHO ARE HOMELESS AND RUNAWAY YOUTH?

## Defining the Population

There is no single federal definition of the terms "homeless youth" or "runaway youth." However, the U.S. Department of Health and Human Services relies on the definitions from the program's authorizing legislation and its accompanying regulations.[6] The Runaway and Homeless Youth Act defines homeless youth for purposes of the BCP as individuals under age 18 (or some older age if permitted by state or local law) who are unable to live in a safe environment with a relative and lack safe alternative living arrangements. For purposes of the TLP, homeless youth are individuals ages 16 through 22 who are unable to live in a safe environment with a relative and lack safe alternative living arrangements. Youth older than age 22 may participate if they entered the program before age 22 and meet other requirements.[7] The accompanying regulations further define homeless youth as being in need of services and shelter that provide supervision and care.[8] The act and regulations describe runaway youth as individuals under age 18 who absent themselves from their home or legal residence at least overnight without the permission of their parents or legal guardians.[9]

Although these current policy definitions are distinct, youth can be homeless and runaways. The American Medical Association's Council on Scientific Affairs argues that the distinctions between the two groups are artificial and may be counterproductive. Their report on this population concludes that most youth on the streets are both runaways and homeless because they have no home to which they are willing or able to return.[10]

Some definitions of runaway and homeless youth may include a sub-population known as "thrownaway" youth (or "push outs") who have been abandoned by their parents or have been told to leave their households. These youth may be considered part of the homeless population if they lack alternative living arrangements. However, the most recent federal study of *runaway* youth — the National Incidence Study of Missing, Abducted, Runaway, and Thrownaway Children-2 (NISMART-2) conducted by the U.S. Department of Justice — includes thrownaway youth in its estimates.[11] The study de-emphasizes distinctions between runaway and thrownaway populations because many youth experience both circumstances, and the categorization of a runaway or thrownaway episode frequently depends on whether information was gathered from the youth (who tend to emphasize the thrownaway aspects of the episode) or their care takers (who tend to emphasize the runaway aspects). Some definitions of runaway and homeless youth, including those used by HHS, include "street youth" because they lack shelter and live on the street and in other areas that increase the risk of sexual abuse, sexual exploitation, drug abuse, and prostitution.[12]

## Demographics

The precise number of homeless and runaway youth is unknown due to their residential mobility. These youth often eschew the shelter system for locations or areas that are not easily accessible to shelter workers and others who count the homeless and runaways.[13] Youth who come into contact with census takers may also be reluctant to report that they have left home or are homeless. Determining the number of homeless and runaway youth is further complicated by the lack of a standardized methodology for counting the population and inconsistent definitions of what it means to be homeless or a runaway.[14]

Differences in methodology for collecting data on homeless populations may also influence how the characteristics of the runaway and homeless youth population are reported. Some studies have relied on point prevalence estimates that report whether youth have experienced homelessness at a given point in time, such as on a particular day.[15] According to researchers that study the characteristics of runaway and homeless youth, these studies appear to be biased toward describing individuals who experience longer periods of homelessness.[16] The sample location may also misrepresent the characteristics of the population generally.[17] Surveying youth who live on the streets may lend to the perception that all runaway and homeless youth are especially deviant. Youth surveyed in locations with high rates of drug use and sex work, known as "cruise areas," tend to be older, to have been away from home longer, to have recently visited community-based agencies, and to be less likely to attend school than youth in "non-cruise areas."[18]

As discussed later in the report, the Runaway and Homeless Youth Protection Act (P.L. 110-378), which renewed the Runaway and Homeless Youth Program through FY2013, authorizes funding for HHS to conduct periodic studies of the incidence and prevalence of youth who have run away or are homeless.

### *Homeless Youth*

A 1998 study in the American Journal of Public Health used the Centers for Disease Control and Prevention's (CDC) 1992 National Health Interview Survey of youth ages 12 to 17 to determine the number of those who were homeless.[19] In the survey, youth were asked whether, in the past 12 months, they had spent one or more nights in a specific type of shelter not intended to be a dwelling place (i.e., in an abandoned building, public place, outside, underground, or in a stranger's home) or a youth or adult shelter. Based on their responses, researchers calculated that 5% of the population ages 12 to 17 — more than 1 million youth in a given year — experienced homelessness. The researchers concluded that the prevalence of staying at a particular dwelling place while homeless was constant across racial groups, socioeconomic status, youth who lived with both parents and those who did not, and youth who lived in cities of varying sizes. However, boys were more likely to experience homeless episodes, especially as these episodes related to sleeping in a shelter or outside.[20]

Measured characteristics of homeless youth vary depending on the source of the sample and methodology. Some evaluations of homeless youth indicate that gender representation varies across sample locations. Surveys from family shelters suggest either even numbers of females and males, or more females (see below for a discussion of the gender of youth using federally-funded Basic Center shelters).[21] Although studies tend to document that homeless youth generally reflect the ethnic makeup of their local areas, some studies show overrepresentation of racial or ethnic minorities relative to the community (black youth are overrepresented at the Basic Center shelters).[22] The history of homelessness among youth also varies by the sample location. Youth in shelters tend to have short periods of homelessness and have not experienced prior homeless episodes while youth living on the streets are more likely to demonstrate patterns of episodic (i.e., multiple episodes adding up to less than one year) or chronic homelessness (i.e., being homeless for one year or longer).[23]

**Table 1. Runaway and Homeless Youth Program Funding, FY2002-FY2008 ($ in thousands)**

| Program | FY2001 Enacted | FY2002 Enacted | FY2003 Enacted | FY2004 Enacted | FY2005 Enacted | FY2006 Enacted[b] | FY2007 Enacted[b] | FY2008 Enacted[c] |
|---------|------|------|------|------|------|------|------|------|
| BCP | 48,338 | 48,288 | 48,298 | 49,171 | 48,786 | 48,265 | 48,298 | 52,860 |
| TLP | 20,740 | 39,736 | 40,505 | 40,260[a] | 39,938[a] | 39,511[a] | 39,539[a] | 43,268[a] |
| SOP | 14,999 | 14,999 | 15,399 | 15,302 | 15,178 | 15,017 | 15,027 | 17,221 |
| Total | 84,127 | 103,023 | 104,202 | 104,733 | 103,902 | 102,793 | 102,864 | 113,349 |

Source: U.S. Department Health and Human Services, *Administration for Children and Families Justification of Estimates for Appropriations Committees*, FY2003, p. H-48; *Administration for Children and Families Justification of Estimates for Appropriations Committees*, FY2004, p. H-45; *Administration for Children and Families Justification of Estimates for Appropriations Committees*, FY2005, p. H-89; *Administration for Children and Families Justification of Estimates for Appropriations Committees*, FY2006, p. D-41; *Administration for Children and Families Justification of Estimates for Appropriations Committees*, FY2007, p. D-41; and *Administration for Children and Families Justification of Estimates for Appropriations Committees*, FY2008, pp. 92, 98; *Administration for Children and Families Justification of Estimates for Appropriations Committees*, FY2009, p. D-42.

Note: BCP and TLP funding are distributed under the Consolidated Runaway and Homeless Youth Program. SOP funds are distributed separately.

a. Includes funding for the Maternity Group Home component.

b. The fourth Continuing Resolution for the FY2007 budget (P.L. 110-5) generally funded programs at their FY2006 levels. However, the FY2006 funding total for the RHYP was slightly lower than the FY2007 total because of an additional transfer of funds from the RHYP accounts to an HHS sub-agency.

c. The FY2008 appropriations includes a 1.7% across-the-board recession on Labor-HHS-Education programs. See page 346 of [http://www.rules.house.gov/1 10_fy08_omni.htm].

### Runaway and Thrownaway Youth

According to HHS's Substance Abuse and Mental Health Services Administration (SAMHSA), approximately 1.6 million youth (7 %) ages 12 to 17 had run away from home and slept on the street in a 12- month period (in 2002). These youth were more likely to be male (5 5%) than female, and nearly half (46%) were ages 16 or 17.[24] The NISMART-2, a study sponsored by the U.S. Department of Justice, estimates that 1.7 million youth under age 18 left home or were asked to leave home in 1999.[25] Of these youth, 68% were between the ages of 15 and 17. Males and females were equally represented in the population.

White youth made up the largest share of runaways (57%), followed by black youth (17%) and Hispanic youth (15%). Over half of all youth left home for one to six days, and 30% traveled more than one to 10 miles. An additional 30% traveled more than 10 to 50 miles. Nearly all (99%) runaway and thrownaway youth were returned to their homes.

Another study estimates a somewhat smaller number of runaway youth—1 million to 1.3 million.[26]

The National Center for Missing and Exploited Children (NCMEC) provides assistance to children believed to be missing, including runaways.[27] From 1990 to December 2007, case managers at NCMEC handled 114,679 cases (i.e., individual children), of which just under three quarters (82,810) involved endangered runaways.[28]

## Factors Influencing Homelessness and Leaving Home

Youth most often cite family conflict as the major reason for their homelessness or episodes of running away. A literature review of homeless youth found that a youth's relationship with a step-parent, sexual activity, sexual orientation, pregnancy, school problems, and alcohol and drug use were strong predictors of family discord.[29] Of those callers who used the National Runaway Switchboard (a federally-sponsored call center for youth and their relatives involved in runaway incidents) nearly one third attributed family conflict as the reason for their call.[30] Runaway and homeless youth also describe abuse and neglect as common experiences. Over 20% of youth in the NISMART-2 reported being physically or sexually abused at home in the prior year or feared abuse upon returning home.[31] Gay and lesbian youth appear to be overrepresented in the homeless population, due often to experiencing negative reactions from their parents when they came out about their sexuality. In five studies of unaccompanied youth in mid-size and large cities, between 20% and 40% of respondents identified as gay or lesbian.[32]

### *Youth in Foster Care*

Youth who run away often have a history of involvement in the foster care system. On the last day of FY2006, states reported over 12,000 (just over 2%) foster children as "runaways."[33] A study of youth who ran away from foster care between 1993 and 2003 by the Chapin Hall Center for Children (University of Chicago) found that the average likelihood of an individual running away from foster care placements increased over this time period.[34] Youth questioned about their runaway experiences cited three primary reasons why they ran from foster care. First, they wanted to reconnect or stay connected to their biological families even if they recognized that their families were neither healthy nor safe. Second, youth wanted to express their autonomy and find normalcy among sometimes chaotic events. Many youth explained that they already felt independent because they had taken on adult responsibilities beginning at a young age. Third, youth wanted to maintain surrogate family relationships with non-family members. Youth in the study were more likely than their foster care peers to abuse drugs and to have certain mental health disorders.

Youth who experience foster care are also vulnerable to homelessness after emancipating from the child welfare system. Each year about 26,500 youth "age out" of foster care, many of whom lack the proper supports to successfully transition to adulthood.[35] Only about two-fifths of eligible foster youth receive independent living services.[36] Of those youth who do receive services, few have adequate housing assistance. Research on youth who emancipate from foster care suggests a nexus between foster care involvement and later episodes of homelessness. In a study of 21-year-olds who had emancipated from foster care in three states, approximately 18% had experienced homelessness since leaving care.[37] A national study of former foster youth found the percentage of the population who experienced homelessness to be much higher—25%.[38]

## Risks Associated with Running Away and Homelessness

Runaway and homeless youth are vulnerable to multiple problems while they are away from a permanent home, including untreated mental health disorders, drug use, and sexual exploitation. In a 1996 evaluation of street youth (ages 13 to 17) in a Hollywood cruise area, about one quarter met clinical criteria for major depression compared to 10% or less of their peers in the general population.[39] However, youth who live on the streets in cruise areas may experience greater challenges than other homeless and runaway youth who stay in other locations. Another study that compared rates for many mental disorders between homeless youth and the general youth population concluded that they were similar, although homeless youth had significantly higher rates of disruptive behavior disorders.[40]

Drug use also appears prevalent among the runaway and homeless youth population. The SAMHSA study found that nearly 30% had used marijuana and almost one quarter used any illicit drug other than marijuana.[41] NISMART-2 reported that 17% of runaway youth used hard drugs (not defined) and 18% were in the company of someone known to be abusing drugs when they were away from home.[42] Runaway and homeless youth are also vulnerable to sexual abuse and exploitation, and are at high risk for contracting sexually transmitted diseases. Some youth resort to illegal activity including stealing, prostitution, and selling drugs for survival. Runaway and homeless youth report other challenges including poor health and the lack of basic provisions such as food.[43]

## EVOLUTION OF FEDERAL POLICY

Prior to the passage of the 1974 Runaway Youth Act (Title III, Juvenile Justice and Delinquency Prevention Act of 1974, P.L. 93-415), federal policy was limited in the area of runaway and homeless youth. If they received any services, most such youth were served through the local child welfare agency, juvenile justice court system, or both. The 1970s marked a shift to a more rehabilitative model for assisting youth who had run afoul of the law, including those who committed status offenses (i.e., running away). During this period, Congress focused increasing attention on runaways and other vulnerable youth due, in part, to emerging sociological models to explain why youth engaged in deviant behavior. The first runaway shelters were created in the late 1960s and 1970s to assist them in returning home. The landmark Runway Youth Act of 1974 decriminalized runaway youth and authorized funding for programs to provide shelter, counseling, and other services. Since 1974, Congress has expanded the services available to both runaway youth and homeless youth. Figure 1 traces the evolution of federal runaway and homeless youth policy.

## Early Years: 1930s-1960s

### Federal Legislation on Homeless Youth.

The federal government first addressed the problem of youth homelessness during the Great Depression when it established programs to provide relief services for children and youth, often accompanied by their families, who left home to find work and became homeless. The estimated number of homeless individuals in 1933 was two million to five million, of whom 20% to 30% were boys.[44] Mayors at this time reported that the transient and homeless populations in their cities were sometimes fed, pushed on to other cities, or placed in jail.

In response to the influx of homeless adults and youth to the nation's cities, the Federal Transient Relief Act of 1933 established a Transient Division within the Federal Transient Relief Administration to provide relief services through state grants. Also in 1933, the Civilian Conservation Corps opened camps and shelters for more than one million low-income older youth. In 1935, President Franklin Roosevelt created the National Youth Administration by executive order to open employment bureaus and provide cash assistance to poor college and high school students. Together, these programs helped to reduce the number of homeless and transient youth. According to the July 1935 Federal Transient Relief Act's Monthly Report, 50,000 young people were homeless and/or transient at that time.[45] The Transient Division was disbanded shortly thereafter.

### Federal Legislation on Runaway Youth

Homeless youth were generally considered a problem that had ended after the Great Depression, but youth running away from home was emerging as a more serious issue. At about the same time the federal government withdrew funding for homeless and transient youth services provided during the Great Depression, it enacted, for the first time, separate and unrelated legislation to assist vulnerable youth — including runaways — through state grants. As originally enacted, the Social Security Act of 1935 (P.L. 74-231) authorized indefinite annual funding of $1.5 million for states to establish, extend, and strengthen public child welfare services in "predominately rural" or "special needs" areas. For purposes of this program (now at Title IV-B, Subpart 1 of the Social Security Act), these were described as services "for the protection and care of homeless, dependent, and neglected children, and children in danger of becoming delinquent."[46] In 1950 (P.L. 8 1-734), Title IV-B was amended to allow state grants to be used to pay the cost of returning a runaway child under the age of 16 to his or her home state from another state. In 1958, the program was again amended (P.L. 85-840) to increase the age of runaways who could receive this aid to 18 and to include 15 days of maintenance (i.e., room and board) for each child in cases where the costs could not be met by his or her parents or the agency institution legally responsible for the care of that child.

The passage of the 1961 Juvenile Delinquency and Youth Offenses Control Act (P.L. 87-274) focused on the environmental and underlying sociological factors of deviant behavior among youth. Unaccompanied minors on the street fit the image of troubled, and potentially delinquent youth. This image was further entrenched as some runaway youth joined the Counterculture Movement of the 1960s.[47] The first runaway centers (Huckleberry House in San Francisco, the Runaway House in Washington, D.C., and branch offices of the Young

Women's Christian Association and Traveler's Aid Society) opened during the late 1960s to provide shelter, counseling, and other services to youth and their families. The centers received little, if any, federal funds, and relied primarily on the donations of churches and other nongovernmental organizations.

## The Runaway Youth Act of 1974

Concerned that an increasing number of runaway youth were entering the juvenile justice system, the Subcommittee to Investigate Juvenile Delinquency of the Senate Judiciary Committee conducted hearings on runaway youth in 1972 to explore the problems facing this population.[48] Testimony from government officials, youth workers, and community leaders focused on the lifestyles of youth, as well as their interaction with police and increasing reliance on runaway centers. Runaway youth were concentrated in areas like the Haight District in San Francisco and New York City's Greenwich Village, often staying in filthy, overcrowded houses (known as "pads") with other youth and adults. Police officers routinely sent unaccompanied youth to juvenile detention centers. The few runaway centers operating in the early 1970s were underfunded, understaffed, and unable to help youth cope with the reasons they ran away. A fractured home life and problems with school were most often cited as motivation for leaving home. Youth who ran away because they were abused or neglected were not always placed under the protection of the state. These youth, like most runaways, had to secure permission from their parents to stay overnight at a runaway center.

The subcommittee also heard testimony regarding the need to establish and federally fund programs to assist runaway youth. At the time, states could only use Social Security Title IV-B funds for runaway youth to return them to their state of origin (not for intrastate transfer). Other federal funding streams that targeted runaway youth were also limited. The Juvenile Delinquency Prevention and Control Act of 1968 (P.L. 90-445) authorized funding for approximately four runaway centers from 1968 to 1972. The primary purpose of the legislation was to provide assistance to courts, correctional systems, schools, and community agencies for research and training on juvenile justice issues.

Although the Senate reacted to the hearings by passing legislation to assist runaway youth, the House did not act. However, two years later, in 1974, Congress passed the Runaway Youth Act as Title III of the Juvenile Justice and Delinquency Prevention Act (JJDPA, P.L. 93-415). A total of $10 million for each fiscal year, FY1975 through FY1977, was authorized to provide temporary shelter, family counseling, and after-care services to runaway youth and their families through what is now referred to as the Basic Center Program. To receive funding under Title III, states had to decriminalize runaway youth and provide services outside of the juvenile justice system. The legislation also included a provision requiring a comprehensive statistical survey of runaway youth.

## Expanding the Scope of the Act

Through the Juvenile Justice Amendments to the JJDPA in 1977 (P.L. 95-115), Congress reauthorized the Runaway Youth Act for FY1978 and expanded its scope to include homeless youth. Such youth became eligible for services provided through the Basic Center Program. Two other programs were later added that targeted specific sub-populations of runaway and homeless youth. Congress established the Transitional Living Program through the Anti-Drug Abuse Act of 1988 (P.L. 100- 690) to meet the needs of older youth ages 16 to 21. The impetus for passing the legislation was the success of demonstration transitional living projects in the 1 980s. The other major program, the Street Outreach Program, was created in 1994 by the Violent Crime Control and Law Enforcement Act of 1994 (P.L. 103-322). The purpose of the program is to serve homeless youth living on the streets. The Runaway and Homeless Youth Act was most recently reauthorized by the Reconnecting Homeless Youth Act of 2008 (P.L. 110-78), which extended the program's funding authorization through FY20 13.

## FUNDING AND DESCRIPTION OF THE RUNAWAY AND HOMELESS YOUTH PROGRAM

### Federal Administration and Funding

The Runaway and Homeless Youth Program is administered by the Family and Youth Services (FYSB) Bureau within HHS's Administration for Children and Families (ACF). The funding streams for the Basic Center Program and Transitional Living Program were separate until Congress consolidated them in 1999 when RHYA was reauthorized by the Missing, Exploited, and Runaway Children Protection Act (P.L. 106-7 1). Under current law, 90% of the federal funds appropriated under the authorization must be used for the Basic Center Program and Transitional Living Program. Of this amount, 45% is reserved for the BCP and no more than 55% is reserved for the TLP. The remaining share of federal funding is allocated for (1) a national communication system to facilitate communication between service providers, runaway youth, and their families; (2) training and technical support for grantees; (3) evaluations of the programs; and (4) HHS efforts to coordinate with other federal agencies on matters relating to the health, education, employment, and housing of these youth. Together, these programs—along with other program activities, except the Street Outreach Program—are known as the Consolidated Runaway and Homeless Youth Program. Although the Street Outreach Program is a separately funded component, SOP services are coordinated with those provided under the BCP and TLP

The 2008 reauthorization law (P.L. 110-378) authorized $140 million for FY2009 and such sums as may be necessary for the Consolidated Runaway and Homeless Youth Program for FY2010 through FY2013. P.L. 110-378 authorized the Street Outreach Program to receive $25 million for FY2009 and such sums as may be necessary for FY2010 through FY2013. P.L. 110-378 also authorized funding for HHS to periodically conduct incidence and prevalence studies of runaway and homeless youth. The studies are authorized to receive such sums as may be necessary for FY2009 through FY2013.

**Figure 2** provides the program funding levels from FY1986 through FY2008 for the BCP and from FY1990 and FY1996, for the TLP and SOP, respectively, through FY2008. No final action has been taken to appropriate FY2009 funding for the Runaway and Homeless Youth Program.

Source: Created by the Congressional Research Service.

Figure 1. Evolution of Federal Runaway and Homeless Youth Policy, 1912-2008.

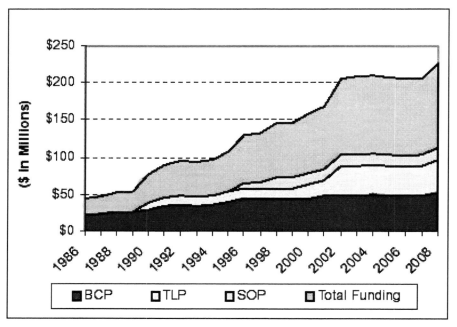

Source: Congressional Research Service.

Figure 2: Runaway and Homeless Youth Program Funding, FY1986 through FY2008

## Basic Center Program

### Overview

The Basic Center Program is intended to provide short-term shelter and services for youth and their families through public and private community-based centers. Youth eligible to receive BCP services include those youth who are at risk of running away or becoming homeless (and may live at home with their parents), or have already left home, either voluntarily or involuntarily. To stay at the shelter, youth must be under age 18, or, as added by the 2008 reauthorization act (P.L. 110- 378), an older age if the BCP center is located in a state or locality that permits this higher age. Some centers may serve homeless youth older than 18 through street- based services, home-based services, and drug abuse education and prevention services.

BCP centers were designed to provide these services outside of the law enforcement, juvenile justice, child welfare, and mental health systems. For FY2007, the program supported approximately 336 BCP shelters in all 50 states, America Samoa, Guam, and Puerto Rico.[49] These centers, which generally shelter as many as 20 youth are located in areas that are frequented or easily reached by runaway and homeless youth. The shelters seeks to reunite youth with their families, whenever possible, or to locate appropriate alternative placements. They also provide food, clothing, individual or group and family counseling, and health care referrals. Youth may stay in a center continuously up to 21 days and may re-enter the program multiple times.[50]

BCP grantees — community-based public and private organizations — must make efforts to contact the parents and relatives of runaway and homeless youth. Grantees are also required to establish relationship with law enforcement, health and mental health care, social service, welfare, and school district systems to coordinate services. Centers maintain confidential statistical records of youth (including youth who are not referred to out-of-home shelter services) and the family members. The centers are required to submit an annual report to HHS detailing the program activities and the number of youth participating in such activities, as well as information about the operation of the centers.

HHS evaluates BCP organizations using the Basic Center Program Performance Standards, which relate to how well the needs of runaway and homeless youth and their families are being met. Nine of these standards address service components (i.e., outreach, individual intake process, and recreational programs) and six focus on administrative functions or activities (i.e., staffing and staff development, reporting, and individual client files).

## Funding

BCP grants are allocated by formula to each state, the District of Columbia, and Puerto Rico and are then distributed (by HHS) on a competitive basis to community-based organizations. The amount of BCP funding available is based on the jurisdiction's proportion of the nation's youth under age 18, and under the law, these jurisdictions receive a minimum of $200,000. Pursuant to the 2008 reauthorization act (P.L. 110-378), HHS is to reallot any funds from one state to other states that will not be obligated before the end of a fiscal year. Separately, each of the territories (U.S. Virgin Islands, Guam, America Samoa, and the Northern Mariana Islands) receive a minimum of $70,000 of the total appropriations. (Prior to the enactment of P.L. 110-378, the states were to receive a minimum of $100,000 and territories received a minimum of $45,000.) Congress appropriated $48.3 million for the BCP in FY2006. See **Appendix Table A-1** for the amount of funding allocated for each state in FY2007 and FY2008.

The costs of the Basic Center Program are shared by the federal government (90%) and grantees (10%). Community-based organizations apply directly to the federal government for the BCP grants. Grants may be awarded for up to three years.

Funding priority is given to organizations that have demonstrated experience in providing services to runaway and homeless youth, and to those who apply for less than $200,000 in funding per fiscal year. Funding for the second and third year, however, depends on the availability of funds and the grantee's satisfactory performance.

## Youth in the Program

BCP grantees serve only a fraction of the more than one million youth who run away or are homeless. According to the FY2007 NEO-RHYMIS report of all grantees, 43,857 youth used BCP services (about 48,400 youth used BCP services in FY2006).[51] Of these youth, 23,618 (53.9%) were female and 20,239 (46.1%) were male (nearly the same percentages as in FY2005 and FY2006). As **Figure 3** shows, the greatest percentage of youth served were ages 15 and 16. The centers also served youth younger than 12 and older than 18. The proportions of youth in each age category were nearly the same as they were in FY2005 and FY2006.

Youth who visited the centers represented a variety of ethnic and racial backgrounds (see **Figure 4**). Although white youth made up the majority of the youth served, black and American Indian youth were overrepresented compared to their share of the general population.[52] Black youth comprised more than one-third of the BCP population in FY2007, but made up 15% of the 10-to-19-year-old population. Similarly, Native American youth comprised about 4% of the BCP population, but are about 1% of the American population ages 10 to 19. Notably, however, not all minorities are overrepresented. The share of Asian youth who used RHY services (1%) in FY2007 is well below their share in the population (3.5%). Hispanic youth are also underrepresented in the population. Hispanic youth of any race comprised just over 16% of the BCP population (not shown in the figure), but are approximately 18% of the general population. The percentages of youth in each racial and ethnic group are almost identical to those reported in the previous two fiscal years.

According to NEO-RHYMIS, at the time of their entrance to the BCP shelters in FY2007, about 70% of youth had lived with their parents. About 60% attended school regularly; however, nearly 20% attended irregularly. Approximately 7.7% had dropped out and the balance of youth had graduated, obtained a GED, were suspended or expelled, or did not know their school status. The greatest share of youth were referred to the shelters by their parents, followed by referrals from law enforcement agencies, self-referrals, referrals by schools, and referrals by child protective services. Nearly all (85.4%) youth received counseling. Youth also received basic support (not defined), life skills training, education, and substance abuse prevention treatment, among other services at the shelters. Upon exiting, most youth (65.2%) planned to live with their parents. However, youth were also exiting to a relative or friend's home (7.8%), the street (5.9%), and foster care (3.6%). Approximately 4% of youth did not know where they would live upon exiting. These proportions are about the same as they were for FY2005 and FY2006. The remaining youth exited to a shelter, another private residence, or a residential program, among other arrangements.

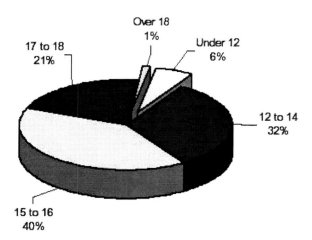

Source: Congressional Research Service analysis of NEO-RHYMIS data.
Note: Based on data from 43,857 youth.

Figure 3. Age of Youth Served by the Basic Center Program, FY2007

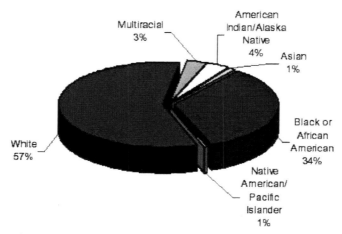

Source: Congressional Research Service analysis of NEO-RHYMIS data.
Note: Based on data from 40,210 youth. More than 3,600 youth did not provide information about their race. Consistent with the Census Bureau classification of ethnicity and race, Hispanic youth can be of any race.

Figure 4. Race of Youth Served by the Basic Center Program, FY2007

As in FY2005 and FY2006, the issues of concern most cited by youth at the time of exiting, in order of frequency, were family dynamics, education, housing, mental health, and alcohol and drug abuse. Almost nine out of 10 youth cited family dynamics as the major issue. Finally, in FY2007, BCP shelters reported turning away 4,039 youth by phone and 331 youth in person due to a lack of bed space

## Transitional Living Program

### Overview

Recognizing the difficulty that youth face in becoming self- sufficient adults, the Transitional Living Program provides longer-term shelter and assistance for youth ages 16 through 22 (including pregnant and/or parenting youth) who may leave their biological homes due to family conflict, or have left and are not expected to return home. In FY2007, 190 organizations received TLP grants.[53] All but five states (Idaho, Nevada, New Hampshire, North Dakota, and Wyoming), Guam, Puerto Rico, and the U.S. Virgin Islands appear to have at least one TLP grantee.[54]

Each TLP grantee may shelter up to 20 youth at host family homes, supervised apartments owned by a social service agency, or scattered-site apartments, and single-occupancy apartments rented directly with the assistance of the agency. The 2008 appropriations law (P.L. 110-278) continues to allow youth to remain at TLP projects for up to 540 days (18 months) or longer for youth under age 18 and adds that a youth ages 16 through 22 may remain in the program for a continuous period of 635 days (approximately 21 months) under "exceptional circumstances." This term means circumstances in which a youth would benefit to an unusual extent from additional time in the program. The new law further authorizes that a youth in a TLP who has not reached age 18 on the last day of the 635-day period may, in exceptional circumstances and if otherwise qualified for the program, remain in the program until his or her 18th birthday.

Youth receive several types of services at TLP-funded programs:

- basic life-skills training, including consumer education and instruction in budgeting and housekeeping;
- interpersonal skill building;
- educational preparation, such as GED courses and post-secondary training;
- assistance in job preparation and attainment;
- education and counseling on substance abuse; and
- mental and physical health care services.

TLP centers develop a written plan designed to help transition youth to independent living or another appropriate living arrangement, and they refer youth to other systems that can coordinate to meet their educational, health care, and social service needs. The grantees must also submit an annual report to HHS that includes information regarding the activities carried out with funds and the number and characteristics of the homeless youth.

### *Funding*

TLP grants are distributed competitively by HHS to community- based public and private organizations for five-year periods. Congress appropriated $39.5 million in FY2007 for the program. Grantees must provide at least 10% of the total cost of the program.

### *Youth in the Program*

For FY2007, NEO-RHYMIS reported that the Transitional Living Program served 3,662 youth (compared to 3,637 youth in FY2006). Of these youth, about 60% were female and 40% were male. Approximately 59% were ages 18 or younger and 41% were ages 19 to 21. About half of the youth were white, 40% were black, and the remaining youth identified as American Indian (4.0%), Asian (9.0%), Native Hawaiian or Pacific Islander (0.7%), or multi-racial (3.8%). Black, American Indian, and Native Hawaiian or Pacific Islander youth were overrepresented, compared to their share of the general population ages 15 to 24.[55] These demographics are consistent with data from FY2005 and FY2006.

Also in FY2007, about one-third of youth in the TLP attended school regularly; almost 23% had dropped out; 22% had graduated from high school; and nearly 8% obtained a GED. The remaining youth either were suspended or expelled, or did not know their school status. According to the FY2007 NEO-RHYMIS report, prior to living at the TLP shelter, youth lived in a variety of locations: the homes of their friends and relatives (25.0%) or parents (19.0%), on the street as a runaway or homeless youth (7.5%), and a BCP shelter (6.6%), among other locations. Youth most often self-referred or were referred to the TLP by a relative or friend. While at the TLP shelter, over three-quarters of youth received counseling, basic support (not defined), life skills training, and employment services, including other services.[56] As in FY2005 and FY2006, youth identified housing, family dynamics, unemployment, education, mental health, and alcohol or drug abuse most frequently as issues of concern upon exiting. Youth reported that at exit, they would live with friends or relatives

(26.9%), independently (25.5%), and with their parents (16.1%), among other situations. About 9% did not know where they would live.

In FY2007, about 1,900 youth were turned away from the TLP by telephone and 55 were turned away in person due to a lack of bed space.

## Outcomes of Youth in the TLP

Efforts are currently underway at HHS to learn more about the youth who are served by the Transitional Living Program. In August 2007, HHS approved a sub-contract to Abt Associates to conduct an evaluation of the TLP at select grantee sites.[57] The study seeks to describe the outcomes of youth who participate in the program and to isolate and describe factors that may have contributed to their successes or challenges, including service delivery approaches, personal characteristics, and local circumstances. HHS (through the Family and Youth Services Bureau) and Abt researchers have conducted three site visits to TLP grantees (in Dallas, Texas; Portland, Oregon; and Wichita, Kansas) and a series of consultations with HHS and outside experts to inform the design of the study.

FYSB has not yet selected the TLP survey sites for the study itself; however, the sites will likely have extensive experience working with runaway and homeless youth and have been awarded continuous TLP funding for at least three years after the survey commences. These sites will work to ensure that after receiving training, staff will be sufficiently capable of administering the survey instruments. The sites will also need to be large enough to capture an adequate sample size.

Youth participants will complete surveys at entry and while receiving services through a survey administered by their TLP programs. They will also complete surveys for up to one year after leaving the program. Youth will self-report the data to a website six months and twelve months after exiting. Evaluators will compare the individual outcomes of each youth to his or her benchmark data. The youth surveys are pending executive branch review, and FYSB expects to begin collecting the data by the end of calendar year 2008. FYSB anticipates making preliminary information available before the last surveys are completed. Further, FYSB expects to maintain the self-reporting website indefinitely as a means of tracking TLP graduates after the formal study is complete.

HHS issued a proposed information collection request for public comment about the evaluation in the *Federal Register* on August 25, 2008.[58]

## Maternity Group Homes

For FY2002, the Administration proposed a $33 million initiative to fund Maternity Group Homes—or centers that provide shelter to pregnant and parenting teens who are vulnerable to abuse and neglect—as a component of the TLP. Congress did not fund the initiative as part of its FY2002 appropriation. However, that year Congress provided additional funding to the TLP to ensure that pregnant and parenting teens could access services (H.Rept. 107-372). A total of $39.7 million was appropriated for the TLP, which included an additional $19.2 million over the FY2001 TLP appropriation to ensure that funds would be available to assist pregnant and parenting teens.

The 2003 amendments to the Runaway and Homeless Youth Act (P.L. 108-96) provided statutory authority to use TLP funds for Maternity Group Homes. For FY2003 through FY2006, the President requested annual funding of $10 million for such homes, separate from the funding for the TLP grants. Congress again did not appropriate separate funds for the program, though funding remained stable at approximately $40 million for the TLP. The Administration's FY2007 budget request sought to implement a $4 million voucher program for 100 pregnant and parenting youth, but no legislation to implement this was proposed or considered during the 109th Congress, and the Administration's FY2008 and FY2009 budgets do not request funding for such a proposal.[59]

Since FY2002, funding for adult-supervised transitional living arrangements that serve pregnant or parenting women ages 16 to 21 and their children has been awarded to organizations that receive TLP grants. Currently, an estimated one-third of TLP grants fund Maternity Group Homes.[60] These organizations provide youth with parenting skills, including child development education; family budgeting; health and nutrition, and other skills to promote their well-being and the well-being of their children.

## Street Outreach Program

### Overview
Runaway and homeless youth living on the streets or in areas that increase their risk of using drugs or being subjected to sexual abuse, prostitution, or sexual exploitation are eligible to receive services through the Street Outreach Program. The program's goal is to assist youth in transitioning to safe and appropriate living arrangements. SOP services include the following:

- treatment and counseling;
- crisis intervention;
- drug abuse and exploitation prevention and education activities;
- survival aid;
- street-based education and outreach;
- information and referrals; and
- follow-up support.

### Funding
The SOP is funded separately from the BCP and TLP and is authorized to receive such sums as may be necessary. Since FY1996, when funding for the Street Outreach Program was first provided, community-based public and private organizations have been eligible to apply for SOP grants. Grants are generally awarded for a three-year period, and grantees must provide 10% of the funds to cover the cost of the program. Applicants may apply for a $100,000 grant each year for a maximum of $200,000 over that period. Approximately $15 million was appropriated to fund 136 grantees in FY2007, many of which operate in coordination with BCPs and TLPs.[61] HHS anticipates that 156 projects will be funded in FY2008.

### Youth in the Program
According to FY2007 NEO-RHYMIS data, street workers with the grantee organizations made 661,286 contacts with street youth (down from 696,146 contacts in FY2006). Of those

youth, most received written materials about referral services, health and hygiene products, and food and drink items.

## Incidence and Prevalence Studies

The 2008 reauthorization law (P.L. 110-378) seeks to determine the number of youth who have run away or are homeless by requiring HHS to estimate at five year intervals—beginning within two years of the enactment of the law (October 8, 2010)—the incidence and prevalence of the runaway and homeless youth population ages 13 to 26. The law also directs HHS to assess the characteristics of these youth. HHS is required to conduct a survey of and direct interviews with a representative sample of the youth to determine past and current socioeconomic characteristics, barriers to obtaining housing and other services, and other information HHS determines useful, in consultation with states and other entities concerned with youth homelessness. HHS is to consult with the federal Interagency Council on Homelessness regarding the study overall. The study must be submitted to the House Education and Labor Committee and Senate Judiciary Committee and made available to the public.

The new law does not specify the methodology for carrying out the studies, except to say that HHS should make the estimate on the basis of the best quantitative and qualitative social science research methods available. Further, if HHS enters into an agreement with a non-federal entity to carry out the assessment, the entity is to be a non-governmental organization or individual determined by HHS to have expertise in this type of research.

## Training and Technical Assistance

In FY2007, HHS allocated approximately $3.6 million of BCP funds and approximately $1.6 million of TLP funds for training and technical assistance, which included funding for a national communications system and the administration of the management information system (known as RHYMIS, discussed in the Congressional Oversight section below).[62]

HHS provides training and technical assistance to RHY grantees through its Runaway and Homeless Youth Training and Technical Assistance Program. Until FY2007, HHS awarded funds to multiple non-profit organizations to provide this assistance in each of the Administration for Children and Families' 10 regions.[63] As of FY2008, training and technical assistance is being provided by one entity. On September 30, 2007, HHS competitively awarded two cooperative agreements to the University of Oklahoma's National Child Welfare Resource Center for Youth Services (NRCYS) to provide training and technical assistance. NRCYS has operated for over 30 years serving public, private, tribal child welfare, and youth services professionals through training and conference events annually.[64]

The two cooperative agreements have distinct assignments.[65] The NRCYS Technical Assistance Center (with an award of $1 million) will provide either one-on-one or in small group settings, specialized attention to specific areas of concern raised by federal staff or RHY grantees to improve grantee performance and/or comply with federal legislation or regulations for the Runaway and Homeless Youth program. The Training Center (with an award of $1.1 million) is designed to provide training and conference services to RHY grantees that will enhance and promote continuous quality improvement of services provided by RHY grantees.

## National Communication System.[66]

A portion of the Consolidated Runaway and Homeless Youth Program funds are allocated for a national communications system (that is, the National Runaway Switchboard) to help homeless and runaway youth (or youth who are contemplating running away) through counseling and referrals and communicating with their families. Beginning with FY1 974 and every year after, the National Runaway Switchboard has been funded through the Basic Center Program grant or the Consolidated Runaway and Homeless Youth Program grant. The Switchboard is located in Chicago and operates each day to provide services to youth and their families in the 50 states, the District of Columbia, Puerto Rico, Guam, and the U.S. Virgin Islands. Services include 1) a channel through which runaway and homeless youth or their parents may leave messages; 2) 24-hour referrals to community resources, including shelter, community food banks, legal assistance, and social services agencies; and 3) crisis intervention counseling to youth. In calendar year 2006, the Switchboard handled almost 114,000 calls, 43% of which were from youth and 35% of which were from parents.[67]

Other services are also provided through the Switchboard. Since 1995, the "HomeFree" family reunification program has provided bus tickets for youth ages 12 to 21 to return home. In FY2002, the Switchboard offered family reunification services to 4,872 youth, of whom 1,170 received free bus tickets to return home or to an alternative placement near their home (such as an independent living program) through HomeFree.[68]

In addition to the National Runaway Switchboard, HHS conducts outreach efforts to the public in three ways.

## Oversight

### *Oversight of Grantees*

ACF evaluates each Runaway and Homeless Youth Program grant recipient through the Runaway and Homeless Youth Monitoring System. Staff from regional ACF offices and other grant recipients (known as peer reviewers) inspect the program site, conduct interviews, review case files and other agency documents, and conduct entry and exit conferences. The monitoring team then prepares a written report that identifies the strengths of the program and areas that require corrective action.

### *Congressional Oversight*

The Senate Committee on Health, Education, Labor, and Pensions and the House Committee on Education and Workforce have exercised jurisdiction over the Runaway and Homeless Youth Program. HHS must submit reports biennially to the committees on the status, activities, and accomplishments of program grant recipients and evaluations of the programs performed by HHS.[69] These reports generally include data on the youth served by the programs which are generated by RHYMIS. The information system is designed to collect information twice during the fiscal year from program grantees on the basic demographics of the youth, the services they received, and the status of the youth (i.e., expected living situation, physical and mental health, and family dynamics) upon exiting the programs. RHYMIS was updated in 2004 to reduce the burden of reporting the data. Known as NEO-RHYMIS, the new system has received routine data submissions from nearly all (99%) Runaway and Homeless Youth Program grantees, including those in FY2006.[70] In prior years, fewer than half of grantees reported on the number of youth served.[71]

The 2003 reauthorization law (P.L. 108-96) of the Runaway and Homeless Youth Act required that HHS, in consultation with the U.S. Interagency Council on Homelessness, submit a report to Congress on the promising strategies to end youth homelessness within two years of the reauthorization, in October 2005. The report was submitted to Congress in June 2007.[72]

As mentioned above, the 2008 reauthorization law (P.L. 110-378) requires HHS to periodically submit to Congress an incidence and prevalence study of runaway and homeless youth ages 13 to 26, as well as the characteristics of a representative sample of these youth. The law also directs the Government Accountability Office to evaluate the process by which organizations apply for BCP, TLP, and SOP, including HHS's response to these applicants. GAO is to submit a report on its findings to Congress.

### *PART Evaluation*

In calendar years 2003 and 2006, the Runaway and Homeless Youth Program was reviewed through the U.S. Office of Management and Budget's Program Assessment Rating Tool (PART) process.[73] The 2003 evaluation concluded that program results were not demonstrated because the RHYP lacked long-term performance measures and time frames for these measures, as well as adequate progress in achieving its annual and long-term performance goals. The PART review also found that no independent evaluations of the program were routinely conducted. However, in 2006 the program was rated effective because it made improvements to its long-term measures for evaluating youth outcomes. According to the PART evaluation, the re-engineering of NEO-RHYMIS has enhanced HHS staff's ability to evaluate these outcomes (see below for more information about changes to NEO-RHYMIS). The 2006 PART also explains that the program has ambitious targets and time frames for its long term measures. For example, the program plans to increase the proportion of youth living in safe and appropriate settings after exiting TLP services to 85% for FY2008, from its initial benchmark of 79%. More accurate NEO-RHYMIS data has enabled HHS to more effectively evaluate the program internally and through contracts. An analysis by the National Opinion Research Center of FY2002 through FY2004 NEO-RHYMIS data on youth using BCPs, identified factors associated with unsafe exits and ranked high and poor RHYP programs by risk levels of youth in their programs.[74] HHS evaluations have affirmed these findings.

# ADDITIONAL FEDERAL SUPPORT FOR
# RUNAWAY AND HOMELESS YOUTH

Since the creation of the Runaway and Homeless Youth Program, other federal initiatives have also established services for such youth. Four of these initiatives—Education for Homeless Children and Youth Program, Chafee Foster Care Independence Program, Shared Vision for Youth initiative, and Discretionary Grants for Family Violence Prevention Program — are discussed below.

## Educational Assistance

The McKinney-Vento Homeless Assistance Act of 1987 (P.L. 100-77), as amended, established the Education for Homeless Children and Youth program in the U.S. Department of Education.[75] This program assists state education agencies (SEAs) to ensure that all homeless children and youth have equal access to the same, appropriate education, including public preschool education, that is provided to other children and youth. Grants made by SEAs to local education agencies (LEAs) under this program must be used to facilitate the enrollment, attendance, and success in school of homeless children and youth. Program funds may be appropriated for activities such as tutoring, supplemental instruction, and referral services for homeless children and youth, as well as providing them with medical, dental, mental, and other health services. Liaison staff for homeless children and youth in each LEA are responsible for coordinating activities for these youth with other entities and agencies, including local Basic Center and Transitional Living Program grantees.

To receive funding, each state must submit a plan to the U.S. Department of Education that indicates how the state will identify and assess the needs of eligible children and youth; ensure that they have access to the federal, state, and local food programs and the same educational programs available to other youth; and resolve problems concerning delays in and barriers to enrollment and transportation. Education for Homeless Children and Youth grants are allotted to SEAs in proportion to grants made under Title I, Part A of the Elementary and Secondary Education Act of 1965, which allocates funds to all states, the District of Columbia, and Puerto Rico based on the percentage of low-income children enrolled in a school or living in the nearby residential area. However, no state can receive less than the greater of $150,000, 0.25% of the total annual appropriation, or the amount it received in FY2001 under this program. The Department of Education must reserve 0.1% of the total appropriation for grants to the Virgin Islands, Guam, America Samoa, and the Commonwealth of the Northern Mariana Islands. The agency must also transfer 1.0% of the total appropriation to the Department of the Interior for services to homeless children and youth provided by the Bureau of Indian Affairs. Amendments to the McKinney-Vento Homeless Assistance Act of 1987 authorized funding for the program through FY2007. In FY2008, program appropriations total $64.1 million.

The No Child Left Behind Act of 2001 (P.L. 107-110) reauthorized and amended the program explicitly to prohibit states that receive McKinney-Vento funds from segregating homeless students from non-homeless students, except for short periods of time for health and safety emergencies or to provide temporary, special, supplemental services. Prior to the reauthorization, homeless children in some districts attended class in separate buildings or schools. Advocates raised concerns that these children, including those enrolled in classes that were equal in quality to the classes attended by their non-homeless peers, were receiving an inferior education because they were physically separated. The act exempted four counties (San Joaquin, Orange, and San Diego counties in California and Maricopa County in Arizona) from these requirements because they operated separate school districts for homeless students in FY2000, as long as: (1) those separate schools offer services that are comparable to local schools; and (2) homeless children are not required to attend them. The Department of Education must certify annually that the school districts meet these requirements.[76]

## Shared Youth Vision Initiative

In 2003, the White House Task Force on Disadvantaged Youth, comprised of the heads of executive branch agencies and their designees, issued a report calling for increased federal coordination to improve service delivery to and outcomes for vulnerable youth. In response to the report, the U.S. Departments of Education, Health and Human Services, Justice, and Labor, and the Social Security Administration, partnered to improve communication, coordination, and collaboration across programs that target at-risk youth groups under a initiative called the "Shared Youth Vision." One of these groups includes runaway and homeless youth.

Together, the agencies have convened an Interagency Work Group and regional forums to develop and coordinate policies and research on the vulnerable youth population. The U.S. Department of Labor (DOL) has led efforts to promote collaboration between the Runaway and Homeless Youth Program and the agency's Workforce Investment Act (WIA) programs. The DOL has encouraged local and state workforce investment boards to implement the strategies of the Shared Youth Vision initiative based, in part, on models already implemented through three WIA programs in California, Oregon, and Washington that provide employment and educational resources targeted for runaway and homeless youth.[77]

## Discretionary Grants for Family Violence Prevention

The Family Violence Prevention and Services Act (FVPSA), Title III of the Child Abuse Amendments of 1984 (P.L. 98-457), authorized funds for Family Violence Prevention and Service grants that work to prevent family violence, improve service delivery to address family violence, and increase knowledge and understanding of family violence. Some of these projects focus on runaway and homeless youth in dating violence situations, through HHS's Domestic Violence/Runaway and Homeless Youth Collaboration on the Prevention of Adolescent Dating Violence initiative. The initiative was created because many runaway and homeless youth come from homes where domestic violence occurs and may be at risk of abusing their partners or becoming victims of abuse.[78] The initiative funds projects carried by faith-based and charitable organizations who advocate or provide direct services to runaway and homeless youth or victims of domestic violence. The grants fund training for staff at these organizations to enable them to assist youth in preventing dating violence. Eight projects are funded at $75,000 annually, for FY2008 through FY20 10, the most recent funding cycle. Grantees funded at least 25% of the total approved cost of the project.

## Chafee Foster Care Independence Program[79]

Recently emancipated foster youth are vulnerable to becoming homeless. In FY2006, approximately 26,500 youth "aged out" of the foster care system.[80] The Chafee Foster Care Independence Program (CFCIP), created under the Chafee Foster Care Independence Act of 1999 (P.L. 106-169), provides states with funding to support youth who are expected to emancipate from foster care and former foster youth ages 18 to 21.[81] States are authorized to receive funds based on their share of the total number of children in foster care nationwide. However, the law's "hold harmless" clause precludes any state from receiving less than the amount of funds it received in FY1998 or $500,000, whichever is greater.[82] The program authorizes funding for transitional living services, and as much as 30% of the funds may be dedicated to room and board. For FY2008, Congress appropriated $140 million for the program. Child welfare advocates have argued that the housing needs of youth "aging out" of foster care have not been met despite the additional funds for independent living that are provided through the CFCIP.[83]

## APPENDIX

**Table A-1. Basic Center Funding by State and Territory, FY2007-FY2008**
**($ in thousands)**

| State | FY2007 Actual | FY2008 Allotted |
|---|---|---|
| Alabama | 500 | 725 |
| Alaska | 194 | 124 |
| Arizona | 806 | 965 |
| Arkansas | 336 | 452 |
| California | 5,185 | 5,546 |
| Colorado | 560 | 749 |
| Connecticut | 401 | 558 |
| Delaware | 120 | 133 |
| District of Columbia | 50 | 100 |
| Florida | 2,500 | 2,766 |
| Georgia | 1,304 | 1,454 |
| Hawaii | 162 | 219 |
| Idaho | 202 | 246 |
| Illinois | 1,764 | 1,934 |
| Indiana | 916 | 987 |
| Iowa | 477 | 478 |
| Kansas | 325 | 445 |
| Kentucky | 573 | 665 |

| Louisiana | 789 | 680 |
|---|---|---|
| Maine | 188 | 224 |
| Maryland | 600 | 881 |
| Massachusetts | 921 | 1,006 |
| Michigan | 2,030 | 1,565 |
| Minnesota | 1,059 | 830 |
| Mississippi | 447 | 467 |
| Missouri | 773 | 915 |
| Montana | 132 | 166 |
| Nebraska | 454 | 381 |
| Nevada | 368 | 404 |
| New Hampshire | 185 | 223 |
| New Jersey | 1,046 | 1,398 |
| New Mexico | 579 | 421 |
| New York | 3,035 | 1,376 |
| North Carolina | 1,203 | 1,376 |
| North Dakota | 100 | 100 |
| Ohio | 1,617 | 1,727 |
| Oklahoma | 504 | 569 |
| Oregon | 631 | 588 |
| Pennsylvania | 1,750 | 1,924 |
| Rhode Island | 136 | 185 |
| South Carolina | 472 | 683 |
| South Dakota | 111 | 142 |
| Tennessee | 763 | 945 |
| Texas | 3,164 | 3,548 |
| Utah | 315 | 412 |
| Vermont | 100 | 100 |
| Virginia | 1,190 | 1,191 |
| Washington | 937 | 1,000 |
| West Virginia | 260 | 300 |
| Wisconsin | 686 | 872 |
| Wyoming | 100 | 100 |
| *Subtotal* | *43,024* | *46,788* |
| America Samoa | 45 | 45 |
| Guam | 45 | 45 |
| N. Mariana Islands | 0 | 45 |
| Puerto Rico | 200 | 603 |
| U.S. Virgin Islands | 0 | 45 |
| *Subtotal* | *290* | *783* |
| **Total** | **43,314** | **43,571** |

Source: U.S. Department Health and Human Services, *Administration for Children and Families Justification of Estimates for Appropriations Committees*, FY2009, p. D-42.

## End Notes

[1] RHYA was most recently reauthorized by the Runaway and Homeless Youth Protection Act (P.L. 110-3783). 42 U.S.C. §470 1 et seq. For additional information about the 2008 reauthorization law, see CRS Report RL34483, *Runaway and Homeless Youth: Reauthorization Legislation and Issues in the 110th Congress*, by Adrienne L. Fernandes.

[2] In 42 U.S.C. §4701 et seq., this program is referred to as the Education and Prevention Services to Reduce Abuse of Runaway, Homeless, and Street Youth Program.

[3] U.S. Department of Health and Human Services, *Administration for Children and Families Justification of Estimates for Appropriations Committees, FY2009*, p. D-36.

[4] U.S. Congress, Senate, Committee on Appropriations, *Departments of Labor, Health and Human Services, Education and Related Agencies Appropriations Bill, FY2008*, Report to accompany S. 1710, 110th Cong., 1st sess., S.Rept. 110-107 (Washington, GPO: 2007).

[5] U.S. Congress, House, Committee on Appropriations, *Departments of Labor, Health and Human Services, Education and Related Agencies Appropriations Bill, FY2008*, Report to accompany H.R. 3043, 110th Cong., 1st sess., H.Rept. 110-231 (Washington, GPO: 2007).

[6] The U.S. Departments of Education and Housing and Urban Development use definitions of homelessness that are different than those used by HHS. The U.S. Department of Justice uses a different definition for runaway youth. For some of these definitions, see CRS Report RL3 0442, *Homelessness: Targeted Federal Programs and Recent Legislation*, coordinated by Libby Perl.

[7] Prior to the enactment of the 2008 reauthorization law (P.L. 110-378), the law did not authorize an older age for youth to stay at a BCP- or TLP-funded site. Further, the law specified that youth ages 16 through 21 were eligible for the TLP program.

[8] 45 C.F.R. §1351.

[9] Ibid. The regulations reference "family" rather than "parent" or "legal guardian."

[10] American Medical Association Council of Scientific Affairs, "Health Care Needs of Homeless and Runaway Youths," *Journal of the American Medical Association*, v. 262, no. 10 (September 1989).

[11] U.S. Department of Justice, Office of Juvenile Justice and Delinquency Prevention, "Runaway/Thrownaway Children: National Estimates and Characteristics," by Heather Hammer, David Finkelhor, and Andrea J. Sedlak, *OJJDP NISMART Bulletin*, October 2002. At[http://www.missingkids.com/en_US/documents/nismart2_runaway.pdf]. (Hereafter U.S. Department of Justice, "Runaway/Thrownaway Children.")

[12] §42 U.S.C. 5732a.

[13] Christopher L. Ringwalt et al., "The Prevalence of Homelessness Among Adolescents in the United States," *American Journal of Public Health*, vol. 88, no. 9 (September 1998), p. 1325. (Hereafter Ringwalt, "The Prevalence of Homelessness Among Adolescents.")

[14] Ibid.

[15] Ibid, pp. 1325-1326.

[16] Ibid.

[17] Andrea L. Witkin et al., "Finding Homeless Youth: Patterns Based on Geographical Area and Number of Homeless Episodes," *Youth & Society*, vol. 37, no. 1 (September 2005), pp. 62-63.

[18] Ibid.

[19] Ringwalt, "The Prevalence of Homelessness Among Adolescents," pp. 1326-1327.

[20] Ibid., p 1327.

[21] Marjorie J. Robertson and Paul A. Toro, "Homeless Youth: Research, Intervention, and Policy," *The 1998 National Symposium on Homeless Research*, (1998), pp. 1-2. At [http://aspe.hhs.gov/progsys/homeless/symposium/3-Youth.htm]. (Hereafter Robertson and Toro, "Homeless Youth: Research, Intervention, and Policy.")

[22] Ibid., p. 4.

[23] Ibid.

[24] U.S. Department of Health and Human Services, Substance Abuse and Mental Health Services Administration, Office of Applied Statistics, National Survey on Drug Use and Health, *Substance Abuse Among Youth Who Had Run Away From Home*, 2002. At [http://www.oas.samhsa.gov/2k4/runAways/runAways.htm]. (Hereafter U.S. Department of Health and Human Services, *Substance Abuse Among Youth Who Had Run Away From Home*.)

[25] U.S. Department of Justice, "Runaway/Thrownaway Children," p. 7.

[26] Jan Moore, *Unaccompanied and Homeless Youth Review of Literature (1995-2005)*, National Center for Homeless Education, 2005, p. 6. At [http://www.cde.state.co.us/ cdeprevention/download/pdf/Homeless%20Youth%20Review%20of%20Literature.pdf].

[27] NCMEC is funded by the Missing and Exploited Children's Program, administered by the Office of Juvenile Justice and Delinquency Prevention in the U.S. Department of Justice. For a discussion of the program, see

CRS Report RL34050, *Missing and Exploited Children: Background, Policies and Issues*, by Adrienne L. Fernandes.

[28] National Center for Missing and Exploited Children, *NCMEC Quarterly Progress Report: October 1-December 31, 2007*, Submitted to the U.S. Department of Justice, January 23, 2008.

[29] Robertson and Toro, "Homeless Youth: Research, Intervention, and Policy," p. 5.

[30] National Runaway Switchboard, "NRS Call Statistics," at [http://www.nrscrisisline.org/ news _events/call _stats .html].

[31] U.S. Department of Justice, "Runaway/Thrownaway Children," p. 8.

[32] Nicholas Ray, *Lesbian, Gay, and Transgender Youth: An Epidemic of Homelessness*, National Gay and Lesbian Task Force and National Coalition for the Homeless, 2006, pp 12-14. At [http://www.thetaskforce.org/downloads/reports/reports/HomelessYouth.pdf].

[33] U.S. Department of Health and Human Services, *AFCARS Report #14 (Preliminary Estimates for FY2005)*. January 2008. At [http://www.acf.hhs.gov/programs/cb/stats_ research/afcars/tar/report14.htm]. (Hereafter U.S. Department of Health and Human Services, *AFCARS Report #14*.)

[34] Mark E. Courtney et al., "Youth Who Run Away from Out-of-Home Care," *Chapin Hall Center for Children Issue Brief*, no. 103 (March 2005), p. 2. At [http://www.chapinhall. org/article_abstract.aspx?ar=1382].

[35] U.S. Department of Health and Human Services, *AFCARS Report #14*.

[36] Mark E. Courtney and Darcy Hughes Heuring. "The Transition to Adulthood for Youth 'Aging Out' of the Foster Care System" in Wayne G. Osgood et al., eds., *On Your Own Without a Net: The Transition to Adulthood for Vulnerable Populations* (Chicago: The University of Chicago Press, 2005), pp. 27-32. (Hereafter Courtney and Huering, "Youth 'Aging Out' of the Foster Care System.")

[37] Mark E. Courtney et al., *Midwest Evaluation of the Adult Functioning of Former Foster Youth: Outcomes at Age 21*, Chapin Hall Center for Children, University of Chicago, December 2007, p. 16. At [http://www. chapinhall.org/article_abstract.aspx?ar=1355].

[38] Ronna Cook, Esther Fleischman, and Virginia Grimes, *A National Evaluation of Title IV-E Foster Care Independent Living Programs for Youth, Phase 2 Final Report*, vol. 1 (1991), Westat, pp. 4-11.

[39] Robertson and Toro, "Homeless Youth: Research, Intervention, and Policy," p. 7. The clinical criteria are found in the Diagnostic and Statistical Manual of Mental Disorders, 3rd Revision, published by the American Psychiatric Association, a handbook used most often to diagnose mental disorders in the United States.

[40] Ibid.

[41] U.S. Department of Health and Human Services, Substance Abuse and Mental Health Services Administration, *Substance Abuse Among Youth Who Had Run Away From Home*.

[42] U.S. Department of Justice, "Runaway/Thrownaway Children," p. 8.

[43] Robertson and Toro, "Homeless Youth: Research, Intervention, and Policy," p. 10.

[44] Eric Beecroft and Seymour Janow, "Toward a National Policy for Migration," *Social Forces*, vol. 16, no. 4 (May 1938), p. 477. (Hereafter Beecroft and Janow, "Migration.")

[45] Ibid., 477.

[46] In 1962 (P.L. 87-543), child welfare services were formally defined under Title IV-B as "public social services which supplement, or substitute for parental care and supervision for the purpose of (1) remedying or assisting in the solution of problems which may result in, the neglect abuse, exploitation, or delinquency of children, (2) protecting and caring for homeless, dependent, or neglected children, (3) protecting and promoting the welfare of children, including the strengthening of their own homes where possible or, where needed, the provision of adequate care of children away from their homes in foster family homes or day-care or other child-care facilities." P.L. 109-288 (2006) removes reference to homeless youth.

[47] Karen M. Staller, "Constructing the Runaway and Homeless Youth Problem: Boy Adventurers to Girl Prostitutes, 1960-1978," *Journal of Communication*, vol. 53, no. 2 (2003), p. 331.

[48] U.S. Congress, Senate, Committee on the Judiciary, Subcommittee to Investigate Juvenile Delinquency, *Juvenile Delinquency*, 92nd Cong., 1st sess., January 13-14, 1972 (Washington: GPO, 1972).

[49] U.S. Department Health and Human Services, *Administration for Children and FamiliesJustification of Estimates for Appropriations Committees*, FY2009, p. D-38. According tothe ACF budget justification, the Northern Mariana Islands and Virgin Islands do not have Basic Center Program grantees, although FY2008 funds are available for new awards to the territory, if desired.

[50] Prior to the enactment of the 2008 reauthorization law (P.L. 110-378), youth could stay at a BCP center for up to 15 days, as authorized under rules promulgated by HHS. See 45 C.F.R. 1351.1(a).

[51] Data on youth served by the BCP, TLP, and SOP are provided in HHS's NEO-RHYMIS reporting system. See [https://extranet.acf.hhs.gov/rhymis/custom_reports.html]. The NEORHYMIS (that is, National Extranet Optimized Runaway and Homeless Youth Management Information System) is explained in the section below on Congressional Oversight. According to the NEO-RHMIS administrator, all BCP, TLP, and SOP grantees reported data for FY2007 (based on December 5, 2007, correspondence with the administrator).

[52] Based on Congressional Research Service analysis of U.S. Census Bureau, Census 2000 Summary File 1, *Table 1: Total Population by Age, Race and Hispanic or Latino Origin for the United States: 2000*. At [http:// www.census.gov/population/cen2000/phc-t9/tab0 1 .xls].

[53] U.S. Department Health and Human Services, *Administration for Children and Families Justification of Estimates for Appropriations Committees*, FY2009, pp. D-38.

[54] See "Locate a TLP Program" on the Family and Youth Services website at [http://www. acf.hhs.gov/ programs/fysb/content/youthdivision/programs/locate.htm].

[55] Based on Congressional Research Service analysis of U.S. Census Bureau, Census 2000 Summary File 1, *Table 1: Total Population by Age, Race and Hispanic or Latino Origin for the United States: 2000*. At [http://www.census.gov/population/cen2000/phc-t9/tab0 1 .xls].

[56] The average length of youth's stay in the TLP is not available.

[57] Based on correspondence with the Department Health and Human Services on March 28, 2008.

[58] U.S. Department of Health and Human Services, Administration for Children and Families, "Proposed Information Collection Activity; Comment Request," 73 Federal Register 50022, August 25, 2008. Comments are due October 25, 2008.

[59] ACF staff stated in correspondence with the Congressional Research Service on March 9, 2007, that HHS does not plan to create a voucher program for pregnant and parenting youth.

[60] U.S. Congress, House Committee on Education and the Workforce, *Runaway, Homeless, and Missing Children Protection Act*, report to accompany H.R. 1925, 1 08th Cong., 1st sess., H.Rept. 108-118 (Washington: GPO, 2003), p. 9.

[61] U.S. Department Health and Human Services, *Administration for Children and Families Justification of Estimates for Appropriations Committees*, FY2009, p. D-44.

[62] U.S. Department Health and Human Services, *Administration for Children and Families Justification of Estimates for Appropriations Committees*, FY2009, p. D-40.

[63] Technical support providers offered assistance through the Regional Training and Technical Assistance Provider System. The providers worked closely with ACF regional office staff to identify grantee needs and review the results of evaluations conducted by HHS staff. Based on these analyses, the provider needs assessments, and grantee requests, the providers offered several types of services, including regional and state-level conferences that address topics of interest to grantees, on-site and telephone consultations, workshops and training on issues of concern, and resource materials.

[64] For additional information, see NCRYS website, [http://www.nrcys.ou.edu/yd/].

[65] This information was provided in correspondence by the U.S. Department of Health and Human Services on October 25, 2007.

[66] HHS reports that it provides information to the public about runaway and homeless youth in multiple ways, including through the National Communications System. Further, the National Clearinghouse on Youth and Families, a FYSB-funded resource center, produces publications for the public about the Runaway and Homeless Youth Program. Finally, RHYA grantees conduct local advocacy and outreach efforts, and public service announcements to attract youth eligible for services. As described in grant announcements for the BCP, TLP, and SOP, grant applicants are evaluated, in part, on the basis of their efforts to establish outreach efforts to youth, including minority sub-groups of youth, where applicable. Based on correspondence with the Department of Health and Human Services on March 20, 2008.

[67] The Switchboard also has a special phone line for hearing-impaired callers and access to AT&T's language translation service. Its website provides information to those seeking non-crisis related information. National statistics on use of the National Runaway Switchboard are available at [http://www.1800runaway.org/news_ events/call_stats.html].

[68] U.S. Department of Health and Human Services, *Report to Congress on the Youth Programs of the Family and Youth Services Bureau for Fiscal Years 2002 and 2003,*October 2004, p. 17. At [http://www.acf.hhs.gov/ programs/fysb/content/docs/0203_report.pdf]. (Hereafter U.S. Department of Health and Human Services, *Report to Congress*.)

[69] NEO-RHYMIS data are available online by state, region, and grantee organization at [https://extranet.acf.hhs. gov/rhymis/custom_reports.html].

[70] This information was provided in correspondence by NEO-RHYMIS technical support staff March 2, 2007. See also U.S. Department of Health and Human Services, *Report to Congress*, p. 2.

[71] U.S. Department of Health and Human Services, *Report to Congress*, p. 2.

[72] U.S. Department of Health and Human Services, *Promising Strategies to End Youth Homelessness, Report to Congress*, 2007. At [http://www.acf.hhs.gov/programs/fysb/ content/docs/reporttocongress_youthhomeles sness.pdf]. This report was required under P.L. 108-96. See 42 U.S.C. 5701.

[73] U.S. Office of Management and Budget, *Detailed Assessment on the Runaway and Homeless Youth Assessment*, 2003 and U.S. Office of Management and Budget, *Detailed Assessment on the Runaway and Homeless Youth Assessment*, 2007. At [http://www.white house.gov/omb/expectmore/summary/10001064.2006.html]. (Hereafter U.S. Office of Management and Budget, PART 2003 or PART 2007.)

[74] U.S. Office of Management and Budget, PART 2007, p. 11.

[75] Other programs assist homeless youth and their families through the McKinney-Vento Homeless Assistance Act, although none are targeted exclusively to runaway and homeless youth. For additional information about these

programs, see CRS Report RL30442, *Homelessness: Targeted Federal Programs and Recent Legislation*, coordinated by Libby Perl.

[76] The Individual with Disabilities Education Act, last amended in 2004 (P.L. 108-446), includes provisions aimed at ensuring special education and related services for children with disabilities who are homeless or otherwise members of highly mobile populations. For additional information, see CRS Report RL327 16, *Individuals with Disabilities Education Act (IDEA): Analysis of Changes Made by P.L. 108-446*, by Richard N. Apling and Nancy Lee Jones.

[77] See notice from Department of Labor to state workforce agencies, available on the DOL website, available at [http://wdr.doleta.gov/directives/corr_doc.cfm?DOCN=2176].

[78] U.S. Department of Health and Human Services, *Domestic Violence/Runaway and Homeless Youth Collaboration on the Prevention of Adolescent Dating Violence Grant Announcement*, April 24, 2007. At [http://www.acf.hhs.gov/grants/open/HHS-2007-ACFACYF-EV-0 103 .html].

[79] For additional information about the program, see CRS Report RL3449, *Youth Trans itioning From Foster Care: Background, Federal Programs, and Issues for Congress*, by Adrienne L. Fernandes.

[80] U.S. Department of Health and Human Services, *AFCARS Report #14*.

[81] For additional information on the Chafee Foster Care Independence Act, see CRS Report RS22501, *Child Welfare: The Chafee Foster Care Independence Act*, by Adrienne Fernandes.

[82] Prior to the passage of P.L. 106-169, states were awarded a share of independent living funds - $70 million-based on the number of children receiving federal foster care payments in FY1984 under the Independent Living Program.

[83] Courtney and Huering, "Youth 'Aging Out' of the Foster Care System," p. 54.

In: Runaway and Homeless Youth
Editors: Josiah Hughes and Isiah Wright

ISBN: 978-1-60741-521-3
© 2010 Nova Science Publishers, Inc.

*Chapter 4*

# RUNAWAY AND HOMELESS YOUTH: RE-AUTHORIZATION LEGISLATION AND ISSUES IN THE 110^TH CONGRESS*

*Adrienne L. Fernandes*

## SUMMARY

The Runaway and Homeless Youth Act (RHYA) was signed into law in 1974 as Title III of the Juvenile Justice and Delinquency Prevention Act (P.L. 93-415). RHYA authorizes funding for programs to support runaway and homeless youth, as well as related training, research, and other activities. These programs and activities are administered by the Family and Youth Services Bureau (FYSB) in the Department of Health and Human Services' (HHS) Administration for Children and Families.

In the second session of the 110th Congress, Congress passed and the President signed into law the Reconnecting Homeless Youth Act of 2008 (P.L. 110-378) to extend existing programs and establish new activities under RHYA for FY2009 through FY2013. The law represents a compromise between provisions that were included in two bills introduced in the 110th Congress: H.R. 5524 and S. 2982. On March 4, 2008, Representative John Yarmuth introduced H.R. 5524, the Reconnecting Homeless Youth Act of 2008, which passed the House on June 9, 2008. On May 6, 2008, Senator Patrick Leahy introduced S. 2982, the Runaway and Homeless Youth Protection Act, which passed the Senate on September 25, 2008. The House approved S. 2982 on September 26, and the President signed it into law as P.L. 110-378 on October 8, 2008.

This report discusses P.L. 110-378 and includes a table with a side-by-side comparison of its provisions to those in H.R. 5524, as well as to the law and regulations as they existed prior to the enactment of S. 2982. The new law amends and adds provisions related to program funding, requirements, and accountability. It extends the authorization of appropriations for

---

* This is an edited, reformatted and augmented version of a CRS Report for Congress publication dated October 2008.

the three programs under RHYA that provide direct services to youth: the Basic Center Program (BCP), Transitional Living Program (TLP), and Street Outreach Program (SOP). Unlike prior law, P.L. 110-378 enables HHS to reallot any unused BCP funds from one state to other states and permits youth to remain in BCP and TLP shelters for a longer period. Another change made by the law requires HHS to regularly submit a report to Congress that describes the incidence and prevalence of runaway and homeless youth. The law also directs the Government Accountability Office to report to Congress on the process by which HHS awards BCP, TLP, and SOP grants.

The provisions of P.L. 110-378 reflect issues raised by policymakers and advocates about RHYA during the reauthorization process. One issue was the amount of funding allocated to grantees under the three direct-service programs. Grantees expressed the concern that although Congress has periodically increased funding authorization for these programs, funding for individual grantees has remained relatively stable over time. A second issue was the lack of outcome data for youth who run away or experience homelessness. Finally, the bill addresses issues related to the educational and workforce needs of runaway and homeless youth.

The Runaway and Homeless Youth Act (RHYA) was enacted in 1974 as Title III of the Juvenile Justice and Delinquency Prevention Act (P.L. 93-415). RHYA authorizes funding for grant programs that provide direct services to youth — the Basic Center Program (BCP), Transitional Living Program (TLP), and Street Outreach Program (SOP) — and related training, research, and other activities. These programs and activities are administered by the Family and Youth Services Bureau in the Department of Health and Human Services' (HHS) Administration for Children and Families. The Basic Center Program provides temporary shelter, counseling, and after care services to runaway and homeless youth under age 18 and their families, while the Transitional Living Program is targeted to older youth ages 16 to 21. Youth who use the TLP receive longer-term housing with supportive services. The Street Outreach Program provides education, treatment, counseling, and referrals for runaway, homeless, and street youth who have been subjected to or are at risk of being subjected to sexual abuse and exploitation.[1]

RHYA has been reauthorized approximately every five years since the 1970s. Most recently, in the second session of the 110th Congress, the President signed into law the Reconnecting Homeless Youth Act (P.L. 110-378) to extend existing programs and authorize new activities under RHYA for FY2009 through FY2013. P.L. 110-378 represents a compromise between provisions that were included in two bills — H.R. 5524 and S. 2982 — to reauthorize RHYA.[2] On March 4, 2008, Representative John Yarmuth introduced H.R. 5524, the Reconnecting Homeless Youth Act of 2008. The bill was referred to the House Education and Labor Committee, but was not taken up by the committee. On June 9, 2008, the House approved the bill by voice vote under suspension of the rules. The version of the bill that was passed contained most of the same provisions as the original version. On May 6, 2008, Senator Patrick Leahy introduced S. 2982, the Runaway and Homeless Youth Protection Act. On May 22, 2008, the Senate Judiciary Committee passed S. 2982, which included an amendment that substituted the introduced version with a similar version of the bill. On September 25, 2008, S. 2982 was approved by the Senate. The Senate-passed version is different from the version that passed the Judiciary Committee and includes many of the same provisions as those in H.R. 5524. The House approved S. 2982 on September 26, 2008, and the President signed it into law as P.L. 110-378 on October 8, 2008.

This report first provides a broad overview of P.L. 110-378, followed by a more detailed summary of the law's provisions. The second section discusses the issues that were raised during hearings in the 110th Congress about runaway and homeless youth, and the provisions in P.L. 110-378 that, in part, address these issues. **Table A-1** at the end of the report provides a side-by-side comparison of P.L. 110-378 with prior law, current regulation, and H.R. 5524. As shown in the table, notable differences include funding authorization levels, the authorization for a national homeless youth awareness campaign (as proposed by H.R. 5524), length of stay at RHYA-funded programs, and the definitions of runaway youth and homeless youth.

## OVERVIEW

The Reconnecting Homeless Youth Act of 2008 (P.L. 110-378) reauthorizes programs for runaway and homeless youth, expands congressional oversight of these programs, and establishes new activities. The major provisions of the law relate to funding for the Basic Center Program, Transitional Living Program, and Street Outreach Program; requirements for grantees that receive BCP and TLP grants; and accountability of programs and activities authorized under RHYA.

- **Funding.** P.L. 110-378 authorizes FY2009 appropriation levels for the BCP, TLP, and related activities that exceed the levels authorized for FY2004 by $35 million (these are the only recent years for which Congress has specified authorized appropriation levels). The law also increases the authorized annual minimum levels of BCP funding available for states and territories. It further requires HHS to reallocate unused BCP funds from one state to another. The amount allocated to states for FY2009 and FY2010 may not be lower than the amount appropriated to the states in FY2008.

- **Requirements.** P.L. 110-378 allows youth to remain in a program funded under the BCP and TLP longer they were able to under the prior law, although the law imposes additional criteria for youth who stay longer at TLP-funded programs. The law also changes the definition of "homeless youth" to permit youth older than age 18 and 22 to stay at BCP- and TLP-funded programs, respectively, but only under certain circumstances. Another change made by the law specifies that in funding grants for research and other projects related to runaway and homeless youth, HHS is to give priority to applicants that serve diverse youth and represent diverse geographic regions of the U.S. (The term "diverse" is not defined.) Other requirements pertain to BCP and TLP plans submitted by grant applicants.

- **Accountability.** P.L. 110-378 requires HHS to promulgate regulations that specify performance standards for public and non-profit entities that receive BCP, TLP, and SOP grants. The law further requires HHS to periodically submit to Congress an incidence and prevalence study of runaway and homeless youth ages 13 to 26, as well as the characteristics of a representative sample of these youth. HHS must consult with the U.S. Interagency Council on Homelessness in developing the study. The law also directs the Government Accountability Office (GAO) to evaluate the process by which organizations apply for BCP, TLP, and SOP, including HHS's response to these applicants. GAO is to submit a report on its findings to Congress.

The discussion below provides more details of these provisions.

# FUNDING

## Authorization of Appropriations

The prior law (P.L. 108-96) to reauthorize the Runaway and Homeless Youth Act authorized funding for all parts[3] of the Runaway and Homeless Youth Act, except the Street Outreach Program, at $105 million for FY2004 and such sums as may be necessary for FY2005 through FY2008. The Street Outreach Program was authorized to receive such sums as may be necessary for FY2004 through FY2008.

For all parts of RHYA, except the SOP and the new incidence and prevalence study provisions, the Reconnecting Homeless Youth Act of 2008 authorizes $140 million for FY2009 and such sums as may be necessary for FY2010 through FY2013. The law authorizes $25 million for the SOP for FY2009 and such sums as may be necessary for FY2010 through FY2013. Finally, the law authorizes such sums as may be necessary for the study for FY2009 through FY2013.

## Allocation for the Basic Center Program

Funding for the Basic Center Program and related training and other activities s allocated among states (including the District of Columbia) and the territories, and is distributed by HHS on a competitive basis to community-based organizations. As the law existed prior to the enactment of P.L. 110-378, each state and territory received a minimum annual allotment of $100,000 and $45,000, respectively, in BCP funds. P.L. 110-378 increases the annual minimum funding available for each state to $200,000 and for each territory to $70,000. The law also provides that funding for each state in FY2009 and FY2010 is to be no less than the amount allotted to that state for FY2008 (the bill is silent on a minimum for territories in those years). Further, unlike prior law, P.L. 110-378 enables the HHS Secretary to reallot any funds that have not been obligated before the end of a fiscal year for a state to the other states. The law does not specify the criteria for re-allotting the funds.

The new law does not change the funding structure for the Transitional Living Program and Street Outreach Program. Funds for these programs are allocated competitively by HHS to community-based organizations.

# REQUIREMENTS

P.L. 110-378 changes program requirements related to (1) the length of time that youth are eligible to stay in Basic Center Program and Transitional Living Program facilities; (2) the definition of homeless youth and runaway youth; (3) BCP and TLP plans submitted by applicants; and (4) applicants that are to be prioritized under the Street Outreach Program.

## Length of Stay

The Reconnecting Homeless Youth Act of 2008 authorizes longer periods in which a youth may stay at a program funded by the BCP or TLP. Current regulation specifies that youth may remain at a BCP shelter for up to 15 days. However, P.L. 110-378 permits youth to stay at a shelter for up to 21 days. The new law continues to allow youth to remain at TLP projects for up to 540 days (18 months) or longer for youth under age 18 and adds that a youth may remain in the program for a continuous period of 635 days (approximately 21 months) under "exceptional circumstances." This term means circumstances in which a youth would benefit to an unusual extent from additional time in the program. The new law further authorizes that a youth in a TLP who has not reached age 18 on the last day of the 635-day period may, in exceptional circumstances and if otherwise qualified for the program, remain in the program until his or her 18th birthday.

## Definition of "Homeless Youth" and "Runaway Youth"

Under the law as it existed prior to the enactment of the Reconnecting Homeless Youth Act of 2008, "homeless youth" for purposes of the BCP was defined as an individual younger than age 18 for whom it is not possible to live in a safe environment with a relative and for whom no other safe alternative living arrangement exists. P.L. 110-378 amends the first clause to define "homeless youth" as an individual younger than age 18, *or an older maximum age* if the BCP center is located in a state or locality with a law or regulation that permits this higher age.

For purposes of the TLP, the prior law defined "homeless youth" as an individual age 16 through 21 for whom it is not possible to live in a safe environment with a relative and for whom no other safe alternative living arrangement exists. P.L. 110-378 changes the first clause of the definition to include an individual ages 16 through 22, *or an age exceeding 22 years old* on the last day the youth is permitted under law to be at the shelter, so long as the participant enters the TLP project prior to reaching age 22. (As mentioned above, P.L. 110-378 permits a stay of 540 days, or up to 635 days if the youth would greatly benefit from being in the program.)

Finally, under current regulation, a "runaway youth" is defined as a person under age 18 who absents himself or herself from home or place of legal residence without the permission of his or her *family*. P.L. 110-378 enacts similar language that defines "runaway youth" as an individual who leaves home or place of residence without the permission of his or her *parent or legal guardian*.

## BCP and TLP Plans

As required under the previous law, applicants for TLP funding were required to submit a plan to the HHS Secretary specifying that they would provide, *directly or indirectly,* shelter and services, among other types of assistance. The Reconnecting Homeless Youth Act of 2008 amends the law to require that applicants provide, by a *grant, agreement, or contract,* shelter, services, and other assistance.[4] Also under P.L. 110-378, applicants for TLP and BCP grants must develop an adequate emergency preparedness and management plan.[5]

## Priority Applicants for the SOP and Research Projects

Under the law as it existed prior to enactment of the Reconnecting Homeless Youth Act of 2008, HHS was to prioritize non-profit private agencies with experience in providing services to runaway and homeless youth, including youth living on the street, when awarding grants under the Street Outreach Program. P.L. 110-378 requires that HHS also give priority to public agencies with experience in serving runaway and homeless youth.

P.L. 110-378 also makes changes to the priority areas for awarding grants for research, evaluation, demonstration, and service projects concerning runaway and homeless youth. Under the prior law, HHS could prioritize projects that addressed one of nine priority areas. P.L. 110-378 modifies the language regarding two of these priority areas. For one of the priority areas, regarding access to quality health care, the law changes the reference from projects addressing *mental* health care to projects addressing *behavioral* health care. For the other priority area, regarding access to education, the law adds that the projects should decrease high school dropout rates, increase rates of attaining a secondary school diploma or its recognized equivalent, or increase placement and retention in postsecondary education or advanced workforce training programs. The law also inserts as a tenth priority area projects that assist youth in obtaining and maintaining safe and stable housing. Finally, P.L. 110-378 makes a change pertaining to applicants that apply for grants to implement projects in one of the priority areas. Under the previous law, HHS was to give priority consideration to applicants with experience working with runaway and homeless youth. P.L. 110-378 adds that HHS is to ensure selected applicants represent diverse geographic regions of the U.S. and carry out projects that serve diverse youth. "Diverse" is not defined in the law.[6]

## ACCOUNTABILITY

The Reconnecting Homeless Youth Act of 2008 includes provisions that seek to improve accountability of programs and activities authorized by RHYA, including requiring HHS to establish performance standards for BCP, TLP, and SOP grantees; directing GAO to evaluate the process by which grants are awarded under the three programs; and requiring HHS to periodically submit a report to Congress that contains estimates of runaway and homeless youth and certain characteristics of the population.

## Performance Standards

The Reconnecting Homeless Youth Act of 2008 requires that within one year after its enactment (October 8, 2009), HHS is to issue rules that specify performance standards for public and non-profit entities that receive BCP, TLP, and SOP grants. In developing the regulations, HHS is to consult with stakeholders in the runaway and homeless youth policy community. The law further requires that HHS integrate the performance standards into the grantmaking, monitoring, and evaluations processes for the BCP, TLP, and SOP.

### Existing Performance Review Processes

As they existed prior to the enactment of P.L. 110-378, the RHYA statute and accompanying regulations did not explicitly set forth performance standards for the grantees. However, grantees were (and are) *collectively* expected to meet certain performance measures established by the Office of Management and Budget's (OMB) Program Assessment Rating Tool (PART) process.[7] The performance measures are as follows:

- achieve the proportion of youth served in the TLP entering safe and appropriate settings directly after exiting care at 85% by FY2008 and maintain this level through FY2010 (this is known as a long-term outcome measure);
- improve funding efficiency by increasing the percentage of youth who complete the TLP by graduating or who leave ahead of schedule because of other opportunities (this is known as a long-term efficiency measure);
- increase the percentage of TLP youth participants who are engaged in community service and service learning activities while in the program (this is known as a outcome measure); and
- increase the proportion of youth who are prevented from running away through BCP in-home or off-site services (this is known as an outcome measure).

Data for these outcome measures are collected from each grantee through the NEO-RHYMIS (National Extranet Optimized Runaway and Homeless Youth Management Information System) reporting system, which includes a range of data elements on the characteristics and short-term outcomes of youth receiving services through the BCP, TLP, and SOP.[8] Further, during the grant application process, described below, applicants must discuss the results or benefits expected from their programs. For example, applicants are advised to identify quantitative outcomes for their proposed projects that will fulfill the program purpose and scope of services, as described in RHYA and the grant announcement.

## Oversight of Grant Review Process

The Reconnecting Homeless Youth Act of 2008 directs the Government Accountability Office to examine the process by which organizations apply for BCP, TLP, and SOP grants. Specifically, GAO is to submit to Congress findings and recommendations relating to (1) HHS's written responses to and other communications with unsuccessful applicants to determine if the information in the responses is conveyed clearly; (2) the content of the grant applications and other associated documents to determine if these materials are presented in a way that gives an applicant a clear understanding of the information that is to be provided and the terminology used in the materials; (c) the peer review process (if any) for the grants; (d) the typical time frame for responding to applicants and the efforts made by HHS to communicate about delayed funding decisions; and (e) the plans for implementation of technical assistance and training authorized under RHYA, and the effect of such programs on the application process for the grantees.[9]

### *Existing Grant Review Process*

Applicants for BCP, TLP, and SOP grants are currently evaluated and rated by an independent review panel made up of non-federal reviewers who are experts in the field of runaway and homeless youth issues.[10] The review panel uses evaluation criteria to assign a score up to 100 for each applicant and to identify the application's strengths and weaknesses. The criteria are established in regulation[11] and described in greater detail in the grant announcements.

As set forth in the grant announcements, these criteria include the extent to which the application

- identifies the services that will be provided, as required by and consistent with RHYA, among other requirements;
- demonstrates the organizational capacity necessary to oversee federal grants through an explanation of the organization's fiscal controls and governance structure, among other requirements;
- identifies quantitative outcomes for the proposed project that will fulfill the program purpose and scope of services as described in RHYA and the grant announcement, among other requirements;
- describes clear and appropriate program objectives that will fulfill the program purpose, as well as a clear need for the proposed project through a discussion of the conditions of youth and families in the area to be served, among other requirements;
- includes an organizational chart that demonstrates the relationship between all positions, including consultants, sub-grants and/or contractors, to be funded through the grant, among other requirements; and
- includes a detailed line-item budget for the federal and non-federal share of project costs and demonstrates how cost estimates were derived.

As further described in the grant announcements, the review panel's assigned scores assist the FYSB Associate Commissioner and program staff in considering applications. Applications are generally ranked in order of the average scores assigned by reviewers; however, the scores, in combination with other factors, determine whether an application is funded. These other factors include, but are not limited to, comments of reviewers and government officials, HHS staff evaluation and input, geographic distribution, previous program performance of applicants, compliance with grant terms under previous HHS grants, audit reports, investigative reports, and an applicant's progress in resolving any final audit disallowance on previous FYSB or other federal agency grants. According to HHS, because RHYA grants are highly competitive, well-qualified applicants may not receive funding.[12]

Further, in some years, applicants with scores in the 90s have not been awarded grants because such a large number of applicants receive scores of 100 or close to 100.

HHS does not have an appeals process for unsuccessful applicants. However, in accordance with HHS's Awarding Agency Grants Administration Manual (AAGAM), unsuccessful applicants are notified by letter that they were not awarded funding, with a full explanation of the reasons the application was not funded.[13] The letter contains a compilation of review comments outlining the strengths and weaknesses of their application as identified by the panel of non-federal reviewers. Compilations are also available for successful applications, however, they are only sent at the request of these applicants. Scores are not automatically sent to any applicants but are available upon request.

## Prevalence and Incidence Studies

The precise number of homeless and runaway youth is unknown due to their residential mobility and other factors, and RHYA, as authorized through FY2008, was silent on whether HHS or any other entity was to approximate this number. Runaway and homeless youth often eschew the shelter system for locations or areas that are not easily accessible to shelter workers and others who count the homeless and runaways.[14] Determining the number of homeless and runaway youth is further complicated by the lack of a standardized methodology for counting the population and inconsistent definitions of what it means to be homeless or a runaway.[15] In response to a 2002 congressional request through the appropriations process,[16] HHS submitted a report to Congress in 2003 that discusses a plan for developing estimates of the incidences of runaway, throwaway,[17] homeless, and street experiences among youth, as well as a plan for regularly monitoring incidence trends.[18]

The Reconnecting Homeless Youth Act of 2008 seeks to determine the number of youth who have run away or are homeless by requiring HHS to estimate at five year intervals, beginning within two years of the enactment of P.L. 110-378 (October 8, 2010), the incidence and prevalence of the runaway and homeless youth population ages 13 to 26. The law also directs HHS to assess the characteristics of these youth. HHS is required to conduct a survey of and direct interviews with a representative sample of homeless youth ages 13 to 26 to determine past and current socioeconomic characteristics; barriers to obtaining housing and other services; and other information HHS determines useful, in consultation with states and other entities concerned with youth homelessness. HHS is to consult with the federal Interagency Council on Homelessness about the studies overall. The new law does not specify the methodology for carrying out the studies, except to say that HHS should make the estimate based on the best quantitative and qualitative social science research methods available. Further, if HHS enters into an agreement with a nonfederal entity to carry out the assessment, the entity is to be a non-governmental organization or individual determined by HHS to have expertise in this type of research. As mentioned above, the law authorized such sums as may be necessary for FY2009 through FY2013 to conduct the study.

The studies must be submitted to the House Education and Labor Committee and Senate Judiciary Committee, and made available to the public.

# ISSUES

During the 110th Congress, the House and Senate conducted hearings on the challenges facing runaway and homeless youth and the federally funded services to assist the population.[19] The issues raised included inadequate levels of funding for RHYA grantees, limited information about the outcomes of runaway and homeless youth, and the need for greater education and workforce opportunities for these youth. The Reconnecting Homeless Youth Act of 2008 incorporates provisions that, in part, address the three issues.

# FUNDING

At a hearing conducted by the Senate Judiciary Committee on April 29, 2008, service providers and advocates for runaway and homeless youth raised concerns that funds appropriated under RHYA have not been adjusted for increases in the cost of living. A provider in Vermont explained that his RHYA-funded programs have been level-funded since 1994, while costs have risen significantly. These same concerns were highlighted at a July 24, 2007, hearing on runaway, homeless, and missing children, conducted by the House Education and Labor Committee Subcommittee on Healthy Families and Communities. Further, the Government Accountability Office described in its February 2008 report on disconnected youth that funding has remained stagnant for federal youth programs, including those funded by RHYA. The report states: "While overall Transitional Living Program funding increased in FY2002 to support a greater number of programs, the amount available to individual local programs — capped at $200,000 — has not changed since 1992. One [runaway and homeless] program director explained that considering increases in the cost of operation, this amount funds only part of one staff rather than three as in previous years."[20]

An analysis of per grantee award amounts from FY2004 through FY2007 indicates that BCP and TLP funding has remained stable or has declined slightly.[21] For example, $44.4 million in BCP funds was awarded to 345 grantees for FY2004, resulting in an average grant of $128,734. For FY2007, approximately $43.3 million was awarded to 336 grantees, with an average grant amount of about $128,821. Average TLP award amounts declined over the period from FY2004 through FY2007. For FY2004, 194 grantees shared $36,744,000 in TLP funds, resulting in an average grant of $189,402. The average grant award decreased to $181,558 for FY2007, when 190 grantees shared $34,496,000 in TLP funds.

In response to concerns about funding, the Reconnecting Homeless Youth Act of 2008 increases the authorization of appropriations in at least one year (FY2009) for the BCP, TLP, and SOP, and increases the minimum BCP awards for states and territories. However, for most programs — including those authorized under the Runaway and Homeless Youth Act — Congress has passed, and the President has enacted, a continuing resolution for FY2009 (P.L. 110-329), which in most cases, provides for the same level of funding as in FY2008. The resolution extends until March 9, 2009, and does not reflect final funding levels for FY2009.

## Youth Outcomes

At the hearings held by the Senate Judiciary Committee and House Education and Labor Subcommittee on Healthy Families and Communities, former runaway and homeless youth discussed the challenges of living on the street, such as the inability to find work and connect to school. One witness at the Senate Judiciary hearing described the assistance he received at a TLP-funded program that now employs him as a manager for the program. He explained that through intensive case management, he was empowered to stop using drugs and to live independently. Yet little is known about the outcomes of runaway and homeless youth generally. Local grantee organizations have limited information about youth after they receive services, and research on whether youth experience homelessness as adults is dated. Some grantees may decide to follow up with youth who received services, but HHS does not require longitudinal data collection. HHS's 2007 report to Congress, *Promising Strategies to End Youth Homelessness*, states that longer-term studies of runaway and homeless youth are challenging because of the youth's transient nature.[22] Further, knowledge about effective strategies for serving these youth is limited[23] and few, if any, studies appear to have been conducted to determine the costs and benefits of these interventions.

To glean more information about the runaway and homeless youth population, the Reconnecting Homeless Youth Act of 2008 requires HHS to determine the incidence and prevalence of runaway and homeless youth and to report on the sociodemographic and other characteristics of the population. Although not a specified goal of the act, this information may help practitioners and social science researchers develop effective interventions for the population.

### *Evaluation of TLP Sites*

Efforts are currently underway at HHS to learn more about the youth who are served by the Transitional Living Program. In August 2007, HHS approved a sub-contract to Abt Associates to conduct an evaluation of the TLP at select grantee sites.[24] The study seeks to describe the outcomes of youth who participate in the program and to isolate and describe factors that may have contributed to their successes or challenges, including service delivery approaches, personal characteristics, and local circumstances. HHS (through the Family and Youth Services Bureau) and Abt researchers have conducted three site visits to TLP grantees (in Dallas, Texas; Portland, Oregon; and Wichita, Kansas) and a series of consultations with HHS and outside experts to inform the design of the study.

FYSB has not yet selected the TLP survey sites for the study itself; however, the sites will likely have extensive experience working with runaway and homeless youth and have been awarded continuous TLP funding for at least three years after the survey commences. These sites will work to ensure that after receiving training, staff will be sufficiently capable of administering the survey instruments. The sites will also need to be large enough to capture an adequate sample size.

Youth participants will complete surveys at entry and while receiving services through a survey administered by their TLP programs. They will also complete surveys for up to one year after leaving the program. Youth will self-report the data to a website six months and twelve months after exiting. Evaluators will compare the individual outcomes of each youth to his or her benchmark data. The youth surveys are pending executive branch review, and

FYSB expects to begin collecting the data by the end of calendar year 2008. FYSB anticipates making preliminary information available before the last surveys are completed. Further, FYSB expects to maintain the self-reporting website indefinitely as a means of tracking TLP graduates after the formal study is complete.

HHS issued a proposed information collection request for public comment about the evaluation in the *Federal Register* on August 25, 2008.[25]

## Education and Employment Outcomes for Runaway and Homeless Youth

On June 19, 2007, the House Ways and Means Subcommittee on Income Security and Family Support held a hearing on disconnected and disadvantaged youth, with a focus on runaway youth. Witnesses described "disconnected youth" as those youth who have weak social networks of family, friends, and communities that can provide assistance such as employment connections, health insurance coverage, housing, tuition and other financial assistance, and emotional support. They also discussed measurable characteristics to indicate whether youth are disconnected, such as the lack of high school or college attendance coupled with not having a job over a specific period of time (e.g., one year).[26]

Runaway and homeless youth are vulnerable to becoming disconnected because of separation from their families, absence from school, and non-participation in the economy.[27] Family conflict — rooted in abuse and neglect, school problems, and drug and alcohol abuse — can compel youth to leave home. Family disconnectedness is also evident among many runaway and homeless youth involved in the foster care system. These youth are brought to the attention of child welfare services because of incidents of abuse and neglect. Further, youth "aging out" of the foster care system experience homelessness at a greater rate than their counterparts in the general population due, in part, to family disconnectedness. Some gay and lesbian youth also experience family disassociation when they come out about their sexuality.

Some runaway and homeless youth spend time out of school while they are away from a permanent home. The FY2007 NEO-RHYMIS survey indicated that about 20% of youth were not attending school regularly before entering the Basic Center Program.[28] Of youth in the Transitional Living Program, 21% had dropped out of school. Some homeless youth face barriers to attending school because of transportation problems and the absence of parents and guardians who can provide records and permission for youth to participate in school activities. Finally, some runaway and homeless youth are removed from the formal economy and resort to illegal activity, including stealing and selling drugs in exchange for cash. Other such youth are too young to work legally or experience mental health and other challenges that make working difficult.

The Reconnecting Homeless Youth Act of 2008 seeks to fund research projects that focus on connecting youth to work and school. The act amends RHYA to require HHS to give priority to research, evaluation, demonstration, and service projects that increase access to education and career pathways for runaway and homeless youth. These projects must be intended to help decrease high school dropout rates, increase rates of attaining a secondary school diploma or its equivalent, or increase placement and retention in postsecondary education or advanced workforce training programs.

# APPENDIX

## Table A-1. Comparison of Changes Enacted by S. 2982/P.L. 110-378 with the Previous Law, Current Regulation (Where Applicable), and H.R. 5524

| Bill Provision and Amendments Made by S. 2982/ P.L. 110-378 to RHYA (and U.S. Code) (The section numbers refer to H.R. 5524) | Previous Law (as it existed prior to the enactment of S. 2982/P.L. 110-378) | Current Regulation (where applicable) | H.R. 5524 (as passed by the House June 9, 2008) | S. 2982/P.L. 110-378 (as signed by the President on October 8, 2008) |
|---|---|---|---|---|
| **Sec. 1. Short Title** | | | | |
| | Runaway and Homeless Youth Act. | | Reconnecting Homeless Youth Act of 2008 (to amend the Runaway and Home-less Youth Act). | (Sec. 1) Same as H.R. 5524. |
| **Sec. 2. Findings** | | | | |
| Finding About Positive Youth Development<br><br>Amends Sec. 302 (42 U.S.C. 5701) | No provision. | | Adds as a purpose that services for runaway and homeless youth should be developed and provided using a positive youth development approach that ensures a young person a sense of (a) safety and structure; (b) belonging and membership; (c) self-worth and social contribution; (d) inde-pendence and control over one's life; and (e) closeness in interpersonal relationships. | (Sec. 2) Same as H.R. 5524. |
| **Sec. 3. Grants for Centers and Services** | | | | |
| Youth's Length of Stay<br><br>Amends Sec. 311(a) (42 U.S.C. 5711) | No provision related to length of stay. However, the law specifies that services provided by | 1351.1(a)<br>"Temporary shelter" under the Basic Center Program is defied as | Safe and appropriate shelter not to exceed 15 days, or not to exceed 21 days, if the center is "located in a state | (Sec. 3) Safe and appropriate shelter not to exceed 21 days. |
| | BCP projects include "safe and appropriate shelter." | "the provision of short term (maximum of 15 days) room and boa-d and core crisis inter-ention services, on a 24- hour basis, by a runaway and homeless youth project." . | or locality with an applicable law or regulation that permits a length of stay in excess of 15 days in compliance with lice-nsure requirements for child and youth serving facilities." | |

**Table A-1. Continued**

| Bill Provision and Amendments Made by S. 2982/ P.L. 110-378 to RHYA (and U.S. Code) (The section numbers refer to H.R. 5524) | Previous Law (as it existed prior to the enactment of S. 2982/P.L. 110-378) | Current Regulation (where applicable) | H.R. 5524 (as passed by the House June 9, 2008) | S. 2982/P.L. 110-378 (as signed by the President on October 8, 2008) |
|---|---|---|---|---|
| Grants for States and Territories Amends Sec. 311(b) (42 U.S.C. 5711) | An annual minimum of $100,000 for each state and an annual minimum of $45,000 for each territory. | | To the extent that sufficient funds are available, and subject to the provision about funding for FY2009 and FY2010 (below), an annual minimum of $150,000 for each state and an annual minimum of $70,000 for each territory. | (Sec. 3) subject to the provision about funding for FY2009 and FY2010 (below), an annual minimum of $200,000 for each state and an annual minimum of $70,000 for each territory. |
| Minimum Funding for FY 2009 and FY2010 Amends Sec. 311(b) (42 U.S.C.5711) | No provision. | | Funding for each state in FY2009 and FY 2010 is to be no less than the amount allotted to that state for FY2008. | (Sec. 3) Same as H.R. 5524. |
| Reallocation of Unused Funds Amends Sec. 311(b) (42 U.S.C. 5711) | No provision. | | The Secretary shall reallot any funds from one state to other states that will not be obligated before the end of a fiscal year. | (Sec. 3) Same as H.R. 5524, with a few minor, non-substantive differences in the text. |
| **Sec. 4. Basic Center Grant Program Eligibility** | | | | |
| Adequate Emergency Prerdness and Management Plan Amends Sec. 312(b) (42 U.S.C. 5712(b)) | No provision. | | Projects must develop an adequate emergency preparedness and management plan. | (Sec. 3) Same as H.R. 5524. |
| **Sec. 5. Transitional Living Grant Program Eligibility** | | | | |
| Provision of Shelter, Servi-ces, and Other Assistance Amends Sec. 322(a) (42 U.S.C. 5714-2(a)) | To qualify for funding, applicants must agree in their plan submitted to the Secretary that they will provide, *directly or indirectly, shelter and services* related to basic life skills and other services. | | Applicants must specify in their plans that they will provide, *directly or by contract,* shelter and services related to basic life skills and other services. | (Sec. 4) Applic-ants must specify in their plans that they will provide, *by grant, agreement, or contact,* shelter and services related to basic life skills and other services. |

# Table A-1. Comparison of Changes Enacted by S. 2982/P.L. 110-378 with the Previous Law, Current Regulation (Where Applicable), and H.R. 5524

| Bill Provision and Amendments Made by S. 2982/ P.L. 110-378 to RHYA (and U.S. Code) (The section numbers refer to H.R. 5524) | Previous Law (as it existed prior to the enactment of S. 2982/P.L. 110-378) | Current Regulation (where applicable) | H.R. 5524 (as passed by the House June 9, 2008) | S. 2982/P.L. 110-378 (as signed by the President on October 8, 2008). |
|---|---|---|---|---|
| Youth's Length of Stay in Program Amends Sec. 322(a) (42 U.S.C. 5714-2(a)) | Not to exceed a continous period of 540 days, except that youth under age 18 may remain in the program until their 18th birthday or the 180th day after the end of the 540-day period, whichever comes first. | | Adds that youth may remain in the program for a continuous period of up to 635 days if they are in a project "located in a state that has an applicable state or local law or regulation that permits a length of stay in excess of the 540-day period in compliance with licensure requirements for child and youth serving facilities." | (Sec. 4) Not to exceed a continuous period of 540 days, or 635 days in exceptional circumstances, except that a youth under age 18 may remain in the program beyond the 635 days (if otherwise qualified for the program and under excetional circumstances) until his or her 18th birthday. |
| Definition of "Exceptional Circumstances" Amends Sec. 322(c) (42 U.S.C. 5714-2(c)) | No provision | | No provision. | (Sec. 4) Circumstances in which a youth would benefit to an unusual extent from additional time in the program. |
| Emergency Preparedness and Management Plan Amends Sec. 322(a) (42 U.S.C. 5714-2(a)) | No provision. | | Transitional Living Program projects must develop an adequate emergency preparedness and management plan. | (Sec. 4) Same as H.R. 5524. |
| **Sec. 6. Research, Evaluation, Demonstration, and Service Projects** | | | | |
| Selection of Grantees Amends Sec. 343(b) (42 U.S.C. 5714-23) | The Secretary is to give *special consideration* to proposed projects relating to research, evaluations, and demonstrations in nine priority areas, including (1) youth who repeatedly leave and remain away from their homes; (2) transportation related to services provided under RHYA; (3) runaway and | | The Secretary is to give *priority* to projects focused on the nine priority areas in current law (with some modif-cations to the descriptions of the projects listed under paragraphs (8) and (9) in current law) as well an addit-ional project under a new paragraph (10): (8) increasing access to quality health care (including *behavioral* health care) for youth; (9) increasing access to education for runaway and homeless youth, including access to educational and workforce programs to achieve | (Sec. 5) Same as H.R. 5524, with a few minor, non-substantive differences in the text. |

**Table A-1. Comparison of Changes Enacted by S. 2982/P.L. 110-378 with the Previous Law, Current Regulation (Where Applicable), and H.R. 5524**

| Bill Provision and Amendments Made by S. 2982/ P.L. 110-378 to RHYA (and U.S. Code) (The section numbers refer to H.R. 5524) | Previous Law (as it existed prior to the enactment of S. 2982/P.L. 110-378) | Current Regulation (where applicable) | H.R. 5524 (as passed by the House June 9, 2008) | S. 2982/P.L. 110-378 (as signed by the President on October 8, 2008) |
|---|---|---|---|---|
| | homeless youth in rural areas; (4) programs that place runaway and home-ess youth with host families; (5) staff training in sexual assault and victimization; (6) innovative methods of developing resources that enhance runaway and homeless youth centers; (7) training for staff and youth about the Human Immunodeficiency Virus (HIV); (8) increasing access to health care (inclu-deing *mental health care*) for youth; and (9) increasing access to education for runa-way and homeless youth. | | outcomes such as decree-sing high school dropout rates, increas-ing rates of attaining a secondary school dip-loma or its recognized equivalent, or incre-asing placement and retention in postsecondary education or advanced workforce training programs; and (10) providing programs, including innovative programs, that assist youth in obtaining and maintaining safe and stable hou-sing, and which may include programs with supportive services that continue after the youth complete the remainder of the programs. | |
| Priority Selection of Grantees Amends Sec. 343(c) (42 U.S.C. 5714-23) | The Secretary is to give priority consideration to applicants with experi-ence work-ing with runaway and homeless youth. | | Adds that the Secretary is to give priority consideration to applicants with experience working with runaway and homeless youth and ensure that appli-cants selected repre-sent diverse geog-raphic regions of the U.S. and carry out projects that serve diverse youth. | (Sec. 5) Same as H.R. 5524, with a few minor, non-substantive differ-rences in the text. |

**Table A-1. Comparison of Changes Enacted by S. 2982/P.L. 110-378 with the Previous Law, Current Regulation (Where Applicable), and H.R. 5524**

| Bill Provision and Amendments Made by S. 2982/ P.L. 110-378 to RHYA (and U.S. Code) (The section numbers refer to H.R. 5524) | Previous Law (as it existed prior to the enactment of S. 2982/P.L. 110-378) | Current Regulation (where applicable) | H.R. 5524 (as passed by the House June 9, 2008) | S. 2982/P.L. 110-378 (as signed by the President on October 8, 2008) |
|---|---|---|---|---|
| **Sec. 7. Estimate of Incidence and Prevalence of Youth Homelessness** *Adds a new Section 345 under Part D (42 U.S.C. 5714-21 — 5714-24)* | | | | |
| Periodic Estimate of Incidence and Prevalence of Youth Homelessness Adds new subsection Sec. 345(a) | The Senate Appropriat-ions Committee request-ed, through S.Rept. 107-84 (to accompany S. 1536), that HHS submit a report to Congress that discusses a plan for developing estimates of the incidences of runa-way, throwaway, home-less, and street experi-ences among youth, as well as a plan for regu-larly Monitoring incide-nce trends. This report was submitted in 2003. | | Not later than two years after this pro-ision becomes effective, and at subse-uent five year intervals, the Secre-tary, in coordination with the U.S. Interagency Council on Homelessness, shall prepare a written report for the House Education and Labor Committee and Senate Judiciary Committee that contains an estimate, obtained using the best quantitative and qualitative social science research methods avail-able, of the incidence and prevalence of runaway and homeless youth ages 13 to 26, and includes an assessm-ent of the characteritics of these youth. | (Sec. 6) Same as H.R. 5524, with a few minor, non-substantive differences in the text. |
| Content of Incidence and Prevalence Assessment Adds new subsection Sec. 345(b) | No provision. | | Each assessment must contain the results of a survey of and direct interviews with, a representative sample of runaway and homeless youth ages 13 to 26 to determine past and current (a) socio-economic characteristics; (b) barriers to obtaining safe, quality, and ffordable housing; comprehensive and affordable health insurance and health services; | (Sec. 6) Same as H.R. 5524. |
| | | | and incomes, public benefits, supprtive services, and connections to caring adults; and (c) other information that the Secretary determines may be useful, in consultation with states, local units of goverment, and national non-govermental organizations concer-ed with homelessness. | |

**Table A-1. Comparison of Changes Enacted by S. 2982/P.L. 110-378 with the Previous Law, Current Regulation (Where Applicable), and H.R. 5524**

| Bill Provision and Amendments Made by S. 2982/ P.L. 110-378 to RHYA (and U.S. Code) (The section numbers refer to H.R. 5524) | Previous Law (as it existed prior to the enactment of S. 2982/P.L. 110-378) | Current Regulation (where applicable) | H.R. 5524 (as passed by the House June 9, 2008) | S. 2982/P.L. 110-378 (as signed by the President on October 8, 2008) |
|---|---|---|---|---|
| Implementation of Assessment Adds new subsection (Sec. 345(c)) | No provision. | . | If the Secretary enters into any agree-ment with a non-federal entity to carry out the assessment, such tity shall be a non-govermental organization, or an individual, determined by the Secretary to have appropriate expertise in quantitative and qualitative social science research. | (Sec. 6) Same as H.R. 5524. |
| **Sec. 8. Sexual Abuse Prevention Program (Note: also known as the Street Outreach Program)** | | | | |
| Priorities in Selecting Applicants Amends Sec. 351(b) (42 U.S.C. 5714-41(b)) | In selecting applicants to receive grants, the Secr-etary shall give priority to non-profit private agencies that have experience in providing services to runaway, homeless, and street youth. | | Same as current law, except that the Sertary is to also give priority to public agencies that have experience in providing services to runaway, homeless, and street youth. | (Sec. 7) Same as H.R. 5524. |
| **Sec. 9. National Homeless Youth Awareness Campign** *H.R. 5524 would have redesignated current Part F as Part G and added a new Sec. 361 under a new Part F* | | | | |
| Purpose *H.R. 5524 would have added a new subse-ction 361(a)* | No provision. | | The Secretary shall, directly or through grants or contracts, conduct a national homeless youth waress campaign for the purposes of (a) incraising awareness among individuals of all ages, socioeconomic backgrounds, and geo-raphic locations about the issues facing runaway and homeless youth, the resources available for these youth, and the tools available for the presention of youth runway and homeless situations; and (b) encouraging parents, guardians, educators, health care professionals, social service professionals, law enforcement officials, and other community members to assist youth in averting or resolving runaway and homeless situations. | No provision. |

**Table A-1. Comparison of Changes Enacted by S. 2982/P.L. 110-378 with the Previous Law, Current Regulation (Where Applicable), and H.R. 5524**

| Bill Provision and Amendments Made by S. 2982/ P.L. 110-378 to RHYA (and U.S. Code) (The section numbers refer to H.R. 5524) | Previous Law (as it existed prior to the enactment of S. 2982/P.L. 110-378) | Current Regulation (where applicable) | H.R. 5524 (as passed by the House June 9, 2008) | S. 2982/P.L. 110-378 (as signed by the President on October 8, 2008) |
|---|---|---|---|---|
| Use of Funds *H.R. 5524 would have added a new subsection 361(b)* | No provision. | | Funds made available for the campaign may be used only for the following: (a) dissemination of educational informa-tion and materials through various media, including television, radio, the Internet, and related technologies; (b) partnerships with national and otherorganizations concerned with homel-essness; (c) in accordance with applic-able laws and regulations, development and placement in media of public serv-ice announcements that educate the public on the issues facing runaway and homeless youth and the opportunities adults have to assist these youth; and (d) evaluation of the effectiveness of the campaign | No provision. |
| Prohibitions on Use of Funds *H.R. 5524 would have added a new subsection 361(c)* | No provision. | | Prohibits the use of funds for the national awareness campaign: (a) to supplant pro bono service time donated by national or local broadcast-ing networks, advertising agencies, or production companies for the campai-gn, or other pro bono work for the campaign; (b) for partisan political purposes, or to express advocacy in support of or opposition to any clearly identified candidate, ballot initiative or regulatory proposal; (c) to fund adve-rtising that features any elected official, person seeking office, cabinet level official, or other federal employee employed pursuant to Section 213 of Section C of Title 5 of the Code of Federal Regulations, as amended; (d) to fund advertising that does not contain a primary message intended to educate the public on the issues facing runaway and homeless youth (or youth considering running away) or the opportunities for adults to help such youth; and (e) to fund advertising that solicits contributions from both public and private sources to support the national awareness campaign. | No provision. |

**Table A-1. Comparison of Changes Enacted by S. 2982/P.L. 110-378 with the Previous Law, Current Regulation (Where Applicable), and H.R. 5524**

| Bill Provision and Amendments Made by S. 2982/ P.L. 110-378 to RHYA (and U.S. Code) (The section numbers refer to H.R. 5524) | Previous Law (as it existed prior to the enactment of S. 2982/P.L. 110-378) | Current Regulation (where applicable) | H.R. 5524 (as passed by the House June 9, 2008) | S. 2982/P.L. 110-378 (as signed by the President on October 8, 2008) |
|---|---|---|---|---|
| Financial and Performance Accountability *H.R. 5524 would have added a new subsection 361(d)* | No provision. | | The Secretary is to conduct (a) audits and reviews of costs of the national awareness campaign pursuant to Section 304C of the Federal Property and Administrative Services Act of 1949 (41 U.S.C. 254d); and (b) an audit to determine whether the costs of the national awareness campaign are allowable under Section 306 of that act (41 U.S.C. 256). | No provision. |
| Report to Congress *Would have added a new Section 361(e)* | No provision relating to a report on a national awareness campaign. However, current law (Sec. 382(a)) requires the | | The Secretary is to include in the report to Congress (as currently required under law) — a summary of the national awareness campaign that describes (a) the activities undertaken | |
| | Secretary to submit a report to Congress bien-nially on the status, activities, and accomplis-hments of entities that receive grants under RHYA.[a] | | by the campaign; (b) steps to ensure that the campaign operates in an effective and efficient manner consistent with the overall strategy and focus of the campaign; and (c) each grant entered into with a corporation, partnership, or individual working on the campaign. | |
| **Sec. 10. Definitions** | | | | |
| Definition of "Homeless Youth" (for the Basic Center Program only) Amends Sec. 387(3) (42 U.S.C. 5732a) | "Homeless youth" is defined as an individual who is not more than 18 years old; for whom it is not possible to live in a safe environment with a relative; and who has no other safe alternative living arrangement. | | Amends the first clause of the current definition to include an individual who is less than 18 years old, or an older maximum age if the BCP center is located in a state or locality with a law or regulation that permits a higher maximum age, in compliance with licensure requirements for child and youth serving facilities. | (Sec. 10) Same as H.R. 5524. |

**Table A-1. Comparison of Changes Enacted by S. 2982/P.L. 110-378 with the Previous Law, Current Regulation (Where Applicable), and H.R. 5524**

| Bill Provision and Amendments Made by S. 2982/ P.L. 110-378 to RHYA (and U.S. Code) (The section numbers refer to H.R. 5524) | Previous Law (as it existed prior to the enactment of S. 2982/P.L. 110-378) | Current Regulation (where applicable) | H.R. 5524 (as passed by the House June 9, 2008) | S. 2982/P.L. 110-378 (as signed by the President on October 8, 2008) |
|---|---|---|---|---|
| Definition of "Homeless Youth" (for the Transitional Living Program only) Amends Sec. 387(3) (42 U.S.C. 5732a) | "Homeless youth" is defined as an individual between the ages of 16 and 21; for whom it is not possible to live in a safe environment with a relative; and who has no other safe alternative living arrangement. | | Amends the first clause of the current definition to include an individual between the ages of 16 and 22 or an age exceeding 22 years old upon exiting the TLP project (as permitted under Sec. 322(a))[b] so long as the participant entered the TLP project prior to reaching age 22. | (Sec. 10) Same as H.R. 5524. |
| Definition of "Runaway Youth" (for the Transitional Living Program only) Amends Sec. 387(3) (42 U.S.C. 5732a) | | "Runaway youth" is defined as a person under age 18 who absents himself or hers-elf from home or place of legal residence with-out the permission of his or her *family*. | No provision. | (Sec. 10) Same as regulation, except that the individual absents himself or herself from home or place of legal residence without the permission of a *parent or legal guardian.* |
| **Sec. 11. Authorization of Appropriations** | | | | |
| RHYA (other than select parts) Amends Sec. 388(a) (42 U.S.C. 5751(a)) | $105 million for FY2004 and "such sums as may be necessary" for FY2005 through FY2008, except for Part E (Street Outreach Program). | | $150 million for FY2009 and "such sums as may be necessary" for each of FY2010 through FY2013, except for Part E (Street Outreach Program) and proposed Part F (National Homeless Youth Awareness Campaign). | (Sec. 11) $140 million for FY2009 and "such sums as may be neces-sary" for each of FY2010 through FY2013, except for Part E (Street utreach Program and Sec. 345 under Part D (Periodic Estimate Assessment). |
| Part E (Street Outreach Program) Amends Section 388(a) (42 U.S.C. 5751(a)) | "Such sums as may be necessary" for FY2004 through FY2008. | | $30 million for FY2009 and "such sums as may be necessary" for each of FY2010 through FY2013. | (Sec. 11) $25 million for FY2009 and "such sums as may be nece-ssary" for each of FY 2010 through FY2013. |

150

**Table A-1. Comparison of Changes Enacted by S. 2982/P.L. 110-378 with the Previous Law, Current Regulation (Where Applicable), and H.R. 5524**

| Bill Provision and Amendments Made by S. 2982/ P.L. 110-378 to RHYA (and U.S. Code) (The section numbers refer to H.R. 5524) | Previous Law (as it existed prior to the enactment of S. 2982/P.L. 110-378) | Current Regulation (where applicable) | H.R. 5524 (as passed by the House June 9, 2008) | S. 2982/P.L. 110-378 (as signed by the President on October 8, 2008) |
|---|---|---|---|---|
| Part F (National Homeless Youth Awareness Campaign) *H.R. 5524 would have redesignated Part F from General Provisions to the National Homeless Youth Awareness Campaign* | No provision. | | $3 million for each of FY2009 through FY2013. | No provision. |
| Part C (National Communications System) and Part D (Coordinating, Training, Research, and Other Activities) Sec. 388(a) (42 U.S.C. 5751 (a)) | In each fiscal year, after reserving the amounts required for Parts A and B (BCP and TLP, respectively), the Secret-ary shall use the remain-ing amount (if any) to carry out Parts C and D. | | No provision. | (Sec. 11) Conforming amendment to exclude Sec. 345 from recei-ving funding that is allocated for Part C or Part D. |
| Sec. 345 (Periodic Estimate Assessment) Sec. 388(a) (42 U.S.C. 5751(a)) | No provision. | | "Such sums as may be necessary" for each of FY2009 through FY2013. | (Sec. 11) Same as H.R. 5524, with minor differences in the text. |
| **Sec. 12. Performance Standards** *H.R. 5524 would have added a new Sec. 390; S. 2982/P.L. 110-378 adds a new Sec. 386A under Part F (General Provisions)* | | | | |
| Establishment of Perfor-mance Standards Adds a new subsection 386A(a) | No provision. | | Not later than one year after this Section becomes effective, the Secretary is to issue rules that specify performance standards for public and non-profit entities that receive BCP, TLP, and SOP grants. | (Sec. 8) Same as H.R. 5524, with a few minor, non-substantive differences in the text. |
| Implementation of Performance Standards Adds a new subsection 386A(c) | No provision. | | The Secretary shall integrate the Perfor-mance standards into the grantmaking, monitoring, and evaluations processes for the BCP, TLP, and SOP. | (Sec. 8) Same as H.R. 5524, with a few min-or, non-substantive differences in the text. |

**Table A-1. Comparison of Changes Enacted by S. 2982/P.L. 110-378 with the Previous Law, Current Regulation (Where Applicable), and H.R. 5524**

| Bill Provision and Amendments Made by S. 2982/ P.L. 110-378 to RHYA (and U.S. Code) (The section numbers refer to H.R. 5524) | Previous Law (as it existed prior to the enactment of S. 2982/P.L. 110-378) | Current Regulation (where applicable) | H.R. 5524 (as passed by the House June 9, 2008) | S. 2982/P.L. 110-378 (as signed by the President on October 8, 2008) |
|---|---|---|---|---|
| Consultation Adds a new subsection 386A(b) | No provision. | | In developing performance standards, the Secretary shall consult with represssentatives of public and nonprofit private entities that receive grants under RHYA, including statewide and region-nal nonprofit organizations (including combinations of such organizations), and national nonprofit organizations concerned with youth homelessness. | (Sec. 8) Same as H.R. 5524, with a few minor, non-substantive differences in the text. |
| Public Comment *H.R. 5524 would have added a new subsection 390(d)* | No provision. | | Before issuing rules to establish performance standards, the Secretary is to provide an opportunity for public comment concerning the standards and maintain an official record of such comment. | No provision. |
| **Sec. 13. GAO Study and Report** *H.R. 5524 and S. 2982 do not specify the section of RHYA in which this language would be inserted* | | | | |
| Study | No provision. | | The Government Accountability Office (GAO) is to conduct a study, and make findings and recommendations, relating to the process for awarding grants under Parts A, B, and E of RHYA, including (a) the Secret-ary's written responses to (and any other methods for communicating with) applicants that do not receive a grant under Part A, B, or E, to determine if the information in the response is conveyed clearly; (b) the structure of the grant application and associated documents (including announcements that grants are available under such parts), to determine if these materials are structured so that the applicant has a clear understanding of what is required in each provision to successfully complete the application, including a clear explanation of terminology required to be used by the | (Sec. 11) Same as H.R. 5524, differences in the text. |

**Table A-1. Comparison of Changes Enacted by S. 2982/P.L. 110-378 with the Previous Law, Current Regulation (Where Applicable), and H.R. 5524**

| Bill Provision and Amendments Made by S. 2982/ P.L. 110-378 to RHYA (and U.S. Code) (The section numbers refer to H.R. 5524) | Previous Law (as it existed prior to the enactment of S. 2982/P.L. 110-378) | Current Regulation (where applicable) | H.R. 5524 (as passed by the House June 9, 2008) | S. 2982/P.L. 110-378 (as signed by the President on October 8, 2008) |
|---|---|---|---|---|
| | | | applicant; (c) the peer review process (if any) used to review the grants (including the selection of peer reviewers) and the oversight of the peer review process by HHS employees, as well as to the extent to which these employees make funding determinations based on the comments and scores of the peer reviewers; (d) the typical time frame and process used by HHS employees, including employee responsibilities, for responding to applicants and the efforts made by HHS staff to communicate with applicants when funding decisions are delayed or not appropriated before the beginning of the current fiscal year; and (e) the plans for, and implementation of, where applicable, RHYA-authorized technical assistance and training programs (authorized under Sec. 342),[c] and the effect of such programs on the grant application process. | with a few minor, non-substantive |
| Report | No provision. | | GAO is to prepare and submit a report to Congress on its findings and recommendations no later than a year after the bill is enacted. | (Sec. 11) Same as H.R. 5524. |

Source: Table prepared by the Congressional Research Service.

a. Section 382(a) pertains to the biennial report to Congress on the status, activities, and accomplishments of entities that receive grants under Parts A, B, C, D, and E of RHYA.

b. Section 322(a) pertains to eligibility for grants under the Transitional Living Program. As amended by S. 2982/P.L. 110-378, youth may remain in the program for a continuous period of 635 days (approximately 21 months) under "exceptional circumstances," or circumstances in which a youth would benefit to an unusual extent from additional time in the program.

c. Section 342 pertains to grants for technical assistance and training made to statewide and regional nonprofit organizations (and combinations of such organizations) to provide assistance to entities eligible to carry out programs, projects, and activities under RHYA.

# End Notes

[1] For detailed program information, see CRS Report RL33785, *Runaway and Homeless Youth: Demographics, Programs, and Emerging Issues*, by Adrienne L. Fernandes.

[2] A third bill, the Runaway and Homeless Youth Act Reauthorization of 2008 was introduced on August 3, 2007, by Representative Raul Grijalva as Title II, Subtitle A of A Place to Call Home Act (H.R. 3409), an omnibus youth policy and child welfare bill. However, the bill was not voted on by the House Education and Labor Committee or the full House.

[3] Part A pertains to the BCP; Part B pertains to the TLP; Part C pertains to the National Communication System; Part D pertains to coordinating, training, research, and other activities; Part E pertains to the SOP; and Part F pertains to general provisions, such as assistance to potential grantees, lease of surplus federal facilities, reports, records, definitions, and authorization of appropriations, among other provisions.

[4] It is not clear whether the language will change the way TLP applicants sub-contract services for runaway and homeless youth, if at all. Prior grant applications for the BCP, TLP, and SOP have asked applicants to submit information about any sub-grants or contracts with other entities that provide services to runaway and homeless youth.

[5] The law does not define how this plan should be carried out, or what is considered "adequate."

[6] The Department of Health and Human Services, through the Family and Youth Services Bureau, has defined diversity in runaway and homeless youth programs to include characteristics such as gender, race, ethnicity, socioeconomic and educational status, sexual orientation, physical capacity, age, personality type, religious and spiritual beliefs, regional customs, and immigrant status. U.S. Department of Health and Human Services, Administration for Children and Families, Family and Youth Services Bureau, *A Guide to Enhancing Cultural Competence of Runaway and Homeless Youth Programs*, January 1994, pp. 5-7.

[7] U.S. Office of Management and Budget, *Detailed Assessment on the Runaway and Homeless Youth Assessment*, 2003 and U.S. Office of Management and Budget, *Detailed Assessment on the Runaway and Homeless Youth Assessment*, 2007, available at [http://www.whitehouse.gov/omb/expectmore/summary/10001064.2006.html]. (Hereafter PART 2003 or PART 2007.)

[8] For additional information about NEO-RHYMIS, see [https://extranet.acf.hhs.gov/rhymis/custom_reports.html].

[9] For information about recent changes to the training and technical assistance programs, see CRS Report RL33785, *Runaway and Homeless Youth: Demographics and Programs*, by Adrienne L. Fernandes.

[10] For additional information about the grant review process, see archived grant funding announcements for the program, [http://www.acf.hhs.gov/grants/grants_archive.html].

[11] 45 C.F.R. 1351.81.

[12] Based on correspondence with the Department of Health and Human Services on September 21, 2007.

[13] Ibid, February 26, 2008.

[14] Christopher L. Ringwalt et al., "The Prevalence of Homelessness Among Adolescents in the United States," American Journal of Public Health, vol. 88, no. 9 (September 1998), p. 1325.

[15] Ibid.

[16] The Senate Appropriations Committee made this request in S.Rept. 107-84 to accompany the Senate version of the Labor, HHS, Education Appropriations Bill for 2002 (S. 1536). Companion legislation (H.R. 3061) was signed into law as P.L. 107-116.

[17] "Throwaway youth" (or "push outs") generally refer to runaway and homeless youth who have been abandoned by their parents or have been told to leave their households.

[18] U.S. Department of Health and Human Services, Office of the Assistant Secretary for Planning and Evaluation, Office of Planning, Research, and Evaluation, Administration for Children and Families, *Incidence and Prevalence of Homeless and Runaway Youth*, May 9, 2003; available at [http://www.acf.hhs.gov/programs/opre/fys/design_opt/reports/incidence/incidence.pdf].

[19] U.S. Congress. House. Committee on Education and Labor. Subcommittee on Healthy Families and Communities. *Runaway, Homeless, and Missing Children: Perspectives on Helping the Nation's Vulnerable Youth*. Hearings. 110th Congress, 1st session, July 24, 2007. Transcript available at [http://frwebgate.access.gpo.gov/cgi-bin/getdoc.cgi?dbname=110_house_hearings&docid=f:36729.pdf]. U.S. Congress. House. Committee on Ways and Means. Subcommittee on Income Security and Family Support. *Disconnected and Disadvantaged Youth*. Hearings. 110th Congress, 1st session, June 19, 2007. Written testimony available at [http://waysandmeans.house.gov/hearings.asp?formmode=detail&hearing=569]. U.S. Congress. Senate. Committee on the Judiciary. *Living on the Street: Finding Solutions to Protect Runaway and Homeless Youth*. 110th Congress, 2nd session, April 29, 2008. Written testimony available at [http://judiciary.senate.gov/hearing.cfm?id=3312].

[20] U.S. Government Accountability Office, *Disconnected Youth: Federal Action Could Address Some of the Challenges Faced by Local Programs That Reconnect Youth to Education and Employment*, GAO-08-313, February 2008, p. 29.

[21] Based on a Congressional Research Service (CRS) analysis of appropriation information and the reported number of grantees, as provided in the U.S. Department of Health and Human Services, Administration for Children and Families, *Justification of Estimates for Appropriations Committees, FY2006 through FY2009.*

[22] U.S. Department of Health and Human Services, *Promising Strategies to End Youth Homelessness, Report to Congress,* 2007. Available at [http://www.acf.hhs.gov/programs/fysb/content/docs/ reporttocongress_ youthhomelessness.pdf]. This report was required under P.L. 108-96. See 42 U.S.C. 5701.

[23] Interventions can include case management, working with the youth's family, and social skills training, among other areas. For a review of research on intervention and prevention of homeless and runaway situations, see Paul A. Toro, Amy Dworsky, and Patrick J. Fowler, *Homeless Youth in the United States: Recent Research Findings and Intervention Approaches,* 2007 National Symposium on Homelesness Research, March 2007. Available at [http://aspe.hhs.gov/hsp/homelessness/symposium07/toro/index.htm].

[24] Based on correspondence with the Department Health and Human Services on March 28, 2008.

[25] U.S. Department of Health and Human Services, Administration for Children and Families, "Proposed Information Collection Activity; Comment Request," 73 *Federal Register* 50022, August 25, 2008. Comments are due October 25, 2008.

[26] For additional information about disconnected and other vulnerable youth, see CRS Report RL33975, *Vulnerable Youth: Background and Policies,* by Adrienne L. Fernandes.

[27] Bob Reeg, "The Runaway and Homeless Youth Act and Disconnected Youth," in Jodie Levin-Epstein and Mark H. Greenburg, eds., *Leave No Youth Behind: Opportunities for Congress to Reach Disconnected Youth* (July 2003), pp. 56-63.

[28] These figures were derived from the report, "Grade Completed at Exit." See [https://extranet.acf.hhs.gov/rhymis/].

In: Runaway and Homeless Youth
Editors: Josiah Hughes and Isiah Wright

ISBN: 978-1-60741-521-3
© 2010 Nova Science Publishers, Inc.

*Chapter 5*

# RUNAWAY, HOMELESS, AND MISSING CHILDREN: PERSPECTIVES ON HELPING THE NATION'S VULNERABLE YOUTH: HEARING BEFORE THE SUBCOMMITEE ON HEALTHY FAMILIES AND COMMUNITIES, COMMITTEE ON EDUCATION AND LABOR, U.S. HOUSE OF REPRESENTATIVES*

## *United States Government Printing Office*

The subcommittee met, pursuant to call, at 3:05 p.m., in Room 2175, Rayburn House Office Building, Hon. Carolyn McCarthy [chairwoman of the subcommittee] presiding.

Present: Representatives McCarthy, Grijalva, Sarbanes, Yarmuth, Lampson, Platts, and Biggert.

Staff present: Aaron Albright, Press Secretary; Tylease Alli, Hearing Clerk; Jody Calemine, Labor Policy Deputy Director; Carlos Fenwick, Policy Advisor, Subcommittee on Health, Employment, Labor and Pensions; Michael Gaffin, Staff Assistant, Labor; Lamont Ivey, Staff Assistant, Education; Brian Kennedy, General Counsel; Deborah Koolbeck, Policy Advisor, Subcommittee on Healthy Families and Communities; Lisette Partelow, Staff Assistant, Education; James Bergeron, Minority Deputy Director of Education and Human Services Policy; Robert Borden, Minority General Counsel; Kathryn Bruns, Minority Legislative Assistant; Cameron Coursen, Minority Assistant Communications Director; Kirsten Duncan, Minority Professional Staff Member; Taylor Hansen, Minority Legislative Assistant; Susan Ross, Minority Director of Education and Human Resources Policy; and Linda Stevens, Minority Chief Clerk/Assistant to the General Counsel.

*Chairwoman McCarthy* [presiding]. A quorum is present. The hearing of the subcommittee will come to order.

---

* This is an edited, reformatted and augmented version of a U. S. Government Printing Office publication dated July 2007.

Pursuant to committee rule 12-A, any member may submit an opening statement in writing, which will be made part of the permanent record.

Before we begin, I would like everyone to take a moment to ensure that your cell phones and BlackBerrys are on "silent."

I would now like unanimous consent to allow the distinguished gentleman from Texas, Mr. Lampson, to be allowed to join us on the dais today and participate in the hearing.

Without objection, so ordered.

I now recognize myself, followed by the Ranking Member, Mr. Platts, from Pennsylvania, for an opening statement.

I am pleased to welcome you all to the Subcommittee on Healthy Families and Communities hearing on runaway, homeless and missing children.

I would like to thank the ranking member, Mr. Platts, for his interest in this important subject.

I would also like to thank my two colleagues on the Healthy Families Subcommittee, Mr. Grijalva and Mr. Yarmuth, for their dedication to the issues of runaway and homeless children.

Mr. Grijalva has taken the lead and urged the appropriation to increase funds for runaway and homeless youth programs, with success, this year. Mr. Yarmuth recently held a town-hall to illuminate the issues of runaway and homeless youth in his district in Kentucky.

We are lucky to have such passionate members on this subcommittee, and I look forward to hearing from the witnesses from your districts today.

Later, 'we would also like to welcome a visitor to hearing today, Mr. Lampson from Texas. We are glad that he will be able to join us later. Mr. Lampson has been personally dedicated to this issue for the last 10 years. He founded the Congressional Missing and Exploited Children's Caucus, which now has over 130 members. Mr. Lampson remains the champion of missing and exploited children in Congress.

We are here today to learn about runaway, homeless and missing children and gain perspectives on how we can help these young people as we begin the reauthorization process.

Although there are no exact figures for the number of runaway and homeless youth in our nation, in 2002 1.6 million young people between the ages of 12 to 17 ran away from home and slept in exposed or poorly sheltered locations.

Runaways may find shelter with a friend or member of the community, but for the children who find themselves on the street, food, shelter, health care, and personal safety needs are not met. Studies of runaway and homeless youth show high rates of emotional and mental health problems. According to the Basic Center Program and Transitional Living Program in 2006, 29 percent were identified as having mental health issues upon exiting care.

In addition, many of the young people who enter shelters have a history with the juvenile justice system, on which we had a hearing just a few weeks ago. These issues are all related, as we have a juvenile correction system that fails to protect youth from shelters and streets.

Runaway children may fall into the missing children category. A study funded by the Department of Justice found that nearly all of the 1.3 million children who went missing in 1999 were reunited with their caretakers.

We will learn of the grassroots activities on these issues, which includes collaboration between those who assist runaway and homeless youth and those who locate missing children.

However, not every child was reunited with caretakers, and that is why we have AMBER alerts, the National Center for Missing and Exploited Children, a Task Force on Internet Crimes Against Children and Law Enforcement Training Center.

Today's topics are difficult. I am looking forward to learning what we do for our runaway, homeless and missing children and recommendations on what we can do through reauthorization to better serve these young people.

I want to thank all of you for taking the time to be here this afternoon.

And now I yield to Ranking Member Platts for his opening statement.

[The statement of Mrs. McCarthy follows:]

## Prepared Statement of Hon. Carolyn McCarthy, Chairwoman, Subcommittee on Healthy Families and Communities

I am pleased to welcome you to the Subcommittee on Healthy Families and Communities hearing on runaway, homeless, and missing children.

I would like to thank the Ranking Member, Mr. Platts for his interest in this important hearing.

I would also like to thank my two colleagues on the Healthy Families Subcommittee, Mr. Grijalva and Mr. Yarmuth for the dedication to issues of runaway and homeless children.

Mr. Grijalva has taken the lead and urged the appropriations to increase funds for runaway and homeless youth programs, with success this year.

Mr. Yarmuth recently held a town hall to illuminate the issues of runaway and homeless youth in his district in Kentucky.

We are lucky to have such passionate members on this subcommittee, and I look forward to hearing from the witnesses from your districts today.

I would like to welcome a visitor to our hearing today, Mr. Lampson from Texas. We are glad that you could join us today. Mr. Lampson has been personally dedicated to this issue to for the last ten years. He founded the Congressional Missing and Exploited Children Caucus, which now has over 130 members. Mr. Lampson remains the champion of missing and exploited children in Congress.

We are here today to learn about runaway, homeless, and missing children, and gain perspectives on how we can help these young people as we begin the reauthorization process.

Although there no exact figures for the number of runaway and homeless youth in our nation, in 2002, 1.6 million young people between the ages of 12 to 17 ran away from home and slept in exposed or poorly sheltered locations.

Runaways may find shelter with a friend or member of the community, but for the children who find themselves on the street, food, shelter, healthcare, and personal safety needs are not met. Studies of runaway and homeless youth show high rates of emotional and mental health problems. According to the Basic Center Program and Transitional Living Program in 2006, 29 per cent were identified as having mental health issues upon exiting care.

In addition, many of the young people who enter shelters have a history with the Juvenile Justice system, on which we had a hearing a week and a half ago. These issues are all related, as we have a juvenile correction system that fails to protect youth from shelters and streets.

Runaway children may fall into the missing children category.

A study funded by the Department of Justice found that nearly all of the 1.3 million children who went missing in 1999 were reunited with their caretakers.

We will learn of the grassroots activity on these issues, which includes collaboration between those who assist runaway and homeless youth and those who locate missing children. However, not every child was reunited with caretakers, and that is why we have AMBER alerts, the National Center for Missing and Exploited Children, a task force on internet crimes against children, and law enforcement training center.

Today's topics are difficult. I am looking forward to learning what we do for our runaway, homeless, and missing children, and recommendations on what we can do through reauthorization, to better serve these young people.

*Mr. Platts.* Thank you, Madam Chair.

I will submit a formal statement for the record, and first just want to commend you for your continuing leadership on issues of importance to our youth, throughout our nation and here, especially dealing with runaway, homeless and missing children. Your hosting this hearing is going to allow us as a committee to be that much better informed and better prepared as we go into the reauthorization process. So thank you for your leadership.

I also want to reference Mrs. Biggert from Illinois, who is also co-chair of the Missing and Exploited Children's Caucus and has been a great leader on these issues for us on the Republican side.

And, Judy, we are glad to have you here with us, as well.

To our witnesses, each of you bring what will be invaluable knowledge to be shared with us. Through your written testimony that you provided and your oral testimony here today, your life experiences, your expertise in this area is so critical for us being better informed.

I look at our job as Congress men and women as being kind of general practitioner. We need to know a little bit about everything and, as an issue is moving forward, become experts on a few things. And, on this committee, dealing with the needs of our nation's children is one of those areas where we are charged with being more experts. The way we become more expert on these issues is through information shared with us, such as you are going to do today.

So I sincerely thank each of you for being here and for making time in your schedules to participate to help us have the knowledge we need to do right by our nation's children and look forward to your testimony.

Thank you, Madam Chair.

[The statement of Mr. Platts follows:]

## Prepared Statement of Hon. Todd Russell Platts, Senior Republican Member, Subcommittee on Healthy Families and Communities

Good afternoon. I'd like to welcome each one of you to this hearing entitled "Runaway, Homeless, and Missing Children: Perspectives on Helping the Nation's Vulnerable Youth." This is the third hearing in a series which we have held that examine the programs authorized by the Juvenile Justice and Delinquency Prevention Act (JJDPA). The Runaway and

Homeless Youth Act and the Missing Children's Assistance Act are Titles III and IV respectively of JJDPA.

The Runaway and Homeless Youth Act authorizes three grant programs to meet the needs of homeless youth. The first, the Basic Center Program, provides emergency short-term shelter for youth, as well as food, clothing, counseling, and referrals for health care. The second program, the Transitional Living Program, assists older homeless youth in developing skills to promote their independence and prevent future dependency on social services. The final program authorizes funding for Maternal Group Homes, which provide a range of services for young mothers such as childcare, education, job training, and advice on parenting to promote their wellbeing and success as a parent.

The Missing Children's Assistance Act coordinates the various federal missing children's programs though the Department of Justice's Office of Juvenile Justice and Delinquency Prevention. In addition, it authorizes the National Center for Missing and Exploited Children, which provides assistance to families and law enforcement officials to help reunite families.

Today, I look forward to hearing from our panel of expert witnesses and learning what their assessments are of the current programs. In Pennsylvania, 40 percent of individuals who become homeless during any given year are youths. It is vital that we provide support early to homeless youth to get them on a path of responsible independence and decrease their risk of entering the juvenile justice system.

Finally, I would like to thank all of the panelists were joining us today. With that, I yield back to Chairwoman McCarthy.

*Chairwoman Mccarthy.* Thank you, Mr. Platts.

And, again, welcome Ms. Biggert. We appreciate you being here. And, also, Mr. Lampson is here.

Without objection, all members will have 14 days to submit additional materials or questions for the hearing record.

Today we will hear from a panel of witnesses.

Your testimonies will proceed in the order of your introduction.

Our first witness, Mr. Chris—I am going to pronounce this wrong—"Kazi" Rolle, comes to us as one of two voices of experience on our panel about homelessness. However, he will also have a message of hope and growth to share through his work on Art Start's Hip-Hop Project, an after-school program for teens which teaches them to turn their life experiences into art through hip-hop. He also has worked on the Hip-Hop Project, which can be seen in the documentary by the same name, with all profits going to support organizations working with young people.

Now I wish to recognize the distinguished gentleman from Arizona, Mr. Grijalva, to introduce the next witness, Ms. Sue Krahe-Eggleston from Arizona.

*Mr. Grijalva.* Thank you very much, Madam Chair and Ranking Member Platts, for holding this very important hearing.

Today, it is my distinct honor and pleasure to introduce a fellow Tucsonan, Sue Krahe-Eggleston, who is director of Our Family Services back home in Tucson. This service, Our Family, provides a comprehensive range, Madam Chair, of services addressing the needs of at-risk youth, children, families, seniors and works with neighborhoods.

For the past 16 years, Sue, in her capacity as executive director, has helped define back home for the community the needs and the attention and the resources that youth in our community need. For that, we are very grateful for her leadership and for her very strong advocacy.

She is nationally renowned and recognized as an advocate for children and family social services and currently serves as a board member of the National Network for Youth. It is my honor to introduce her.

Thank you very much, Madam Chair, and look forward to the testimony of all our witnesses and welcome them, as well.

I yield back.

*Chairwoman McCarthy.* And I thank you.

Now I wish to recognize the distinguished gentleman from Kentucky, Mr. Yarmuth, to introduce the next witness, Mr. Rusty Booker.

*Mr. Yarmuth.* Thank you, Madam Chair.

It is my distinct privilege today to introduce a young man of incredible strength and courage, Rusty Booker.

I met Rusty about 3 weeks ago at a forum I hosted on disconnected youth in our mutual hometown of Louisville, Kentucky. Rusty spoke of his experience with abuse, how he ran away at age 12 and about his placement in five different foster homes.

The power of his story comes not simply from the hand that he was dealt but the way that he played it. So often, when we think of disconnected youth, we think, often correctly, of helplessness and victimization.

But this exceptional young man has long since left behind helplessness and the role of a victim. After a childhood of neglect, he took control of his life, set himself on a path toward adult success.

He is determined to get a high school degree and join the police force. Also, at the age of 17, he has dedicated himself to helping others who suffered like he did, reaching out to kids on the street.

Rusty is the success story. I thank him for being here to share his story. He has demonstrated an awful lot of courage in his life and today is one more chapter in displaying courage.

I also want to thank Safe Place for ensuring he could be here today.

I yield back.

*Chairwoman McCarthy.* Thank you.

Our next witness, Mr. Steve Berg, is the vice president for programs and policy of the National Alliance to End Homelessness. Prior to coming to Washington, Mr. Berg spent 14 years as a legal service attorney. Mr. Berg will speak to us today about what the research on runaway and homeless youth tells us.

Mr. Yarmuth from Kentucky will also introduce our next witness, Mr. Ernie Allen.

*Mr. Yarmuth.* Thank you again, Madam Chair. It is my big day here today. Big day for Louisville, too.

You would be hard pressed to find someone who so consistently has shown more devotion to the nation's missing and exploited children than the next witness to be introduced.

My friendship with Ernie Allen goes back many years, to his time in Louisville. He has always shown a selfless dedication to serving our community as our city's director of health and public safety, director of our county crime commission and now, as founder, president and CEO of the National Center for Missing & Exploited Children.

He serves all our communities today, having helped recover well over 100,000 missing children, increasing the recovery rate from 62 percent in 1990 to 96 percent today. Not despite, but because of, his success, Ernie knows as well as anyone the vast challenges still ahead of us.

And so, Madam Chair, it is my honor to introduce a true humanitarian and an example for all of us, my friend, Ernie Allen.

*Chairwoman McCarthy.* Thank you very much.

Now I wish to recognize the distinguished gentleman from Texas and our guest today, Mr. Lampson, to introduce the next witness, Ms. Beth Alberts.

*Mr. Lampson.* Thank you, Madam Chair, and I certainly thank you for allowing me to participate in the hearing today.

As founder and co-chair of the Congressional Caucus on Missing and Exploited Children, thanks to the suggestion from Ernie Allen a number of years back, I really am pleased to be able to welcome Beth Alberts here.

Beth is the CEO of Texas Center for the Missing. It is a not-forprofit organization, established in 2000 by Houston executive Doreen Wise in memory of her son, Gabriel, after his 4-month disappearance and tragic loss. The center has one goal: to keep vulnerable children and adults safe.

And since July 2001, Ms. Alberts has served as the director of the Houston Regional AMBER Plan, the largest regional AMBER Alert system in the country.

Ms. Alberts also serves as the coordinator for both the Southeast Texas Child Abduction Response team, which is a multi-jurisdictional, multi-discipline team of 70 different agencies prepared to respond to endangered/missing child cases, and the Southeast Texas Search and Rescue Alliance, a consortium of volunteer search and rescue teams and missing children's organizations, providing support to law enforcement agencies and families of the missing.

Ms. Alberts serves as the secretary of the board of AMECO, Inc.—it is an international consortium of missing children's organizations—and is a board member of the Harris County Department of Education's Safe and Secure Schools and sits on the Children's Assessment Center Partnership Council.

A busy, busy lady, one that we have tremendous appreciation for her for caring, for her willingness to help and give back so much of herself and for being here today.

Welcome.

And, thank you, Madam Chair.

*Chairwoman McCarthy.* And I thank you.

For those of you that have not testified before, you will see in front of you a lighting system. Each witness will be able to speak for 5 minutes. The warning lights are green. Then, when you have yellow, you have a minute left. When it turns red, I will let you go a little bit, but if you go too long, you will hear a light tapping, which will get louder.

That goes the same for the members sitting at the dais. Especially for us, right?

The first witness we want to hear from is Mr. Rolle, if you would?

## STATEMENTS OF CHRIS "KAZI ROLLE", CREATOR, ART START'S HIP–HOP PROJECT

*Mr. Rolle.* Mike check, one, two, one, two. Peace and love.

My name is Kazi, also known as Chris Rolle. I was born on a little island called Nassau, in the Bahamas. My mother was a Jamaican immigrant who was trying to get to America, because it was easier for a Bahamian to get to America than coming straight from Jamaica.

At 6 months of age, she left on that journey and left me with her friend. Her friend and her husband were very abusive. And I lived there for 4 years. And at 4 years old, I was found wandering the streets, and, subsequently, the Department of Social Services in the Bahamas took me out of that home and placed me in the Children's Emergency Hostel for orphans.

Catherine Brown, who was a social worker there, she and I developed a relationship, and in 1982 I was fostered by her and her family. And the adjustment was very difficult. I had numerous behavioral problems. I always like to say she tried to give me heaven and I gave her hell.

But she trucked on with me, and I was officially adopted in 1988, on November 4th, still posing a lot of behavioral challenges. And the family didn't have the know-how or the resources to provide me with the emotional healing and help that I needed.

And, in 1990, I was forced to have to go back to the orphanage. And in the orphanage, all the boys in my room, we got in trouble and we were asked to leave the orphanage. Some kids were adopted, and I went on to a psychiatric ward for unruly children.

While I was there, the psychiatrist, his analysis came to the conclusion that a lot of the stuff I was dealing with was based on the fact that I missed my mother. I couldn't understand why these strangers were doing so much for me and my own mother could give me away.

So we contacted the American embassy, sent a letter to her and found that she wanted me. We sent a one-way ticket, and I came here on December 22nd, to America, in 1990.

We had a tumultuous reunion, and I found myself 2 years later on the streets of Brooklyn. Wherever I laid my head was my home, and got in a lot of trouble.

I was involved in street pharmaceutical corporations and family organizations that were one color, if you understand what I am saying. And they were my family.

After being incarcerated a few times, I decided that I needed to get my life together, and I leaned on the people and the resources that I knew. I was a part of a theater company called Tomorrow's Future Theater Company, Elaine Robinson, and she helped me to get into a school called Public School Repertory Company, which was a last-chance high school for kids who were interested in the arts.

There I found a guy by the name of Scott Rosenberg, who founded an organization called Art Start, which was an arts education organization. And he just gave me the opportunity to just use my voice and use music and art. And I found that it was really a healing tool, to be able to put my life and all the things I was going through in music and art.

I created a play called "Brooklyn Story," and I shared it with people across the tri-state, and it moved a lot of young people. And just to put it out there, I think that was the beginning of my healing and a change for my life.

Scott also supported me in creating my own program, because I made a commitment that I have got to give back. I understand what these kids are going through and I understand the journey, now. And I need to give back the same way that there were people along the way that took the time out to give to me.

In 1995, I appeared on numerous shows for just gaining all these awards and recognition for doing all of this work. In 2000, I made it all the way to the Oprah Winfrey Show, to basically just say that this young brother has overcome some obstacles and was once homeless and now speaks at Harvard and across the world about how hip-hop can really heal and change lives.

In 2007, this year, May 11th, a movie was released, executive produced by Bruce Willis and Queen Latifah, that chronicled my journey and the creation of this program, and a lot of lives were moved based on that.

I am here today to just basically say that the step-parents, the organizations like Art Start, like the Hip-Hop Project, Network for Youth, all of the programs across the country that are trying to really reach our missing children, kids like myself, who were homeless and living in orphanages, they need the resources.

They need the resources to do this work, because I could have been that kid crawling through somebody's window or robbing somebody, because when you don't have, you have to try to get it by any means necessary. And the only reason there was a change in my life, because there were programs and there were people and institutions that had some type of resources and a heart to try to help me.

And those people need the resources and help to continue to do that work, because all young people need a place to call home.

[The statement of Mr. Rolle follows:]

## Prepared Statement of Chris "Kazi" Rolle, Creator, Art Start's Hip-Hop Project

I was born in a little Island called Nassau in the Bahamas. My mother was a Jamaican immigrant who was trying to get to Amercia via the Bahamas , due the fact there were less obstacles for Bahamians seeking to come to United States than there were for people coming from here country.

At 6months old, my mother left me in the care of friends to venture to the United States in hopes of opportunity. She had left three kids before with my grandmother in Jamaica. She never returned for me. In 1980, the Bahamian Department of Social Services substantiated reports that I was living in an abusive situation. At four years old, I was found wandering in the streets of and was subsequently institutionalized at the Children's Emergency Hostel for orphans.

Catherine Brown, a social worker at the hostel, developed a relationship with me and in 1982, I was fostered by here and her family. The adjustment was very difficult—they said that I presented numerous behavioral problems at home and in school, as I could not understand how strangers could love me when my own mother abandoned him. Thank fully Mrs. Brown trucked on. I was officially adopted on November 4th 1988.

I still got into a lot of trouble and posed ongoing challenges. Due to lack of the proper resource to help me with my emotional issues, the family came their wits end in dealing with me. In 1990, I was placed in the Ranfurly Home for Children. While in the Ranfurly Home, I was placed in a psychiatric ward for unruly children. It was determined by the Department of Social Services that my challenges were directly related to my early childhood experiences— as a result, the American Embassy was contacted to locate my biological mother and on December 21, 1990, reunited with her in New York City, USA.

From 1990-1992, I's relationship with my biological mother was highly tumultuous. By 1992, at age 16, I found himself homeless once again, on the streets of New York City. From 1992-1994, Wherever I laid my head was my home. Gangs were my family. Warm train station was my apartment. Street Pharmaceutical Corporations became was my employers. Five discount was how I shopped for clothing. It was all bout survival. I found my self incarserated numerous time. I was on a road to nowhere. All the people who said that I wouldn't amount to nothing were being proved right.

In 1994, at age 18, I finally decided to get my life together. I enrolled in Public School Repertory Company, a "last chance" performing arts high school and I discovered that I had a passion for music and theatre, and realized the power of the arts as an outlet for healing. I wrote a play based on my life story called a Brooklyn Story.

At Public School Repertory, I connected with Art Start—an arts-based youth organization he also began writing, directing and acting for the award winning urban theater company, Tomorrow's Future. My play, A Brooklyn Story, earned me a New York Governor's Citation and a Martin Luther King, Jr. Award. In 1995, I received the CBS Fulfilling the Dream Award for my play and my work in schools and homeless shelters advocating education and drug abuse prevention.

In 1999, having personally experienced the healing power of the arts, I chose to dedicate my life to providing a similar outlet for under-served youth. I created The Hip Hop Project, an award-winning program that connects New York City teens to music industry professionals to write, produce and market their own compilation album on youth issues. The program attracted Russell Simmons and Bruce Willis, whose support contributed largely the success of the program. In 2000 I was featured on the Oprah Winfrey Show in a segment called People Who Are Using Their Lives. In 2005 he passed the torch of leadership of the Hip Hop Project one of my students, and joined the organization's Board of Trustees.

I say all of this to say that I was that kid. Homeless. No where to go. Pocket had rabbit ears. I had nothing. I was at the bottom. Rock bottom. Being homeless. Not have a family. Not having resources, influenced my choices. If no one was there to give it to me, I am going to have to take it. Steal it. Whatever. By any means necessary. You feel me?

We need more support for the programs like Art Start, Tomorrow's Future theater group, The Hip Hop Project and all of the wonderful people who take their time to help people like myself.

We also need to get the word out in a big way to caring community members, parents, and young people themselves that millions of youth experience homeless-ness in the United States each year. All of the step and extend family members who step up to the plate, they need all the support, resources and services available to assist them. These programs, families and those working to bring about awareness desperately need federal funding, cause these are expensive undertakings. Every youth in the nation deserves a place to call home.

[Additional material submitted by Mr. Rolle follows:]

Please Join Us for

# Shining the Light
## on
# Youth Homelessness

## A Reception by the National Network for Youth
### with Honorary Co-sponsors
### Congresswoman Carolyn McCarthy & Congressman Todd R. Platts

Presenting Clips from

# The Hip Hop Project*

*Proceeds from the film go to support organizations serving homeless youth.

### Kazi and a panel of homeless youth will speak

Tuesday, July 24, 2007 • 6:30 - 8:30 pm

Rayburn House Office Building • Room B369
U.S. House of Representatives

The Hip Hop Project is a feature-length documentary released this spring about Chris "Kazi" Rolle, a formerly homeless youth who created an award-winning artist development program that connects teens to music industry professionals to write, produce, and market their own music.

**Food for this event is sponsored by Youthcare, Seattle WA**

*Chairwoman McCarthy.* I thank you for that testimony. Mrs. Eggleston?


## STATEMENT OF SUE KRAHE–EGGLESTON, EXECUTIVE DIRECTOR, OUR FAMILY SERVICES

*Ms. Krahe-Eggleston.* Good afternoon.

In addition to serving as the Our Family executive director, I am also a member of the board of directors of the National Network for Youth, the nation's leading organization on youth homelessness. I am testifying on behalf of both organizations today.

Our Family delivers the full continuum of runaway and homeless youth programs, including a street outreach program, a drop-in center, a shelter and family reunification program for minor-age youth, a transitional living program for older youth and supervised apartments for homeless young families.

My agency could not offer this programming without the federal RHY funds. Arizona only appropriates a small amount of targeted money for homeless youth, but many states do nothing. The national system of support for this population is wholly reliant on federal funds. Accordingly, RHY must be reauthorized.

In addition, Congress should raise authorization and appropriation levels, both to start new programs in underserved communities, as well as provide a cost of living increase to current grantees, which have operated at the same funding levels year after year after year, despite inflation.

The causal factors for homelessness among young people in Tucson match those across the country. Our agency has supported youth in all manners of dire circumstances, and I want to give you some examples.

There is a 14-year-old boy named John, who felt safer living in a tunnel than with his abusive parents. Then, there is a 16-yearold gay young person by the name of Paul dropped off at our shelter by his mom, with his belongings in a plastic bag, saying to us, "Take him."

Then think about Angie, a young mom standing outside the hospital in Tucson with her four-pound little infant, not knowing where she was going to go. Then, lastly, there is Precious, a 21year-old mom of two, living in her car because the children's father had been incarcerated.

These are all stories of Tucson, but they could be stories of any community across our country.

Yet we also see incredible resilience in our youth, young people whose running away is an expression of their most basic right to survive, young people seeking better options, young people craving for caring adults and supportive peers for the first time, or longing to mend those old family ties.

Our Family helps youth tap their inherent strength and mobilize those assets for the youth's recovery and ultimate well-being.

Now, turning to policy considerations, my written statement includes 18 of the RHY reauthorization recommendations that the National Network of Youth has put together. They are the outcome of a consultation process we took with the grantee community.

I will mention just two. First, we recommend the act require a process for developing performance standards for RHY programs so that all grantees would work towards common performance expectations. Secondly, RHY grantees seek a process to request reconsideration of unsuccessful applications when there is a good cause.

We look forward to working with Representative Yarmuth and the subcommittee leadership in developing the RHY reauthorization bill. To complement RHY, we call on Congress to pass measures that respond to the needs of homeless youth, which surpass the scope of the RHY.

Among them, Congress should pass Representative Biggert's forthcoming Homeless Education Bill. Also, Congress should pass H.R. 601, the Homeless Student Aid Bill.

RHY programs have never intended to be the tools to end youth homelessness. The act forms the safety net for unaccompanied youth and must be continued, with increased funding. But if we are to prevent and end youth homelessness, we must go way beyond RHY.

We need more publicly funded resources for family substance abuse, mental health and strengthening of family services. We need a child welfare systems that permits youth to remain in care until they research the developmental age of adulthood, rather than the artificial legal age of majority.

We need to support reentry of youthful offenders, such as the one that Representative Grijalva will be proposing. Permanent housing targeted to youth is also required.

We are pleased to support Representative Hinojosa's forthcoming Place to Call Home Act. It contains the solutions I just identified and much, much more. It is a policy blueprint for preventing and ending youth homelessness. We call on Congress to follow its design.

Youth-serving organizations, young people and concerned community members will continue to fight for the day when there will be indeed a place to call home for all youth. Until then, the Runaway and Homeless Youth Act must remain available for the millions of young people in America each year without a safe place to live.

And I thank you.

[The statement of Ms. Krahe-Eggleston follows:]

## Prepared Statement of Sue Krahe-Eggleston, Executive Director, Our Family

### Part I—About Our Family

Sue Krahe-Eggleston is the Executive Director of Our Family, a community-based organization in Tucson, Pima County Arizona which offers services in four main areas, including youth services. Youth programs include street outreach, youth center, shelter, and transitional living for runaway and homeless youth.

### Part II—Unaccompanied Youth Primer

Runaway and homeless youth are the most vulnerable of our nation's disconnected youth. Between one million and three million U.S. youth experience an unaccompanied situation annually. Unaccompanied youth become detached from parents, guardians and other caring adults due to a combination of family and community stressors. Data specific to Pima County also point to large numbers of homeless, at-risk youth in the region, with the same causal factors and risk factors as their peers nationally.

### Part III—Runaway and Homeless Youth Act Reauthorization

The federal Runaway and Homeless Youth Act (RHYA) has established funding streams to support outreach, family reunification, shelter, and transitional living programs targeted to unaccompanied youth, all in an effort to provide a basic level of support for these vulnerable young people regardless of the state in which they are living.

Federal RHYA programs are a substantial and reliable funding stream to Our Family and other RHYA grantees. For organizations in many states, RHYA funds are the only resources available explicitly to serve unaccompanied youth. RHYA is the sole federal law targeted solely to unaccompanied youth. Without RHYA, many unaccompanied youth in communities across the nation would go completely without support.

Our Family urges Congress to reauthorize and strengthen the programs and authorities of the Runaway and Homeless Youth Act. We offer 18 recommendations for RHYA reauthorization. These recommendations were identified after an intensive consultation process with the RHYA grantee community convened by the National Network for Youth, the membership association of RHYA agencies.

## *Part IV—Beyond RHYA*

The Runaway and Homeless Youth Act, while a critical federal law that must be continued and fully funded, is no substitute for the aggressive interventions necessary to eliminate the very factors causing unaccompanied situations among millions of the nation's youth, or to respond to the resources and services needs of currently unaccompanied youth that surpass the scope and purpose of the Act. We call for action in juvenile justice, elementary and secondary education, postsecondary education, workforce investment, and other areas. We support the Place to CallHome Act.

## *Part I—About Our Family*

Our Family makes Southern Arizona a better place to live, to grow up, and to grow older with a continuum of services to people in every stage of life. Last year, more than 29,000 at-risk children, youth, families, seniors and disabled adults used our services, which include counseling, education and mediation, housing, mediationand help for people in crisis.

Our Family provides services in four main areas—counseling, education and prevention, youth services, and services to older and disabled adults.

Our youth services include:

- Teens in Transition helps homeless and near-homeless youth 13-21 stay in school and gain the skills to succeed, through case management, counseling, education and career planning, housing, and help with basic needs.
- Reunion House offers brief-stay shelter, respite and family reunification services to youth ages 12-17, including systems youth who are awaiting placement and homeless youth who want to come off the street.
- CommonUnity is a complex of safe, supervised apartments and a community of support for homeless young mothers ages 18-21 with up to two children. Life-skills classes and case management help residents break cycles of poverty and crisis and create a support network among themselves.
- Skrappy's is a drug- and alcohol-free youth center. Young people from all back-grounds participate in youth-led media arts and theater projects, dance classes, health fairs, volunteer projects and community activism, as well as concerts.
- Street Outreach goes where homeless, runaway and street youth gather and helps them come off the streets.

Of the more than 29,000 individuals who used Our Family's services last year, six percent were age 12 or under, 54 percent were 13-17, 16 percent were 18-21, 18 percent were 22-59, and 6 percent were 60 or older.

Our Family is a $4.2 million organization with 100 employees, as well as an active corps of volunteers. It is accredited by the Council on Accreditation of Services for Families and Children Inc. and licensed as a behavioral healthcare institution by the Arizona Department of Health Services. Services are available in English and Spanish.

Our Family, created in October 2005 by the merger of Family Counseling Agency and OUR TOWN, has a combined history of more than 75 years of service to the greater Tucson community.

Our Family invites Members of Congress and Congressional staff in Arizona or visiting the Tucson area to visit our agency. For more information, please visit www.ourfamilyservices.org or call (520) 323-1708.

## Part II—Unaccompanied Youth Primer

### Unaccompanied Youth Basics

Runaway and homeless youth are the most vulnerable of our nation's "disconnected" youth. We refer to these two populations collectively as "unaccompanied youth." Like other disconnected youth, unaccompanied youth experience separation from one or more of the key societal institutions of family, school, community, and the workplace. Their disconnection is accentuated by their lack of a permanent place to live, which is not only disruptive in and of itself, but also indicative of the larger socioeconomic instability they are experiencing.

Between one million and three million of our nation's youth experience an unaccompanied situation annually, according to various estimates derived from government studies and data sets. Some of these estimates do not include young adults ages 18 and older within their scope.

Unaccompanied youth become detached from parents, guardians and other caringadults—legally, economically, and emotionally—due to a combination of family and community stressors.

Family Stressors—Many of our nation's unaccompanied youth are compelled to leave their home environments prematurely due to severe family conflict, physical, sexual, or emotional abuse by an adult in the home, parental neglect, parental substance abuse, or parental mental illness. For other youth, the values and traditionswith which their families operate prescribe that the young person separate economically from the family unit upon reaching the legal age of majority or after graduation, in some cases regardless of whether the youth is actually prepared for independent adulthood. Others are expelled from the home due to parental inability to accept the sexual orientation, parenting status, mental or addictive disability, or normal adolescent behavior of their child. For still other young people, their familiesare simply too poor to continue to bear the financial burden of providing for the youth's basic needs. Others are abandoned as their parents are incarcerated. Youth in families that are experiencing homelessness may be separated from the family unit—and become homeless on their own—so that emergency shelter or domestic violence services can be secured for the remaining family members, or to squeeze most of the family into means of habitation that are too small for all of its members.

Community Stressors—State custodial systems—including child welfare, juvenile justice, mental health, addiction treatment, and developmental disabilities—which have responsibility for ensuring the safety and protection of children and youth who are not properly cared for by parents and guardians—are failing in general to accept older youth into their custody due to financial limitations and policy disincentives. Many of the young people who do come in contact with public custodial systems arenot adequately prepared for independence and residential stability during their period of custody nor provided an aftercare arrangement to support them after the custodial relationship has ended. Many of these young people have no home environment to which to return. Youth with mental illness, addiction, and other disabilities face discrimination when searching for an independent living arrangement.

Many unaccompanied youth who are psychosocially prepared for independentadulthood are not economically ready for self-sufficiency. Inadequate educational preparation, lack of employment skills, short or non-existent work histories, language barriers, and undocumented immigration status all contribute to the relegation of many youth to unemployment or to low-wage jobs—neither of which generate income sufficient for acquiring affordable housing.

Policy barriers also stand in the way of permanency for unaccompanied youth. Insome jurisdictions, youth below the age of majority are prohibited from entering into leases or other contracts on their own behalf. "One strike" laws prohibit individuals with criminal histories from residency in public and assisted housing and prohibit juvenile ex-offenders from returning to their families. And, federal, state, and local public and assisted housing programs rank young people low, if at all, among their priority populations for assistance.

Regardless of the causal factor, unaccompanied youth, when left to fend for themselves without support, experience poor health, educational, and workforce outcomes which imperil their prospects for positive adulthood. This results in their long-term dependency on or involvement in public health, social service, emergency assistance, and corrections systems.

### *Youth Homelessness in Arizona and in Pima County*

### Youth Homelessness in Arizona
According to the U.S. Department of Health and Human Services, NationalExtranet Optimized Runaway and Homeless Youth Management Information System (NEO-RHYMIS), 943 youth were involved with Runaway and Homeless Youth Act emergency (BCP) and transitional (TLP) programs in Arizona in the 2004-2005 federal fiscal year. Of this population, 67 percent were white, 6 percent were American Indian, 0.42 percent were Asian, 10 percent were African American, 0.32 percent were Native Hawaiian or other Pacific Islander, and 16 percent did not reportracial information. Within the population of those reporting ethnicity (804), 14 percent were Hispanic. 42 percent were male and 58 percent were female. Girls are more prevalent in every age group of youth except for youth under the age of 12, where there are more boys than girls. The vast majority (81 percent) of Arizona youth who receive services through a BCP or TLP in that same time period entered the program from a private residence; more than half of these youth came from the home of a parent or legal guardian. Two percent of youth came from correctional institutions, two percent came from residential programs, four percent came from other shelters, two percent came from other living situations, less than one percent came from the military, and 10 percent came from the streets. 53 percent were attending school regularly, and 3 percent had already graduated or obtained a GED. The rest were not regularly attending school. 24 youth seeking BCP or TLP services in Arizona were turned away during this time period.

### Youth Homelessness in Pima County
Data specific to Pima County also point to the large numbers of homeless, at-risk youth in our region. Pima County demonstrates a number of factors that indicate significant need for the proposed services. First, there is a high number of runaways in our county. In 2003, 3,036 runaways were reported in Pima County, accounting for 20 percent of all juvenile crime

reported. This number amounts to two percent of Pima County's total juvenile population. Second, runaways face a pervasive drug economy in our region. The county lies 70 miles from the Mexican border in a high impact drug corridor. Drugs flow across the border and are distributed nationwide. Runaway and homeless youth, always at risk for involvement in drug use and drug sales, are at an especially high risk in Pima County.

Tucson's need for Runaway and Homeless Youth services is further demonstrated by a Homeless Youth Survey administered in the spring of 2005 by the Tucson Planning Council for the Homeless Youth Committee and Arizona State University's School of Social Work. Information was gathered through 30 minute in-person and telephone interviews using an 18 page questionnaire that covered the following domains: demographics; housing and living situations; education; employment and income sources; sexual orientation, practices and risk behaviors and abuse; physical health, mental health, and substance abuse; use of, access to, and knowledge about community services, modes of transportation, social networks and personal issues; and personal/familial legal concerns. In total 458 surveys were completed. The information obtained indicates, from the youth themselves, what are the most pressing issues for Tucson's runaway and homeless youth. (Homeless in Tucson by LeCroy and Milligan, 2005.)

Homeless youth interviewed ranged from 13-18 years old and were predominantly Hispanic/Latino/a or white, heterosexual, non-married and female. The majority of youth (76 percent) lived in Tucson before becoming homeless. Over 60 percent of the youth had been homeless at least twice during their young lives, with an average 3.5 times in 2005, up from 1.92 times in 2002. Over half of the youth had spent at least one year of their life homeless and, at the time of the survey, half had been homeless for more than 180 days. The average age at which youth first became homeless was 14. Nine percent self-reported homosexuality and 7 percent reported bisexuality. The main reasons cited for leaving home the first time included running away because of problems (24 percent), being removed by Child Protective Services (21 percent), and being kicked out or told to leave the home (20 percent). Over 75 percent of the youth said they would not continue to be homeless if they had a choice.

Forty percent of the youth spent the night prior to the interview at a friend's house, 14 percent spent the night in an unstable environment (e.g., park, wash, car, street, backyard), and 13 percent spent the night at a family member's house. Notably, 10 percent of the youth did not know where they would be sleeping the night of the interview. Half of the youth (50 percent) were currently enrolled in school or some other type of educational/training program, down slightly from 2002 when 56 percent of youth surveyed were enrolled in school and/or an educational program. Of those not currently attending school, the main reasons reported were lack of a permanent address and/or difficulties with transportation.

Many of the youth had experienced significant trauma before age 18, and were still suffering its effects. 63 percent reported experiencing verbal/emotional abuse, 52 percent said they had witnessed domestic violence occur in their household, 50 percent reported witnessing drug/alcohol abuse, 44 percent reported experiencing physical abuse, 42 percent experienced neglect, and 25 percent reported being sexually abused (19 percent of females, 6 percent of males) before the age of 18. When asked whether abuse/neglect was ever a factor in their leaving home, 60 percent of the youth said yes. Alarmingly, 28 percent said that they had attempted suicide in the past, up from 19.5 percent in 2002. These statistics substantiate the tenuous, high-risk situation that faces RHY in Tucson, the risk factors they face for having unsuccessful adulthoods, and the critical nature of getting services to them.

## Our Family's Homeless Youth Profile

Data collected on homeless clients who received case management services at Our Family between 7/1/05 and 6/30/06 (n=82) reflect similar patterns to the County and the State. The average number of runaway episodes was four. The current status of youth entering the program included: 35 percent at home; 35 percent runaway; 17 percent homeless; 9 percent throwaway, 8 percent other/street. Substance use was a prevalent problem indicated at intake: 35 percent smoke cigarettes; 55 percent use beer, wine or wine coolers; 45 percent use hard liquor; 35 percent had 5 or more servings of alcohol on the same occasion; 40 percent use marijuana; 10 percent use cocaine; 10 percent use methamphetamines, 5 percent use over the counter drugs above recommended dosage; 2 percent use inhalants; 40 percent use alcohol and marijuana on the same occasion; 5 percent used two or more drugs (excluding alcohol and tobacco) on the same occasion; 30 percent have been asked to sell drugs and 12 percent have sold drugs. Approximately 30 percent of the youth said they had been physically abused by a parent or guardian. 5 percent reported being sexually abused by parents and another 12 percent reported being sexually abused by a parent's partner. Almost all of them listed emotional abuse, and 30 percent said that a household member abused alcohol or drugs. In addition 30 percent had poor grades in school, 60 percent had been charged with a misdemeanor, 5 percent with a felony, and 26 percent were depressed.

## Trends in Homeless Youth Population Observed by Our Family

Our Family's Reunion House Basic Center Program (RH) has seen double the number of youth 12-17 who are school dropouts at intake. These young people have been absent from educational services often for a semester or more and as such are a grade or two behind their peers. A number of these youth profess to have no desire to continue their education, seeing school as a useless and stressful environment.

Our Family's Teens In Transition TLP (TNT) has noted a continuing high demand from couples coming in for services where the female is significantly younger than the male. Because of the male partner's age these couples are unable to access housing options and homeless couples services targeted to underage youth. There appears to be no defined reason for this shift but it is noteworthy and provides a considerable challenge when attempting to provide housing for these individuals and their children.

Our Family's CommonUnity TLP (CUP) has continued to see increasing numbers of 22-24 year old mothers and their infant children on street who are coming in to seek services. CUP must turn these mothers away, as they are too old for the program. They are referred out to other providers who often have considerable waiting lists or are limited in their effectiveness with younger adults. Domestic and Relationship Violence issues remain prevalent, with approximately 92 percent of the young parents coming into CUP dealing with the effects of relationship and domestic violence in their lives.

The Street Outreach Program (SO) continued to see an increase in the number of youth dealing with death or loss of a parent or guardian in their lives due to substance abuse. In many cases these issues directly relate to the initial destabilization of the youth with their families.

The Homeless Youth Services at Our Family continued to see a steady increase in the numbers of Lesbian, Gay, Bisexual, and Transgender (LGBT) youth requesting services. This is due in part to increased awareness through outreach to LGBT organizations as well as establishing a positive rapport and reputation among LGBT youth. This also highlights the number of LGBT youth who run away, are kicked out, or who otherwise become homeless and need the services we offer.

CommonUnity and Teens in Transition Programs have seen increases in the number of parenting youth that have inquired about transitional/independent living services.

Tucson youth service providers also report an explosion of methamphetamine use—a trend mirrored nationally.

## Barriers Facing Pima County Homeless Youth

The Homeless Youth Committee of the Pima County, Arizona Plan to End Homelessness has identified the following major barriers that impede homeless youth in their transition back to permanent housing and to successful adulthoods. (Plan to End Homelessness, Pima County, Arizona, Spring 2006.)

- While Tucson's youth services are extensive, they are not enough to meet these needs. Homeless youth ages 18 through 24 have few, if any, emergency and transitional housing options. Whether they are "legally" adults (i.e. over 18) or not, Pima County homeless youth are at best uncomfortable, and at worst subject to victimization, in adult shelters or service environments.
- Youth of all ages have almost no affordable addiction treatment options: in part because there is little funding to serve them, in part because agencies which do offer youth treatment are oversubscribed, and in part because youth simply do not feel comfortable engaging in therapeutic environments with older adults.
- LGBT youth, many of whom have already been victimized, have no dedicated, safe emergency or transitional housing alternatives.
- And all youth making a transition to independence need serious—and now seriously underfunded—life and job skills training, adequate housing, and often counseling.

Our Family has identified the following additional barriers, based on our observation of the daily struggles of our residents and program participants:

- Some homeless youth and young adults are unable to access HUD-funded homeless assistance services because their homeless living arrangement, usually "couch surfing," does not qualify as "homeless" under the HUD definition.
- Many of our participants are unable to pursue the postsecondary education and training they desire—and that is imperative to move them to high-wage employment in high-growth sectors—because they must forego education in order to maintain employment, which is their sole source of income.
- Homeless young families expend considerable resources on childcare; subsidized child care slots are precious in our community.
- Permanent housing to which our youth may transition is in short supply. Youth and young adults are low on priority lists, or even the community's radar screen as a subpopulation in need of housing assistance.
- Youth access to mental health services is a major challenge; there is simply insufficient publicly funded mental health treatment and support options for adolescents and for adults.

- Reentry of youth offenders into the community is uneven, and certainly far behind in program development compared to the system of support for transitioning foster youth.

## Runaway and Homeless Youth Act Program Basics

The federal government, through the Runaway and Homeless Youth Act (RHYA) has established funding streams to support outreach, family reunification, shelter, and transitional living programs targeted to unaccompanied youth, all in an effort to provide a basic level of support for these vulnerable young people regardless of the state in which they are living. RHYA programs have the purposes of preventing victimization and ensuring basic safety of unaccompanied youth and ensuring their access to family reunification, housing, education, employment training, health care, and other social services.

The RHYA Basic Center Program (BCP) provides grants to community-based, faith-based, and public organizations to support family strengthening efforts, including counseling, home-based services for families with children at risk of separation from the family, and emergency and respite shelter (no greater than 15 days) for youth under the age of 18.

The RHYA Transitional Living Program (TLP) provides competitive grants to community-based, faith-based, and public organizations to support longer-term residential services (up to 18 months) and life skill supports to youth ages 16 through 21 who are unable to return home safely. TLPs assist youth in successfully transitioning into responsible adulthood and self-sufficiency and connecting them to education, workforce, and other supports. This program includes maternity group homes, which are residential arrangements for pregnant and parenting youth who are fleeing from abusive homes. Maternity group homes assist these youth in accessing housing, prenatal care, parenting classes, child care, and educational services.

The RHYA Street Outreach Program (SOP) provides competitive grants to community-based and faith-based organizations to support street-based outreach and education to homeless children and youth who have been sexually abused or who are at risk of commercial sexual exploitation.

RHYA basic centers and transitional living projects serve nearly 50,000 youth in all 50 states. RHYA street outreach projects make over 2.3 million contacts with youth annually.

The Runaway and Homeless Youth Act also authorizes funds for the National Runaway Switchboard, a national communications system for runaway youth and their families; regional training and technical assistance for grantees; an information clearinghouse; a management information system; research and evaluation; and peer monitoring of grantees.

Congress first enacted the Runaway and Homeless Youth Act in 1974 as Title III of the Juvenile Justice and Delinquency Prevention Act. It was most recently reauthorized in 2003. RHYA programs are administered by the Family and Youth Services Bureau within the U.S. Department of Health and Human Services (HHS).

## Part III—Runaway and Homeless Youth Act Reauthorization

## Need for the Runaway and Homeless Youth Act

Federal RHYA programs are a substantial and reliable funding stream to Our Family and other RHYA grantees. For organizations in many states, RHYA funds are the only resources available to serve unaccompanied youth explicitly. More important, they are the sole federal programs targeted to unaccompanied youth. Without RHYA, many unaccompanied youth in communities across the nation would go completely without support.

More RHYA Capacity is Needed across the Nation. The basic living needs of too many of our nation's unaccompanied youth are not being met through state and local child welfare systems or permanent housing and homeless assistance programs. Furthermore, few states have established funding streams targeted to unaccompanied youth. RHYA basic center and transitional living projects served approximately 55,000 youth in FY 2005, yet estimates of the U.S. unaccompanied youth population are one million at minimum, suggesting that at least approximately 950,000 of the nation's unaccompanied youth are not able to access RHYA services.

## Effectiveness of the Runaway and Homeless Youth Act

RHYA Projects are Cost Effective Alternatives to Custodial Care and Arrest. The average cost of serving a youth in a transitional living project of $11,877 is less than half the minimum cost of serving youth through the child welfare or juvenile justice systems; with annual costs ranging from $25,000—$55,000 per youth depending on the state. Law enforcement officials are the referral source for 20 percent of youth entering basic centers.

RHYA Projects Use Federal Funds to Leverage Community Resources. RHYA projects succeed due to partnerships created among families, schools, community-based organizations, faith communities, law enforcement agencies, businesses and volunteers.

RHYA Projects Raise the Achievement Level of Unaccompanied Youth. The last federally-funded evaluations of the Basic Center Program and the Transitional Living Program found that they produced positive outcomes for participating youth in the following areas:

## Family Strengthening

- Basic center youth reported lessened rates of family conflict and parental physical abuse.
- Transitional living youth reported that the program helped them better manage communication and maintain positive relationships with their families.

## Education

- School participation among basic center youth doubled after basic center services commenced, compared to the participation rate 30 days prior to accessing a basic center.
- The proportion of youth in transitional living projects attending college was three times that of homeless youth who were not in a TLP.

## Employment

- Employment rates of youth in basic centers increased by 24 percent.

- 60 percent of transitional living youth were employed part-time or full-time, compared to 41 percent of homeless youth not participating in a TLP.

### *Runaway and Homeless Youth Act Reauthorization Recommendations*

The Runaway and Homeless Youth Act is scheduled to sunset in 2008 and merits extension. In addition, new issues affecting unaccompanied youth and unaccompanied youth service providers have emerged that require a Congressional response. Our Family urges Congress to reauthorize and strengthen the programs and authorities of the Runaway and Homeless Youth Act in a timely manner. We offer the following recommendations for RHYA reauthorization. These recommendations were identified after an intensive consultation process with the RHYA grantee community.

### Funding

1. Reauthorize and increase authorization levels for Runaway and Homeless Youth Act programs. The runaway and homeless youth consolidated account should be authorized at the $200 million level in FY 2009 and "such sums as may be necessary" in each of FY 2010 through FY 2013. The runaway prevention account should be authorized at the $30 million level in FY 2009 and "such sums as may be necessary" in each of FY 2010 through FY 2013.

   Funding levels for RHYA programs are inadequate for meeting the need for such services. With estimates of unaccompanied youth at the low-end of one million, and the RHYA basic center and transitional living programs reaching only 55,000 youth annual, at least 900,000 of the nation's unaccompanied youth do not have access to the supports and services that RHYA programs offer. For these unserved youth, their unaccompanied episodes are prolonged; they are at heightened risk of victimization, poor health, school failure, and unemployment; and they are thwarted from attaining safe, productive, and healthy adulthoods.

2. Increase the RHYA Basic Center Program allotments for small states and for territories. The minimum BCP allotment for states with small youth populations should be increased to $200,000. The maximum BCP allotment for U.S. territories should be increased to at least $100,000.

   BCP formula allotments to states with small youth populations are limited to $100,000. This amount makes it difficult for HHS to fund more than one basic center in each such state, even though the geographic swath of many such states tends to be wide. BCP allotments to territories are limited to $40,000. This amount is hardly enough to act even as seed money for basic centers in territories to leverage non-RHYA funds.

3. Permit HHS to redistribute unexpended BCP funds to other BCP applicants for a one-year grant period, after which time the amount should be returned to the BCP general pool for re-allocation. RHYA grantees and applicants would benefit from greater transparency and standardization in the manner in which HHS reallocates "unrequested" BCP allotments from states lacking applicants to "excess" BCP applicants from states with qualified applicants requesting a total of funds that exceed the state's allotment.

## RHYA Project Admission and Length of Stay Criteria

4. Limit basic centers to providing shelter services to individuals who are less than 18 years of age, with an exception that basic centers located in states with child-caring facility licensure laws that permit a higher age may serve up to the age permitted by the state law. RHYA grantees and applicants would benefit from clarification on the maximum age of youth permitted to receive emergency shelter through a basic center. The current RHYA permits basic centers to provide emergency shelter to youth "not more than 18 years of age," which some interpret to mean ages 17 and under and others interpret to mean through age 18. To resolve confusion in the field, we recommend that the maximum age for emergency shelter services through a BCP be extended to youth "who are less than 18 years of age," which is in alignment with the maximum age used in the formula for allocating BCP funds. However, grantees should be given the discretion to serve youth over age 17 if the child-caring facility licensure law in which the basic center is located permits a higher age.

5. Allow extensions in length of stay in basic centers from 14 days to up to 30 days and in transitional living projects from 18 months through 24 months, on a case-by-case basis, provided that the state child-caring facility licensure law applicable to the basic center permits a longer length of stay. RHYA grantees report difficulty in ensuring safe exists for some of their program participants within the timeframes required by current law. The grantees then find themselves in the situation of either keeping the participant at the basic center or transitional living project with other than federal funds, or triggering an unsafe exit by the youth. Providing grantees limited flexibility to keep some of their participants in service beyond the target exit period would allow a greater level of individualized support for those unaccompanied youth at greatest risk of unsafe program exits.

## RHYA Applicant Eligibility, Use of Funds, and Funding Conditions

6. Add public entities as eligible applicants for Street Outreach Program funds. Eligibility for the Street Outreach Program (SOP) is limited to private nonprofit organizations, whereas public organizations as well as private nonprofit organizations may apply for BCP and TLP funds. Extending SOP eligibility to public organizations would provide public entities receiving either BCP and/or TLP funds the opportunity to build a longer continuum of RHYA services by also competing for SOP funds.

7. Clarify that RHYA funds are to be distributed to organizations and not directly to program participants. The President's FY 2007 budget request included a proposal to reserve a portion of Transitional Living Program (TLP) funds for vouchers directly to participants to purchase maternity group home services on their own. Appropriations Committees in both chambers the 109th Congress, in consultation with their authorization committee counterparts, concluded that a voucher arrangement was neither contemplated by the statute nor in the best interest of either the pregnant and parenting youth or unaccompanied youth service providers. Accordingly, the committees rejected the proposal in report language to accompany the FY 2007 Labor-HHS-Education appropriations bills. Current law should be amended to clarify

that RHYA funds are to be made available for distribution to organizations and not directly to program participants.

8. Allow transitional living projects to use RHYA funds for facility renovation. Renovation costs should not exceed 15 percent of the total first-year award. The current RHYA permits use of BCP funds for facility renovation, but does not permit TLP funds to be used for facility renovation. A parallel use of funds for renovation should be extended to TLP grantees.

9. Require basic centers and transitional living projects to have in place written emergency management and crisis response plans as a condition for receiving federal RHYA awards. Hurricanes Katrina and Rita focused national attention on the need to ensure more effective responses to emergencies and crises, including by congregate care providers. The 109th Congress recently amended the Older Americans Act and the Promoting Safe and Stable Families Act to ensure that federally-funded congregate care providers funded through these programs have emergency management and crisis plans in place. A parallel requirement should be established for RHYA basic centers and transitional living projects.

## Federal Program Management

10. Require HHS to develop performance standards for RHYA direct service grantees. The HHS Secretary shall provide an opportunity for public comment on the performance standards. At one time, HHS had developed program performance standards for basic centers, and was in process of developing program performance standards for TLP and SOP grantees. These standards provided guidance to grantees on the minimum expectations of program performance. HHS has suspended standards development or activation lacking clear instruction in the RHYA statute to support them.

11. Require HHS to develop a process for accepting and considering appeals for reconsideration from unsuccessful RHYA applicants. The HHS Secretary shall provide an opportunity for public comment on the appeals process. The RHYA statute does not prescribe, and HHS has not established, an orderly process for accepting or considering appeals for reconsideration from unsuccessful RHYA applicants. Lack of a formal process has led to lack of transparency whether or how reconsiderations are made.

12. Add a finding on the applicability of positive youth development to the organization and delivery of services to unaccompanied youth. Inclusion of a finding on positive youth development in the RHYA statute is important for encouraging grantees to apply youth development principles to the development and implementation of their projects.

13. Add a statutory definition of "runaway youth" identical to the definition of such term in the Code of Federal Regulations. The RHYA statute does not include a definition of "runaway youth." However that term is defined in the Code of Federal Regulations (45 CFR 1351.1) as "a person under 18 years of age who absents himself or herself from home or place of legal residence without the permission of his or her family." For the convenience of policymakers, RHYA grantees, and the general

public, the current regulatory definition of "runaway youth" should be inserted into statute.

## National Activities

14. Require HHS to develop each fifth year, directly or via contract, a national estimate of the prevalence of unaccompanied situations among youth and young adults. The nation lacks a single, reliable source of data on the prevalence of unaccompanied situations among youth. The dearth of data impairs federal, state, and local public policy decision-making, community needs assessment, service organization and delivery, and performance measurement.

15. Require HHS to establish research, evaluation, and demonstration priorities each two years and to provide an opportunity for public comment on such priorities. The RHYA grants HHS authority to make grants for research, evaluation, demonstration and service projects. RHYA grantees, youth, advocates, and other stakeholders have limited to no input into the identification or prioritization of issues to be studied or evaluated.

16. Require HHS to conduct, directly or via contract, a study demonstrating the economic and social benefit of providing emergency housing, transitional housing, permanent housing and supportive services to unaccompanied youth, and the extent to which that housing and services offsets the costs of allowing such conditions to persist for young people. While it is intuitive that interventions which resolve unaccompanied situations among youth are more cost-effective to the public in the long-term than ignoring the problem, there is yet to be conducted an authoritative cost-benefit analysis to "prove" this assertion. A cost-benefit study would be instructive to policymakers about the type and level of investments in health and human needs programs for children, youth, and families.

17. Authorize HHS to conduct, directly or via contract, a public information campaign to raise awareness of the unaccompanied youth population and their service and support needs. Unaccompanied youth are a largely invisible or misunderstoodpopulation. Lack of public awareness of this group of young people, their life circumstances, and the interventions available to support them and end their homeless situations, allows homelessness to persist among the nation's youth.

18. Amend the Higher Education Act to authorize forgiveness of educational loans for workers in RHYA grantees with at least five consecutive years of service. Nonprofit and public organizations supporting unaccompanied youth face a number ofworkforce challenges, including difficulty recruiting and retaining employees for long terms of service, compensating employees at competitive wages, and attracting employees with postsecondary education. Student loan forgiveness is a strategy that has been deployed with success in other sectors to recruit and retain workers in shortage occupations and should be extended to the unaccompanied youth service sector.

### PART IV—Beyond RHYA

The Runaway and Homeless Youth Act, while a critical federal law that must be continued and fully funded, is no substitute for the aggressive health and human needs interventions necessary to eliminate the very factors causing unaccompanied situations among millions of the nation's youth, or to respond to the resources and services needs of currently unaccompanied youth that surpass the scope and purpose of the Runaway and Homeless Youth Act. A comprehensive response to the causal factors of and ultimate solutions to unaccompanied situations among youth is required. We call the Education and Labor Committee's attention to a number of opportunities beyond RHYA reauthorization within its jurisdiction where decisive impact could be made for unaccompanied youth.

### Juvenile Justice

There is a clear intersection between the juvenile justice system and youth homelessness, in terms of both youth entry into the system due to their homeless and youth exit from the system into homelessness. We urge the Committee to use the reauthorization of the Juvenile Justice and Delinquency Prevention Act to break the connection between juvenile justice and youth homelessness. We call for repeal of the valid court order exception to the JJDPA deinstitutionalization of status offenders requirement. We also call for the establishment of a youth offender reentry grants program.

### Elementary and Secondary Education

Youth experiencing homelessness encounter difficulties enrolling in and attending School. These barriers include legal guardianship requirements, residency requirements, lack of necessary immunization, academic, or other records, and inadequate transportation to their schools of origin from their temporary living arrangements. As a result, many homeless young people struggle in obtaining education, or fall out of the educational system altogether. Congress has responded to the educational needs of homeless children and youth by establishing laws and a grant program (the EHCY program) which ensure that children and youth experiencing homelessness shall have a right to enroll, attend, and succeed in school. We urge Congress to reauthorize and strengthen the Education for Homeless Children and Youth program during No Child Left Behind reauthorization.

### Postsecondary Education

Postsecondary education offers students experiencing homelessness and others hope for escaping poverty as adults. The Higher Education Act has the potential to assist disconnected youth to graduate from high school, apply for and access postsecondary education, and complete their degrees—if they can access the network of HEA programs and services. The most basic access barrier facing homeless students is the very ability to apply for student financial assistance. We Urge Congress to approve the FAFSA Fix for Homeless Kids Act (H.R. 601, Biggert), legislation that would allow youth to be considered independent students for purposes of applying for financial aid (the Federal Application for Federal Student Aid) if they have been verified as an unaccompanied homeless youth by a school district homeless liaison, shelter director, or financial aid administrator.

We also encourage the establishment of a supportive services program for disconnected postsecondary students and the establishment of a grant program to colleges and universities so that they may assist homeless students in retaining campus or off-site housing during periods when the institutions are closed.

## Workforce Investment

Income is a necessary tool which unaccompanied youth must possess in order for them to pay for housing and thus exit homelessness. Workforce services for youth entail far more than job readiness training and job placement. Because of their developmental stage, youth require comprehensive, intensive employment and training programs that involve the following: job skill training, including classroom training, on-the-job training, and apprenticeships; training in life skills and work-related values; exploration of life options, including career paths that are non-traditional for a youth's gender, race, culture and/or social class; meaningful connections between youth and their peers, adults, and communities; opportunities for youth to assume leadership roles and develop responsibility, self-reliance, initiative and the desire and ability to participate in decisions affecting their lives; opportunities that take into account the life circumstances of youth, such as housing, health, and transportation; and connections to postsecondary education and training opportunities. Like other systems, unaccompanied youth are experiencing difficulty accessing workforce services in their communities. We urge the Committee to use the reauthorization of the Workforce Investment Act to help connect unaccompanied youth to the workforce. We ask that runaway and homeless youth organizations be added as members of local Youth Councils. We also call for an assurance that Youth Councils permit unaccompanied youth to participate in workforce services without parental consent.

## Place to Call Home Act

In February 2007, the National Network for Youth announced a long-term campaign to end youth homelessness. A Place to Call Home: The National Network for Youth's Permanency Plan for Unaccompanied Youth. Our Family supports the Place to Call Home Campaign.

The signature public policy component of the campaign is the Place to Call Home Act, comprehensive legislation to prevent, respond to, and end runaway and homeless situations among youth. The bill includes provisions in the homeless assistance, housing, child welfare, juvenile justice, public health, education, workforce investment, teen parenting, and immigration areas. Representative Rube´n Hinojosa (DTX) will introduce the bill imminently. We encourage Members of Congress to join as original co-sponsors to the Place to Call Home Act.

*Chairwoman McCarthy*. Thank you very much.

Mr. Booker?


# STATEMENT OF RUSTY BOOKER, FORMERLY HOMELESS YOUTH

*Mr. Booker*. Hi. My name is Rusty Booker. I am 17. I was born and raised in Louisville, Kentucky. I just want to thank all of you for giving me an opportunity to share my story with you.

I was born to a mom, 17. Living with my mom and stepfather was difficult. My stepfather came home every night drunk and would beat my mom. My brother and I didn't sleep well, not knowing if we would be next.

At age 8, my parents finally divorced, and my mom started drinking. She never laid a hand on my brother and I. Drinking was her way of forgetting the past.

I was sent with my stepfather and his wife at age 9. The abuse soon started afterwards. My brother soon came afterwards. I was placed in foster care and then, very quickly and unbelievably, back with my stepfather.

Months after I was placed back with my stepfather, I started sending letters to my previous foster family from an abandoned house's mailbox, so my stepparents wouldn't know. A month or so after the letters, I built the courage to run.

I contacted my previous foster family, and they told me to look for a Safe Place instead of going back home. I went to a library that had a Safe Place sign on the front. I was 12 at the time, and until that day didn't know what Safe Place was but glad that there was a public place, like the library, where I could get help.

They took me to the YMCA Safe Place Services shelter in Louisville. When I got to the shelter, the staff welcomed me. I felt safe for the first time in many years.

They did an intake, provided me clothes, hygiene products and clean linens. The next morning, I had a warm breakfast and I met with a caseworker who would change my life forever, Mr. Bill.

When we talked, at first I had a hard time connecting with him and getting solutions, but it wasn't long before I was sharing my life story with him. The shelter determined that going home was not going to be possible, and I understood.

Within 2 weeks, they arranged for me to be placed in a foster home with a loving family. But I still had problems, and over the next several years I was placed in psychiatric hospitals and along with that came therapy and meds.

Then came another foster home, group homes, even jail. I started using drugs. And, after witnessing my friend get shot in a deal gone bad, I thought to myself, "Nobody asked me what I wanted." I felt like I was to blame, and powerless to change my life. I had no family, no home and, at this rate, no future.

After another failed foster home, I went to Safe Place again and asked for help. I knew the shelter was there for me. Again I felt safe and understood. I met with Ms. Missy and told her everything that I had been through. She didn't judge me or laugh at me. She understood me and made me feel wanted.

The next day I met Mr. Quan, a man with a story for every lesson he learned that I needed to learn or had already but in a rougher way. He, too, understood me. He has taught me very many ways of how to not let little things get blown way out of proportion.

And then there is Mr. Bill. When I met with him again after several years, I gave him a hug. I felt so relieved to see someone I knew that really cared about me and loved me more than anyone I knew at the time.

I am not really going to put his business out on Front Street, but I will say that he has been through a huge amount of things that other kids and myself can relate to.

Mr. Bill, Ms. Missy and Mr. Quan and the other wonderful and amazing staff at Safe Place Services are keeping me drug-and alcohol-free. I don't know the last time I have felt this good about myself.

To some, these people I mentioned may just be ordinary people, but to me and 600 other kids a year in Louisville, these people are heroes. Mr. Bill even gave up his vacation to bring me to D.C. so I could testify.

There are 14 kids at the Safe Place Services right now who have experienced many of the same things that I have. I would like to be able to convince kids that Safe Place is a first step to getting help and the shelter is a place where they can feel safe and begin to solve their problems.

Many times, when I was younger, I wanted to run for help, but when I was in a rural area there weren't many places to go. Louisville is a smaller city, compared to here in D.C. or L.A. or even Atlanta.

Kids all around the country, thousands of kids, feel like I did. No one understands them, and they need a place to turn. I hope that they, too, will be able to get to find a Safe Place site, get to a shelter, feel safe and have a bed, a warm meal and someone to talk to instead of roaming the streets or bumming money.

I am asking for your help to make a difference for kids just like me, because every kid deserves a second chance. I plan to finish my GED and plan to go to college and get a degree in law enforcement.

Thank you for letting me share the experiences I have had. I know I am headed in the right direction. I used to always ask myself, "Why me?" Maybe this is why. Maybe what I have been through can make a difference for someone else. I hope you will make it possible for kids like me to have these programs in their city.

Thank you.

[The statement of Mr. Booker follows:]

## Prepared Statement of Rusty Booker, Formerly Homeless Youth

My name is Rusty Booker. I'm 17 years old. I was born and raised in Louisville, KY. I just want to thank all of you for giving me an opportunity to share the story of my life with you.

My life was never easy. I was born to a mom of 17. Living with my mother and stepfather was so difficult. My stepfather came home every night, got drunk andbeat my mom. My brother and I didn't sleep well not knowing if we would be next. At age eight my parents divorced and my mom started drinking. She never laid a hand on my brother and me. Drinking was her way of forgetting the past. I was sent to live with my stepfather and his wife at age nine. The abuse started then. Belts, ping pong paddles, even his hand all against flesh. I wouldn't be able to sit while my bottom and legs were marked with bruises. My brother soon came afterwards. I was placed in foster care and then back with my stepfather. Months after I was placed back with my stepfather. I started sending letters to my previous foster family from an abandoned house's mailbox so my stepparents wouldn't know. A month or so after the letters, I had built the courage to run.

I contacted my previous foster family and they told me to look for a Safe Place instead of going back home. I went to a library that had a Safe Place sign on the front. I was 12 at the time and until that day didn't know what Safe Place was but was glad that there was a place like the library where I could get help. They took me to the YMCA Safe Place Services shelter in Louisville. When I got to the shelter the staff welcomed me. I felt safe for the first time in many years. They did an intake and got me clothes, hygiene products and clean linens. The next morning I had a warm breakfast and it was good. I met with a caseworker who would change my life forever—Mr. Bill. When we talked, at first I had a hard time connecting with him and getting solutions, but it wasn't long before I was sharing my life's story with him.

The shelter determined that going home was not going to be possible and I understood. Within two weeks, they arranged for me to be placed in a foster home with a loving family. But I still had problems and over the next several years, I was placed in a psychiatric hospital and along with that came therapy and meds. Then came another foster home, group homes, even jail. I started using drugs and after witnessing my friend getting shot because of drugs, I thought to myself, nobody asked me what I wanted. I felt like I was to blame and was powerless to change my life. I had no family, no home and at this rate, no future. After another failed foster home, I went to Safe Place again and asked for help.

I knew the shelter was there for me. Again I felt safe and understood. I met with Ms. Missy and told her everything that I had been through. She didn't judge me or laugh at me. She understood me and made me feel wanted. The next day I met Mr. Quan, a man with a story for every lesson he learned that I needed to learn or had already but in a rougher way. He too, understood me. He has taught me verymany ways of how to not let little things get blown way out of proportion. And then there is Mr. Bill. When I saw him again after several years, I gave him a hug. I felt so relieved to see someone I knew that really cared about me and loved me more than anyone I know. I'm not really going to put his business out to the public, but I will say that he has been through a huge amount of things that other kids and me can relate to. Bill, Ms. Missy and Mr. Quan and the other wonderful and amazing staff at Safe Place Services are keeping me drug and alcohol free. I don't know the last time I have felt this good about myself.

To some, these people I mentioned may just be ordinary people, but to me and six hundred other kids a year in Louisville, these people are heroes. Mr. Bill even gave up his vacation to bring me to DC so I could testify today.

There are 14 kids at the Safe Place Services right now who have experienced many of the same things that I have. I would like to be able to convince kids that Safe Place is a first step to get help and the shelter is a place where they can feel safe and begin to solve their problems. Many times when I was younger, I wanted to run for help, but when I was in a rural area there weren't many places to go. Louisville is a smaller city compared to here in DC or LA or even Atlanta. Kids all around the country, thousands of kids, feel like I did. No one understands them and they need a place to turn. I hope that they, too, will be able to get to find Safe Place sites to get to a shelter, feel safe, and have a bed, food, someone to talk to instead of roaming the streets, bumming money or doing anything just to survive.

I'm asking for your help to make a difference for kids just like me, because every kid deserves a second chance. I plan to finish my GED and plan to go to college and get a degree in law enforcement. Thank you for letting me share the experiences I have had. I know I'm headed in the right direction. I used to always ask myself "Why me?" Maybe this is why. Maybe what I have been through can make a difference for someone else. I hope you will make it possible for kids like me to have these programs in their city.

[Additional material submitted by Mr. Booker follows:]

## NATIONAL SAFE PLACE

Safe Place offers the first step to help for any young person at risk of abuse, neglect or serious problems. The testimony presented by Rusty Booker to the US House of Representatives, Healthy Families and Communities subcommittee of the Labor and Education Committee addressing Runaway and Homeless Youth issues represents just one young man who was the victim of serious circumstances and made the decision to ask for help. His courage and determination to alter the path on which he was headed represents that of many other young people. More than 205,000 youth have also made the decision to seek help at a Safe Place location or contacted a youth shelter agency after learning about Safe Place at their school.

Businesses and community buildings such as fire stations and libraries are designated as "Safe Place" sites. Any youth in crisis can walk into one of the nearly 16,000 Safe Places across the country and ask an employee for help. These locations display the yellow, diamond-shaped Safe Place sign on their location. Inside, employees are trained and prepared to assist any young person asking for help. Youth who go to a Safe Place location are quickly connected to the nearby youth shelter. The shelter then provides the counseling and support necessary to reunify family members and develop a plan to address the issues presented by the youth and family.

In addition to providing youth in crisis immediate access to help and safety at community locations, the visibility of Safe Place signs makes the community more aware of some of the issues that young people experience. As consumers enter their neighborhood market or convenience store, the Safe Place sign is a constant reminder that keeping young people safe is everyone's responsibility. Safe Place provides an opportunity for the entire community to get involved in helping to solve some of the serious issues that face young people and getting their life back on track. According to Suzanne Quinlan, Human Resources Director for Louisville area Dairy Queen corporate stores, "You could not pay us enough to take down the Safe Place sign. Even if we only get one child, it is important that both kids and parents can easily find Safe Places."

The success of Safe Place is based on public/private collaborations between businesses, school systems, fire departments, law enforcement, and a network of volunteers. An estimated 250,000 employees at Safe Place locations nationally are trained and ready to help a child or teen. Transit systems in 45 cities designate their buses as mobile Safe Place sites. When a youth boards a bus asking for help, the driver contacts the dispatch office and a trained supervisor is immediately sent to transport the youth to the shelter.

National Safe Place, headquartered in Louisville, KY provides youth shelters across the nation with the infrastructure, materials and training to establish and maintain a Safe Place program. Agencies operating Safe Place receive all of the tools for successful implementation. National corporations such as Sprint, Southwest Airlines, and CSX partner with National Safe Place to offer support benefiting youth in Safe Place communities through cause marketing campaigns, awareness and education initiatives and in-kind contributions.

National Safe Place currently partners with 140 shelters in 40 states. An equal number of runaway youth shelters could establish the program, but have not because of limited resources. Safe Place expands the reach of youth shelters, offering additional front doors in the community where a youth can get help in his or her own neighborhood. Often young people must quickly run from a dangerous or threatening situation. Having a Safe Place nearby makes it possible for them to do so.

Safe Place is a proven, nationally recognized program. Its success is contingent upon each generation of young people understanding that the Safe Place sign is a symbol of immediate help and safety and that seeking help is a better resolution to their crisis than running. Efforts must be made to bring Safe Place to the 10 states where it is not available and to incorporate this outreach program within more shelters. Safe Place is a cost-effective initiative. Businesses and public organizations are willing to support the program to foster the safety of young people and the community. Safe Place also empowers young people to seek help earlier in their crisis before it escalates; thus it is easier for shelter staffs to affect a positive resolution in a shorter period of time. In many instances, it eliminates inappropriate placements in the juvenile justice or other such systems, saving tax payer dollars.

Rusty Booker testified on behalf of other runaway and homeless youth in similar situations. We must make an effort to raise the awareness of the services provided by runaway and homeless youth shelters. Safe Place does that. An investment of resources for Safe Place will benefit many other young people like Rusty.

*Chairwoman McCarthy.* Thank you, Rusty.

Mr. Berg?

## STATEMENT OF STEVEN R. BERG, VICE PRESIDENT FOR PROGRAMS AND POLICY, NATIONAL ALLIANCE TO END HOME LESSNESS

*Mr. Berg.* Thank you, Madam Chair. Thank you.

I would like just start by saying thank you for holding this hearing. I know every person who is on this panel who has done specific things to move this issue forward, move the issue of homelessness forward. And we are grateful for that and for what so many other members of Congress have done.

I am here to talk a little bit about some of the research numbers about this problem. We have submitted our written testimony, which I would refer people to. Part of that is a bibliography which makes a pretty good reading list for people who want to dip into the issue even further.

Let me just make a few quick points here, by way of summary. The first point, it is a couple of bad news and a couple pieces of good news.

The first piece of bad news is this is a sizable problem. I mean, the number you recited, 1.6 million people, young people, every year, this does not include people who are staying with relatives or staying with friends. It is young people who are in shelters, who are on the streets or who are staying temporarily with strangers in often dire circumstances.

A striking finding of the research is that for more than half of these young people, no one was looking for them while they were going through this experience. There were not people making police reports or posting things. They were on their own, in many cases, abandoned by families or what supports they had.

And the other thing is substantially fewer than half were in shelters during these experiences. The rest, a small number of the 1.6 million, was living with strangers. For the most part, young people were surviving on the streets. They were surviving in abandoned buildings. They were surviving outside.

The second piece of bad, but mixed, news is that many of the young people how have these experiences, there are mixed and complex and difficult histories. Severe conflict within the family is a near-universal experience. Also prevalent are issues of abuse and neglect, issues of abandonment, issues of substance abuse, more often with the parents than with young people. Issues of mental health and poverty is a common occurrence.

The involvement with the juvenile justice system is very common. The involvement with the child welfare system is very common. These add up to the fact that prevention of homelessness for young people, while extremely important and, the research shows, doable, is difficult.

The good news, and I hope you take this from the hearing and the witnesses that have preceded me, is that young people are resilient. They go through these experiences, but the research shows what many people who work in the field know from experience, which is that despite incredible hardship and incredible experiences, people, when they are given the chance, do recover from the trauma and do go on to lead very useful and, indeed, in many cases, exemplary lives.

The other piece of good news is we have a pretty clear idea of what the interventions are that bring about those good results. We could always have more on this, and one of the probably areas where there is more research needed is sort of individual rigorous evaluations of individual program models.

But, from the research that exists, we see that a stable residence, a connection and attachment to a caring adult and the supportive services that build on the strength of these young people and that address the problems that they have get good results. So sort of programmatically, we are aware of the answers and we can put them into place.

The final point I would like to make, and the research bears this out, is the urgency of this question. I think sometimes in this day and age we are all a little too used to the idea of homelessness and have lost, to some extent, the idea that homelessness for anyone is an immediate and crucial problem that needs to be dealt with as a crisis, an individual emergency in each case.

I think certainly for young people this is the case. I think the stories you hear will back this up. What I can say about the research is, the longer young people stay homeless, the worse their troubles get.

Every night is an additional risk of drug abuse and addiction, of being the victims of crime or of turning to crime, of sexual abuse, of physical abuse. Every night that young people stay homeless increases the risk of deteriorating mental health conditions, higher risks of suicide, the longer people stay homeless.

These are young people who are in grave danger. But, on the other hand, every night, young people are moved from the streets into programs that prevent those dire consequences from happening. We know what the programs are. We have good federal policies in place.

We will be working with the committee staff to make them even better through reauthorization, but the main point is we need to get behind these programs and make sure they are funded and available to everyone.

Thank you.

[The statement of Mr. Berg follows:]

## Prepared Statement of Steven R. Berg, Vice President for Programs and Policy, National Alliance to End Homelessness

Thank you, Chairwoman McCarthy, Ranking Member Platts, and the honorable members of this subcommittee on behalf of our Board of Directors and partner members for providing this opportunity to address the subcommittee on research findings concerning youth homelessness in the United States. I would like to start by congratulating this subcommittee on its important work in addressing the need of homeless and other vulnerable youth in our nation. The National Alliance to End Homelessness believes that ending youth homelessness is well within our reach. The population is small enough for our collective effort to eradicate this social crisis among our states.

The National Alliance to End Homelessness is a nonpartisan, nonprofit organization that was founded in 1983 by a group of leaders deeply disturbed by the appearance of thousands of Americans living on the streets of our nation. We have committed ourselves to finding permanent solutions to homelessness. Our bipartisan Board of Directors and our 5,000 nonprofit, faith-based, private and public sector partners across the country devote ourselves to the affordable housing, access to services, and livable incomes that will end homelessness. The Alliance is recognizedfor its organization and dissemination of evidence-based research to encourage best practices and high standards in the field of homelessness prevention and intervention and we wish to share our insights with you today.

As our name implies, our primary focus is ending homelessness, not simply making it easier to live with. We take this idea very seriously. There is nothing inevitable about youth homelessness in the United States. We know more about youthhomelessness and how to address it than we ever have before, thanks in part to extensive research. We know a great deal about the pathways into homelessness for youth, the characteristics of youth who experience homelessness, and interventions and program models which are effective in offering youth reconnection to family, community, and stable housing.

We have been asked today to summarize the research available on the characteristics and experiences of homeless youth, the causes of youth homelessness, and the solutions to youth homelessness. We will also point out the limitations of the research, and identify some research questions that we believe need to be addressed.

### Overview of research

### Demographics and Experiences of Youth Homelessness

Homeless youth are typically defined as unaccompanied youth aged 12 to 24 years who do not have familial support and are unaccompanied, and who are living in shelters, on the streets, in a range of places not meant for human habitation (e.g. cars, abandoned buildings) or in others' homes for short periods under circumstances that make the situation highly unstable (so-called "couch surfing").｜Youth homelessness is essentially caused by a breakdown in families, where environments of abuse, neglect, or youth abandonment are exacerbated by larger systemic issues such as poverty, unemployment, poor housing, and lack of community and economic support in rural and urban neighborhoods.｜Youth turn to shelters and the streets as an often rational choice to avoid violence, abuse, neglect, and abandonment but the alternative can be hard lives riddled with poor health and exploitation by unscrupulous adults.|

Two major incident studies by the U.S. Department of Justice and Professor Ringwalt and colleagues estimate that the number of youth below the age of 18 who flee from their home, are barred from home by their guardian, or experience homelessness ranges from 1.6 to 1.7 million in the course of a year. Additionally, an unknown number of young adults aged 18 to 24 experience homelessness each year. Some youth will remain away from their home for only short periods of time (a few nights) while others will experience long periods of homelessness and become street-dependent. Street-dependent youth often sleep exclusively outdoors, in public places, or in abandoned buildings, form their own unique culture and family structure withother street-dependent youth, and often rely on street economies such as prostitution, drug sales, theft, or begging to meet their basic needs.|However, street-dependent youth represent a small minority of the total homeless youth population.\Local programs funded by the federal Runaway and Homeless Youth Act (Department of Health and Human Services) served over 500,000 homeless and runaway youth in 2005. Homeless youth can be found in urban, suburban, and rural areas throughthe United States and few differences have been found when urban, suburban, and rural youth are compared.

A 1999 study by the U.S. Department of Justice, the Second National Incidence Studies of Missing, Abducted, Runaway, and Thrownaway Children, estimated 1,682,900 youth had a runaway/throwaway episode that year. Of these youth, 37 percent were actively sought by their caretakers and 21 percent were reported toauthorities for purposes of locating them. This study underscores that a majority of runaway and homeless youth (63 percent) are never reported or sought after by their parents or primary caretakers.

There is little gender disparity among various homeless youth groups, except that youth living on the streets are more likely to be male. While youth from all races and cultures run away, become homeless or are thrown away by parents, shelterand housing programs report a significant disproportionate representation of American Indian and African-American youth.

Also, gay, lesbian, bisexual, and transgender youth have been found to be over-represented in homeless and street populations with estimates ranging from 11 to 35 percent. Compared to heterosexual homeless youth, gay, lesbian, bisexual, and transgender homeless youth also are exposed to greater victimization while on the streets.

Background information on homeless youth show that they tend to come from low-income communities and their families are disproportionately poor or working class. Many grew up in single-parent households or blended families.

Contrary to stereotypes about homeless youth, studies have not consistently shown that substance abuse is characteristic of a majority of runaway youth. Whilemany studies show use and abuse of drugs or alcohol, research is inconclusive that homeless youth are more prone to dependency. However, studies of homeless youth have shown high rates of parental alcohol or drug abuse (24 to 44 percent) which likely contributes to youth homelessness. Additionally, most homeless youth are still in school but may have experienced difficulties, discipline actions, and delays. One 2005 study showed that 79 percent of youth were attending school on a regular basis before entering shelter.

Additionally, homeless youth are at elevated risk for mood disorders, suicide attempts, and post-traumatic stress disorder. High rates of behavioral disorders are also noted. Regardless of the assessment method used or the sample, homeless youth are more likely to experience mental health and behavioral disorders than adolescents in the general population.

Numerous studies have indicated that once homeless, youth often engage in sexual behaviors that put them at high risk for both sexually transmitted diseases and pregnancy. Most studies indicate that a portion of the homeless youth population engages in survival sex which is the trading of sexual acts for basic needs like a place to stay. A significant number of homeless girls are also pregnant or parenting. One national, representative sample study published in the American Journal of Adolescent Health found that 48 percent of street youth and 33 percent of shelter youth had histories of pregnancy or impregnating someone, as compared to 10 percent of a nationally representative sample of housed youth.

Homeless youth may be characterized by the length of time spent homeless—recent runaways, transitionally or episodically homeless, homeless and shelter using youth, and street-dependent youth who may travel. Evidence suggests that differences may exist between subtypes of homeless youth, and therefore, unique, targeted interventions may be merited.

In summary, research has given us insight into some fairly constant variables that cut across most homeless youth groups. The common characteristics of their experience prior to becoming homeless include:

- Abuse and neglect histories
- Parental alcohol and substance abuse
- Poverty (except runaways)
- Broken family relationships (single parent, blended, or no parental contact)
- Severe family conflict
- Difficulty with educational success and advancement despite enrollment in school.

Research has also given us a warning that the longer youth remain homeless, the greater their likelihood of experience a host of troubles, including:

- High rates of sexual activity
- Acute medical problems
- Alcoholism and alcohol/chemical addiction
- HIV
- Mental health diagnosis & institutionalization
- Suicide
- Physical violence
- Sexual assault.

### Pathways to Homelessness for Youth

Research offers information about the pathways into homelessness for youth. Studies show that there are often multiple factors which cause a youth to leave home: severe family conflict, physical abuse, sexual abuse, neglect, substance abuse, mental health disabilities, and abandonment. Youth consistently report severe family conflict as the primary reason for their homelessness but also report multiple barriers to reunification. Behavioral issues on the part of the youth may be a source of the conflict, but this is certainly not always the case.

Beyond the individual and family problems, youth homelessness is also fed by lack of affordable housing, poverty, and child welfare and juvenile correction systems that fail to protect youth from shelters and the streets.

A sizable minority of homeless youth have had histories of foster care or juvenile justice placements and still end up homeless before their 18th birthday. According to the 2007 National Symposium on Homelessness Research, the percentage of homeless youth who report previous placement in foster care or an institutional setting ranged between 21 and 53 percent across studies. A longitudinal study by the University of Chicago found that 14 percent of former foster youth became homeless after being discharged from care. Another large representative sample study of foster youth aging out of care by Professors Fowler and Ahmed noted that 17 percent of homeless youth had experienced literal homelessness during the 3.6 years after exiting care. One predictor of future homelessness for foster youth is whether the youth had repeatedly run away from placement. By contrast, feeling very close to at least one family member reduced the odds of becoming homeless by nearly 80 percent.

Homelessness may not be a surprising result given the multiple placements and school transfers experienced by foster youth. One study by Casey Family Programs found that more than 30 percent of foster youth experienced eight or more placements with foster families and group homes and a majority experienced seven or more school changes between elementary and high school age. In addition to residential instability, many foster youth face mental health problems and developmental or behavioral challenges. The Northwest Foster Care Alumni Study by Casey Family Programs found that foster youth experience anxiety disorders, depression, panic disorders, and social phobias at two to four times the rate of the general population.

### Solutions to Youth Homelessness

There is a growing body of evidence about what works. We know interventions that work to restore youth and offer them a pathway out of homelessness. The past ten years of research and study have provided some indication of methodologies which result in positive outcomes for youth to prevent or end homelessness.

Most homeless youth do not experience long-term homelessness. Homeless youth often go home, find relatives, or make it on their own as young adults. In a 2004 study by Professor Paul Toro of 249 homeless youth as compared to a matched sample of 149 housed youth, ages 13 and 17 years, conducted longitudinally over seven years, most of the adolescents returned fairly quickly to their family of origin. Nearly 93 percent were no longer homeless after seven years of study. However, not all were successfully reunified with parents. One third lived with their families, about 20 percent lived with relatives or friends, and over a third (34 percent) lived on their own. Therefore, the pathway out of homelessness sometimes focuses on parents, sometimes focuses on kin and extended family, and sometimes focuses on independent living.

Studies of what works focus on three areas. The first is early intervention/prevention that seeks to avert a homelessness episode or to ensure that a family separation does not result in an out-of-home placement that so often leads to long term homelessness. The second is interventions with youth who are already homeless, to rapidly reunite them with their families while strengthening the families to achieve more stability. The third is independent housing options other than reunification for youth who will not be able to return to their families. The implication of these threestrategies is that the first and best option is to try to reconnect youth with their families, and only after this fails should independent living options be considered.

Initial early intervention and prevention services which focus on mental health and family systems can often meet the crisis needs of a family and prevent homelessness and/or foster care placement.

Two forms of mental health services have been identified that show positive results in decreasing youth anti-social behavior and aggression: multisystemic therapy (MST) and functional family therapy (FFT). Both have indicated that youth recipients have significantly fewer out-of-home placements and decreased recidivism to the juvenile justice system.

Multisystemic Therapy is an intensive family- and community-based treatment that addresses multiple aspects of serious antisocial behavior in adolescents. MST uses family members to design the treatment plan and attempts to encourage behavior changes by using strengths in various areas of the youth's life (family, peers, school, and neighborhood). Evaluations of MST have demonstrated the following benefits:

- decreased recidivism and re-arrests;
- reduced adolescent alcohol and drug use;
- reduced long-term rates of crime for serious juvenile offenders;
- improvements in family functioning;
- decreased behavior and mental health problems for youth; and
- favorable outcomes at cost savings in comparison with usual mental health and juvenile justice services.

Functional Family Therapy is so named to identify the family as the primary focus of intervention. Therapists employing FFT believe they must do more than simply stop antisocial or unhealthy behavior, they must motivate families to change by identifying their strengths, helping build on those strengths in ways that enhance self respect, and offering recommendations on particular pathways for improvement. Data show that when compared with other forms of community intervention like probation support, residential treatment, and alternative therapeutic approaches, FFT is highly successful. In randomized trials FFT was shown to have reduced recidivism for a wide range of anti-social or criminal behavior. In addition, studies have shown it to reduce the cost of treatment.

Youth who are experiencing abuse or neglect at home could also be diverted away from costly out-of-home placements and homelessness through Family Group Conferencing or Family Group Decision Making programs. In these early intervention and prevention programs extended family, kin, and important people in the life of the youth come together to implement a plan for the continued safety, nurturance, and permanency of the youth. These programs show remarkable success in stabilizing youth. Research on Family Group Decision Making found reductions in re-abuse, increased family involvement, decreased residential instability, and more extended families accepting care of the youth.

Program models have proven effective at reuniting homeless youth, even those with troubled histories, with their families.

Originally designed to assist young people who have been diagnosed with mental health disabilities and their families, Intensive Case Management (ICM) works with a family (in conjunction with teachers and other helping professionals) to develop an individualized comprehensive service plan. Case Managers who are professional and specially trained conduct an assessment and assist in coordinating supports and services necessary to help children and adolescents live successfully at home and in the community. The case loads are small (1 to 10 or 1 to 12) and offer round-theclock access. Intensive Case Management services have been used successfully with homeless youth. One study published in the Journal of Emotional and Behavioral Disorders noted that homeless youth receiving Intensive Case Management services showed improved psychological well-being, less aggression, and satisfaction with their quality of life.

Both shelter and outreach services can be used as a gateway to exit homelessness. A 2002 study by Professor Thompson and colleagues compared 261 runaway and homeless youth who received services through emergency shelter and crisis services with 47 at-risk youth receiving services from a long-term day treatment program. The study found that both groups experienced positive changes in their family relationships, runaway behavior, school behavior, employment, sexual behavior and self esteem. The study noted that there were no significant group differences in the amount of change they experienced, leading one to observe that the less-costly shelter system had as positive return in positive outcomes for youth as the more expensive day treatment programs.

Some youth will never be able to return to their families, and there are successful housing programs that not only meet the housing needs of such youth, but also have programming that addresses their development needs and helps them to build relationships with adults and with the community.

Multiple housing models exist for youth but they have limited capacity in most jurisdictions. Examples of youth housing models include: host homes, shared housing, community-based group homes, dormitories, scattered site transitional housing, single-site transitional housing, permanent scattered site housing with supportive services, and foyer (employment-focused) housing. These models incorporate life skills training, connection to caring adults, and opportunities for growth, mistakes, and positive youth development. Many homeless youth rely on such housing options when family members are unwilling or unable to care for their nurturance and welfare. Most homeless youth never receive housing benefits because of lack of supply and long waiting lists.

### *Limitations of the research and unanswered questions*

There is an extensive body of study and research on the characteristics and demographics of homeless youth, as well as the pathways or antecedent factors leading up to a youth turning to life on the streets. Unfortunately, there are limitations to existing research and we are left with remaining questions.

One problem is that studies that have examined homelessness among adolescents have often cast the problem as individual vulnerability instead of examining the broader environmental factors involved. This has created the tendency by research to focus on the youth behavior in risky situations while homeless, rather than on the adult behaviors that often propel youth from their homes or on interventions and supports that could end youth homelessness. Additional research that focuses on child welfare, juvenile justice, and economic or social network failures that have a role in youth homelessness may allow us to address these causal factors.

Further, little research has been conducted on the inherent characteristics possessed by youth which make them resilient to negative outcomes despite their homelessness. Homeless youth are resilient and creative and often exit homelessness after short periods of time. While it is important to understand the deficits of homeless youth, a greater understanding of their strengths and assets could lead us to new interventions that build upon these strengths to help young people gain residential stability and escape life on the streets.

There is little research that helps clarify the distinction between youth who remain on the streets or hop between shelters and those that remain housed with friends and relatives, either stably or unstably. Further research is needed to understand which program models, resources, or intervention methods best equip "couch surfing" youth with the opportunity to find stable homes and brighter futures.

There are several programmatic models and methodologies which may hold promise in working with youth. However, there is little rigorous research that verifies results. School-based programs that offer youth a safe way to access services or receive one-to-one counseling and support may help prevent and end homelessness, but we have found little evaluation of such programs. We also know that a minority of homeless youth experience chemical or alcohol addiction, yet we do not know whether out-patient support groups or residentially-based treatment geared toward adolescents is more effective. Most of the research on chemical and alcohol addiction is focused on adults. Further, given the high rates of adult sexual exploitation, molestation, and assault of homeless youth, it would be helpful to have a better understanding of the level of support, outreach, case management, and housing stability that are needed to effectively escape prostitution and the commercial sex industry. Another area of youth homelessness that has been under-examined is the experience of undocumented youth who may flee to America to escape abusive, violent, or neglectful families in their home countries. We do not know the dimensions of this problem, or what solutions are workable.

Finally, Congress has funded an array of services, housing and shelter for vulnerable and homeless youth, although not enough to meet all of the need. While we are able to point to some interventions that offer solutions, the vast array of service systems have yet to be rigorously evaluated. It would appear that critical research and study in this area is in its own adolescent phase—able to produce some solutions but not fully matured. When evaluations have been done on local service systems or specific programs, rigorous experimental designs have generally not beenused and often lack comparative data to allow cross-system comparison.

## *Implications*

After a reviewing the current body of research and studies on youth homelessness, the Alliance wishes to offer the following implications, as a framework for this sub committee in crafting public policy to end youth homelessness:

1. Youth by definition are still developing and require attachment to and the support of caring adults. Homeless youth are unique in that they represent a population of homelessness that is impacted by physical, emotional, and cognitive development. Any consideration, intervention, or program model must consider how positive youth development is both retarded and enhanced through our programmatic responses.
2. Youth homelessness is as much about societal and system failures as individualand family breakdown. The pathways to homelessness for youth are about breakdown of families, abuse and neglect, but also community systems (including economic conditions, social networks, housing stock, and child welfare systems) contributing to youth living on the streets of America.

3.  Our targeted response should be tailored toward the length of time spent homeless. Recent runaways and couch surfing youth should be quickly served to find alternative family placements, while shelter and street-dependent youth require intensive case work and access to housing models grounded in life skills training and opportunity for growth, with rapid stabilization in housing as the highest possible priority.

4.  We know some of what works and Congress should invest in those interventions that have shown positive outcomes. Those typically tend to be mental healthservices, intensive case management services, respite care tied to family reunification counseling, and housing coupled with life skills training and positive youth development services.

5.  We can end homelessness for youth, and prevent untold suffering, hardship and expense in so doing. With coordination of services between child welfare systems and community-based organizations centering on family, health, and housing this isa social condition that is not inevitable.

Thank you again and we look forward to working with you to confront and end youth homelessness.

# SOURCES

Cauce, A. M., Morgan, C. J., Wagner, V., Moore, E., Sy, J., Wurzbacher, K., Weeden, K., Tomlin, S. & Blanchard, T. (1994) Effectiveness of intensive case management for homeless adolescents: Results of a 3-month follow-up. *Journal of Emotional and Behavioral Disorders, 2*, 219-227.

Courtney, M., Dworsky, A., Ruth, G., Keller, T., Havlicek, J. & Bost, N. (2005). *Midwest Evaluation of the Adult Functioning of Former Foster Youth: Outcomes at age 19.* Unpublished report. Chicago, IL: Chapin Hall Center for Children.

Fowler, P. J., Ahmed, S. A., Tompsett, C. J., Jozefowicz-Simbeni, D. M. & Toro, P. A. (2006) Community violence, race, religiosity, and substance abuse from adolescence to emerging adulthood. *Unpublished manuscript, Department of Psychology, Wayne State University.*

Green, J. M. & Ringwalt, C. L. (1998). Pregnancy among three national samples of runaway and homeless youth. *Journal of Adolescent Health, 23*, 370-377.

Promising Strategies to & Youth Homelessness: Report to Congress, U.S. Department of Health and Human Services, Administration for Children and Families, Administration on Children, Youth, and Families, Family and Youth Services Bureau.

Ringwalt, C. L., Greene, J. M., Robertson, M. & McPheeters, M. (1998). The Prevalence of homelessness among adolescents in the United States. *American Journal of Public Health, 88(9)*, 1325-1329.

Robertson, M. J. & Toro, P. A., Homeless Youth: Research, Intervention, and Policy, 1998 National Symposium on Homelessness Research.

Second National Incidence Study of Missing, Abducted, Runaway and Thrownaway Children (NISMART II), U.S. Department of Justice, 2002, Washington, D.C.

Thompson, S. J., Pollio, D. E., Constantine, J., Reid, D. & Nebbitt, V. (2002). Short-term outcomes for youth receiving runaway and homeless shelter services. *Research on Social Work Practice, 12(5),* 589-603.

Toro, P. A., Dworsky, A. & Fowler, P. J., Homeless Youth in the United States: Recent Research Findings and Intervention Approaches, 2007 National Symposium on Homeless Research, Draft from February, 2007.

Chairwoman McCarthy. Thank you, Mr. Berg.
Mr. Allen?

## STATEMENT OF ERNIE ALLEN, PRESIDENT AND CEO, NATIONAL CENTER FOR MISSING AND EXPLOITED CHILDREN

*Mr. Allen.* Madam Chair, members of the committee, I particularly want to express my gratitude to my friend, Congressman Yarmuth, and to the great leadership of the Congressional Caucus on Missing and Exploited Children, Chairman Lampson and cochair Congresswoman Biggert.

I want to report to the committee that the progress in the search for America's missing children is extraordinary. More missing children come home safely today in this country than at any time in the nation's history, and that is because the leadership of Congress and the leadership of law enforcement, we have been able to build a national network.

Today, images and information are transmitted instantly across the nation. There are 50 state missing children clearinghouses. Because of the AMBER Alert and the leadership of great nonprofit organizations like the Texas Center for the Missing, we are mobilizing the eyes and ears of the public.

Law enforcement is better prepared. There is more technology, more resources. The good news is, it is working. The bad news, as you all know, is that 2,000 children will be reported by their parents to the police as missing today somewhere in the United States.

And, the bad news is, despite all our progress and despite a recovery rate in the upper 90s, thousands of children each year still don't make it home. Our national center, which is now 23 years old, at your mandate operates a National Missing Children's Hot-line.

We are currently handing about 300 calls a day. We have handled 2.2 million over our history. And let me say the long partnership with the runaway and homeless youth community is extraordinarily important, because, for example, we link with the National Runaway Switchboard.

When the kid calls our hotline, we pass them immediately to the National Runaway Switchboard. And when the parent or a member of the public calls the National Runaway Switchboard, they send it to us. It is that kind of cooperation that I think is essential in this issue.

We are focusing aggressively on issues like the long-term missing. There are still thousands of children who have not been identified, many of whom are deceased and whose remains have not been identified, bringing closure for these families.

We are working with the FBI and others to provide direct, on-scene response, technical experts to help law enforcement, who may waste valuable time because they don't know what to do. So there is enormous progress.

An area of perhaps greater challenge is the area of child sexual exploitation. And let me just say a few words about that. This is an issue that has exploded with the advent of the Internet. In 1998, the Congress asked our center to establish what it called the 911 for the Internet, a cyber tip line. Last week, we handled our 500,000th report, and these reports are of online enticement of children, child pornography, child sex tourism, a range of child sexual exploitation offenses.

The good news is that these reports have led to thousands of arrests and successful prosecutions. The bad news is that this problem has proliferated. For example, child pornography has become a multi-billion dollar commercial industry and the victims are getting younger and younger. Our staff has reviewed 8 million images and videos in an attempt to identify the children.

And what we have learned is that of the offenders how have been identified, 39 percent have had images of children younger than 6 years old. Nineteen percent have had images of children younger than 3 years old.

This is an enormous challenge. Law enforcement is doing more today than ever before. The FBI, ICE and other agencies are gearing up the Internet crimes against children task forces around the country are doing extraordinary work, but law enforcement is under-resourced, under-manned and is tackling a problem that is far greater than any of us ever thought.

The last thing I would want to point out is that a couple of years ago, in the PROTECT Act, the Congress asked for us to take on a pilot project to do background screening for youth-serving organizations.

We have done that, and we have found that even though these applicants are being fingerprinted and know they are being subject to national criminal history background checks, fully 3 percent of the applicants have had criminal histories, many of them serious criminal histories involving crimes against children.

Background screening needs to be continued. This needs to be a national effort for youth-serving organizations that is fast, accurate fingerprint based and either free or as close to free as we can get it.

Thank you, Madam Chair.

[The statement of Mr. Allen follows:]


## Prepared Statement of Ernie Allen, President and CEO, National Center Formissing and Exploited Children

Madame Chairwoman and members of the Subcommittee, as President of the National Center for Missing & Exploited Children (NCMEC), I welcome the opportunity to appear before you to discuss issues affecting our nation's children. NCMEC joins you in your concern for the safety of the most vulnerable members of our society and thanks you for bringing attention to the problems facing America's families and communities.

Let me first provide you with some background information. NCMEC is a not-for-profit corporation, mandated by Congress and working in partnership with the U.S. Department of Justice as the national resource center and clearinghouse on missing and exploited children. NCMEC is a true public-private partnership, funded in part by Congress and in part by the private sector. Our federal funding supports specific operational functions mandated by Congress, including a national 24-hour toll-free hotline; a distribution system for missing-child photos; a system of case management and technical assistance to law enforcement and families; training programs for federal, state and local law enforcement; and programs designed to help stop the sexual exploitation of children.

In recent years, our nation has become outraged by the abductions of children like Jessica Lunsford, Jetseta Gage, Erica Pratt, Shasta Groene, Samantha Runnion, Elizabeth Smart, and many others. Their stories have unleashed fear among parents everywhere who are asking, "How safe is my child?"

The response is, "Safer than ever before."

More missing children are coming home safely today than at any time in our history. Law enforcement is responding more swiftly and effectively. There is a national network in place. Parents are more alert, more aware, and talking to their children about their safety.

Yet that is not enough, and there are some inescapable facts. Hundreds of children still do not make it home each year, and many more continue to be victimized by acts of violence. In fact children are the most victimized segment of our society.[1] Further, research has consistently shown that crimes committed against children of all ages are the most underreported of any victim category.[2]

How has NCMEC responded to this?

We have worked with law enforcement on more than 133,000 missing-child cases, and played a role in reuniting more than 115,000 children with their families. We have a 96.2 % recovery rate, up from 62% in 1990. We have analyzed more than500,000 reports of crimes against children on the Internet, and referred them to law enforcement, resulting in hundreds of arrests and successful prosecutions.

Here are some of the services we provide:

- Hotline: Since 1984 our 24-hour, national and international toll-free hotline has received more than 2 million calls, or, on average, nearly 300 calls per day, intaking new cases and receiving leads on current cases, which are triaged according to urgency of the information and the case, and referred to the investigating law enforcement agency. Information from callers about runaway children is immediately transmitted to the National Runaway Switchboard.
- Case Management: NCMEC Case Managers serve as the single point of contact for the searching family and provide technical assistance to locate abductors and recover missing children.
- Case Analysis and Support: Using NCMEC databases, external sources, and geographic databases, our analysts track leads, identify patterns among cases, and help coordinate investigations by linking cases together. In 2006 NCMEC created the Attempted Abduction Program to analyze attempted abduction trends and patterns and collect information to assist law enforcement during investigations. Currently, no other national organization aggressively tracks attempted abductionsacross the United States.

- Forensic Imaging: NCMEC provides age-progressed photographs of missing children and reconstructed facial images of unidentified, deceased children. Since 1990 NCMEC has age-progressed the photographs of almost 3,300 children; these new photos played a role in helping to identify and recover 768 children. Of the 117 facial reconstructions performed by NCMEC forensic artists for law enforcement, 29children have been identified.

- Cold Case Team: NCMEC works with families, law enforcement, and medical examiners to resolve long-term missing children cases, cases of unidentified human remains of victims believed to be children and young adults, and "cold" child homicide cases. Former homicide detectives review each case, develop a set of recommendations regarding the investigation, and, if requested, provide forensic resources. NCMEC is currently handling 468 cases of long-term missing children, 201 cases of unidentified human remains, and 7 "cold" child homicide cases.

- Photo Distribution: NCMEC is actively distributing photos of missing children via a wide array of resources, including franked envelopes of members of Congress. Three hundred and fifty public and private sector companies and organizations partner with us to distribute photos, at no cost to NCMEC or taxpayers.

- Team Adam: Created in 2003, Team Adam is a rapid, on-site response and support system that provides no-cost investigative and technical assistance to local law enforcement. It consists of 62 retired federal, state and local investigators experienced in crimes-against-children investigations. NCMEC has deployed Team Adam 296 times in 43 states, which has helped to resolve 321 cases of missing children.

- AMBER Alerts: NCMEC offers technical assistance and training, in concert with the U.S. Department of Justice, to all state AMBER Alert programs. We also disseminate AMBER Alert messages to secondary communications distributors, such as cell phone service providers.

- Website: In 1997 we launched our website, www.missingkids.com. The use of the web has enabled us to transmit images and information regarding missing children instantly across America and around the world. The response has been overwhelming. On the first day of operation, our website received 3,000 "hits." Today, we receive more than 1 million "hits" every day, and are linked with hundreds of other sites to provide real-time images of breaking cases of missing children. To demonstrate the value of this in a real-world sense, a police officer in Puerto Rico searched our website, identified a possible match, and then worked with one of our case managers to identify and recover a child who had been abducted as an infant from her home seven years earlier.

- Publications: NCMEC has designed, written, edited and published manycollaterals and publications for law enforcement, other child-serving professionals, and the general public. Since 1984, NCMEC has published more than 42 million copies of its publications.

- Training: Each month, in our Jimmy Ryce Law Enforcement Training Center, NCMEC brings in police chiefs and sheriffs for training in the policy and practical aspects of missing and exploited child investigations. In addition, we are also training state and federal prosecutors, police unit commanders, and many others. We also conduct on-site training sessions for hospital staff in preventing infant abductions.

- International Cases: NCMEC plays a key role in international child abduction cases, handling all cases of children abducted out of the United States, as well as acting as the State Department's representative on incoming cases under the HagueConvention on the Civil Aspects of International Child Abduction. Since September 1995, we have handled 8,264 international child abduction cases, resulting in the resolution of 4,714 cases. We are using the Internet to build a network to distribute images worldwide in partnership with Interpol. We also provide attorney referrals and other assistance to American parents whose children were abducted to another country.

- While NCMEC's initial mandate was missing children's issues, NCMEC has also been a leader in the fight against child sexual exploitation. As technology has evolved and provided those who sexually exploit children with more sophisticated and insidious tools to prey on their vulnerability, the challenges of protecting our children have increased in complexity and number. The mission and resources of NCMEC have responded to this challenge in the following ways:

- Exploited Child Division: In 1997, in response to the increasing prevalence of child sexual victimization, NCMEC officially opened our Exploited Child Division (ECD). ECD is responsible for the receipt, processing, initial analysis and referral to law enforcement of information about these crimes. As technology continued to advance and the use of computers became more widespread, Congress recognized the need to provide the public with a central reporting mechanism for crimesagainst children on the Internet—and came to us.

- CyberTipline: In response to Congress' request, NCMEC launched the CyberTipline, www.cybertipline.com, in 1998. The CyberTipline serves as the national online clearinghouse for investigative leads and tips and is operated in partnership with the Federal Bureau of Investigation ("FBI"), the Department of Homeland Security's Bureau of Immigration and Customs Enforcement ("ICE"), the U.S.Postal Inspection Service, the U.S. Secret Service, the U.S. Department of Justice's Child Exploitation and Obscenity Section and the Internet Crimes Against Children Task Forces, as well as state and local law enforcement. Leads are received in seven categories of crimes:
  - possession, manufacture and distribution of child pornography;
  - online enticement of children for sexual acts;
  - child prostitution;
  - child-sex tourism;
  - child sexual molestation (not in the family);
  - unsolicited obscene material sent to a child; and
  - misleading domain names.

These leads are reviewed by NCMEC analysts, who visit the reported sites, examine and evaluate the content, use search tools to try to identify perpetrators, and provide all lead information to the appropriate law enforcement agency. The FBI, ICE and Postal Inspection Service have "real time" access to the leads, and all three agencies assign agents and analysts to work directly out of NCMEC and review the reports. The results: in the 9 years since the CyberTipline began operation, NCMEC has received and processed more than 500,000 leads, resulting in hundreds of arrests and successful prosecutions.

- CyberTipline for Internet Service Providers: In 1998, Congress passed the Protection of Children from Sexual Predators Act,[3] which requires that providers of electronic communication services report apparent child pornography on their systems to NCMEC. To facilitate this new role, NCMEC created a separate reporting mechanism through which these providers can swiftly and efficiently transmit the images and related information to NCMEC for analysis and referral to law enforcement. In response to this congressional mandate, NCMEC handles approximately 500 reports per week.

- Child Victim Identification Program (CVIP): CVIP was formally created in 2002 in response to the Supreme Court's decision that federal laws prohibiting child pornography only apply to images of real children and not to images that simply appear to be children.[4] CVIP analysts assist law enforcement and prosecutors by maintaining a catalog of information about identified child victims, which can be used to provide the evidence required to get a conviction in court. The program also serves to assist law enforcement in rescuing children who are currently being abused but whose identity and location are unknown. To date, CVIP has processed more than eight million images and movies, and has cataloged information about more than one thousand child victims who have been identified by law enforcement agencies around the world.

- Here is but one example of CVIP's success: our analysts received images of several young girls whom they did not recognize from previous images. The photos were taken in various rooms in a home. By scrutinizing the background in each image, our analysts detected clues to the location of the girls: an ad for a local convenience store, an envelope with the name of a storage facility, and a Girl Scout uniform. A team of federal, state and local law enforcement used this information to find the girls and arrest their abuser. He was the grandfather of two of the girls as well as their legal guardian. He was convicted and given a sentence of 750 years in prison. None of the girls had told anyone about what he had done to them. Their abuse would be continuing today if no one had tried to find them.

- Partnerships with Internet Industry: Last year, six Internet industry leaders, AOL, Yahoo, Google, Microsoft, Earthlink and United Online, created a TechnologyCoalition to work with NCMEC to develop and deploy technology solutions that disrupt the ability of predators to use the Internet to exploit children or traffic in child pornography. The Technology Coalition brings together the collective experience, knowledge and expertise of its members and represents a significant step towards making the world safer for our children.

- NetSmartz411: This is a first-of-its-kind, online service operated by NCMEC toanswer questions about Internet safety, computers and the web. It is provided at no cost to the public, in partnership with the Qwest Foundation. Concerned parents, children, or anyone, can directly access the NetSmartz411 library to search for information as well as contact NCMEC experts to ask questions related to online safety and the Internet.

- Safety Education Campaigns: NCMEC has partnered with federal agencies, industry leaders and public service organizations to create campaigns to educate parents and children about Internet safety. These safety messages include "Help Delete Online

Predators," "Don't Believe the Type," "Type Smart. Post Wisely" and "Think Before You Post."

- In recent years, Congress has asked NCMEC to undertake a number of new challenges and responsibilities beyond its core functions. We have welcomed them andbelieve that NCMEC is well suited to take on these tasks. Further, we consider these initiatives to be an integral part of our mandate as the national resource center and clearinghouse on missing and exploited children. These new challenges include the following:

- LOCATER: Congress asked NCMEC to develop and implement a program to enhance basic law enforcement technology in responding to missing child cases. NCMEC created LOCATER, a web-based program which enables police to create high-quality color posters for local distribution when a child disappears as well as disseminate that information online to other law enforcement agencies, the media and other outlets. NCMEC has approximately 4,000 active LOCATER users.

- NetSmartz Internet Safety Resource: When Boys & Girls Clubs of America launched its effort to create technology centers in all of its clubs, Congress asked that NCMEC develop a state-of-the-art Internet safety resource to ensure that these centers could be used safely by children. Thus, NetSmartz was born—an interactive, educational safety resource for children, parents, educators and law enforcement that uses age-appropriate, 3-dimensional activities to teach children how to stay safer on the Internet. NetSmartz is now available at no cost to other youth organizations, schools, and the general public at www.netsmartz.org. Since its inception, 16 state Attorneys General have recommended the use of NetSmartz in their public schools; currently, all 50 states have schools that use NetSmartz.

- Background Checks for Non-Profit Child-Serving Organizations: In response to Congress' request in 2003,[5] NCMEC launched a pilot program to conduct national criminal history background checks on applicants for volunteer positions with non-profit organizations that provide services to children. Because it is a fact that child molesters will seek legitimate access to children, these organizations are particularly attractive to predators. To date, our Background Check Unit (BCU) has conducted over 33,000 fitness determinations based on criminal histories. A startling number of applicants were found to have lied about not having criminal histories, which included violent crimes and crimes against children. This project has demonstrated not only the need for fingerprint-based checks of the national criminal history database, as opposed to name-based checks of state databases, but also the need to make these comprehensive checks available at the lowest possible cost to ensure that these organizations are able to provide the best protection to the children they serve.

- Hurricanes Katrina and Rita/National Emergency Child Locator Center: The Department of Justice asked NCMEC to lead federal and local efforts to recover the more than 5,000 children displaced during Hurricanes Katrina and Rita in 2005. Team Adam consultants were deployed to the affected areas to serve as an on-site rapid response and support system, providing investigative and technical assistance to local law enforcement. Team Adam consultants also set up safe areas for missing children in the evacuee shelters and, working directly from these shelters, electronically transmitted information and photos of the children directly to NCMEC headquarters. To manage the volume of Katrina/Rita-related calls, NCMEC created a dedicated Katrina/Rita Missing Person Hotline which we operated in addition to our existing Call Center Hotline. In the aftermath of the hurricanes, NCMEC handled more than 34,000 Katrina/Rita-related calls. NCMEC's relationship with the media proved vital to our efforts—because of the ongoing television coverage of NCMEC's Katrina/Rita Operation, millions of people saw the photos of displaced children and got information that led to their reunification. As a result of NCMEC's expertise and ability to rapidly mobilize critical resources, all (100%) of the more than 5,000 missing/displaced children cases reported to NCMEC in the aftermath of the storms were resolved within 6 months.

- In 2006, Congress passed legislation to create the National Emergency Child Locator Center at NCMEC [6] to similarly handle all future such disasters. We have developed a Disaster Response Plan and are actively working with the Department of Homeland Security, the Federal Emergency Management Agency and the American Red Cross to establish policies and procedures necessary for the Center's operation.
- The Financial Coalition Against Child Pornography: At the request of Senator Richard Shelby, NCMEC brought together leading banks, credit card companies, third party payment companies and Internet service companies, in a joint effort to eradicate the multi-billion-dollar commercial child pornography industry from the Internet.
- Sex Offender Tracking Team: At the request of the U.S. Marshals Service, under its mandate per the Adam Walsh Child Protection and Safety Act,[7] NCMEC created the Sex Offender Tracking Team (SOTT) to serve as the central information and analysis hub to help locate non-compliant registered sex offenders. Analysts provide information upon request to federal, state and local law enforcement agencies. In addition, SOTT analysts compare NCMEC's attempted abduction data, online predator data, and child abduction data to identify potential linkages with non-compliant sex offenders being sought by law enforcement. This information will be used to create more effective prevention and response strategies regarding these offenders.
- The legacy of missing and exploited children in the United States can be seen in new laws, heightened public awareness, improved response from law enforcement, and unprecedented national attention to prevention and education. The recent resurgence of awareness of this ongoing problem is a call to action to all law- and policymakers across the country. Enormous progress has been made to better protect our nation's children in the past 20 years, but our children deserve even more.
- Since 1984, per your mandate and with your support, NCMEC has been proud to serve as America's national resource center and clearinghouse for missing and exploited children.
- Madame Chairwoman, we are deeply grateful for the Subcommittee's leadership and support, and, as always, stand ready to work with you and your committee to bring more missing children home and keep every child safe.

*Chairwoman McCarthy*. Thank you, Mr. Allen.
Ms. Alberts?

## STATEMENT OF BETH ALBERTS, CEO, TEXAS CENTER FOR THE MISSING

*Ms. Alberts*. Thank you so much for letting me come from the small state of Texas today to talk to you.

During 2006, there were more than 650,000 children reported missing in the United States and more than 60,000 of those are in my home state of Texas. Of these Texas cases, at the end of 2006, 5,182 of those children remained missing. Those are the kinds of things that make me lie awake at night and wonder if we are ever going to get all of those kids back.

I beg you, when you are looking at the issue of missing and homeless children, not to differentiate between them, even if a child left home voluntarily. Any child who is away from home, from a stable, loving environment, is a child at risk.

No child chooses to be marginalized. Children never knowingly choose to expose themselves exploitation and victimization. A child who chooses to run away is always running to a better place, they hope, than the place they have been. They do not consciously choose to become vulnerable to predators and exploiters.

Children who live on the street have three ways to support themselves: They steal from us, our communities; they sell drugs; and they sell themselves. Many resort to all three, creating yet more victims.

It has also been said that children are our most valuable resource, but this is seldom reflected in our practices as a society. With our national focus on terrorism, we worry more about an enemy we cannot see, cannot know and whose motives we cannot understand than those who threaten our children daily.

Make no mistake, the animals who prey on our children are terrorists of the worst order, and they target our most vulnerable citizens, those who represent our future, our children.

Predators systematically and methodically threaten and terrorize our children on all fronts, whether they are runaway or homeless children, those threatened by their own family members or by pornographers who line their pockets with the profits from the sale of innocents.

Our defense must be no less systematic and methodical. The primary motive for stranger abduction is sexual assault of the child, and child molesters have on average 117 victims prior to their first arrest.

Children are no longer safe from these terrorists online, on the streets, in their homes or even in their beds. And what is our response? Very little response, until that particular chicken comes home to roost in our backyard. And then we are outraged and we pick up the mantle and carry on.

But we must act now, before another young life is lost, before another child loses the very innocence that defines childhood.

There is good news. There is hope. There are concerned citizens working together, such as the member organizations of the Association of Missing and Exploited Children's Organizations and the National Center who work tirelessly to ensure that no stone is left unturned in the battle to protect our children and to punish the guilty.

The AMBER Alert program has been so successful and has accomplished so much. The multi-jurisdictional, multi-discipline child abduction response teams now are poised to take this critical notification system one step further by providing for an immediate, full-scale response to a critical missing child incident.

The attorney general's Project Safe Childhood has begun successful efforts to pull together teams to wage war on Internet predators. And as a response to continued threats to our kids, small, independent efforts are popping up across communities daily.

I am very proud of the staff and volunteers of the Texas Center for the Missing for being on the front lines, providing both leadership and training to others in the field for all of these critical programs.

Unhappily, I must report to you that not one of these programs is adequately funded and few, if any, receive a penny of government funding at the local, state or national level. Local grassroots efforts are the most effective method for delivering prevention efforts and saving children's lives.

If only a fraction of our war on terror dollars was devoted to the protection of our children, we could dramatically reduce the number of children traumatized.

Margaret Mead said, "Never doubt that a small group of thoughtful, committed citizens can change the world. Indeed, it is the only thing that ever has."

I believe that we at the Texas Center for the Missing, through our extensive collaborative partnerships, and through our champions like Congressman Lampson, that we have begun to have a tremendous impact on this problem. But true social change does not happen in isolation. It happens through the concerted efforts of a diverse group of caring, committing citizens focusing on a complex issues and seeing, really seeing, not just the forest, but the trees.

We must ensure the replication of these collaborative networks 10,000-fold are our country and the world to save both our children and ourselves from a future more bleak than we can imagine.

Thank you.

[The statement of Ms. Alberts follows:]

## Prepared Statement of Beth Alberts, CEO, Texas Center for the Missing

### *The problem*

During 2006 there were 662,228 children reported missing in the United States and 60,729 in my home State of Texas (The National Crime Information Center, 2007). In Texas, 5,182 of those cases remained active at the end of 2006, and I lie awake at night wondering if we will be able to recover all of those missing children.

Any child who is away from a stable and loving home is a child at risk. No child chooses to be marginalized. Children never knowingly make a choice to expose themselves to exploitation and victimization. A child who chooses to run away is always running from a bad place to what they hope is a better place. They do not consciously choose to become vulnerable to predators and exploiters. It has often been said that children are our most valuable resource, but this is not reflected in our practices as a society.

The National Runaway Switchboard reports between 1.6 and 2.8 million youth run away in a year and that youth aged 12 to 17 are at higher risk for homelessness than adults.[8] Despite these startling statistics, law enforcement training academies are not required to provide any

Amber Alert or missing persons investigative tools, training, or resources. Local nonprofit agencies must fill the void.

## *The solution: Local nonprofit leadership and collaboration*

Harris County, Texas, represents Texas Center for the Missing's largest client base. Harris is the largest of the 13 counties in Texas Center for the Missing's primary service area and has a larger population than 24 states in U. S. From 2005 to 2006, the number of children reported missing rose from 11,648 to 14,809 and in Harris County alone, from 8,905 to 11,134—both of these represent more than a 25% increase! Might I repeat, this is a 25% increase in just one year. Despite these alarming numbers, there is no dedicated funding for local prevention efforts or law enforcement investigation and response.

Yes, there is some good news. Strategic partnerships are being formed across the United States and North America. Collaborative efforts like Project Safe Childhood and regional Child Abduction Response Teams are set to have a significant impact through both prevention and recovery of missing children. However, neither of these vital projects is funded. Local organizations are required to tap into their already stretched budgets to provide the people, the time, the resources, and the coordination to make these efforts successful.

## *Roles of Texas Center for the Missing: A model for local efforts*

Texas Center for the Missing offers, or coordinates the delivery of, services to meet the needs of the entire spectrum of missing persons issues. I would encourage other communities to implement a similar comprehensive community child safety plan that should include:

- Programs to educate parents and caregivers in the ways to safeguard children on the streets and on the Internet, and exactly what to do, step-by-step, if a child does go missing;
- Encouraging families to discuss safety issues and to create their own emergency response plan;
- Programs to educate our children in ways to stay safe in our community and on the Internet, and alternatives to running away;
- Fast public notification of a missing child via the Amber Alert for abducted children, or other systems for those missing children who were not abducted;
- Timely, coordinated responses to endangered missing child incidents; and
- Follow-up and aftercare for victims and families.

Texas Center for the Missing's advocacy and support services for victims and their families include guidance in reporting and finding a missing or abducted child, guidance in finding a runaway child, a resource database for abduction survivors and their families, and liaison support between families and law enforcement including case management, reunification, and information and referral services.

## *Amber Alert*

The National Center on Missing and Exploited Children reports that there are 121 Amber Alert programs across the United States credited with recovering 236 children. In the 13-county Houston Region, covering more than 12,000 square miles and a population of more than 5.5 million people, we have issued 65 Amber Alerts representing 70 children. Of these, children in 58 cases were recovered safely, 3 were found deceased, and 4 remain missing. This is an 89% success rate and exemplifies what a powerful tool the Amber Alert can be.

The Amber Alert has made a huge difference in missing child cases; however, it is imperative to understand what the Amber Alert is and what it is not. The Amber Alert is a very effective tool for law enforcement to enlist help in tracking down an abductor, the abductor's vehicle or the missing child. It is a way for the media and the general public to assist in the recovery of an innocent child and a malicious predator.

The Amber Alert is not a panacea. It will never replace a thorough, efficient, and effective law enforcement investigation. It will not replace vigilant supervision of children by trusted adults nor will it replace missing child prevention and education programs. It will not replace adequate prison sentences and good criminal justice supervision of probationers or parolees and, in particular, child sex offenders. Rapists and child molesters are serial offenders. It is well documented within the mental health community that most sex offenders are beyond rehabilitation ("compared to non-sex offenders released from State prisons, released sex offenders were 4 timesmore likely to be rearrested for a sex crime."[9]).

Law enforcement officers are the only ones who can issue an Amber Alert for an abducted child. It is a critical element in the resolution of a child abduction, but it is only a part of what we must do to keep children safe. We must each do our part by protecting children and responding when they are in danger. It is my fervent hope that someday soon we will not need the Amber Alert, the Child AbductionResponse Team or a National Missing Children's Day because all of our community's children will be safe.

### Southeast Texas Child Abduction Response Team (SETCART)

The Southeast Texas Child Abduction Response Team (SETCART) is an effort to bring seasoned investigators, tenured prosecutors, search-and-rescue volunteers and victims' advocates together to work the most urgent child abduction cases. TheSoutheast Texas Child Abduction Response Team will enable the immediate deployment of all necessary resources for qualifying cases and therefore positively impact these serious, life-threatening scenarios.

Texas Center for the Missing and the Houston Regional Amber Alert are providing leadership for the development and implementation of the Southeast Texas Child Abduction Response Team. Our effort was the first in Texas and serves theregion that historically has the most missing child cases in the state. With over 150 law enforcement agencies in the Southeast Texas region, this is a Herculean effort that requires unbiased leadership and strong relationships within the community. Currently, more than 70 law enforcement agencies in our region have signed on to SETCART.

SETCART is a multi-disciplinary, cross-jurisdictional, pre-planned and coordinated response to cases of endangered missing children and child abductions based upon a highly successful model system operating in Florida. While Florida has a state mandate and state funding with which to implement their CART process, Texas is not so fortunate. SETCART is a grassroots-driven effort in which participation is purely voluntary for all of our member agencies.

### Missing Persons Response Kit

Texas Center for the Missing has also developed a Missing Persons Response Kit for law enforcement agencies so that they have at their fingertips the tools and contacts to provide the fastest, most effective response in the critical period after a child is missing. Amber Alert and Missing Persons Investigation training is provided upon delivery of each resource kit. Contents of the Resource Kits can be found in Appendix A.

### Southeast Texas Search and Rescue Alliance (SETSARA)

One of the greatest achievements of Texas Center for the Missing has been the coordination of the Southeast Texas Search and Rescue Alliance (SETSARA): a coalition of volunteer search-and-rescue groups and law enforcement partners. Prior to the creation of SETSARA, law enforcement had little confidence in the professionalism of search-and-rescue experts and, therefore, did not access this importantresource. To compound the issue, there was a mutual feeling of distrust among the individual search-and-rescue groups so that communication was limited and duplication of efforts was common. Now local groups work together to offer effective and efficient search resources to law enforcement and the community.

Formed in 2001, SETSARA provides its membership with search training and public safety agencies (e.g., law enforcement, fire department, and wildlife agencies)with awareness, education, and search services. By providing necessary resources to law enforcement (and only the resources they need and request), we enable law enforcement agencies to focus on what they do best—the investigation.

### Association of Missing and Exploited Children's Organizations (AMECO)

AMECO is an organization of member agencies in the United States and Canada who provide services to families with missing and exploited children. Our missionis to build and nurture an association of credible, ethical and effective non-profit organizations that serve this vulnerable population.

In partnership with the National Center on Missing and Exploited Children and the International Center on Missing and Exploited Children, the member organizations of the Association of Missing and Exploited Children's Organizations, of which Texas Center for the Missing is one, serve hundreds of thousands of children andfamilies each year.

These passionate, professional, caring staff and volunteers work diligently to protect children. Most of us feel it is a mission, a calling, and not just a job. However, we are truly fighting an uphill battle. Two things threaten the work we do: a lack of awareness on the part of the community and legislators about the severity of the problem, and the lack of funding to support these critical life-saving efforts.

Our greatest challenge has been that funding dollars are scarce while demand for our services continues to increase!

### Crime-Stoppers

Another collaborative partnership that Texas Center for the Missing has found to be successful is working with the local Crime Stoppers organization. Crime Stoppers of Houston works closely with Texas Center for the Missing and the Houston Amber Alert to maximize the publicity of open Amber Alert cases on the anniversary of the child's abduction. The press conferences convened by Crime Stoppers of Houston provide another tool for law enforcement agencies to secure leads in a cold case.

### The Internet Threat

I believe the battle to protect our children has moved, largely, from the street to the Internet. This is not good news. Unfortunately, the Internet has re-defined who is accessible and expanded the victim pool exponentially. A single predator can communicate with hundreds of children and set them up for victimization. Predators share their victims with other predators and manipulate children to self-exploit by sending explicit photos across the internet which are then shared among these heinous criminals.

Locally, Texas Center for the Missing participates in the US Attorney's Southern District Office efforts to implement this vital program. Prevention is key to educate children on the dangers they face online, as well as how to avoid self-exploitation. The very simple concept that, "Digital is forever." is often lost on the most impressionable in our society—young teenagers who are looking for "safe" ways to rebel against their parents and expand their boundaries as young adults. To address this issue, Texas Center for the Missing has developed a cadre of internet safety education programs which are modeled closely upon the National Center for Missing and Exploited Children's NetSmartz program. Preventing a child from being abused or exploited is the ultimate goal in all of our educational programs. A complete list of our educational programs can be found in Appendix B.

### Project Safe Childhood

Guided by the leadership of the Attorney General, Project Safe Childhood (PSC) aims to combat the proliferation of technology-facilitated sexual exploitation crimes against children. The threat of sexual predators soliciting children for physical sexual contact is well-known and serious; the danger of the production, distribution, and possession of child pornography is equally dramatic and disturbing. The response to these growing problems must be coordinated, comprehensive, and robust. It must aim to investigate and prosecute vigorously as well as protect and assist victimized children. At the same time, it must recognize the need for a broad, community-based effort to protect our children and to guarantee to future generations the opportunity to grow safely into adulthood.

Project Safe Childhood is a definite step in the right direction, pulling together diverse teams working together to keep children safer online, to snare Internet Predators and prosecute them to the fullest. Unfortunately, the predators are cunning, incredibly technologically savvy and highly adaptable to all of the obstacles we place in front of them. We must arm ourselves better against this crime on all levels or we will remain seriously outgunned. As Attorney General Gonzales says, "We can not prosecute our way out of this problem." Sadly, this program, too, is unfunded.

# JENNY'S STORY[*]

*In January, 2006, a petite, 15-year-old girl from League City, TX, was lured away over the Internet by a 26-year-old man who lived in her area. He picked her up, took her to his house, drugged and raped her and shared her with two of his friends, one of whom carved Xs with a razor blade from one of her pelvic bones across to the other. 18 months later she and her fam-ily are still struggling with their recovery while having to deal with the court, the DA's office and the fact that one of the perpetrators of this heinous crime is on the run and may never face justice. This traumatized victim and family strive everyday to get their lives back to normal.*

*Many civilians as well as law enforcement officers do not feel that internet lures are a danger or on some level believe that a child who leaves of their own volition is not endangered or does not deserve emergency response. Jenny's story exemplifies how a child's single poor choice can lead to a nightmarish experience that becomes a life sentence for and her entire family.*

### Next steps

The U. S. Attorney General's Project Safe Childhood, Jessica's Law, which has been passed in various states across the country, and the recently passed Adam Walsh Child Protection and Safety Act provide even greater support of programs to arm children and families as well as punish those who would rob our children of their innocence.

We are fortunate to have all of the partnerships and programs discussed in this document, but it will take all of us, working together, to truly protect our children. In the past, we could let our children play in the front yard without standing guard over them. In the past, we could put our children to bed at night and comfortably expect to find them safely there the next morning. Unfortunately, these two simple acts, and many more, can no longer be taken for granted. We have seen children snatched out of their yards and their school and play areas, off the streets in our communities, and from their very homes, that place we all think of as a haven.

# RACHEL

*Robert Cooke, whose daughter Rachel has been missing since January 2002 says "When I first met the director of Texas EquuSearch, he told me my wife Janet and I are now in a special club. It's a club no one wants to join. It's a club of sorrow and grief. It's the club of parents and families of missing children.*

*The club is full of emotions. There is anger at the person who took your loved one. The worst feeling of all is helplessness. What can I do? What haven't I done? We've posted flyers and passed out bumper stickers and buttons, but nothing has brought our Rachel home.*

*Many sleepless nights occur in the club. When you are able to sleep and you awake, you wake up to a reality far worse than any nightmare. The guilt is overwhelming. Why was I not there to protect her? Why didn't I teach her how to protect herself? I am her father; it was my job to protect her. Well, I say it's time to reduce the membership drive for this club".*

### Funding

Nothing to which I have ever been exposed has affected me as deeply as this issue. I have never been more convinced that working together, caring people can make a difference. I have never been more convinced that we can, we must, do more to protect our children and keep their families from joining "the club."

Unfortunately, most people believe that the missing children problem is solely the province of law enforcement and is already well-funded by our tax dollars. As a result, concerned citizens are unaware of the need to support this effort. The truth is a very different story.

Did you know that there are no designated funds for our Amber Alert system? There are no monies at the local, state or federal level to help offset the costs associated with administering this important effort. Each year in the thirteen-county Houston-Galveston region, populated by more than 5 million people, 12,000—15,000 children are reported missing, and Texas Center for the Missing is responsible for all costs associated with administering the Amber Alert in our high-need region.

### Legislation and other public policy issues to pursue
- Comprehensive Funding Tied to Collaborative Efforts
- Establish Statewide Minimum Standards for Certification for Search and Rescue Volunteers
- Give parole officers the right to enter sex offenders residences so law enforcement officers do not have to wait hours for warrants when looking for an abducted child

### Conclusion
Regardless of the circumstances under which a child is missing or homeless—abduction, runaway or thrownaway—each of those children, dulled by that trauma, represents a bright future—our future. However, we must devote resources to helping them regain the innocence and sense of hope that will inspire them to become an active, caring part of the communities in which we live. Otherwise, we have condemned them and ourselves to less—less quality of life, less security, less of a safety-net for those closest to us.

When I was a child, I dreamed of having a child, loving and nurturing a young life. When I realize that dream and had my two daughters, I poured my heart and soul and most of my energy into protecting them and raising them. They were my number one priority, as they should be.

Too often children are not the number one priority of their parents, or of the communities and society in which they are reared. Lip-service is paid to them in grand speeches and editorials, and through poorly funded programs that address piecemeal programs instead of servicing the spectrum of comprehensive needs.

Ultimately, we are judged not on what we say but what we do, and children learn from us too—not from listening to what we say but by watching and emulating what we do, and recognizing where they fall in our priorities. I believed while raising my young children that the world was, at least generally, a safe place. I wonder what young mothers think now.

Unfortunately, adults no longer represent figures of authority to our children, those to whom respect is due. Adults are seen as threats to, or targets of, children. However, we must not blame the child. The child learns by example, by our actions not our proselytizing.

We can blame the media, the celebrities, and law enforcement, but we are the ones who must bear the brunt of the blame—parents, grandparents, citizens of the communities in which our children grow up, decision-makers and policy-makers. We must ask ourselves each day "Am I putting the welfare of our children first?"

We are fortunate in the Houston area to have a comprehensive network of organizations that mobilize and deploy resources to help save children. Most areas don't. However, would it not be better to eliminate the problem of missing children by putting child predators on notice that we won't tolerate them targeting our children, and if they do, we will hunt them down like the animals they are?

Predators like Joseph Smith, who murdered Carlie Brucia in Florida in 2004 and will never be released from prison, will never victimize another child, but those like him are legion. Our best defense against his type are more, and better-funded, programs like the ones AMECO Organizations offer to parents and children in how to reduce the ways for them to become victims.

Each time a child has been abducted—my heart is crushed, and I want to rewind the clock to see what could have been done differently to prevent the tragedy. But all I can do is help when I can and stay steadfast in my convictions that we can reduce these incidences. Working in the missing child field has changed my life forever. I am convinced there is no more challenging or rewarding work, nor has my contribution to any field been more important. Together we can save lives and childhood's innocence.

For the victim and family involved in an abduction or Internet luring case—the victimization is a "life sentence". Their lives are normal the day before the incident, but during and after it there lives will never be the same again.

[Additional materials submitted by Ms. Alberts follow:]

# APPENDIX A.—LAW ENFORCEMENT MISSING PERSON RESOURCE KIT INVENTORY LIST

## Pre-Planning

- When It's Not an Amber Alert: Developing a Missing Child Response Plan
- Law Enforcement Policy and Procedures for Reports of Missing and Abducted Children

## Amber Alert

- Houston Regional Amber Plan Brochure
- Missing Children, the (Houston) Amber Alert and You
- Website Overview (www.amber-plan.net)
- User Name and Password
- Navigating the Online Web Activation System
- Contact Information
- Houston Regional Amber Plan (includes After Action Report Form)
- Texas Amber Alert Network
- Amber Alert (National) Brochure
- Amber Alert Fact Sheet
- Amber Alert Best Practices Guide for Public Information Officers
- Amber Alert Best Practices Guide for Broadcasters and Other Media Outlets

## Local Resources and Investigative Checklists, Alert Systems, and Guides

- Resources for Law Enforcement—Texas Center for the Missing
- Investigative Checklist for First Responders
- Alzheimer's and Related Disorders Missing Person Checklist
- Lost Person Questionnaire
- A Child is Missing Flyer
- Critical Reach Alert System Packet
- FBI's Child Abduction Response Plan: An Investigative Guide
- Missing and Abducted Children: A Law Enforcement Guide to Case Investigation and Program Management
- Recovery and Reunification of Missing Children: A Team Approach

## Texas Checklists, NCIC, DNA Tools, and Clearinghouse Services

- Basic Checklist for Working Unidentified Person Cases (Texas)
- NCIC $M Messages
- Information on the Texas Missing Persons DNA Database
- Texas Missing Persons CODIS DNA Database Sample Collection Kit
- Sexual Assault Medical Examinations Reimbursement Form for Law Enforcement Agencies
- Laboratory of Forensic Anthropology and Human Identification: Case Submission Information
- Texas DPS Missing Persons Clearinghouse Brochure
- Texas DPS Special Crimes Service Overview
- Texas DPS Missing Persons Clearinghouse State and Federal Missing Persons Statutes

## National Resources

- National Center for Missing and Exploited Children (NCMEC) Resources for Law Enforcement Professionals
- NCMEC Nationwide Support Services
- Association of Missing and Exploited Children's Organizations (AMECO) Membership List
- National Association of Search and Rescue (www.nasar.org)
- Safe Return: Alzheimer's Disease Guide for Law Enforcement
- Resources/Websites of U.S. Departments
- NCMEC General Information and Publications
- National Training Available

## Family Resource Packet

- When Your Child is Missing: A Family Survival Guide
- Texas Crime Victims' Compensation Application Form (English)

- Texas Crime Victims' Compensation Application Form (Spanish)
- Victim Support Resource Database (Greater Houston Area)
- A Family Resource Guide on International Parental Kidnapping
- Alzheimer's Association Brochure
- SafeReturn—Wandering: Who's at Risk?
- Covenant House-Texas Flyer

### *Discs and Software*

- Simple Leads Management System
- Federal Resources on Missing and Exploited Children: A Directory for Law Enforcement and Other Public and Private Agencies

## *Texas Center for the Missing Programs*

**S.A.F.E. Child Puppet Show** is for children under 10 years old and features Detective Buddy who teaches Billy and his friend, Barb, how to stay safe with real-life examples.

**Missing Child Prevention Training for Caring Adults** is specifically designed to teach parents, childcare providers, concerned community leaders, and educators how to keep children safe from abduction and internet lures.

**Internet Safety Training** consists of multi-media presentations developed in three formats geared toward: (1) parents/adult caregivers, (2) 6th-12th graders, and (3) elementary-aged children.

**Alzheimer's Wandering Prevention Training** is for caregivers whose loved ones suffer from any form of dementia to deter the highly dangerous pattern of wandering.

**Casework/Case Management** includes: general safety information, child ID kits, Crime Victims' Compensation Advocacy, search-and-rescue resources, and law enforcement liaison services.

**Houston Amber Alert** is administered by Texas Center for the Missing. We train law enforcement on the local Amber Alert system, provide 24-hour support for alert issuance, and deploy trained search-and-rescue experts upon request.

**Southeast Texas Search and Rescue Alliance** is a consortium of search-and-rescue experts. Texas Center for the Missing coordinates the training and deployment of these vetted search-and-rescue volunteers through an alliance of member organizations dedicated to finding the missing.

713.314.3673 • Fax: 713.522.7386
www.thetexascenter.org

*We offer help, and hope, to the missing and their families.*

## *Programs (cont.)*

**Southeast Texas Child Abduction Response Team** is a multi-discipline, cross-jurisdictional, coordinated response to endangered missing children and child abductions based upon a highly successful model in Florida. By coordinating the resources that already exist in our 13-county region, we can bring all relevant assets of the 150+ law enforcement agencies and myriad social services together to find an at-risk child, apprehend predators, and reduce the number of children affected in the future.

## *Frequently Asked Questions*

**How much does each presentation cost?**
All programs are provided to the community at no charge. However, a suggested donation of $50 per presentation is greatly appreciated.

**How long does each presentation last?** The S.A.F.E. Child Puppet Show lasts approximately 20 minutes, and requires 30 minutes to set-up. All other presentations are typically one hour, but can be shortened or expanded depending on your organization's needs.

**How many people can each presentation serve?**
Texas Center for the Missing is only limited by the size of your meeting space and the audiovisual equipment capabilities at your location.

**What are the reservation procedures?**
Contact us at 713.314.3673 or support@tcftm.org to schedule your presentation.

**Are programs available in Spanish?**
Some materials are available in Spanish. Currently, we require a volunteer translator from the requesting organization to interpret the presentations.

**How do I request child identification kits?**
Child identification kits are distributed at all educational events. In addition, you can contact us directly (713.314.3673 or support@tcftm.org) to receive this critical resource for recovering children quickly and safely.

*Chairwoman McCarthy.* Thank you very much.

There are many of us that sit on the Education Committee that feel very strongly—before I came here, I was a nurse, so I kind of look at things holistically. And many of us are looking at those young families from when the child is born to be able to reach out and give help to them at that particular time, hopefully so that we won't be running into problems later on, working with the parents and certainly working with the newborn child.

But, with that, Rusty and Mr. Rolle, I guess I would want to hear from you. You have been through the justice system, you have been through foster homes, you have been through homeless shelters.

Where do you feel could be an improvement as far as where did the system drop both of you? Where did we lose you, as a society? What could have been done, or what do you think could have been done? Because I am sure you probably thought about that, if somebody had gotten to you at an earlier age to work with you, or did you have to go through it, just grow out of it, or with the help that you got?

Could you put your mike on?

*Mr. Rolle.* Today, I had a conversation with Vicki. She runs the Network for Youth. And I didn't know of half of the services that were in New York City. And I didn't know how to get to the place that would have told me where the services was.

I kind of just stumbled on people in the community just trying— when I got kicked out of my mother's house, I was walking down the street and a friend of mine who was in the theater group said, you can stay at my house. I had this big bag of stuff in my hand, and he said, what happened? I told him what happened. But that was only because I was a part of that group.

And this was out of our own pocket. We met at the local school, so it was just her ingenuity, trying to figure out how to do something, because she just had a heart. Even myself, with the work that I do. So a lot of it is, I guess, public awareness, or in entertainment we say marketing, to be known.

I don't know, sitting on the subway, I can see a place, see signs or see something that is attractive to a young person that he can say, all right, if need something, I could call this number. And I never knew of any places like that. So I think that was missing.

And then for me, personally, I think where I got lost a little bit was the arts in the school for me, being in school—not so much the arts, but a place to kind of just talk, if that makes sense. When I heard him speak, it touched me, because I feel like that is why I couldn't pay attention in school, or I acted out, was because I didn't have a place that I could talk about those things.

Who wants to hear about some kid, what he is dealing with? So that is where I kind of got lost.

*Chairwoman McCarthy.* Thank you.

Rusty?

*Mr. Booker.* I guess I could say, going through everything I went through, I guess I can say I always felt like I could go to Safe Place to get what I needed done.

*Chairwoman McCarthy.* How did you find out about the Safe Place, just to go to them?

*Mr. Booker.* When I was 12, my previous foster mother told me about it and she told me to go to the library and ask for it. And it took me a couple of hours. I sat there thinking, because I was kind of scared about what was going to happen afterwards, after I got there.

But I finally got the courage to walk up there and ask for it. And, like I said, when I got there, I talked to somebody and within 2 weeks I was with that previous foster mother that had told me about it.

And I don't feel like the state really did anything after I left there to find me somewhere to go. They just stuck me back in an abusive home. And there, I just went downhill. I once again was in that home and it wasn't doing anything for me.

I had nobody to talk to, was roaming the streets, selling drugs, doing drugs, just doing whatever I pleased. And nobody was ever there for me.

*Chairwoman McCarthy.* And I guess just a follow-up question, for the rest of the panel, especially with what kind of background checks are we doing for the foster homes that these kids are going into?

And what are we doing as far as when you talked about the first thing I was talking about—obviously, we should be fingerprinting those that are working with children. We should be doing the same thing with the elderly, in nursing homes.

I happen to think we should be going both ways, because there is a lot of abuse in nursing homes, also. But I will go back with what is the answer? When these kids go into foster homes and they turn out to be bad homes and these kids have no place to go?

*Mr. Allen.* Madam Chair, clearly, there are an extraordinary number of committed, dedicated people doing great work. I mean, what we hear around the country is there just aren't enough. And there are inadequate resources to support these alternative programs and been the basic social services programs.

And state and local governments are just overwhelmed with the sheer magnitude of the problem. And I think this is a very complex answer, and it is one that involves more resources and also involves—you talk about background screening.

We have dealt with these cases all the time that make it to us and we just have to build systems where the protection of the child is paramount in all of this. And I think there are ways to do that, but it is complicated.

*Chairwoman McCarthy.* I will finish up with this. I know back in New York many years ago, actually, my neighbor took in foster children for a long time. One of the problems that she came across was back then every 2 years, even though the children were with her, happy, they had to be moved out so there would be no attachment. Thank goodness we have outgrown that, hopefully to a large extent.

With that, Mr. Platts?

*Mr. Platts.* Thank you, Madam Chair.

My thanks again to all of our witnesses and, Rusty and Mr. Rolle, or Kazi, if you prefer, especially the two of you, being willing to come and share your personal experiences and stories. It certainly helps us better understand the real-life aspect of these issues.

And I commend your courage in doing so and through your efforts of ensuring that your challenges result in positive outcomes for others. And that through your efforts here today and not just today in testifying, but in your work, in your community, in your efforts, that you are going to make a difference for others. And so I especially thank you.

And I would like to recognize, and I don't know if he is comfortable, and I don't know who he is, so if he is not, but if Mr. Bill, as referenced here, if you would like to stand and be recognized on behalf of all of those who work with children. [Applause.]

We appreciate your helping Rusty to be here and, as I say, in kind of being recognized on behalf of all of our men and women throughout the country who are working on behalf of youth to improve and ensure the safety of their lives, so thank you.

Mr. Allen, I want to follow up, and you talked about it in your written testimony and in your oral testimony, about the background checks, this effort to try to ensure that predators don't get access through a legitimate program. Did you say 3 percent on average?

*Mr. Allen.* We have done in the pilot that was set up under the PROTECT Act, the FBI runs the records, and then we do fitness determinations so that we communicate to the youth organization on a red-light, yellow-light, green-light basis.

We have reviewed 25,000 applicants, and of that number, roughly 7 percent had criminal records and slightly less than 3 percent had what we considered disqualifying criminal records. This is in every case knowing that they are being fingerprinted and knowing that they are going to be subjected to a national FBI-based criminal history background check.

*Mr. Platts.* Given that that is 3 percent of that 25,000, so we are talking a significant number, that are seeking access to children that shouldn't be, what happens once you make the identification?

I guess, does law enforcing in any way follow up on that information? Are those who obviously present information either falsely, that they have no reason—I imagine some of those 3 percent in their adjudication probably are prohibited from having contact with children.

Is there any specific follow-up mechanism to ensure that not just they are prevented from being in that program, because the worry is they will go to another program and not get caught?

*Mr. Allen.* Yes. Now, I think the key point in all of this is in many of these instances, these offenders have not done something wrong by applying to be a volunteer, absent some kind of violation of their parole condition or probation condition, but where possible, where actionable, we are making sure that the appropriate law enforcement agency gets that information.

*Mr. Platts.* Because by them having it, there may be something in their parole that says no contact and the fact that they actively sought would then be evidence that they are violating that parole.

*Mr. Allen.* Yes.

*Mr. Platts.* Okay, related to that, and, Ms. Alberts, I think it was in your testimony you talked about access to parolees and parole officers being given more access on a timely manner where there is belief that perhaps a child has been abducted or sexually abused by someone on parole.

*Ms. Alberts.* Absolutely. There are several cases. If you will recall, the Jessica Lunsford case, that was a case right there where she was in that parolee's residence, that had they not had to wait for a warrant, something could have been hopefully avoided at that time.

We just felt that, in working with our law enforcement agencies, that the probation and parole officers have rights of access to the domicile for welfare checks or those kinds of things. And why not in a case, during those critical first hours that a child is missing, if we can close in and close that gap, I think that would be phenomenal.

*Mr. Platts.* I assume that most of that is probably going to be driven by state law in most prosecutions.

*Ms. Alberts.* Right, right.

*Mr. Platts.* Although there are federal prosecutions as well. And I guess I was under the belief that someone on parole basically gave up their right to privacy while they are on parole. But your understanding is that if they go in for other reasons, but they still have to——

*Ms. Alberts.* My understanding is that in order to come in in a circumstance like this, it still has to meet the probable cause in order to justify a warrant. That is my understanding. I am not an attorney, but that is what my law enforcement folks are telling me.

*Mr. Platts.* I see my time has expired. I am not sure if we will have a chance to come back with a second round. If not, again, I want to thank each of you.

Is it okay if Ms. Eggleston had a follow-up I think?

*Chairwoman McCarthy.* Oh, sure.

*Ms. Krahe-Eggleston.* Many of the RHY providers are licensed by the state. So in Arizona, and I speak about my own state, every staff member that works, or volunteer that works in our programs have to be fingerprinted and have to go through a background check.

Yes, we do get those few that knowingly apply for positions. The challenge we have is the time line to get that information back. It is a drudgerous process. So even a good person coming to volunteer that has no background until they are cleared, we can't let them work with our young people.

So the challenge we have is the time line. It can take 3 to 6 months and it costs, $60, $80 a pop to have it done. So, for us, most of us are licensed. Most of us that provide the services within the RHY umbrella meet those criteria, but it is a time line issue more than anything else.

*Mr. Platts.* Thank you.

Thank you, Madam Chair.

Chairwoman *McCarthy.* You are welcome.

*Mr.* Grijalva?

*Mr. Grijalva.* Thank you, Madam Chair.

And, as my colleague Mr. Platts mentioned, let me thank Mr. Booker and Mr. Rolle. Your persistence and your strength is something that I respect and admire very much. Thank you for your testimony.

Ms. Krahe-Eggleston, a couple of questions. Do you have any data, or even an idea, of the percentage of homeless young people in the centers that you have that have aged out of foster care?

*Ms. Krahe-Eggleston.* Congressman, I could tell you an approximate, but I could gather that information for you specifically and get that to you in writing. We see a lot of street kids that have aged out of the system, by choice sometimes. They don't want to be involved with the system. They have been involved with the system that has been very difficult for them for a long time.

The foster care system isn't always a friendly system, to say the least. So most of them would rather not be involved with the system, and as soon as they turn 18, they disappear.

But the Chafee funds that came in a few years ago picked up a lot of those kids. But I can get you that information.

*Mr. Grijalva.* Thank you.

Your agency operates a residential program for homeless young families. Tell the committee a little bit about that and about what I perceive to be an increasing need for that kind of residential service.

*Ms. Krahe-Eggleston.* The young families that we see, whether they are single-parent families or intact young families, just trying to get by in today's time, it is very, very difficult. The housing costs, just the day-to-day living costs, become insurmountable. In the service delivery system we have, we have young couples.

We have couples that are under the age of 21 or 24 sometimes, but mostly under the age of 21, that choose to have children and they are a couple. And some are married, some are not. But they are a couple.

Being able to serve them is a huge gift to our community, and it is one that the need for that kind of service has become more and more apparent as time has gone by. I think we see that across the country with that.

Of course, single moms, single dads, raising kids at age 19 years old is a huge challenge today. We see it.

*Mr. Grijalva.* Thank you.

And one other question, if I may. Some examples of how your agency provides positive youth development principles to the young people that you work with. I think this legislation, this authorization, is also about youth development. It is not just a safe harbor. There are things that need to occur as part of that safe harbor.

*Ms. Krahe-Eggleston.* For me, the biggest issue around positive youth development is having the kids involved with every step of their process within the system. People can't decide what is going to happen to a 16-year-old by themselves. That 16-year-old or 15-year-old or 18-year-old needs to have a voice in what happens to them, for them, with them.

Also, getting the kids involved at all levels of our organization is really important, and most of us within the RHY community, kids are on our boards. Young people serve on our advisory committees. They have a say in how the program operates and what services they need.

*Mr. Grijalva.* Thank you very much.

*Ms. Krahe-Eggleston.* You are welcome.

*Mr. Grijalva.* A final question. Mr. Berg, you mentioned in your oral testimony, I don't know how to describe it, but you become desensitized, tolerate, benign acceptance of the idea or the concept of homelessness, and, in this specific instance, homeless youth.

We talked about outreach. We talked about getting information to those persons that need it. But how do we combat that attitude? I sense it as well. There is a margin of tolerance—"Oh, they are homeless"—and you kind of walk away from it.

*Mr. Berg.* Yes, thank you, Mr. Grijalva. I agree. I think hearings like this are helpful. The more community-based kind of hearings, I think the more people can hear from, particularly in the issue of youth homelessness, from young people themselves who have gone through these things.

I think that is very effective. I know I constantly talk to members of Congress and their staff who us sort of wonky, D.C. types can talk until we are blue in the face, but what they remember is talking to a person who had been homeless and suddenly realizing that this just wasn't some number on a page.

We struggle with that all the time. The other part is we need policies that are directed at immediate solutions, short-term solutions, getting people off the streets and into some sort of stable housing, fast. And we need to have performance measures for providers that include those.

I know the National Network for Youth has been in favor of that. Those are some of the things that will be helpful.

*Mr. Grijalva.* Thank you, Madam Chair.

*Chairwoman McCarthy.* You are welcome.

Mrs. Biggert?

*Mrs. Biggert.* Thank you, Madam Chairman.

One of the first situations I think that caused me to get so interested in these types of programs was having a neighbor who had a daughter that was troubled and was a runaway. And they never found her, never heard from her. My neighbor died not too long ago, and I think that was the thing that was so troubling to her, was never to know what had happened to her child.

And for all of the good work that all of you do on this, I noticed that, Mr. Allen, you have a cold case where you are still working on finding those missing children that have been gone for a long time.

*Mr. Allen.* Congresswoman, the media spotlight dims and the world forgets, but these families don't forget. And so we have a team that is actively looking at these long-term cases, trying to look for new leads. We have resolved, having worked more than 5,000 of these cases, resolved about, as I recall, 368.

All but 12 of them were resolved through identifying a deceased child. And while that doesn't bring a live child home, at least it brings closure. But I think it is important.

These are long, long-term cases. And in 12 of the cases, where law enforcement had run out of leads, the child was found alive and was brought home. So it is really important that we not forget about these kids that are out there.

*Mrs. Biggert.* Thank you, and thanks for all you do on that.

And then, Mr. Berg, how do you reach runaways? Or any of you that are in these services, and I know so many times that they are ready to come home if they can find a way home or a pathway to connect with their families again. How do you encourage that? How do they get to know about the services?

*Mr. Berg.* Yes, I think one of the things is the runaway and homeless youth programs of course include a very active street outreach program that I think is very effective and reaches lots and lots of people and are very effective where there is a family ready to take a child back.

I would note parenthetically that there are many situations where that is not the case, where the outreach is a good first step, but there is nothing behind it. And that is why more of the kinds of programs, transitional programs and permanent housing options, are very necessary.

But I think people in the field have really developed this sort of art and science of outreach to a very great extent. There are a lot of very skilled practitioners who carry this out.

Partly, it is knowing that there are options available and just making sure that people know what those are. I mean, the story about sort of not having a place to find about what sort of services are available I think is sort of a common one.

*Mrs. Biggert.* Well, one of the bill that I am working on is to provide for homeless children who are emancipated and are not working with their parents, or there is no connection. And right now, they cannot get scholarships to college because the parents can't or won't sign the form and they won't disclose their finances, which of course they wouldn't be using for their child's education, anyway.

Do you have any idea how many youth could take advantage of something like this?

*Mr. Rolle.* I had a couple of things, but just on that particular point, the state of California, they did something very similar where they wanted to talk about foster care, because it is very, very high there. And one of the things that I found when I emancipated is I didn't know where to go to go to the next level.

And I think that I am creating a network for the people in positions like yourself to look down at all of these people doing this work and connect them, because sometimes we don't know about each other.

And if there is a network of I don't have them, you have them, and we both kind of converse about what are the things that we can help each other on, I think that is very important. And a lot of times everybody is fighting for the money. There is not enough money. So if there is enough money, then we are, like, we can work more together.

So I think that is very important, especially for emancipated youth, because they are the ones who feel the jails, fill the cemetery, the strip clubs, because those girls, a lot of them go to college. They are the ones that are in the clubs, trying to go to college, really, trying to find a way. And the innovation is not there, and I think that was wonderful, what Ms. Eggleston said about having the young people involved.

Because young people, that is who evolved us as human beings. They are the ones that think innovatively and come with new ideas. And one of the feelings for most young people is that we don't matter.

I think she said an excellent point about terrorism. We know that that matters in America, but we don't feel as young people that we matter, by the way the funding goes, that there is not a feeling or a marketing from the government to say that young people matter and we don't want them homeless, we don't want them running away from home.

That feeling is not there, so I think innovation and having more strong voices of young people to say something about it.

*Mr. Berg.* If I could just add on that particular piece of legislation. I hope everyone, other members of the committee, are aware of this particular piece of legislation.

I can't tell you the numbers, but it is maybe not like the worst-off kids, but the idea that young people who have been abandoned by their parents can't go to college because there is nobody to sign the financial aid forms, I find that personally offensive. And I am glad it has been dealt with.

*Mrs. Biggert.* I hope all the members know, because if they sign up as co-sponsors, we can get it through much faster. So, thank you.

I yield back. Thank you.

*Chairwoman McCarthy.* Thank you.

Mr. Yarmuth?

*Mr. Yarmuth.* Thank you, Madam Chair.

And to all the professionals on the panel, thank you very much for being here. Thanks for all you do to help with this serious national problem.

Kazi, thank you for your story and for all you do.

Rusty, you did a great job and your community is very proud of you, and I am very proud to be your Congressman, so thank you for everything you have done today.

And Mr. Platts beat me to introducing Bill, but I will say that this morning, I was talking to Bill, and he mentioned the fact that when he was younger and people were deciding what to do, that all of his friends were becoming lawyers and politicians. I don't know who all those people were. But the implication may be that he hadn't chosen the right path, but I know he knows he did. And I know today Rusty is grateful that he did, and so are we.

Kazi mentioned something that leads me to a topic that came up in our forum that we held a few weeks ago. And that was the fact that even in a community like Louisville, which has national Safe Place headquarters and a wide array of services that are available to homeless and runaway youth, that there is no continuum of contact with the young people who are disconnected.

And they go from one service, where they do get some help or attention, and then they are back into the community and disconnected once again and they go through a series of these encounters with services. But nobody is there to kind of help them through the entire process.

Any of the professionals who would like to comment on that, and with specific reference to whether they know of any models for providing some kind of continuum.

*Ms. Alberts.* I like to think we are, and I think that what you have heard today in talking about the partnerships and collaborations, I think that is the key. You will notice in my written testimony, one of the things I said was to tie funding to collaborative efforts so that people don't feel like it is okay to operate in isolation when they hit a particular point on a spectrum of services.

There needs to be a requirement that you know what came before for the child and what needs to come after, because children fall through the cracks. They get a little bit of this and they get a little bit of that. And they try to make a patchwork quilt out of it, and there are huge, gaping gaps in those services.

This is a pet peeve of mine. I have been in nonprofit management for 27 years, and the reason we have the program that we have at the Texas Center for the Missing is that I recognize the need to make sure that if we are not doing it, somebody is doing it, all along, from the beginning to the end of those programs, because it is the only true way to make a difference. It is the only way to save those kids who need help.

And communication, collaboration, partnerships, whatever it takes. And no territoriality. There is no my piece of the pie needs to be bigger than your piece of the pie.

I don't know who the author of the quote is. It is unknown, but it says it is amazing what you can get accomplished when nobody cares who gets the credit.

*Mr. Yarmuth.* Did you want to respond, Ms. Krahe-Eggleston?

*Ms. Krahe-Eggleston.* I would really like to.

*Mr. Yarmuth.* Sure.

*Ms. Krahe-Eggleston.* I have the honor of working in a community that works very hard at collaboration for the young people that we serve. We have a small group of providers of the types of services that I referred to today. There is four or five of us in town, and we meet every week or every other week, at least, and talk about the cases that we have.

The money only goes so far, so we try not to duplicate services. We really have those conversations across the board that our case managers have.

Good case management, to me, is the key, building that relationship with the young person and being able to maintain that. Funding that we get our service that we get that are narrow based, where there is a finite beginning and end, it doesn't do our young people any good.

What does the best for your young people is a continued involvement over the long haul. It is the relationship Rusty talked about with his workers. It is the relationship that the young people we are involved with—in our young moms program, we have been involved with moms for the last 6 years and we know, and they stay with us a couple years, we know where 97 percent of those young women are today and keep in touch with them regularly.

That is the key to success.

*Mr. Yarmuth.* I would like to also maybe add another element to this discussion, and that is the connection between the juvenile justice system and the social services that are available for the homeless, because obviously many of the kids who are homeless and runaways end up in an encounter with the juvenile justice system.

Is this something that your experiences has shown that works or is there sometimes too great a disconnect between the judicial system and the social service aspect?

*Mr. Allen.* Just a brief comment, and I think these folks know better than I, but when I got into this, when we got into it, in the 1970s, the whole premise was you would have the law enforcement system over here that is viewing these kids in one way. You have the social services system over here that is viewing these kids in another way. And the kids get caught in the cracks.

And so our whole beginning in this effort in Louisville 30 years ago was to create a police-social work team, to kind of blur the traditional lines and the traditional turf battles between jurisdictions, between units of government and, frankly, I think there are models all over the country where that is working and working very well.

And when you put people together, they can share information, even though their mindset and their approaches are different.

*Mr. Rolle.* I had just something real brief on that. I think that one of the key things is the innovation. And the reason why I say innovation, there is a song by a guy named Justin Timberlake. He had a song called I am bringing sexy back. But if you translate that into the work that we are doing, it is old ideas in a new time.

Even the funding that is for stuff like this is, to my understanding, the same amount that it has been many, many years ago, and the economy is just different. So even finding the people working in social services, and I know a lot of them, they are burnt out.

Their bosses don't even care, because their salaries don't really— so that feeling that you get burnt out doing this work. People need things. They need you to be excited about coming to work and that is why they fall through the cracks in the juvenile justice system.

For people doing this youth work, there needs to be innovation in how we deal with them. We need to make the job, for lack of better words, in the way that I know how to translate it, is sexy. People need to feel like I want to be involved with the youth and giving back. So that is one thing.

And another thing, something that you asked earlier, I think, when we fall through the cracks is in the foster home, when you go back there, there is not—I think that instead of just placing them in a home, the whole house should now go under some type of training.

In New York City, there is a place called Harlem Children's Zone, and that is a great model for a lot of things that he is talking about. But, the Harlem Children's Zone, they provide training from birth, when the baby is still in the womb, for certain families, so that those families can have that training.

And it is sexy to go there and the whole environment. The funding is there, the whole environment says that, all right, our youth matter. So I would just say innovation is the key word.

*Mr. Yarmuth.* Thank you, Madam Chair.

*Chairwoman McCarthy.* You are quite welcome. When you were talking about burnt out, I am thinking of my nurses, all over the country. We are trying to work on that, too.

Mr. Sarbanes?

*Mr. Sarbanes.* Thank you, Madam Chair, for holding the hearing.

I wanted first to salute Representative Biggert for her work on these issues. In particular, we have been working recently on the McKinney-Vento funning, which is critical in a whole host of areas in terms of keeping families together and combating homelessness among young people. And Representative Lampson, who has obviously been right on the forefront of dealing with issues of missing children.

Can you quantify the extent to which the issue is about communication and coordination and collaboration for purposes of finding kids who have fallen through the cracks, versus real services that have to be provided through affirmative outreach?

Because what I gather from the discussion is there is a certain amount of this which is just making sure that we are in touch with each other better, so that when kids disappear or run away, or are lost or missing, there is a communication infrastructure in place that allows you to find them and get them back home.

But there is another dimension, which is reaching out to kids on a continuous basis and having resources behind that so that you can not just get them reconnected, but support that so that they don't fall into the cracks again. And I don't know if you can quantify how that splits out.

You will probably say that they are too interrelated to separate, but I don't know if anybody wants to comment on that.

*Ms. Krahe-Eggleston.* I think for education purposes, the thing that helps the most is people just knowing what is going on. The schools are a great place to connect with young people. If they know there is a safe place out there within their school structure and the school is aware of what is going on in the communities, they are a huge help.

We have found that over and over and over again. Youngsters as young as 8, 9, 10 years old, know that there is a principal or a teacher or somebody that has the information about a service, whether it be in regards to homelessness or a multitude of services.

But the school system, I have found, is probably one of the best ways to get the information out so that teachers know that there are services out there, so that those other significant people in the little ones' lives start young enough that notice things going on with a child and his family. And teachers are great at that.

Sometimes, they don't know the resources that are out there. So, in my book, it is really important that the education process is a community-wide process about the services that are out there and what needs to happen, but, as well, it is our responsibility to get that information out.

We spend a lot of time in the schools, mostly middle schools and high schools, but we get information out to all the counselors on a regular basis, and I think that is part of that prevention and early intervention piece that may avoid those children hitting the streets at age 16 or 14.

*Mr. Sarbanes.* The other question I had is that in the larger committee, Education and Labor Committee, we have had numbers of hearings over the last few months on the issue of economic insecurity in the country. And I would imagine that you all can sense the interplay between this predatory culture on the one side and the economic insecurity of any families on the other.

And as economic insecurity is heightened in the society, it leads to increased pressures on families. It helps break down families in ways that then makes them much more vulnerable to the predatory side of our society. And if you could comment on that, if you are seeing the trends of that sort of interplay between this culture and economic insecurity.

*Mr. Rolle.* I experienced that. It wasn't in this country, but coming from a poor country, the reason why I was in that abusive situation was really based on that. The lady that my mother left me with, my mother got stuck in America and she couldn't leave.

So the lady that I lived with, I was there too long and I became another expense. And the stress of that, and then her husband leaving, was the reason why I became the stress release. When the resources are there for people—she was a stepparent—so when the resources are there for people like her. And it goes even deeper, because the reason there are not resources for people like her is because the agencies that do the work feel as if they don't have enough resources and then it trickles down.

Even the brother here, he said when his father left and his mother was dealing with it, she had to go through her healing, she needed to know that there were resources and a place for her, because of what she was dealing with trickled down to him, and it goes on.

*Ms. Krahe-Eggleston.* Many, many of our young people are homeless due to economic issues, whether it means a parent became incarcerated and all of a sudden there is no more money at home, or that mom had another baby and you are 16, you are 17, just go fend for yourself.

The economic issues are huge, and we have many, many young people that live 10 to an apartment, just to try and get by. And they are okay, they are doing their best to get by.

A lot of our young moms come to us with a garbage bag of clothes and that is it, and a baby on their hip, and have no place to go. Think about affording just diapers today. Just think, if you have been to the grocery store lately and bought a box of diapers, think about living on minimum wage, having to pay a portion of childcare if you don't qualify and having to pay for food, housing. Just the day-to-day living is almost impossible. And it is very hopeless for many of them.

*Mr. Sarbanes.* Thanks for your testimony.

*Chairwoman McCarthy.* Mr. Lampson?

*Mr. Lampson.* Thank you, Madam Chair.

Wow, what magnificent stories. It is hard to know where to start and I wish I were a member of your committee. It would be fun to work with on one hand. On the other hand, you would probably reach a little bit of a level of frustration because there probably are more questions than there are answers to give.

But as I was listening to everybody's stories, the things that I thought of were some luck involved on the part of finding the right people, just happening across the right thing that Mr. Booker came across the Safe Place. And I want to ask you a question about Safe Place in just a minute.

I keep writing down, time and time again, commitment. I write down the word "money." Our children are an investment. We are choosing, it seems like, to postpone that investment, and instead of trying to make the resources available now, as difficult as it is, we are choosing to not do it and then we are choosing to pay for people to stay in prison or hospitals or to support the criminal activity that they are getting away with.

For me, right now, it is hard to find the answers to the questions in listening to what you all are doing. I found, when I visited a Boys and Girls Club—I happened to have been in

Galveston, Texas, about 2 years or so ago, when a truant officer brought a 12-year-old little girl in, and I got to sit in on the interview there with her and found out what difficulties that she was facing.

She didn't have anyone to listen to her about her problems with education. She thought all the teachers hated her, didn't like her, weren't willing to help her. She thought she was dumb, stupid, couldn't pass classes. She was making F's in every subject.

And through the course of the conversation with her, we found out that she did have some interests. She was interested in astronomy and, interestingly enough, she actually picked up a book on calculus to, she said, try to help herself understand some of that. And here is a 12-year-old reading a calculus book, and I don't even know what calculus is. Knowing then that students, kids, have great opportunities if we would but see it in them.

And I want you to talk some more, Ms. Eggleston, if you don't mind. You talked abut this catch-22 of getting kids caught in a situation where they have to maintain employment in order to stay afloat financially. Employment prevents them from being able to go into school and taking opportunities, whether it is secondary or post-secondary, any of them.

What can policymakers do to help right this lack of—what are the specific things that you would tell us to try to put into words, policy?

*Ms. Krahe-Eggleston.* One of the first things I would do is talk about true age, of being able to be independent. I don't know how many of you are parents, but I know my children, when they were 18, weren't able to support themselves.

We forget that these children are our children as well, and that magic age of 18 across our country is a falsehood, as far as I am concerned. So, for me, taking a policy look at what is the age of majority, because that dictates a lot of things in our world.

Again, I think about my own family, and these are no different. To me, that is really important. The other issue is being able to afford to do all those things that the affordability is impossible. Finding jobs that pay well isn't easy. A living wage is not $8 an hour. I don't know any community where you can live on $8 an hour, to be honest, if you are a single mom trying to raise a child.

A lot of our issues around unaccompanied and disconnected young people, these are people that don't have support systems. These are people that don't have you or me or an aunt or uncle. We find that we play that role for so, so many.

We supplement rents all the time for young people. We help pay utilities. We try and take care of the young people that are lucky enough to touch the service delivery system. There are a lot that don't. There are a lot that don't.

So how do we expand that safety network? I mean, that is a resource issue. A lot of us raise a lot of money in our own communities to supplement what we get from what comes from our federal friends.

*Mr. Lampson.* Well, the specifics are the things that are going to be hard. Changing the age of majority, maybe. Minimum wage, we already——

*Ms. Krahe-Eggleston.* You are working on that.

*Mr. Lampson* [continuing]. Have done.

I want to talk at some point in time, and my time is up, but, Mr. Booker, I do want to find about Safe Place, because we have Project Safe Place in my congressional district.

And I want to find out the comparisons. I know that it started in Louisville, Kentucky, at the YMCA, a great project. And then, obviously, some work that Ms. Alberts is doing on pornography that we would also like to question about.

But I just want to thank the chairwoman for allowing me to participate in this committee hearing today.

Thank you so much. It is a great set of presenters.

*Chairwoman McCarthy.* Thank you, Mr. Lampson.

Just to let you know, we are going to go through, if it is all right with the witnesses, another set of questions. Not everybody wants to ask questions, but some of us do.

As I told the witnesses earlier, I have a markup, so if I get up and leave, it is not anything that you said, and one of my colleagues will take over the chair.

One of the things, listening to all of this, how much federal money do you actually get for the shelters themselves, or how do you operate the shelters? Where do the bricks and mortar come from?

*Ms. Krahe-Eggleston.* Well, I can speak for myself. I think I will speak for many of the shelters across the country. Our communities are wonderful supporters of the service that we do.

The federal money that we receive does not cover the cost of the services. It is the seed money that opens the door for other things. The shelter-specific money, in my case, covers about half of the ongoing expenses within our agency.

I find money through private sources, through grants, through fees, through any other way I can to supplement those dollars. But the federal money is a base that we work from.

*Chairwoman McCarthy.* The other reason that I am asking is because I sit on Financial Services, and with that we are starting a new program this year that will follow through, and I have to look into it and I have to bring it up to my chairman on that particular committee.

But being when we are talking about, especially those that are transiting from "a young teenager" to that 18 to 21, when that seems to be the most vulnerable time for a lot of these young people, that there should be some sort of housing that could come out of HUD.

*Ms. Krahe-Eggleston.* Well, every community deals with that difference. CDBG has been, for years, a good friend for many of us in helping to fund bricks and mortar, at least in our community, using our community section eight has been a place that we also used.

Those kind of resources are out there if you can get to them. In our community, the one I come from, it is very friendly for those things, but every community isn't that way.

*Chairwoman McCarthy.* But from that transition age, from 18 to 21, is it better for them to have their own apartment, because you had mentioned at 18 it is kind of hard to be on your own, or would it be better that there would be almost like a group home type thing, with three or four young people together and maybe one house mother, house dad?

*Ms. Krahe-Eggleston.* There are many, many wonderful program models, including all that you said. There are apartment complexes across the country that have developed it. Kids have their own little piece of that apartment complex. There are housing units that are, again, the example you gave, many kids live there and there are staff members that come and go.

I think the key to all this is that caring adult more than anything else. All these programs are just different environments. Is there one that works for every child, absolutely not.

*Chairwoman McCarthy.* Does anyone else have any?

The other thing, just going through, thinking about what each and every one of you has said, from a young child, teenage years, foster homes, shelters. We also deal with juvenile justice on this committee.

Last week, we passed mental parity. Hopefully, we will have resources out there to help, again, more students.

But when a young person is in the juvenile justice system, or a young person might even be in prison, they come out and they are homeless. And they would have a record, which there is a big debate going on in Congress, because a lot of times then they can't get a job.

Prison, if you really look at the term, means rehabilitation, depending on what the crime was, obviously. But a lot of our young people that do go to prison, and I talk to my correction guys all the time, one of the things that they are lacking is they need mental health, most of them, and they need to get a high school education because most of them have learning problems.

So, again, when I say I look at things holistically, my mind is going from one pot to the other pot and how do we bring it all together? I think we have our work cut out for us on this committee on how we are going to be able to pull these things out.

And one of the things that Mr. Platts and I have tried to do on this committee is to have more joint hearings. When we did juvenile justice, we brought in the Juvenile Justice Committee also, so we had a joint hearing so we can try and figure out, how can we work together? And I hope that we will be able to continue doing that in the future for other hearings.

Mr. Platts?

*Mr. Platts.* Thank you, Madam Chair.

As a parent, one of the things that has just been, I guess, startling in both the testimony, again, written and oral, is just the numbers. The national numbers of 600,000-plus missing in a year, the 1.6 million-plus runaways.

In the survey, Ms. Krahe-Eggleston, that you referenced in your testimony, that 6 percent are 12 or under in a typical year, seeking your services, and especially startling that 28 percent had attempted suicide.

As a nation, the alarm bell should be going off, when you look at number after number, and certainly each of you understand that. And we need to do a better job at it.

I don't know if you can give me an answer on how we can do a better job, and it is the funding side. For the various programs, I don't know if you have available to you today or a ballpark of what you spend per child that you serve in a year on average and what percentage, in a percent standpoint, or a dollar standpoint, is from either the federal government specifically from these programs that we are talking about reauthorizing and funding or from taxpayers, federal state and local.

And that may not be something that you readily have available.

*Ms. Alberts.* I can tell you right off the bat, it costs us about $10 per client per year, and we get zero of any kind of government funding. It is all private.

So the passion I hope that you hear in my testimony and what I am talking about, it is there always and this is to me why I lie awake at night. It is not only these missing kids and the roughly 4 to 8 percent that will never be located in our country, but the fact that I, unfortunately at times throughout the year wonder where my next paycheck is going to come from.

Because, again, I am going to use that patchwork quilt corollary for our budget is like that. We are literally scrambling constantly, looking for funds and trying not to do what unfortunately I have seen programs do in the past, which is mission drift and have their mission follow funding as opposed to seeking funds that actually do fit the mission.

But none of these things are easy answers. Like I said, 27 years of nonprofit management, and these social issues are dramatic. I really applaud your efforts to bite off a big piece of this, but, again, I am going to tell you, It is communication and collaboration, as well as funding and caring, committed folks that will stay in the field.

*Ms. Krahe-Eggleston.* In my written testimony, there are some examples of cost-benefit on a national, especially with the Transitional Living Services. So you could pull some of that information, or we could get you some more on that line.

But, most of us, it is a combination of resources that make this work. Because the RHY funds have been flat for so very long, in order to continue to do the work we do, we have to figure out ways to supplement other ways.

And if I just want to add a little bit to something that was just mentioned, I know I am taking up your time. But the issue of work force is a huge issue for us. And I know that there are some issues on the table around college and waiving—

*Mr. Platts.* Forgiveness and things?

*Ms. Krahe-Eggleston.* That would be a huge gift in our field. You would have more people coming to our field. And that work force issue is one that as an executive director I am challenged with daily, daily.

*Mr. Platts.* Thank you.

*Mr. Rolle.* Can I just say to that?

*Mr. Platts.* Yes, sure.

*Mr. Rolle.* I just want to second the last thing she said. Go back to that innovation, it means innovator. That is the same work that I do with the Hip-Hop Project. The Hip-Hop culture has transcended from this subculture within the United States to a global culture, and all of the young people respond to that.

One of the things—Madam Chairperson just left—that she said was that she tried do this kind of joint work, meaning bringing the stuff that is going on in the jails with the social services.

So it is the same thing we are finding in education, that a lot of people don't want to get in education, or kids don't think that that is cool, to be in education and understand their work. So a lot of the work that I am doing within hip-hop is to try to explain to these artists, and work with young people before they become these successful artists that their work is joint.

Jay-Z, do you know who Jay-Z is? Somebody like Jay-Z, who is like God out there in the realm of hip-hop and the idol of those guys who are going to jail, half of the reason they are going to jail is they want to be the next Jay-Z. But they don't know that Jay-Z may not realize the power that he has.

If he said, "We are going to go to school." Or the fact, if he was here today, the power and influence that he can have with what he has within the culture of hip-hop that is global to really say something and do something.

So I just say that I second what she says in that the field of education, the field of social work, is not cool to get into mainly because people don't feel that they can take care of their families. It is something that they are doing unless there is just a passion there.

*Mr. Platts.* And I see my time is up.

And maybe just a final comment, Mr. Chairman, and it kind of follows on Kazi's kind of broad picture here, is that while today's hearing is specifically the Runaway and Homeless Youth Act, Missing Children's Assistance Act, that issues, mental health parity that the chair had referenced.

There is legislation that Danny Davis and I are sponsoring, education begins at home. It is about teaching parenting skills to low-income new parents, to how to establish a good home setting for their newborns, their children, counseling services in our schools.

All those in the end relate to kind of the underlying problems that drive to this issue. And that while we are focused on these acts, that we also need to be advocates and pursuing those issues, as well.

Thank you, Mr. Chairman.

Mr. *Grijalva* [presiding]. Thank you, sir.

And let me turn to Mr. Yarmuth for any additional questions you might have.

*Mr. Yarmuth.* Thank you, Mr. Chairman. I just have one thing I would like to pursue.

We talk a lot about numbers in this topic, and I think the value of this hearing is to hear from Kazi and Rusty, people who put a human face on these stories, but numbers are important when we are talking about legislation and planning and budgeting and so forth.

But I would like to ask Mr. Berg, is the methodology we use to kind of make estimates about homeless, runaway kids in this country adequate, or are there some things that we ought to be doing to give us a better, more accurate picture of what we are dealing with?

*Mr. Berg.* You can draw some conclusions from the evidence that exists, but I think there is definitely a need for a better job of knowing how big the problem is and some of the other dimensions of it. I think the adult homeless system has been working a lot on that over the last few years.

The system that is in place in the runaway, homeless youth programs is good and provides a lot of good data, but not everyone is in that system. I think there is a lot to be said to getting a better handle and investing a little bit on getting a better handle on the size of the problem.

*Mr. Yarmuth.* Mr. Allen, you have dealt with this, too. What are your thoughts?

*Mr. Allen.* Yes, I think there is a significant need for better data across the board. In the area of missing children, what is called runaway, thrown away children, the Justice Department research, it is done once a decade. So we are still citing data from 1999 research, which was released in 2000.

One of the things that we are working on now with various parts of the Justice Department is I think it is very important that there be an annualized data set, drawn from existing data sources.

One of the problems right now is that the NCIC reports, the National Crime Information Center, reorts at the FBI really don't break out reported missing children by usable categories. So it is a huge challenge, but frankly I think there ought to be numbers in this field, just like there are numbers in the Uniform Crime Reports that tell us how many burglaries and how many auto thefts there are a year. Because we need to be able to track this year to year to have a better sense of whether we are making progress or not.

*Mr. Yarmuth.* Okay, thank you very much.

Thank you, Mr. Chairman.

Oh, I am sorry.

*Ms. Alberts.* I just want to second that emotion. This is the only field that had the dearth of information and data. When I ran the substance abuse program, I could wake up on any day and tell you roughly how many kids were using what drug in the high schools. The data, particularly funding sources, they want that data. They don't want it to just be anecdotal, I know we are doing great stuff and here is why. We need that data.

Thank you, that is huge.

*Mr. Berg.* And I think this relates to what Mr. Grijalva said before, which is the feeling of sort of like we have had this problem forever and we just learned to tolerate it.

On homelessness, people support doing something about homeless. They support it a lot, but they believe there is nothing that can be done, which is not the case. But we need to be able to have data to show people, show the public, that we are succeeding at this. We have programs that work. We can have whole communities that are reducing the number of homeless people.

Without a functioning data system, or without a very good data system, you won't be able to make that case.

*Mr. Yarmuth.* Thank you, Mr. Chairman.

*Mr. Grijalva.* Thank you, sir.

And let me turn to Mrs. Biggert for any questions she might have.

*Mrs. Biggert.* Thank you, Mr. Chairman.

I just wanted to ask Rusty, after you have listened to all of the talk here, if you have any ideas on how best to spread the word about the Safe Place for other children who have found themselves in the same situation. From all this talk, I think you were very fortunate to have found that place.

*Mr. Booker.* I think so far they are doing good, but they could make a lot of improvements. The public signs that they have in Louisville, they have them on TARC buses, the libraries. Safe Place, White Castle donated $30,000 to Safe Place, and that White Castle was made a place where a child or a teenager can go and ask for a Safe Place to get help.

But I feel that there are more places and more things that can be done, and we all need to work together to see what can be done.

*Mrs. Biggert.* Well, I really was taken by your story, and I have to ask you, did your brother had the opportunities that you had? Did he do all right?

*Mr. Booker.* My brother is currently locked up until he is 18. And, yes, he did have some of the opportunities I had, but he really had nobody to help him after he got through those opportunities.

*Mrs. Biggert.* A while back, after Columbine, we had a task force here of members of Congress. We heard from a lot of experts and did field hearings. But the one thing that was so true is that violence begets violence and it usually starts with the back of a hand, and that is usually a parent.

We see all the things that happen and they are so terrible, so I really applaud you for finding your way and hope that there will be a lot of other children that will be able to do that.

Thank you for being here.

I yield back.

*Mr. Grijalva.* Thank you.

*Mr. Lampson, questions?

*Mr. Lampson.* Thank you, Mr. Chairman.

I wanted you to talk about Safe Place, and you did, so thank you, you got that in.

*Ms. Alberts,* we spend, $7,000, $8,000 a year on a child in school. What does the state of Texas appropriate each year for programs for children who are not in school?

*Ms. Alberts.* Not enough.

*Mr. Lampson.* Do you have any idea?

*Ms. Alberts.* We usually fall pretty low on the totem pole. There are no specific funds in the state of Texas for the type of work that we do.

*Mr. Lampson.* No specific funds available for what you are doing.

*Ms. Alberts.* No. We have worked a lot in the runaway community with Covenant House and some of the law enforcement agencies, and there are some small bits of money that they piece together, but there is nothing comprehensive.

*Mr. Lampson.* How do they get it? Do they get it through grants?

*Ms. Alberts.* Yes, yes.

*Mr. Lampson.* As far as an appropriation that would go to every county or to every child, there is not. Do you know of any programs at the federal level?

*Ms. Alberts.* No, I am not familiar with any program that looks at that at all, that deals with that, that services that.

*Mr. Lampson.* And what about at the federal level? Is there anything that anyone knows about? Obviously, there is some appropriation at the National Center for Missing and Exploited Children, but is there anything that filters down to Child Protective Services or other programs that will be able to grab hold of a child and help point them into a program?

When I mentioned the little girl a while ago, we got her into three different places to live. And the little-bitty bit of funds that they had ran out and all three programs closed while she was participating. We had to get one and move her to another and so on.

People try, they are, but if they don't have the resources to be able to do it, it is not going to succeed.

What were you going to say, Ms. Eggleston?

*Ms. Krahe-Eggleston.* Many states do nothing, many states and local communities.

There are a few states, and I am not sure of the specifics. I can tell you which states do and don't. I can get that information to you.

In Arizona, we have about less than $0.5 million a year that is spread out amongst our communities.

*Mr. Lampson.* What is the best state that you know of? And is there one that could be piloted, or could be copied, where we find some way that we might do something that would be beneficial?

*Ms. Krahe-Eggleston.* I don't know that I can tell you that right now, but I can give that to you.

*Mr. Lampson.* I would appreciate it if you would. Would you all rather see grant programs and let the people somehow or other apply for money? Or would you like to see some kind of mechanism to get money into specific agencies that might be able to help locally? Would you comment on that? Anybody, all of you.

*Ms. Krahe-Eggleston.* What would I like? Any of those would be nice.

I think recognizing those groups in the communities that have experience. I think the challenges that we have with grants, state grants, have to do with procurement issues and laws around how money can be sorted out through the states. At least in our state, there are laws around how money can be allocated.

It just can't go to any program. You have to go through a process to get it. Private money, we are always applying. Most of us apply a lot to a lot of private—you heard White Castle. White Castle does stuff in Kentucky. Our local electric company in Tucson does a lot for a lot of us. We need all of them.

*Mr. Lampson.* Ms. Alberts, were you going to say something?

*Ms. Alberts.* I was going to say, one of the things that we talked about, I thought about something after we finished. The Harris County Sheriff's Office is the only agency in our area that has a specific runaway division. They actually have a squad of officers to deal with that problem, and it is very successful in how it can be, given its scope.

And they are tied in well with the social service agencies in the area. But I think runaway and homeless youth, I think looking at what happens to a child, the bulk of the resources for a law enforcement agency are spent picking up those runaways and taking them home.

That is another of those areas where it is not against the law to run away. There is nothing that can be done. Occasionally a judge will say somebody has to do community service or something. I think that is another one of those places that we might look at trying to figure out how to intervene there.

*Mr. Allen.* A quick comment, and I think this is more historic, and these folks may be able to correct me. But what we hear from the runaway community is that the Runaway and Homeless Youth Act is helpful in terms of a certain level of support, but particularly in the areas of the more difficult problems, the chronic runners, there becomes a place where there really aren't resources to address the kids with the most serious needs.

We hear from communities all the time, that they are funding for shelters for the first time a kid runs, or for the early part of the episode. But the really longer term, the chronic, the most serious challenge. Really, this is the problem that is answered simply through resources.

*Mr. Lampson.* If there were going to be a comprehensive study, who would do it? Who should do it? About what you were speaking of a little while ago, Mr. Allen?

*Mr. Allen.* Are you talking about data? Are you talking about a study of what the best models are and where the gaps are?

*Mr. Lampson.* Both.

*Mr. Allen.* Well, historically, as it relates to data, what the government has done has been to go to universities and God bless universities and the work they do, but that is expensive. I think we need to develop a systematized way to capture data, reported data, and interpret it.

For example, that is what we are trying to do on the whole area of missing children. There are police reports all the time. Maybe we don't have it for all 50 states, but maybe it can be extrapolated——

*Mr. Lampson.* Would the National Center be the appropriate place to go for that, or would one of the federal agencies?

*Mr. Allen.* I think the National Center, with the National Institute of Justice, or the Bureau of Justice Statistics or somebody like that, the people who are already capturing data.

As it relates to the runaway and homeless youth community, I am not sure, but I think that same model can be replicated. In terms of who should develop the models for identifying where the gaps are, I think you go to the leadership of the national runaway community and you gather the experts and you say this is where services are adequate, this is where services are not. Here is the void and here is what it would cost to fill that void, based upon the numbers of kids who are identified in these services.

*Mr. Lampson.* Thank you.

Thank you, Mr. Chairman.

*Mr. Grijalva.* Let me on behalf of the chair, the ranking member and the members of this committee thank each and every one of you for your testimony. It is invaluable as we go through this reauthorization process.

Much of what was said, I personally felt that the issues that we talked about and the chair mentioned it, not only this reauthorization, but how we are conscious with every piece of legislation that we are working with, that we are integrating this group of young people into that process, be it health care, be it education, be it the issue of economics, be it the issue of reentry for people coming out of the justice system. I think all those are valuable things that we need to be conscious of as we go along.

But, with that said, let me thank you very much as we go forward.

As we conclude this hearing, I would like to invite everyone to the reception that is being sponsored by the National Network for Youth, shining a light on youth homelessness. Mr. Platts and Chairwoman McCarthy are serving as honorary co-sponsors of this event.

One of our witnesses, Kazi, will speak with homeless youth of D.C. and share clips from the documentary, the Hip-Hop Project. It is going to be in room B-369 of the Rayburn Building, of this building, at 6:30.

As previously ordered, members will have 14 days to submit additional materials for the hearing. Any member who wishes to submit follow-up questions in writing to the witnesses should coordinate with majority staff within the requisite time.

And, with that, without objection, this hearing is adjourned. Thank you.

[The prepared statement of Mr. Altmire follows:]


## Prepared Statement of Hon. Jason Altmire, a Representative in Congress from the State of Pennsylvania

Thank you, Madam Chair, for holding this hearing on runaway, homeless and missing children.

It is estimated that between 1 million and 1.7 million youth experience homeless-ness on a yearly basis. Some of these children are homeless for a few nights while others are homeless for long periods of time. Youth who become homeless run a high risk of being physically or sexually abused and are also more likely than their peers to engage in high risk behaviors.

Title III of the Juvenile Justice and Delinquency Prevention Act authorizes federal programs that help combat youth homelessness. As Congress reauthorizes the Juvenile Justice and Delinquency Prevention Act I hope that we study how to improve the programs authorized by title III.

Thank you again, Madam Chair, for holding this hearing. I look forward to continuing to work with you on this important issue. I yield back the balance of my time.

[Whereupon, at 5:05 p.m., the subcommittee was adjourned.]


## End Notes

* Jenny's name has been changed to protect her identity.
[1] Children as Victims: 1999 National Report Series. Washington, D.C.: Office of Juvenile Justice and Delinquency Prevention, Office of Justice Programs, U.S. Department of Justice, May 2000, page 6.
[2] David Finkelhor and Richard Ormrod. Reporting Crimes Against Juveniles. Washington, D.C.: Office of Juvenile Justice and Delinquency Prevention, Office of Justice Programs, U.S. Department of Justice, November 1999, page 3.

[3] P.L. 105-314.

[4] Ashcroft v. Free Speech Coalition, 535 U.S. 234 (2002).

[5] The Prosecutorial Remedies and Other Tools to end the Exploitation of Children Today (PROTECT) Act, P.L. 108-21.

[6] Defense Appropriations Bill, P.L. 109-295.

[7] P.L. 109-248.

[8] Hammer, H; Finkehor, D. & Sedlak, A. (2002). Runaway/Thrownaway Children: National Estimates and Characteristics. National Incidence Studies of Missing, Abducted, Runaway and Thrownaway Children. Office of Juvenile Justice and Delinquency Prevention.

[9] Report on the Recidivism of Sex Offenders Released from Prison in 1994. U.S. Departmentof Justice-Office of Justice Programs: Bureau of Justice Statistics.

In: Runaway and Homeless Youth
Editors: Josiah Hughes and Isiah Wright

*Chapter 6*

# LIVING ON THE STREET: FINDING SOLUTIONS TO PROTECT RUNAWAY AND HOMELESS YOUTH, HEARING BEFORE THE COMMITTEE ON THE JUDICIARY UNITED STATES SENATE, ONE HUNDRED TENTH CONGRESS*

## *United States Government Printing Office*

The Committee met, Pursuant to notice, at 10:06 a.m., in room SD–226, Dirksen Senate Office Building, Hon. Patrick J. Leahy, Chairman of the Committee, presiding.

## OPENING STATEMENT OF HON. PATRICK J. LEAHY, A U.S. SENATOR FROM THE STATE OF VERMONT, CHAIRMAN

*Chairman Leahy.* Good morning. We're going to talk today about youth homelessness. It's an issue on which we should share a common concern. America is the wealthiest Nation in the world and the problem of youth homelessness is shockingly high. This is not just in larger cities, but smaller communities and rural areas, as is much of the area I represent in the State of Vermont.

We're going to hear from several witnesses who are going to speak firsthand about the challenges young people face when they have nowhere to go. They also show the potential within young people who face the most harrowing obstacles, if they're given a chance. One of

---

* This is an edited, reformatted and augmented version of a U. S. Government Printing Office publication dated April 2008.

these homeless went on to become an Oscar-nomi-nated actor; another now works with homeless youth in my home State of Vermont and is on his way to great things. So, I look forward to hearing from all of these witnesses.

Homeless youth is a problem around the world. It affects these young people most directly when they're homeless, but it really affects and endangers the future as well, theirs and everybody else's. There remains a problem, and our wealthy country means we need to redouble our commitment and our efforts. We need to support those in small towns and communities across the country who work on this problem every day and see it firsthand.

Now, the Justice Department estimated that 1.7 million young people either ran away from home or were thrown out of their homes in 1999. 1.7 million. Another study suggested a number closer to 2.8 million in 2002. Now, whether you're talking about 1 million or 5 million, young people become homeless for a variety of reasons, including abandonment, running away from an abusive home, having no place to go after they've left State care.

An estimated 40 to 60 percent of homeless kids are expected to experience physical abuse, 17 to 35 percent experience sexual abuse while on the street. Homeless youth are also at greater risk of mental health problems. Now, many receive vital services in their communities, but a very large number of them remain a hidden population.

The Runaway Homeless Youth Act is the way in which the Federal Government helps communities across the country protect some of our most vulnerable children. It was first passed the year I was elected to the Senate. That was 1974. We have reauthorized it several times over the years. I've worked with Senator Specter, Senator Hatch, and others on both sides of the aisle, and I hope we can reauthorize it again this year.

Now, some have tried to end these programs, but a bipartisan group of Senators said no. This law, the programs it funds and provides a safety net that gives young people a chance to build lives for themselves. It helps reunite youngsters with their families.

Considering the increasingly difficult economic conditions as we go into a recession being experienced by so many families around the country, now is the time to recommit ourselves to these programs, not to let these programs expire.

Under the Act, every State receives a basic center grant to provide housing and crisis services for runaway and homeless youth and their families. Community-based groups around the country can apply for funding through the Transitional Living Program and Sexual Abuse Prevention Street Outreach Grant program, to provide longer term housing to homeless youth between 16 and 21, but also to help them become self-sufficient.

In Vermont, the Vermont Coalition for Runaways, the Homeless Youth, the New England Network for Child, Youth, and Family Services, and Spectrum Youth and Family Services in Burlington all receive grants under these programs. They've all provided excellent service.

Recently we learned that the street outreach programs in Vermont served nearly 10,000 young people. Think of that number. We are a State of only 600,000 people and we helped 10,000 young people. Replicate that in the other 49 States or in a country of 300 million.

So, the topics are difficult. They deserve our attention. We have a distinguished panel of witnesses today of the people working directly with youth in the streets today in rural places like Vermont, those who are lending their names and voices to a worthy cause. It's necessary that we find ways to approach this.

[The prepared statement of Senator Leahy appears as a submission for the record.]

So what I'm going to do, I'm going to introduce each witness and ask them to speak, and then we'll go into questions.

Djimon Hounsou is an Academy Award-nominated actor. He's an advocate on behalf of homeless youth. We had a chance to chat prior to this hearing and he was kind enough to not correct my French when we were speaking French. He's best known for his roles in films such as Amistad, when I first saw him, the film, In America, and Blood Diamond, which, as difficult as it is to watch, I would urge everybody to see to see what's happening the world today. He's won numerous awards, including an NAACP Image Award and a National Board of Review Award. He testifies today based on personal experience. He was born in West Africa. He moved to Paris at age 13 in order to get a better education. While living in France as a youth, he became homeless. So we will begin, Mr. Hounsou, avec vous.

## STATEMENT OF DJIMON HOUNSOU, ACTOR AND ADVOCATE, LOS ANGELES, CALIFORNIA

*Mr. Hounsou.* Thank you, Chairman Leahy and members of the Committee for this opportunity to speak on behalf of the Runaway and Homeless Youth Act, which serves our country's troubled and neglected adolescents that are so in need of our assistance.

My name is Djimon Hounsou and I can address this issue personally, having experienced the very problem that we are discussing.

It is known to some that this cause is of personal importance to me and connects on a deeply intimate level. While I stand before you today accomplished and successful in the eyes of society, I haven't always been so fortunate. After leaving my home at an early age and moving to France, I lived on the streets for some time, fighting for survival and searching out for nothing more than my daily necessities for a meager existence. I lived out my days in hunger and desperation.

So this cause is not merely some distant charity that I contribute to from my home due to feelings of guilt or goodwill, but my concern comes from an intimate understanding of the situation that these children face.

This issue is as relevant today as it was in 1991, at the last hearing on the matter. We cannot ignore this crisis any longer. The mostly silent problem of homeless and disconnected youth in our country will not simply disappear.

The RHYA is important because kids need to dream. The hopes and dreams of homeless youth who live on the street, however, are stifled and crushed and there is no room left for a vision of the future. When you lack the basic necessities required for survival, everything else fades away and you are left with nothing but the aching desire for food and shelter. I believe in the beauty and importance of our youth and I believe that we have the responsibility to protect and nurture the generation beneath us to preserve our future and theirs. Therefore, we need to champion causes such as the RHYA and the National Network's Place to Call Home campaign, and find other ways to help safeguard and teach our youth.

It is a sad state of affairs when the richest country in the world has over 2 million children and adolescents living on the streets. This should not be seen as a crisis, but a crime. It should not be taken lightly or overlooked. It is wonderful that we live in such a generous country that is able to help so many others in need around the world, but let us not forget the people closest to home.

Now, the question is not whether we can afford to fund such a cause, the question is how can we afford not to? The homeless children of our country and the kids that have run away who choose to live on the streets rather than to deal with their family lives deserve not only a better, brighter future, but a better today.

In summary, I urge the Committee to quickly reauthorize the Runaway and Homeless Youth Act so that community-based organizations can provide a much-needed safety net for youth in runaway and homeless situations.

I also encourage you to support the National Network for Youth's Place to Call Home campaign, a comprehensive public policy platform that seeks to prevent and end homelessness among our youth. If we have learned anything over the last 30 years, it is that young people's chances of becoming productive, contributing members of society are greatly increased when they are given the opportunity to realize and pursue their dreams. We need to guard and preserve the innocence and purity of the youth of our country and help cultivate and encourage their hopes and dreams. Without a home, food, and clothing, children do not have even the opportunity needed to rise above their circumstances.

So I thank the Chairman and members of the Committee for taking leadership on the important issue of runaway and homeless youth, and I look forward to answering any questions you may have.

Thank you.

Chairman *Leahy*. Thank you very much.

[The prepared statement of Mr. Hounsou appears as a submission for the record.]

*Chairman Leahy*. Mark Redmond will be our next witness. He's the executive director of Spectrum Youth and Family Services in Burlington, Vermont. He's worked there since 2003. Is that correct?

*Mr. Redmond*. That's correct.

*Chairman Leahy*. He spent almost 27 years volunteering and working for various nonprofit organizations on behalf of homeless, runaway, and at-risk youth, including the Domos Foundation Stamp for Connecticut and Covenant House in New York. Mr. Redmond's book, The Goodness Within: Reaching Out to Troubled Teens With Love and Compassion, was published in 2004. He's also written articles and essays that have been featured in major nationwide publications. He received his bachelor's degree from Villa Nova, his master's degree from New York University.

Mr. Redmond, you and I also chatted briefly this morning, and I'm delighted to have you here. Please go ahead.

## STATEMENT OF MARK REDMOND, EXECUTIVE DIRECTOR, SPECTRUM YOUTH AND FAMILY SERVICES, BURLINGTON, VERMONT

*Mr. Redmond*. Thank you, Chairman Leahy and members of the Committee, for this opportunity to address the fundamental role of the Runaway and Homeless Youth Act in serving young people in our country who are disconnected from family and other supports, many of whom end up living on the streets.

I'm the executive director of Spectrum Youth and Family Services in Burlington, Vermont. We're the largest provider of services to homeless and at-risk youth in the State. We've been in existence since 1970. In fact, Senator Leahy was one of our early board members. We're also a longstanding member of the National Network for Youth.

The Act authorizes three distinct programs. Spectrum is the only nonprofit in Vermont which receives funding for, and provides services in, all three areas. The first program within the continuum is called Street Outreach. We hire professional, credentialed adults and college students from nearby St. Michael's College and the University of Vermont, and our staff are out every day connecting with scores of homeless youth in Burlington. Some of them are living in abandoned box cars down by Lake Champlain, some of them live in the woods out by the lake, others live behind restaurants on Church Street. Our staff are out there every day. They know them by name. They're distributing sandwiches, blankets, sleeping bags, clothing, gloves, anything to meet their most basic needs.

Our outreach staff use these contacts to build trusting relationships with youth so we can get them off the streets and into our shelter. We also have a drop-in center as part of our outreach program, right off the main pedestrian mall in downtown Burlington. Every day of the year, homeless youth can come in and receive a free hot lunch, free hot dinner, change of clothing, shower, do their laundry, and there's a free health clinic right next door run by the Community Health Center of Burlington where they can see a doctor a nurse.

We have four job developers on staff to help kinds find jobs. We have a full-time teacher on staff to help them get their GED or their high school diploma. We even have a part-time person to help kids get into college. We have licensed mental health and substance abuse counselors on staff because we know that mental illness, alcoholism, and drug addiction are prevalent among this population.

The second program model of the Act is called Basic Center. Basic Center funds support our 12-bed shelter, which is right above the drop-in center. That, too, is open every day of the year. From the moment a youth arrives, the message is: how can we support you in developing a plan that will get you off the streets permanently? Our shelter staff also work closely with young people's families to support reunification, if that is possible.

The third component of the Act is called the Transitional Living Program. At Spectrum, this consists of a nine-unit SRO, single-room occupancy, building which is a few blocks away from the shelter. If a young person is in our shelter and cannot be safely reunified with his or her family, he or she then transitions over to the longer term SRO where they get a Section 8 lease and their own room. They can stay there for up to 18 months. A few years ago we developed an after-care support, allowing you to successfully graduate from the SRO, to receive a Section 8 voucher to take out into the housing market.

Other young people will go into a college dorm, they'll go into Job Corps, or State safe and stable living situations. Just a month ago, we even had one young man who, 2 years ago was homeless, living in a truck, came to Spectrum, went through our programs, and after he graduated he decided he wanted to become a Marine. Two weeks ago, he graduated from Paris Island boot camp, and today he's a Marine. So, our mission is to help homeless youth develop a plan that leads to self-sufficiency and independent living.

The Runaway and Homeless Youth Act supports all of this work that we do, which is why it's so important to reauthorize it before it sunsets in September. A few recommendations that would strengthen the Act. First, the small State minimum for Basic Center should be increased to $200,000. It's only $100,000 now. That's all that the entire

State of Vermont receives right now, and Spectrum only receives $18,000 of that. So, it's very difficult to operate a program on so little money.

Second, the authorization levels for the consolidated account should be $200 million, and the Street Outreach programs authorized at $30 million. Spectrum has been level-funded since 1994, so you can only imagine how costs have risen in 14 years, while the grant amount stays the same. With more funding available, we could assist youth in exiting the streets, connecting them to school and to the workforce.

Finally, please extend the amount of time a young person can remain in a transitional living program from the current 18 months to 2 years.

Thank you, Senator, for this opportunity to speak to you today. I look forward to answering any questions you may have.

*Chairman Leahy.* Thank you very much.

[The prepared statement of Mr. Redmond appears as a submission for the record.]

*Chairman Leahy.* I should note for anybody who's watching us, when you talk about the number of homeless people in Burlington and sleeping out, I was showing some of you a picture earlier that my grandson took in our home of Vermont just 6 weeks ago with a 10-foot snow bank behind it from where they'd been plowing our driveway. Vermont is not a southern State. We can have temperatures literally 10, 15 degrees, 20 degrees below zero in the winter-time, as well as very severe weather. This is just to put in context what being homeless there can be. I never know each week when I go home what the weather is going to be because it changes and it can be severe.

Now, Michael Hutchins is a residential manager at the Spectrum Youth Co-Op in Burlington, Vermont. Mr. Hutchins, I hope you won't mind that I'd point out that you've overcome addiction, post-traumatic stress disorder, and homelessness. I mention those things because you're not speaking in the abstract when you speak here. You had a drug overdose in 2002. After that, you became a client at Spectrum's Runaway and Homeless Youth Shelter, and 3 years later became part of their residential team. You're currently enrolled at Springfield College's School of Human Services in St. Johnsbury, Vermont, working a bachelor of science degree in human services, with concentration in addiction studies. Again, an example of having people who are testifying here, not speaking about some abstract concept.

Mr. Hutchins, it's all yours.

## STATEMENT OF MICHAEL HUTCHINS, RESIDENTIAL MANAGER, SPECTRUM YOUTH AND FAMILY SERVICES, BURLINGTON, VERMONT

*Mr. Hutchins.* Thank you very much. I work as a residential manager at Spectrum Youth and Family Services. At the Youth Co-Op, we house up to six teenaged youth, ages 15–19, who are in the foster care system. I can identify with the youth that I have the opportunity to work with because I know what it is like to be homeless, and I know how difficult it is to be struggling with addictions and mental health issues, as these young men are.

I first came to Spectrum in May of 2002 as a client in the shelter. Just 1 week prior to my arrival, I had barely survived a drug overdose in the club that I worked at down in Orlando,

Florida. Unlike the experiences of most runaway and homeless youth, there had been no immediate family conflict between my adoptive mother and myself.

My mother is a renowned psychologist who has specialized in child and family counseling for almost as many years as I am old. She had a lot of work to do when she adopted me, as I had 6 years' worth of physical and sexual abuse that had occurred while I was in the care of my biological mother. My experience of abuse is common among youth who experience homelessness. Studies have shown that between 40 and 60 percent of homeless youth have experienced such abuse during their childhood. So, my adoptive mother was my saving grace and I'm very lucky to have her as my parent.

The large part of the problems I encountered down in Florida, most specifically the addiction and the homeless and the overdose, were due to the fact that I wanted to prove my independence, not just to myself, but to anyone and everyone who might have said I wasn't going to make it out on my own.

Back then, going back home to Vermont from Florida, getting support from my family was not really an option for me, as I was trying to figure out who I was, what I believed in, what I wanted to do with my life, and without my decisions being influenced by my mother's opinions.

Another factor that played a part was the fact that, as an adopted adolescent who hadn't heard from his biological mother in years, I wasn't sure if I felt that I belonged to anybody. So after a 3-month binge on narcotics, my body finally fell out from beneath me. I went into seizures on the ground outside of the club and my heart had stopped beating on the way to the emergency room. The EMTs had to resuscitate me in the ambulance and I awoke in a hospital bed several hours later, alone, homeless, broke, and terrified. The only thing that I possessed in that moment was the realization that I wouldn't be alive much longer if I didn't get help.

So with the help of family members and friends of the family who work in the field of human services, the referral to Spectrum came swiftly to my list of options. My other choices included joining the military, moving to Philadelphia to live near my brother, or staying in Orlando and risking death yet again. So I chose Spectrum because I wanted to be closer to home and people that I know who cared about me.

So once I arrived at Spectrum and made the decision to stay dedicated to getting my life on track and clear of narcotics, it only took me 2 months to earn my way out of the shelter and into Spectrum's transitional living program, the SRO.

During my 18-month stay there, I went through intensive inpatient treatment at Conifer Parks Drug Rehabilitation Center in Schenectady, New York, intensive outpatient treatment in the form of group therapy which met three times each week at a Burlington facility called Day One, and attended Alcoholics Anonymous and Narcotics Anonymous meetings nearly twice a day for several months.

Everyone on my Spectrum treatment team—my case manager, counselor, doctor, and the workers in the jobs program and the education department—as well as all the residential managers who worked in the shelter and the SRO, all helped me achieve my ultimate goal: to live independently in the community as a self-sufficient young adult.

Once I successfully completed the three phases of the SRO program, I moved into an apartment with a friend that I'd made while working as a seasonal worker at a video game store. About a year and a half later, after working as a shift supervisor at a McDonald's restaurant and assistant store manager at the video game store, it didn't really take me long to realize that, as proud as I was to have the managerial skills that I had learned, it wasn't rewarding enough work.

So I remembered a conversation I had with our residential director, Elise Brokaw, and I'd asked her if she thought I would make a good staff member some day. She told me to give it a year out on my own and then to come back and talk to her and she'd be glad to have me on board.

So as soon as I got hired at Spectrum, I quit my job at the video game store and after 6 months of working part-time respite I was taken on as full-time staff. I have worked there for almost 3 years. It's been amazing to watch these young individuals work on treatment goals similar to those that I had once set for myself. It is highly rewarding to be able to assist and support them through their difficult struggles. Now instead of helping people make decisions on which video game to buy or whether to super-size their meal, I am able to help them make important decisions about their lives.

When a youth tells me that I don't understand what they're going through, I can tell them now that I know exactly how they are feeling. I believe my experience as a Spectrum client gives hope to the youth that I work with so they can see proof that success through this program is, indeed, possible. I've even had them ask me if I thought they would make a good staff member someday, so things have come around full circle.

I can only hope that the youth that I work with, as well as the thousands and thousands of homeless and runaway youth in this Nation today, will be able to share their own success stories like mine, and encourage others to improve the quality of their lives as well.

Without the funding that the Runaway and Homeless Youth Act provides to organizations like Spectrum nationwide, those success stories might never occur. If Spectrum Youth and Family Services had not existed on May 19, 2002, I would not be standing before you today.

So I profess to you that I believe in this system wholeheartedly, and I implore you to not only reauthorize this Act before it expires, but to focus in the years to come on how we as a Nation can improve the quality of the lives of youth who believe they don't have a brighter tomorrow.

*Chairman Leahy.* Thank you, Mr. Hutchins. I appreciate you being here. We'll have questions in a few minutes.

[The prepared statement of Mr. Hutchins appears as a submission for the record.]

*Chairman Leahy.* Victoria Wagner, is the president and CEO of the National Network for Youth, a national membership organization that represents the needs of homeless youth to policymakers and lawmakers. Prior to working with the National Network for Youth, Ms. Wagner served as the CEO of Youth Care, a multi-million dollar agency devoted to homeless and runaway youth from 1985 to 2004. Is that correct?

*Ms. Wagner.* That's correct.

*Chairman Leahy.* She served on the boards of numerous organizations, including the International Forum for Child Welfare, the Child Welfare League of America's International Committee, and the Council on Accreditation.

Again, in keeping with the previous three, she can speak from experience. Ms. Wagner was a former runaway herself. She's devoted her career to changing the lives and circumstances of runaway and homeless youth.

Ms. Wagner, the floor is yours.

# STATEMENT OF VICTORIA A. WAGNER, CHIEF EXECUTIVE OFFICER, NATIONAL NETWORK FOR YOUTH, WASHINGTON, D.C.

*Ms. Wagner.* Well, thank you, Mr. Chairman. It's a pleasure to be here with such a distinguished panel.

As you said, my roots in this really were 40-some years ago. I was sexually abused for 2 years by a stepfather. I ran away from home as a result of that. The Runaway and Homeless Youth Act did not exist. There was no one there to reach out a hand, there was no one there to help troubled youth.

As a result, I went in front of a judge and I was locked up for a year for nothing more than running away. During that year, I decided that it was important to me to try to change what happened to runaway youth and I've spent my career doing that. I deeply, deeply believe in the Runaway and Homeless Youth Act. It is the only source of money in this country that allows a young person to walk in the door of a program without going through a State, without going through police, or some other kind of gatekeeper and get help.

We need to fund it at much higher levels. We need to make sure that there are not long waiting lists. Behind me sits the executive director of one of the oldest runaway programs in the country, Sasha Bruce Youthwork. It is one mile from here. It has a waiting list of a year for young people to get into transitional housing. I find that, personally, deeply disturbing.

As you said, the National Network for Youth represents 400 organizations across the country. Between them, they serve 2.5 million young people annually. Last year, we launched a sweeping campaign called the Place to Call Home campaign that looks at legislative issues, policy issues, and program issues that relate to runaway and homeless youth.

As you said, it's difficult to know the size of the homeless youth population. Some estimates are 1.7 million, some estimates are higher. What I know personally is that it is a crime to have a young person on the streets of America that's homeless. Young people—not surprisingly—they still report family conflict, drug and alcohol problems within the home, and increasingly family poverty, as reasons for leaving home.

When I worked as a street outreach worker and an executive director, we heard stories of young people literally being left by their families during a move and the children having nowhere to go.

The National Network has submitted written testimony, as I'm sure you know, with a number of policy recommendations, but I would like to highlight some of our priority recommendations.

The first of those, which I don't think should be a surprise, is to ask HHS every fifth year to do a national estimate of the prevalence of runaway and homeless episodes among youth. It's very difficult to have appropriate guidance and funding when our numbers are such a guesstimate, and I honestly think they are a guess-timate.

There was a study done by HHS in 2003 that recommended doing such prevalence studies every 5 to 10 years. Nothing has been done since that. We would really urge you to make that part of this reauthorization.

Obviously, my second priority is to reauthorize the Runaway and Homeless Youth Act. We certainly echo Mr. Redmond's recommendations on the funding levels. I would certainly ask for higher if I thought there was any chance. I believe that a country that's been—

*Chairman Leahy.* So would I.

*Ms. Wagner.* Yes. Okay. Well, why don't we, you know, divert some funds from other places and take care of our children, is what I would say.

The Runaway and Homeless Youth programs are remarkably successful. When Djimon and I had breakfast this morning, we were talking about what works. Is there something that works? Well, these programs work. That is what is so appalling, that we know that they work and yet we don't fund them. They decrease drop-out rates, increase young people going into college, help families get back together, and reduce physical abuse. They do many, many positive things. Last year, they served 740,000 young people. Of those, only 7 percent were provided housing because of lack of funding for housing.

My third priority recommendation is to develop performance standards. There are performance standards now for Basic Centers. We believe that performance standards are necessary across all three of the programs.

And finally, my last recommendation is to ask for an appeals process. Over the last 3 years, in more communities like those you represent, we have seen a greater need. We are seeing more and more grants go in, and often what is written gets missed by reviewers. I personally have had calls from a number of organizations saying, I answered this question on this page and yet I was turned down. There is no process now for a grantee to appeal that decision? We would be happy to talk with you about our technical recommendations, but that's our fourth recommendation.

There are certainly solutions. I see that I'm out of time.

*Chairman Leahy.* Everyone's whole statement will be made part of the record.

*Ms. Wagner.* Okay.

*Chairman Leahy.* Including any recommendation.

*Ms. Wagner.* Our biggest recommendations, I've just given you, and all of our written recommendations you have. But thank you very much for letting me testify.

Chairman *Leahy.* I think it would be safe to say you don't see the problem going away.

*Ms. Wagner.* True.

[The prepared statement of Ms. Wagner appears as a submission for the record.]

*Chairman Leahy.* Senator Specter has been a tremendous help in these programs throughout his years, both as a member of this Committee and as a member of Appropriations. As often happens, most of us have four or five committee meetings going on at the same time. I know I have several others. He is stuck in one. But he wanted me to welcome Mr. Kilbane.

Jerome Kilbane has worked for community-based organizations since 1988, assisting homeless, runaway, and at-risk youth. He's currently the executive director of the Covenant House in Pennsylvania, and Senator Specter wanted you to testify. He's held that position since 1999. In fact, you are responsible for starting up in Pennsylvania, in Philly, as I recall. From 1994 to 1999, he held various positions with the Covenant House in Atlantic City, New Jersey, including associate executive director. He received both bachelors and master's degrees from St. Johns University.

Mr. Kilbane, thank you for coming. Go ahead, please.

## STATEMENT OF JEROME KILBANE, EXECUTIVE DIRECTOR, COVENANT HOUSE PENNSYLVANIA, PHILADELPHIA, PENNSYLVANIA

*Mr. Kilbane.* Good morning. Thank you, Chairman Leahy and members of the Committee, for allowing me to testify today.

As you said, my name is Jerome Kilbane. I'm the executive director of Covenant House in Pennsylvania, located in Philadelphia. Covenant House International has been serving homeless and run-away youth since 1972. We serve kids under the age of 21. We began working with homeless and runaway youth 2 years before the actual enactment of the Runaway and Homeless Youth Act.

But since its inception, Covenant House has served over one million homeless youth throughout all of our sites. Last year alone, through Covenant House International, 65,000 kids were served. Sixty-five percent of the kids who come to Covenant House are between the ages of 18 and 21. They are the youth who are between the youth system and the adult system. Often, they are overlooked and invisible.

Covenant House Pennsylvania, as you stated earlier, was started in 1999. Since that time, we have served probably 10,000 kids. But last year, 3,500 young people came to our doors and received services. We provided emergency shelter and support services for over 500, and it looks like this fiscal year that number will be up 20 percent.

We have a continuum of services, as many of the providers do, that starts with street outreach. Our major therapeutic tool is not our services, it's our relationships. It's beginning to reach out to kids to say, you have a place to go to, that you're worth more than being on the street. I think that is the message that we have to send to all of our young people.

It may surprise many to learn that there is a large homeless population in the State of Pennsylvania. Homeless youth are largely invisible, as I said, and they're homeless for many reasons. Over half of the kids who come to Covenant House either age out of the foster care system or are abandoned. They're essentially thrown to the streets.

At last count, there were 40 transitional housing beds in the entire State, in the entire Commonwealth of Pennsylvania. We served 500 young people in our shelter alone. The math just doesn't add up.

We are beginning a project to expand the transitional housing beds for youth in the City of Philadelphia by building an 18-unit program in the Kensington section. That gives 30 beds. But the reality of it is, again, it is not nearly enough.

I think what was stated earlier is that programs work. Over 80 percent of the kids who left our transitional housing program moved to a safe, stable living environment. You know, our kids do not need sympathy, they need empathy and choices and the support to do it.

I was going to talk about a young lady who was given a scholarship through St. John's University who came to us homeless, was abused, and has recently graduated. But I want to talk a little bit about an experience I had. About a year ago, I got a phone call by a young man who had been to Covenant House. His name was Wesley. Wesley's goal after being through our crisis center was to enter the military. I got a phone call saying that he was killed in Iraq and we, Covenant House, was the last known address. I thought to myself the tremendous responsibility that we had, that when he was writing down what was the most important thing in his life, he said a homeless shelter.

I cannot talk to you about the importance of this funding. The reality of it is, we'll give statistics about the numbers of kids on the street tonight, but the reality of it is, it's because of this funding that there are tens of thousands of kids who do not need to be on the street, who have a place to go. That is something that we need to celebrate. It's only because of you and the support that you've given to us, and the need to reenact this legislation.

I cannot say enough that this makes a difference in thousands of kids' lives who have no other place to go, who have no one else to turn to. It's because of that that I think that's one of the things that we can say that we're proud of. So I'd like to thank you for your support and to ask, please, I come with my hat in my hand and I beg and ask you to please, please, support us again.

[The prepared statement of Mr. Kilbane appears as a submission for the record.]

*Chairman Leahy.* Thank you.

I hope nobody will think this is political to say, but as a matter of priorities, you talk about the young man who was killed in Iraq, the amount of money we've spent in Iraq this week so far—it's not even noon on Tuesday—would fund all these programs several times over. At some point in our country, in thinking about our youth, we'd better start thinking about what our priorities are as a Nation. That's something that is not a Democratic or Republican view, but as Americans we have to start asking, what are our priorities?

I look at my children. Our son, Mark, went in the Marine Corps out of Burlington High School. I look at our children, our grand-children, and others. They have families with a stable life. But I also know a lot of people, and have met a lot of people both when I was a prosecutor and since I've been in the Senate, who do not have, the people you've talked about.

Mr. Hounsou, you mentioned in your testimony the issue of homeless children. It's one that you can personally relate to. It's not just as some who take on a cause du jour, you do this because it means something to you.

When you were a teenager, struggling with homelessness—and I realize it was in a different country—but what kind of programs or assistance would have been most helpful to you?

*Mr. Hounsou.* Well, Mr. Chairman, my recollection, is that while I was growing up in France and was homeless, was that there was no facility that was geared towards homelessness. All I remember is that during the hard times that I was on the street, and those times were mostly the wintertimes when I didn't have enough warm clothes to sustain the harsh weather outside, I found myself mostly—being sent to a juvenile—sort of the juvenile prison to spend the night. So my experience was, within the course of 3 or 4 years before I was discovered on the street by a fashion designer and my life sort of turned around eventually. But there was no structure in place when I was growing up in France. There was no structure for homelessness, for homeless youth.

Another one of the things that I found difficult for homeless youth is that I think we all have the sort of understanding that when you're homeless, you ought to be—the outlook is you're dirty, long hair, haven't washed for a long time, and don't have clean clothes on. So that is society's image of the homeless. But I think one thing that most of us are missing is that young men and women, mostly within the age of 16, 17, 18 years old, are always trying to look their best, while going out, searching for a minimum to eat, searching out for help to find a place to sleep.

So, obviously we're all trying to look somewhat clean as we're searching for a better tomorrow. So I think most people look at that as, well, you're not really homeless, you look quite decent, you look quite clean, you're not really homeless. But there was no structure really in place to educate you, or someone to champion you, or to direct you in the right place, to the right facilities, or to the right people, to someone that can help. So that was my experience, growing up in France.

*Chairman Leahy.* You talk about, to get a warm place to sleep they had to put you in a juvenile prison.

*Mr. Hounsou.* Right.

*Chairman Leahy.* Were there no mentors?

*Mr. Hounsou.* There was no mentor. You were just given a letter. I was just given a letter to go to a juvenile prison to spend the night, and that was it. Yes.

*Chairman Leahy.* Were you treated differently because of the color of your skin, as homeless?

*Mr. Hounsou.* I can't really say that, in the sense that I didn't know any other homeless. I certainly wanted to distance myself from being with the group of homeless, because I didn't see any solution coming out of being in a group of kids that can't find means or ways to get out of the streets. It was not necessarily helpful, so I was just navigating through the city and trying to find help or assistance.

*Chairman Leahy.* But there wasn't anything like a shelter you could go knock on the door and say, here, I want to do something.

*Mr. Hounsou.* No.

*Chairman Leahy.* I want school, I want a job, I want whatever, can you help me out.

*Mr. Hounsou.* No. There weren't any shelters of the sort, no.

*Chairman Leahy.* Would that have made a difference?

*Mr. Hounsou.* That would have made a tremendous difference. I think there were probably some structures in place in France, but not to my knowledge at the time. I think that probably now it's definitely better today than it was before, but there weren't any shelter facilities, no.

*Chairman Leahy.* And you weren't separated by language. Your first language is French.

*Mr. Hounsou.* Yes. My first language is French, so it was not a question of language.

*Chairman Leahy.* Let me then switch continents. Mr. Redmond, you serve a predominantly rural area in your work. For those who are watching, the largest city in Vermont is 38,000 people. Where I live, in a town of 1,200 people, it is more typical in Vermont. I live on a dirt road. My nearest neighbor is half a mile away—in this case, my son and daughter-in-law. That sets up a different thing. But you still have a lot of runaway and homeless youth, as you talked about.

Can you refer to some of the particular problems within a rural area, how you reach out to these homeless, these runaway youths? Because if we have about 10,000 in Vermont, they're not all in the Burlington area, which has at least a certain urban core to it. They have to be all over the State.

*Mr. Redmond.* Right. That's true. Thankfully, Kreig Pinkham's here today. He's head of the Vermont Coalition of Runaway and Homeless Youth Programs. There is a whole network of programs around the State that are there to help. Because you're right, they're not all in Burlington; they're in St. Johnsbury, they're in Brattleboro, they're in Bennington. So there's a series of smaller programs. Spectrum is the largest one. For a certain percentage of kids,

Burlington becomes the downtown, and Church Street in Burlington is the downtown of the downtown. That's why we're right there. We're a block away from that, so that's important.

So I think you're right. There are different challenges with a rural setting and those programs adapt in the way that they can. The program model we have was recently replicated in St. Johnsbury, which is probably the second or third largest in Vermont, because they saw the success that we were having. So I think the key to this Act is to provide enough flexibility so a State that has, like in Philadelphia, a high concentration of homeless youth, it can do what works there, and in a State like Vermont, can replicate programs that fit them the best.

*Chairman Leahy.* Let me go into it a little bit further. You mentioned St. Johnsbury. Even that has a basic defined downtown. We don't have a downtown where I live. It's spread out over a large area. Not untypical of other parts, like the Northeast Kingdom where my wife was born, places of that nature, how do you find homeless? Where do they go?

*Mr. Redmond.* Where do kids go from those communities?

*Chairman LEAHY.* Yes.

*Mr. Redmond.* They're linked into—I mean, word of mouth is the biggest. Kids will hear about programs through the police, through counselors. But word of mouth among other homeless youth is the biggest network. So they will know where these different resources are. Some cities have apartments, supportive apartment programs. So finding them is never a problem. I mean, the beauty of the Act also has an outreach component, and that's key for us.

As I said earlier, we have these staff and college students who are out every day and they know where these kids are, and they're connecting with them. These are young people who haven't had a good experience with adults, they haven't had a good experience with agencies and different institutions. So that's why I think it's key to engage them with young people— we hire college students— who can really connect with them and build relationships. A lot of it is just the relationship building part that's the key to the work, in my opinion.

*Chairman Leahy.* Well, then let me go to somebody who has experienced all parts of this, Mr. Hutchins. What I understand from your testimony, you were helped by some of these programs. What type of assistance—if you had to go and pick any one type of assistance, what was most valuable to you?

*Mr. Hutchins.* I think the 18 months that I spent in the transitional living program helped me the most because it provided me stability. I wasn't, you know, moving back and forth from place to place or sleeping on people's couches. I had, you know, my own room. I paid rent. I had my own key to the door. I had a secure, safe place to stay and reside while I worked on my issues.

*Chairman Leahy.* What about counseling? Did you get that during that time?

*Mr. Hutchins.* Yes. Sometimes twice a week. Usually we try to get our youths to see counselors once a week.

*Chairman Leahy.* When you're talking to homeless youth and they can see you dressed like you are now, in a suit and tie, you might get the, "what the heck do you know, how do you know?" Obviously, you can go to your own experience and say. But is there anything that—when you sent to Spectrum, any piece of advice or help that you find yourself going back and passing on to people who you're now trying to help or is it all varied from person to person?

*Mr. Hutchins.* Everyone's experience varies. What they need to do to get their lives on track will vary. But I think the biggest piece of advice is, you really need to want it.

*Chairman Leahy.* Do what?

*Mr. Hutchins.* You really need to want to get your life back on track. We don't just hand youth a brand-new life, and here you go. It's a lot of work. You really need to dedicate yourself, and it's incredibly worth it once you get through.

*Chairman Leahy.* Well, let me follow that a bit. Suppose you have a young person, an alcoholic, drug dependence, extremely angry from whatever put them there. It could have been a situation like Ms. Wagner or somebody else had. It's one thing when, in a case like you had, you wake up in a hospital and you say, this kind of sucks, you know. There's got to be something better than this, because the morgue is two floors down. I could have ended up in there, too.

But is there some way of reaching, before someone reaches that point? That's pretty cataclysmic. When I was State's Attorney in Burlington in Chittenden County, we saw some of these homeless youths. But I did see them in the morgue. I did see them in the morgue. They hadn't sought the help. You said your heart stopped a couple of times. Their hearts stopped and stayed stopped.

Is there anything you can do to reach them before they hit that point? What I'm trying to reach for is, is there a way of convincing somebody you really want to turn your life around before they reach that conclusion on their own?

*Mr. Hutchins.* I think that's something we all try to figure out, how to stop someone from hitting that ultimate rock bottom. But it's really hard to get someone to really want to turn their life around until they've experienced that. So, unfortunately, people hit rock bottom and stay there. It's something I struggle with every day when I am working with someone who is, you know, not making the greatest decisions for themselves.

I know from my experiences, me standing there and wagging my finger at them and telling them what not to do is only going to make them go out and do it. It's always a difficult task to figure out, you know, what's going to motivate them, how to get them motivated to turn things in a different direction and figure things out for themselves and become empowered and realize that they can be independent and make good decisions for themselves.

*Chairman Leahy.* Finger wagging. Dealing with even younger children, I understand what you're saying. But I imagine the temptation must be there to say, listen up, I was there, pay attention, and to hit the right point.

That sort of leads me to the next question. Ms. Wagner, you talked about your running away. They locked you up. Is that still happening today?

*Ms. Wagner.* Oh, it's definitely still happening, yes. In the mid 1980s, there was a technicality placed in the Juvenile Justice Act called the Valid Court Order exception that created a loophole in the core requirement a for no longer locking up runaways and other kids for status offenses. Status offenses could be truancy, running away, things that if you or I did wouldn't be a crime. In 2004, over 400,000 young people were arrested or held in custody because of those kinds of status offenses.

*Chairman Leahy.* Give me that number again.

*Ms. Wagner.* Four hundred thousand. So in a lot of ways, I mean, we haven't totally turned back the clock. The really, really good news is that we have the Runaway and Homeless Youth Act. I guess I would like to add that having someone on the street to reach out a hand to a young person, I think, makes a critical difference. But the fact that we're still locking up young people is ab-solutely appalling, and worse is that they are locked up often for long periods of time.

*Chairman Leahy.* Now, we have NIS–MART, too. For those who aren't used to acronyms, it's the Department of Justice that funds the National Incidence Studies of issuing, abducted, runaway, and thrown-away youth. I have to read it to remember all the words on it.

Tell us a little bit about that study. Is it adequate or can we make it better?

*Ms. Wagner.* Well, I think there are some big pieces missing from that study. For one thing, kids who didn't return home weren't counted, so if you remained homeless, you weren't counted in that study. It only included young people under 18. It didn't look at street youth—we've talked all the way through this, that home-less youth do not look like homeless adults. They don't sit with shopping carts or match the image Djimon spoke of. It's different. They often go from place to place, they couch surf. They become invisible and they try to blend in.

*Chairman Leahy.* It could be a kid going back and forth to school.

*Ms. Wagner.* Certainly. Kids that go to school, kids that sleep on their best friend's couch, kids unfortunately that turn tricks on the street because the first person they find is a john that will pick them up, all of those kinds of kids. But they are invisible. They do not get counted. They do not come to attention. We need a study that is a really thorough prevalence study that helps identify those kids and tells us what is the nature of this problem and how do we address it?

*Chairman Leahy.* Can such a study be done? Assuming adequate funding and all, can it be done?

*Ms. Wagner.* I think it can be done. In 2003, there was a report—a pretty thorough report released by HHS looking at different methodologies of studies, looking at costs for those studies, looking at how they could be done. There has been some work done very recently in New York with Colombia University. The University of Washington has looked at how to pilot a study. We honestly looked at an earmark to try to do a study. However that study is done, I don't think you can make adequate funding and policy decisions without being able to really say how many young people are homeless on the street.

*Chairman Leahy.* Well, we've talked a lot about rural areas. Mr. Kilbane, in Philadelphia, which of course has a lot more population than our whole State, do you know how many homeless are living in your city? Do you know how many young people need services and are not getting them?

*Mr. Kilbane.* No. I cannot give you an exact count, for a variety of reasons. One, is that we can say there are probably anywhere between 5,000 to 7,000 kids in care—in the Child Welfare system, for example—in the City of Philadelphia. A portion of those are going to age out and you have, I guess, some studies that have shown a 50 percent chance of being homeless if you age out of the foster care system. So, we can look at that.

We are the largest provider of—

*Chairman Leahy.* Explain what you mean by ``age out'' just so that—

*Mr. Kilbane.* Sure. Essentially, once you turn the age of 18 you're no longer eligible to receive support through the Child Welfare system across the country. Now, many cities, towns, or States have a process where young people, if not adopted, move from the foster care system into adulthood. There is some attempt to transition them, but often they are under-funded and under-serviced so many of the kids ending up becoming homeless. We want a 51-bed program in Philadelphia. We averaged, in the last 6 months, a census of over 60. So, I have more kids than I have beds for. But because we have an open intake policy which says anyone who shows up at our doors the first time is admitted, no questions asked, as long as they're under the age of 21. I think we have a moral obligation to accept them.

So I can give you—and I think what's been established—is a guesstimate. It's a guesstimate. But the reality of it is, is that we are serving predominately youth between the ages of 17 and a half and 21. I'm not even talking about kids who are under the age of 18, so there might be many, many more. One of the realities is, because we are 80 percent privately funded, Covenant House is, that niche population that no one really is serving enough of, is that group between 18 and 21. So, we have kind of—

*Chairman Leahy.* How do people find out about you?

*Mr. Kilbane.* I think what was said was very profound: half of the youth who come to Covenant House are referred by other kids. So, they're our best spokepeople. About 10 percent of the kid who come to our Basic Center or our crisis center are there through our outreach program. You asked the question about, you know, how do we get kids who are in need, how do we get them to make the right choices? The only answer that I've been able to come up with is that we have to be present to them. What that means is, I can give you a statistic that says about 40 percent of the kids who go through our crisis center move from the crisis center to a safe, stable living environment.

Of the other 60 percent, overwhelmingly most of them return back to the crisis center. What that means is, the programs that say ''three strikes, you're out'' or put a limit on that don't work. We forget, I think, at times that we're dealing with adolescents, and adolescents are very difficult. They want to make their own decisions. They're going through tremendous turmoil, often. And I'm talking about adolescents who are in stable living environments. So when you place stress, homeless—

*Chairman Leahy.* Even the Chairman was an adolescent at one time and I can think of some things I would have wrung my kids' necks if they'd done the same thing. If they see this transcript they're going to say, ''Dad, what was that?'' [Laughter].

*Mr. Kilbane.* I think that we need to be present to them so that when they're ready to make that decision we say, welcome, come in. We can't say, no, you're out. Now, we can say to them, look, you have to make right choices and expect natural consequences of those choices. But I think the reality of it is, being present to them really helps with success. What we do know is that repeated attempts at trying to straighten your life out, your success rate goes up.

*Chairman Leahy.* Would everybody else agree with that? Ms. Wagner, you're shaking your head yes.

*Ms. Wagner.* I've actually been involved—when I was in my previous job at Youth Care, we did a number of research projects for the University of Washington and really looked at a process of young people that the more times they tried, they stayed in care longer and longer, and how important it is to have open-door policies. There's a lot of research that I wish you had time to hear that we'd be happy to provide you.

*Chairman Leahy.* Well, when we close this out, we'll keep the record open. If there are other things you want to add, send it to the Judiciary Committee and we'll add it to the record.

Mr. Hutchins, do you find that same thing, the more they try, the better the chance that they may succeed?

*Mr. Hutchins.* I think one of the best examples is in our shelter. The basic expectation is, you get up on time, you do a chore, you come back for curfew on time, you go to bed on time.

If those basic expectations aren't met, you get a certain accumulation of points before it counts as one strike. So, you have a bit of time before you can accumulate three strikes.

Then you have to face being not in the shelter for a night to kind of get a little bit of a wake-up call and say, I'm not doing what I need to be doing. This is going to happen again when I go back, so maybe when I go back I should do the things that I'm supposed to do. People sometimes go back out there for a night a couple times, but eventually they learn. It's all about the learning process. So, the more times, the better the success.

*Chairman Leahy.* Do you agree with that, Mr. Redmond?

*Mr. Redmond.* Yes. It's interesting, listening to Jerome's statistics. We are very similar, even though they're two different locales: 44 percent of our kids in our shelter do make it to safe and stable housing. The other 50-plus percent, is it the second time, the third time, the tenth time? Who knows? Why does it click on the tenth time for one kid and it clicked on the first time for another? Who knows. But I think they're all correct. It's important that we be there to give kids multiple chances to succeed.

*Chairman Leahy.* Mr. Hounsou, you have spoken about this. You must hear from people. I would assume you hear from kids who have made it. Do you?

*Mr. Hounsou.* Oh, yes. I've heard from kids that were homeless. Also, it's a tragic problem in the sense that homeless kids meet other homeless kids, and basically they end up either in prostitution, because there's no other way of coming out and being self-sufficient, and to be self-sufficient, you do kind of have to have a place to sleep so that you can allow yourself to dream about your future and what you want to accomplish tomorrow. But drug abuse and prostitution is the number-one thing that hits homeless kids.

*Chairman Leahy.* Well, let us hope that—I'll be at a meeting with 20 or 50 other Senators later today. I'm going to be talking about this hearing. Let's hope we get reauthorization, but let's also do it in a flexible enough way that if we find things that work better than other things, that we can put the emphasis on that. This country ought to be able to afford it. Some of us, like myself, feel that this country can't afford not to do this, because we lose part of our soul if we don't.

We stand in recess. Thank you.

[Whereupon, at 11:14 a.m. the hearing was adjourned.]

[Questions and answers and submissions for the record follow.]

# SUBMISSIONS FOR THE RECORD

Senator Russell D. Feingold
Senate Judiciary Committee
Hearing on "Living on the Street: Finding Solutions to Protect Runaway and
Homeless Youth"

Mr. Chairman, thank you for holding this hearing on the critical topic of protecting runaway and homeless youth. This is a very important issue that affects thousands of families throughout the country, including in my state of Wisconsin.

The lack of affordable and safe housing for all Americans is a key contributor to homelessness among adults and young people and much more needs to be done to create additional affordable housing in our country. Increasing numbers of Americans are facing housing affordability challenges and I have heard from many Wisconsinites concerned about the lack of affordable housing, homelessness, and the increasingly severe cost burdens that families have to undertake in order to afford housing.

There are a number of steps that Congress should take this year to provide Americans with more stable affordable housing options and one such step is to reauthorize the Runaway and Homeless Youth Act (RHYA.) While the lack of affordable housing contributes to homelessness among our youth, many other issues also impact homelessness among young people ranging from instability at home and abusive situations to disengagement in school and a lack of space in shelters. Homelessness affects millions of young Americans every year and we must do a better job of addressing the educational, housing, and health care needs of these young people through the reauthorization of the RHYA.

Effectively addressing the causes of homelessness requires a multifaceted approach that incorporates supportive services, housing placement, and assistance in locating employment and educational opportunities. The various programs in RHYA, including the Basic Center Program, the Transitional Living Program, and the Street Outreach Program, provide this sort of multifaceted approach that combines immediate shelter needs with counseling, educational, and other services. Advocates who work on homelessness issues in Wisconsin have told me about the important funding that RHYA provides for their work throughout the state and have let me know how much more difficult it would be to get their work done without the RHYA programs.

Shelter is one of our most basic needs and too many young Americans are struggling to have that basic need met. Much more needs to be done to prevent these young people from running away or becoming homeless in the first place, including improving the quality of schools and employment opportunities as well as providing counseling services for families. We must also take steps to improve and reauthorize the RHYA programs to provide better opportunities for those youth who have run away or are homeless to help bring stability and safety to their lives.

I look forward to working with the Chairman and this Committee in the coming weeks and months to reauthorize the RHYA and improve the delivery of housing and supportive services to our young people in Wisconsin and throughout the country.

Committee on the Judiciary
United States Senate

Written Testimony
Hearing on "Living on the Street: Finding Solutions to Protect Runaway and Homeless Youth

Tuesday, April 29, 2008

Dirksen Senate Office Building Room 226
10:00 A.M.

Testimony Submitted by: Janet Garcia
Deputy Director Governor Napolitano's Office for Children, Youth and Families
Director, Division for Children

## Introduction

Thank you for this opportunity to submit written testimony regarding the reauthorization of the Runaway and Homeless Youth Act (RHYA). I strongly urge expeditious action to strengthen, update and reauthorize this vitally important program.

In my current position with the Governor's Office for Children, Youth and Families, Division for Children, my duties include overseeing the implementation of the Juvenile Justice and Delinquency Prevent Act (JJDPA) in Arizona. As I am sure you are aware, the Runaway and Homeless Youth Program was originally authorized as part of the 1974 JJDPA as an alternative to criminalization of youth who were in difficult family and personal situations, often beyond their control. Although the Runaway and Homeless Youth Act became a stand alone program some time ago, the importance of these programs in meeting the requirements of the JJDPA act cannot be overemphasized. By providing youth with safe alternatives and services including reunification and strengthening of families or, when that is not possible, assisting youth to develop independent living skills, complete education and find stable employment RHYA programs prevent youth from becoming involved with the juvenile justice system.

Prior to taking my current position in 2005, I was the Executive Director of Tumbleweed Center for Youth Development (Tumbleweed). Tumbleweed is a community-based non-profit agency located in Phoenix, Arizona, serving runaway, homeless abused, abandoned and delinquent children. During my 20 years with the agency, we developed a continuum of services for at-risk, runaway and homeless youth. The agency received funding from the Basic Center, Transitional Living and Street Outreach Programs authorized under the Runaway and Homeless Youth Act. In addition to our programs for runaway and homeless youth, Tumbleweed operated programs for youth in the child welfare and juvenile justice systems. This array of services and range of youth system involvement allowed me to observe first hand the interaction between programs and the potential consequences of failing to address the needs of runaway and homeless youth.

During my tenure at Tumbleweed, I had the pleasure of partnering closely with other Arizona programs serving runaway and homeless youth including Open Inn, Inc. based in Tucson and serving communities in Southern and Northern Arizona and Our Family Services serving the Tucson area. Both of these programs are funded by the Runaway and Homeless Youth Program and provide a range of services to youth and their families.

I have also had the opportunity to visit approximately 10 programs in California, Oregon, Washington and Alaska as a **Peer Monitor** for federally funded Runaway and Homeless Youth Programs. This experience has allowed me to observe the crucial function that these program have in each of these states. While the state operated services for children vary widely from state to state, the need for this safety net of programs that are directly available to youth and families in crisis is apparent in every case.

### Importance of runaway and homeless youth programs to Arizona & the Nation

Runaway and Homeless Youth funding supports programs in Arizona that are key building blocks in our efforts to respond to the needs of vulnerable youth and to strengthen families and communities. For example, Tumbleweed's eight bed shelter, funded by the **Basic Center Program**, provides shelter and services to over 200 runaway youth each year. Through aggressive outreach and services to families, approximately 90% of these youth are reunited with family, be it a parent or an extended family member. Nearly 90% of youth who are contacted 30 days later remain with their family. Were it not for the intervention of this program many of these youth would have entered the child welfare system, the juvenile justice system, or, worst of all, joined the culture of the street where victimization, addiction, mental illness and hopelessness are rampant. Our office is a funding partner for agencies serving runaway and homeless youth in Arizona because we believe strongly that the best way to address juvenile delinquency is to prevent entry into this system by offering effective support to youth and families so that they can stay together as a functional family unit.

Unfortunately, there are youth in our communities who come from families too fractured to reunite. Sometimes parents are physically not available because they are incarcerated or deceased. In other cases, parents have mental health and addiction issues and are unable to care for their teenage children. Other families push their child out because of disagreements over lifestyle or economic hardship. When families cannot or will not complete the job of raising their children and no other supports are available the consequences are severe to both the individual youth and to the community. These young people have not learned the skills to succeed in the community and are at great risk of victimization, school dropout, unemployment and poverty. All of these factors increase the likelihood of dependence on government services and/or involvement in the criminal justice system.

The **Transitional Living Program** provides a safety net for youth who do not have a family to assist them. Through the safe housing, support and services offered through this program, youth who are homeless are proving that they can be successful. I had the opportunity recently to visit

Tumbleweed's Young Adult Program, a federally funded Transitional Living Program. Remarkably, 7 out of the 15 residents who are ages 16 and 17 had completed their GED or High School Diploma and were in post-secondary training and education programs. The remaining 8 were all actively involved in secondary education programs. With a relatively small investment, these youth will have the skills and the education to be contributing members of the community.

Finally, the **Street Outreach Program** provides the mechanism for reaching out to the most disconnected of Runaway and Homeless Youth. For many youth, reaching out to other adults is unthinkable because the adults who they have trusted have violated that trust in extreme ways on multiple occasions. For some youth, choosing the streets with all of the danger and hardship that this choice brings is preferable to taking the risk that they will again be injured by those who purport to care for them. The Street Outreach Program allows staff, including trained peers, to locate disenfranchised youth, provide basic comfort services and, over time, develop a relationship that can lead to the development of trust, the return of hope, and a reconnection to supportive services.

Across the nation, we know that youth who age out of foster care are more likely than their peers to become homeless. This trend holds true in Arizona. The Governor's Office for Children, Youth and Families and the Interagency and Community Council on Homelessness are working together with our Child Welfare System to strengthen the link between Street Outreach Programs and the Foster Care Independence Act funded Chafee Independent Living Program to assure that when homeless youth are identified, they are able to take advantage of the services of this system for youth aging out of care and that services are coordinated to avoid duplication.

**Recommendations**

As you consider the reauthorization of the Runaway and Homeless Youth Act, I urge you to consider the following:

- It is critically important that the funding level for these programs is increased. I urge you to authorize the consolidated account which funds the Basic Center Program and the Transitional Living Program at $200 million and the runaway prevention account which funds the Street Outreach Program at $30 million for FY 2009.

  Current funding levels for RHYA programs does not allow for services to be provided to many of the youth and families who desperately need them. Nationally, only about 50,000 of the estimated 1 to 3 million runaway and homeless youth receive residential services provided by the Basic Center and Transitional Living Program. In Arizona, there are an estimated 5,000 runaway and homeless youth. The latest report published in December, 2006 by the Arizona Department of Economic Security on the Current Status of Homelessness in Arizona reported only 24 emergency shelter beds and 34 transitional shelter beds are available for unaccompanied, homeless youth in the state of Arizona giving the state the capacity to serve approximately 700 or 14% of the homeless youth in our state.

  My experience with Arizona programs and with programs I have visited in our region is that most programs receive only 25% to 45% of their funding from RHYA programs. The remainder is leveraged from other state, local, public and private funding sources. An increase in funding will allow Arizona and other states to more adequately meet the demand for services in their community.

- The Reauthorization of the Act should emphasize the utilization of a **Positive Youth Development** approach in the delivery of services. This approach which emphasizes the active participation of every youth in every aspect of their lives is supported by adolescent development science and is considered best practice for serving all youth and especially youth in at-risk situations. The basic tenants of Positive Youth Development include that:

  1) Youth need positive adult role models in their lives;
  2) Youth need others to believe in their potential by having high expectations of them and;
  3) Youth need to be actively engaged in decision making regarding their lives and their community.

These are things that we as parents strive to offer our own children and that we must also strive to offer all young people in our community.

- It is important that we work to educate ourselves and the public about the issue of youth homelessness and the services that are most effective in assisting young people in this situation to long-term success. First, it is important that a process be in place to regularly and systematically develop a reliable estimate of the number of unaccompanied youth in our nation. It is important that we have in place meaningful evaluation of various models for emergency, transitional and permanent housing for unaccompanied youth and of programs of outreach to bring youth into services. And, finally, it is important that both the scope of youth homelessness and the programs that work to serve them be communicated widely so that the public is educated on this largely invisible and widely misunderstood population.

Thank you for this opportunity to submit testimony on this important issue. I would be pleased to provide any further information that would be helpful in your consideration of the Reauthorization of the Runaway and Homeless Youth Act.

**Contact Information:**

Janet Garcia
Governor's Office for Children, Youth and Families
1700 W. Washington, Suite 101
Phoenix, AZ 85007
jgarcia@az.gov
(602) 542-1227

4

Testimony of

Djimon Hounsou

Actor and Advocate

---

**Before the United States Senate Committee on the Judiciary**

**Hearing on "Living on the Street: Finding Solutions to Protect "Runaway and Homeless Youth**

**Tuesday, April 29, 2008**

Thank you, Chairman Leahy and members of the Committee, for this opportunity to speak on behalf of the Runaway and Homeless Youth Act, which serves our country's troubled and neglected adolescents that are so in need of our assistance. My name is Djimon Hounsou and I can address this issue personally, having experienced the very problem that we are discussing.

It is known to some that this cause is of personal importance to me and connects on a deeply intimate level. While I stand before you today, accomplished and successful in the eyes of society, I haven't always been so fortunate. After leaving home at an early age and moving to France I lived on the streets for some time - fighting for survival and searching for the daily necessities. I lived out my days in hunger and desperation. So this cause is not merely some distant charity that I contribute to from my home due to feelings of guilt or good will. My concern comes from an intimate understanding of the situation that these children face.

This issue is just as relevant today as it was in 1991 at the last hearing on the matter. We cannot ignore this crisis any longer. The mostly silent problem of homeless and disconnected youth in our country will not simply disappear.

The RHYA is important because kids need to dream. The hopes and dreams of homeless youth who live on the streets, however, are stifled and crushed, and there is no room left for a vision of the future. When you lack the basic necessities required for survival everything else fades away and you are left with nothing but the aching desire for food and shelter. I believe in the beauty and importance of our youth, and I believe that we have a responsibility to protect and nurture the generation beneath us to preserve our future and theirs.

Therefore, we need to champion causes such as the RHYA and the National Network's Place to Call Home Campaign, and find other ways to help safeguard and teach our youth. It is a sad state of affairs, when the richest country in the world has over two million children and adolescents living on the streets. This should not only be seen as a crisis, but a crime, and should not be taken lightly or overlooked. It is wonderful that we live in such a generous country that is able to help so many others in need around the world, but let us not forget the people closest to home. The question is not whether we can afford to fund such a cause. The question is how can we afford not to? The homeless children of our country and the kids that have runaway who choose to live on the streets rather than deal with their family lives deserve not only a better, brighter future, but a better today.

In summary, I urge the Committee to quickly reauthorize the Runaway and Homeless Youth Act so that community-based organizations can provide a much-needed safety net for youth in runaway and homeless situations. I also encourage you to support the National Network for Youth's Place to Call Home Campaign, a comprehensive public policy platform that seeks to prevent and end homelessness among our youth. If we have learned anything over the last 30 years, it is that young people's chances of becoming productive, contributing members of society are greatly increased when they are given the opportunity to realize and pursue their dreams.

We need to guard and preserve the innocence and purity of the youth of our country, and help cultivate and encourage their hopes and dreams. Without a home, food, and clothing children do not have even the opportunity needed to rise above their circumstances.

I thank the Chairman and members of the Committee for taking leadership on the important issue of runaway and homeless youth and I look forward to answering any questions you may have.

Embargoed: April 29, 2008

U. S. Senate Committee on the Judiciary Hearing

Tuesday, April 29, 2008

The Reauthorization of the Runaway and Homeless Youth Act

**Oral Testimony**

Michael Hutchins

Residential Manager, Spectrum Youth and Family Services

Hello. My name is Michael Hutchins; I live in Burlington, Vermont, and I am 25 years old. I currently work as a Residential Manager at the Spectrum Youth Co-op, a group home in which Spectrum Youth and Family Services houses up to six male youth, ages 15-19. While I myself have never been through the foster care system, as these young men have, I do know what it is like to be homeless and I know how difficult it is to be struggling with addictions and mental disorders, as these young men are.

I first came to Spectrum in May of 2002, as a client in the shelter. Just one week prior to my arrival, I had barely survived a drug overdose at the nightclub I worked at down in Orlando, Florida. After a three-month binge on narcotics popular to the circuit culture—such as ecstasy, cocaine, crystal meth, Special K, and GHB—my body finally fell out from beneath me. I went into seizures on the ground outside of the club; my heart had stopped beating on the way to the emergency room and the EMT's had to resuscitate me in the ambulance. I awoke in a hospital bed several hours later, alone, homeless, broke, and terrified. The only thing I possessed in that moment was the realization that I wouldn't be alive much longer if I didn't get help.

With family members—and friends of family members—that work in the field of Human Services, a referral to Spectrum came swiftly to my list of options; other choices included joining the military, moving to Philadelphia near my brother, or staying in Orlando and risking death yet again. I chose Spectrum, because I wanted to be closer to home and people I knew. Once I arrived at Spectrum and made the decision to stay dedicated to getting my life on track and clear of narcotics, it only took me two months to earn my way out of the shelter and into Spectrum's transitional living facility: the Single-Room-Occupancy program. During my 18 month stay at the SRO, I went through intensive inpatient treatment at Conifer Park's drug rehabilitation center, intensive outpatient treatment in the form of group therapy which met three times each week at a Burlington facility called "Day One," and attended Alcoholics Anonymous and Narcotics Anonymous meetings nearly twice a day. Everyone on my Spectrum treatment team—my case manager, my counselor, my doctor, my workers from the JOBS Program and the Education Department—as well as all the residential managers who worked in the shelter and the SRO, all helped me achieve my ultimate goal: to live independently as a self-sufficient young adult out in the community. Once I successfully completed the three phases of the SRO program, I moved into an apartment with a friend I had made while working as a seasonal worker at a video game store.

While living with my friend and successfully paying rent, bills, and previous debts, I first attained employment as a Shift Supervisor at the local mall's McDonald's restaurant, and not too long after that I returned to the video game store as an Assistant Store Manager. It did not take long for me to realize that as proud as I was to be in a managerial position, I definitely did not want to be in retail for the rest of my life. It was around this time that I recalled a conversation I had with Elise Brokaw, our Residential Director, in which I asked if she thought I would be a good staff member some day. Her reply was, "let's give it a year out there on your own, and then come see me. We'd be glad to have you." I applied for part-time respite work at the Co-op and gave my two week notice to my store manager the second I was hired at Spectrum. Despite having never worked in the Human Services field, I had incredible confidence that having been through the program myself would be an incredible asset and an efficient tool I could use while working with youth whose shoes I had been so recently standing in.

Now that I have worked here at the Co-op for almost three years, it has been amazing to watch these young individuals work on treatment goals similar to those I had once set for myself; it is highly rewarding to be able to assist and support them through their difficult struggles. Now, instead of helping people make important decisions on which video game to purchase, I am helping people make important decisions about their lives. When a youth tells me that I don't understand what they're going through, I can tell them that I know exactly how they are feeling. I believe my experience as a Spectrum client gives hope to the youth I work with; they can see proof that succession through this program is indeed possible, and I've even had a few of them ask me if I thought they would make good staff members themselves some day.

I can only hope that the youth that I work with, as well as the thousands and thousands of homeless and runaway youth in this nation today, will be able to share their own success stories and encourage others to improve the quality of their lives as well. Without the funding that the Runaway and Homeless Youth Act provides to organizations like Spectrum nationwide, those success stories might never occur; if Spectrum Youth and Family Services had not existed on that 19th day of May, in 2002, it is more than probable that I would not be standing before you this very minute.

I profess to you today that I believe in this system whole-heartedly, and I implore you to not only reauthorize this act, but to focus in the years to come on how we, as a nation, can improve the quality of the lives of those youth who believe there will be no brighter tomorrow.

Thank you very much for your time.

# Illinois Collaboration on Youth

*Administrative Office:*
   200 N. Michigan Ave. Suite 400 Chicago, IL 60601 312/704-1257 Fax 312/704-1265
*State Office:*
   321 ½ S. 6th Street Suite 200 Springfield, IL 62701 217/522-2663 Fax 217/522-2676

**UNITED STATES SENATE
SENATE COMMITTEE ON THE JUDICIARY
HEARING ON "LIVING ON THE STREET: FINDING SOLUTIONS TO PROTECT
RUNAWAY AND HOMELESS YOUTH"**

**WRITTEN TESTIMONY IN SUPPORT OF REAUTHORIZATION OF THE RUN-
AWAY AND HOMLESS YOUTH ACT
Tuesday, April 29, 2008
Washington, DC**

The **ILLINOIS COLLABORATION ON YOUTH (ICOY)** provides this written testimony in support of programs and services for unaccompanied youth, and the direct service organizations that serve them.

The Illinois Collaboration On Youth is a statewide membership organization, which advocates on behalf of young people and their families, and provides support for organizations and individuals that serve them within their communities. ICOY is comprised of more than 60 youth service organizations throughout Illinois, each providing critically needed services for youth and their families in their local communities. These direct service organizations provide services to many youth and their families who have experienced and been affected by homelessness and periods of unaccompaniment. The need to maintain and increase access to these services is imperative – there are not enough services available to meet the need of the young people who are attempting to access these supports.

Programs that serve youth who have runaway or are experiencing homelessness (RHY) are critical. Without this frontline intervention and support, many young people would fall through the cracks of the system and have nowhere to turn. RHY programs are geared to intervene prior to youth entering the child welfare or juvenile justice system. We know that keeping youth with their families (when possible) and in communities of origin, with the necessary supports, diminishes the possibility that they will need to enter the more costly and restrictive juvenile justice, child welfare or mental health systems. From programs that reach out to youth while they are on the streets, to those that reunite youth with families and provide counseling and supports to keep the family together, to those that offer transitional living services to support youth who have no other choice than to live independently, these programs promote the positive and healthy development of young people within their communities.

In order for youth service organizations to be able to continue to provide these services effectively -- outreach to unaccompanied youth on the streets, family reunification and support, education and life skills, and transitional living services -- there are some specific areas that need to be addressed. These areas include funding, best practices when working with youth and families, and research and public education on experiences of youth who are in unaccompanied situations. Specifically, ICOY supports:

- expeditious passage of the Reauthorization of the Runaway and Homeless Youth Act;

- increased authorization of appropriation levels to $30 million for the runaway prevention account, and $200 million for the RHY consolidated account;

- inclusion of positive youth development as a critical component in the development and delivery of services to unaccompanied youth; and

- research studies on the national prevalence of situations of unaccompanied youth and young adults.

In addition, direct service organizations that are funded by the federal government to perform these services need to continue to partner with and be supported by the Department of Health and Human Services, Administration for Children and Families, Family and Youth Services Bureau (FYSB). Historically, this partnership has benefited the federal government, the direct service organizations, and the youth and families served. In addition to supports, direct service RHY organizations also need an avenue to communicate concerns regarding the competitive grant process, so as to ensure accuracy and accountability in funding decisions for both direct service providers and FYSB. Toward this end, ICOY supports:

- development of performance standards for the RHY direct service organizations;

- provision of opportunities for research and demonstration projects that are conducted every two years; and

- development of a standardized appeal process for unsuccessful RHY funding applications.

The Illinois Collaboration On Youth is greatly appreciative of this opportunity to provide this written testimony to the Senate Judiciary Committee.

**Contact:** Denis Murstein, Executive Director
(312) 704-1260

**United States Senate**
**Senate Judiciary Committee**
**Written Testimony – Illinois Collaboration On Youth**

**Testimony of**

Jerome Kilbane

Executive Director, Covenant House Pennsylvania

---

Before the United States Senate Committee on the Judiciary

Hearing on the "Living on the Street: Finding Solutions to Protect "Runaway and
Homeless Youth

Tuesday, April 29, 2008

---

Chairman Leahy and the members of the Committee, thank you for giving me the
opportunity to speak to the crucial role the Runaway and Homeless Youth Act plays in
serving the many suffering children who have too often been discarded by family and
main-stream society.

My name is Jerome Kilbane and I am the Executive Director of Covenant House
Pennsylvania, located in Philadelphia, Pennsylvania. Covenant House Pennsylvania is an
affiliate of Covenant House International and a member of the National Network for
Youth.

Covenant House International has been serving runaway and homeless youth under the
age of 21 since its creation in 1972 in New York City's Lower East Side. Covenant
House's creation precedes the enactment of the Runaway and Homeless Youth Act and
responded to the same issues that Congress eventually did recognize through RHYA's
enactment. However it is as true today as in 1972, that the need for services for homeless
and runaway youth far outstrips the supply. We miss a great opportunity to prevent youth
from becoming totally disconnected from mainstream society and from becoming
chronically homeless by underfunding this statute and not amending it to respond to
changing needs of America's at-risk youth. We are in a time of budget cuts and
economic tightening. Now more then ever, we should recognize the value of
preventative services which help young adults become productive and healthy adults.
What Covenant House, and what the RHYA does, is try to intervene in a young persons
life when they are in crisis and help them stabilize and reach their potential. Our
investment in these youth will bring us positive returns. If we do not meet the needs of
these at-risk youth, they are likely to enter the more costly child welfare and juvenile
justice systems or linger on the street without the skills or resources to make it on their
own.

Since its inception, Covenant House International has served over one million young
people in need throughout all of its sites. Last year alone, Covenant House International
worked with 65,000 youth on the street who had nowhere else to turn but here in their

most desperate moment. 65% of the total youth CH serves are between 18-21 years of age, a rather invisible population that are too old for the Child Welfare System and too young for the adult system. Covenant House is the bridge for this gap, serving an extremely unique population.

Of those 65,000 served last year, Covenant House Pennsylvania provided services for 3,525 young people. Covenant House Pennsylvania has been providing services to runaway, homeless and at-risk youth under the age of 21 in the Philadelphia area since 1999. Covenant House Pennsylvania is now the largest provider of shelter and services to homeless and runaway youth in the Commonwealth.

Covenant House has built a continuum of services that meets the complex needs of homeless and runaway youth. Similar to the continuum of services funded by the RHYA, our continuum consists of Street Outreach, a Crisis Center, and a Transitional Living Program. I would like to report that in 2007, our Outreach and Community Service Center had contact with over 3000 youth. Our Crisis Center served 500 youth and our transitional living program served 24 youth.

Covenant House's continuum is designed to help youth move from the street to independence, which begins with our Street Outreach Program and Community Outreach Center. In Fiscal Year 2007, these programs made contact with over 3,000 different young people throughout the Philadelphia area. The next step in our continuum is our Crisis Center, a 51-bed emergency shelter in the Germantown neighborhood of Philadelphia. This program operates from a policy of Open Intake, which means any young person under 21 who comes through our doors for the first time is admitted, no questions asked. In Fiscal Year 2007, 500 unduplicated young people, with an average daily census of 38 youth in the shelter. The third step in our continuum is our transitional living program, "Rights of Passage", currently an 8-bed facility near Temple University. Last year 90% of the youth served in the Crisis Center were 18 years or older. Most could not return home and because of factors such as unemployment, limited education and a lack of independent living skills had little chance of making it on their own. This is where our Rights of Passage Program has been crucial.

5 years ago, an 18-year old girl came to our doors, scared and hungry. Her family had moved to out of state and left her behind. She had been raped, and found herself with nowhere to turn. A friend had suggested Covenant House and although she was hesitant to enter a shelter, she came in. This shy young woman stayed with us for a few months, before applying for a scholarship program through and partnership with Saint Joseph's University. She was selected, and received a full scholarship. Last May, she graduated with a bachelor's degree in Business Administration, acquired a job at a local mortgage firm, and has been volunteering her time with Covenant House Pennsylvania's Young Professionals.

While youth have varying paths to homelessness, it is important for this Committee to understand that a large number of youth who we served are foster care alumni.

Over 40% of the young people we serve annually have been involved in the Child
Welfare System, and 21% have "aged-out" of foster care. It should shock Congress and
the general public that so many youth who were removed from their families for their
own protection and care are being raised by a system that then releases them to
homelessness when they turn 18. We understand the stress that most child welfare
systems are under and that it is the infants and young children who receive much of the
public's attention, but we should be very concerned that our child welfare systems are
producing so many homeless youth. I do not suggest these stressed agencies be punished,
but rather that they are held accountable for the fate of the youth they raise AND that
increased funding is provided through the RHYA to respond to the needs of these
vulnerable youth. In 2005, the Commonwealth of Pennsylvania had 5,611 children in
foster care over the age of 16, with 942 "aging-out" of care. In 2006, the City of
Philadelphia alone had 1205 children in foster care over the age of 17, with over 300
"aging-out" of care. This is a significant number of youth who are highly vulnerable to
becoming homeless and for whom we have the opportunity to intervene and limit their
cost to society and maximize their ability to become productive and contributing
members of society.

At last count, there were under 40 transitional living program beds in the entire
Commonwealth of Pennsylvania specifically serving runaway and homeless youth. With
500 young people in shelter at Covenant House in Philadelphia alone, there is an obvious
disconnect between the number of young people in need and the number of transitional
beds available. We also are aware that there are many large rural areas that have no
shelters or transitional living programs for homeless youth, and that this disconnect
between need and supply can lead to devastating consequences. Covenant House
Pennsylvania has begun a campaign to construct a brand new 30-bed "Rights of Passage"
facility in the Kensington neighborhood of Philadelphia to help address this problem.
While this project will increase the number of transitional living beds in the
Commonwealth by about 75% it still does not meet the need of the homeless youth in
Philadelphia or the rest of the state.

It is imperative that the Runaway and Homeless Youth Act is reauthorized before it
expires later this year. We are in a unique position where we actually know what services
and supports work and help young adults get off the street and into work and stable
housing. The outreach, basic center, and transitional living continuum of services is a
good one that is effective, but we must provide greater access to youth in need, and this
would require increased funding. In closing, I would make the following suggestion to
strengthen this legislation:

- The Federal Government should provide more help to youth aging out of the
  foster care system. Meaningfully addressing the needs of this population has the
  potential to greatly reduce the number of homeless young adults. This could be
  done through increasing the funding for Chafee Foster Care Independence Act
  and require that states dedicate some of those funds to meet the housing needs of
  aging out youth. Similarly, these goals could be met through passage of the Place
  To Call Home Act [H.R. 3409].

**Statement Of Senator Patrick Leahy (D-Vt.),
Chairman, Senate Committee On The Judiciary
Hearing On "Living On The Street:
Finding Solutions To Protect Runaway And Homeless Youth"
April 29, 2008**

Today the Committee turns to the topic of youth homelessness. It is an issue about which we should share a common concern. The prevalence of youth homelessness in America is shockingly high. It is a problem that is not limited to large cities, but affects smaller communities and rural areas, as well.

We will hear from several witnesses who can speak first-hand about the significant challenges that young people face when they have nowhere to go. These witnesses also show the potential that is within young people who face the most harrowing obstacles, if they are given a chance: One has gone on to become an Oscar-nominated actor, and another now works with homeless youth in my home state of Vermont and is on his way to great things. I look forward to learning from all of our witnesses their perspectives concerning what we can do to help keep our nation's youth safe.

Homeless youth is a problem around the world. It affects those young people most directly, but affects and endangers the future of us all. That it remains a problem in the richest country in the world means we need to redouble our commitment and our efforts. We need to support those in small towns and communities across the country who work on this problem every day and see it firsthand.

The Justice Department estimated that 1.7 million young people either ran away from home or were thrown out of their homes in 1999. Another study suggested a number closer to 2.8 million in 2002. Whether the true number is 1 million or 5 million, young people become homeless for a variety of reasons, including abandonment, running away from an abusive home, or having no place to go after being released from state care. An estimated 40 to 60 percent of homeless kids are expected to experience physical abuse, and 17 to 35 percent experience sexual abuse while on the street, according to a report by the Department of Health and Human Services. Homeless youth are also at greater risk of mental health problems. While many receive vital services in their communities, others remain a hidden population, on the streets of our big cities and in rural areas like Vermont.

The Runaway and Homeless Youth Act is the way in which the Federal Government helps communities across the country protect some of our most vulnerable children. It was first passed the year I was elected to the Senate. We have reauthorized it several times over the years and working with Senator Specter, Senator Hatch and Senators on both sides of the aisle, I hope that we will do so again this year. While some have tried to end these programs, a bipartisan coalition has worked to preserve them and all the good that they do. I remember when Senator Specter came to the Senate in the early 80's and his leadership in saving these programs as the chair of our Committee's subcommittee on juvenile justice. This law and the programs it funds provide a safety net that helps give young people a chance to build lives for themselves and helps reunite youngsters with their families. Given the increasingly difficult economic conditions being experienced by so many families around the country, now is the time to recommit ourselves to these principles and programs, not to let them expire.

Under the Act, every State receives a Basic Center grant to provide housing and crisis services for runaway and homeless youth and their families. Community-based groups around the country can also apply for funding through the Transitional Living Program and the Sexual Abuse Prevention/Street Outreach grant program. The transitional living program grants are used to provide longer-term housing to homeless youth between the ages of 16 and 21, and to help them become self-sufficient. The outreach grants are used to target youth at risk of engaging in high-risk behaviors while living on the street.

In Vermont, the Vermont Coalition for Runaway and Homeless Youth, the New England Network for Child, Youth, and Family Services, and Spectrum Youth and Family Services in Burlington all receive grants under these programs and have provided excellent services. In one recent year, the street outreach programs in Vermont served nearly 10,000 young people. Reauthorizing this law will allow them to continue their enormously important work.

These topics are difficult but deserve our attention. We have a distinguished panel of witnesses today, and they bring with them unique and personal perspectives about this important issue. From the people working directly with the youth on the streets today in rural places like Vermont, to stars lending their names and voices to a worthy cause, finding solutions to this growing problem is an effort we can all support. I thank our witnesses for being here today and look forward to their testimony.

# # # # #

National Alliance to
END HOMELESSNESS

www.endhomelessness.org
IMPROVING POLICY | BUILDING CAPACITY | EDUCATING OPINION LEADERS

1518 K Street, NW, Suite 410 | Washington, DC 20005
Tel 202.638.1526 | Fax 202.638.4664

## Testimony to the Senate Judiciary Committee

### By

### The National Alliance to End Homelessness
### Nan Roman, President

*Living on the Street: Finding Solutions to Protect Runaway and
Homeless Youth
Hearing: April 29 2008
Testimony Submitted May 8, 2008*

The National Alliance to End Homelessness is a nonpartisan, mission-driven organization committed to preventing and ending homelessness in the United States. The Alliance analyzes policy and develops pragmatic, cost-effective policy solutions. We work collaboratively with the public, private, and nonprofit sectors to build state and local capacity to make homelessness rarer and briefer for individuals and families. We provide data and research in order to inform policy debates and educate the public and opinion leaders nationwide.

The Alliance appreciates the leadership of Chairman Leahy, Ranking Member Specter and the Committee in addressing the needs of homeless youth. The Runaway and Homeless Youth Act (RHYA) is one of the few federal programs targeted specifically to homeless children and youth. The RHYA supports local communities' critical outreach, shelter, family reunification, and transitional housing options for youth who are homeless.

The Alliance encourages you to strengthen the Runaway and Homeless Youth Act to better assist communities in targeting limited public resources toward those interventions that provide the best outcomes for vulnerable, homeless youth. To that end we recommend the following for consideration and inclusion in the reauthorized statute.

## Research

Basic research is lacking on the number of homeless youth, their characteristics, and the nature of their homelessness experience. Similarly lacking is comparative evaluation of the various interventions that can help youth end their homelessness. While the RHYA programs successfully meet some of the emergency needs of homeless youth (to the extent of their funding), if we are going to make progress on ending youth homelessness, more information is needed.

The first step is to create a baseline of the number of homeless youth, as well as how they experience homelessness (how many stay homeless only a day or two; how many for weeks; how many never reunify with family; etc.). Further, we need to know what interventions end homelessness for distinct subpopulations of homeless youth, including recent young runaways, couch hopping disconnected and homeless youth, and street-dependent young adults. Finally, we need to know how homelessness among youth affects their use of other publicly funded systems including mental health, child welfare, corrections, and substance abuse treatment, in order to assess the effectiveness of various interventions. This type of research has led to improvements in the adult homelessness system, which have in turn resulted in decreases in homelessness among adults in many cities across the nation.

While the U.S. Department of Housing and Urban Development collects data on homeless people through both point-in-time surveys and management information systems, these efforts generally overlook homeless youth, leading to significant under-counting of the population. Research examining the national prevalence and incidence of youth homelessness was last conducted in the 1990's and did not include youth over the age of eighteen.

In order to help us improve our homeless youth programs, make them more outcome-oriented, and maximize their effect, the Alliance recommends that the following research projects be included in the RHYA reauthorization.

### *Recommendations:*

> *The U.S. Department of Health and Human Services should, every five years, conduct a national estimate of the prevalence of homelessness among youth and young adults ages 12 to 24.*
> *The U.S. Department of Health and Human Services should conduct a study assessing reductions in the use of publicly funded systems of care (mental health, child welfare, corrections, substance abuse treatment, etc.) resulting from interventions funded through the RHYA, as well as the cost savings associated with such reductions.*
> *The U.S. Department of Health and Human Services should examine the outcomes (in terms of recidivism to homelessness, repeat incarcerations, mental health hospitalizations, and in-patient substance abuse treatment) of key housing models. Outcomes should be examined for the two years following the program intervention.*

## Special Populations

Although research on homelessness is inadequate, it does indicate that minority and special needs populations are disproportionately represented. In particular, African American and American Indian youth; youth with mental illness; pregnant and parenting youth; and lesbian, gay, bisexual, and transgender youth are overrepresented in the homeless youth population. To ensure that the needs of these youth are met, communities should identify the presence and prevalence of such groups among their homeless youth population and use federal resources to proportionately meet their needs. Included among the strategies to meet the needs of such special populations may be programming that is culturally competent, special outreach and staffing strategies, staff and board training programs, innovative interventions, and more.

### Recommendation:

> As part of the application process for funding from the RHYA programs, prospective grantees should demonstrate their ability to meet the needs of special homeless youth populations in their community, including: youth of color; youth with disabilities; pregnant and parenting youth; and gay, lesbian, bisexual, and transgender youth. Such youth should receive any special outreach and services required to address their particular needs.

## Authorization level

Even the data currently available indicates that the RHYA programs are woefully oversubscribed and fail to meet the need for critical emergency services. The Congressional Research Office reports that of the 740,000 efforts youth made to access assistance from the programs during 2007, only 50,000 were met with emergency shelter or housing assistance. Not only is it a tragic squandering of the promise of these young lives, but failing to address the needs of youth in crisis can result in a lifetime of expensive public-sector interventions in the areas of mental health and addiction treatment, health care, and corrections. Increased resources for RHYA are required to address even the most basic needs of homeless youth.

### Recommendation:

> We recommend authorized appropriations levels of $200 million for FY 2009 for the homeless youth consolidated account (and such sums as may be necessary in subsequent years); and $30 million for FY 2009 for the runaway prevention account (and such sums as may be necessary in subsequent years).

3

## Performance standards

The Family and Youth Services Bureau (FYSB) of the U.S. Department of Health and Human Services has developed performance standards for the Basic Center Program funded under RHYA. The Alliance recommends that FYSB also develop performance standards for the remaining RHYA programs. They should include rapid return to stable housing. Development of standards should be accomplished in consultation with grantees, service providers, experts, and consumers, and should be subject to public comment. Such standards will improve the outcomes of the programs over time.

### Recommendation:

> The U.S. Department of Health and Human Services should develop performance standards for RHYA direct service grantees. Such standards should include rapid return to stable housing.

## Appeals

The lack of a formal funding appeals process impedes the transparency of funding decisions. The appeals process should not be burdensome or lengthy, and the Administration should be given the authority to structure the policies and procedures to ensure ease and accessibility.

### Recommendation:

> The U.S. Department of Health and Human Services should develop a process for appealing funding decisions.

## Length of Stay

Current data collected by the U.S. Department of Health and Human Services under the Runaway and Homeless Youth Management Information System (RHYMIS) indicates that the average length of stay for youth in shelter is over the 14 days allowed by the RHYA. Fourteen days is not long enough for programs to deal with the complex family issues, stabilize youth in crisis, reunify youth with their families, or find suitable placements. This time limit should be extended.

### Recommendation:

> Allow extensions from the statutory limit of 14 days to 30 days for stays in Basic Center Programs, when allowed by state law, in order to increase outcomes of family unification and appropriate mental health treatment for homeless youth.

4

## Eligibility age

In order to achieve standardization across the country, it is necessary to clarify the age of those youth who are eligible to be served by RHYA-funded Basic Youth Centers.

### *Recommendation:*

> ➢ *Specify that a young person is able to receive assistance from Basic Center Programs up to his or her 19th birthday, when this is not in conflict with State law.*

Our nation cannot afford to squander its young people. The Runaway and Homeless Youth Act programs support a critical network of organizations that are often all that stands between vulnerable youth and disaster. We should use our increasing knowledge to improve the programs, focus them more squarely on outcomes, and adequately support them both to meet all emergency needs and to become the vehicle for eventually ending youth homelessness in our nation.

The National Alliance to End Homelessness is deeply grateful for the Committee's leadership and support on the reauthorization of the Runaway and Homeless Youth Act, and thanks you for the opportunity to submit testimony. We look forward to working with Congress to secure timely passage of the Runaway and Homeless Youth Act.

**Committee on the Judiciary**
**United States Senate**

**Written Testimony**
**Hearing on "Living on the Street: Finding Solutions to Protect Runaway and Homeless Youth**

**Tuesday, April 29, 2008**

**Dirksen Senate Office Building Room 226**
**10:00 A.M.**

**Testimony Submitted by: Kreig Pinkham**
**Director of Vermont Coalition of Runaway and Homeless Youth Programs**

My name is Kreig Pinkham and I am the Director of the Vermont Coalition of Runaway and Homeless Youth Programs (VCRHYP), a coalition of thirteen community-based service agencies that provide a safety net for runaway and homeless youth in Vermont. In that role, I also Chair both Vermont's State Advisory Group on Juvenile Justice and National Network for Youth's National Council on Youth Policy. I'm submitting this testimony in support of the reauthorization of the Runaway and Homeless Youth Act.

The Runaway and Homeless Youth Act is central to VCRHYP's history and service approach. The Coalition was formed 26 years ago as three community youth service agencies agreed to collaborate around a limited amount of federal runaway funding then available to the state of Vermont. While the funding was never adequate to support the full array of services at any one of these agencies, it provided the cornerstone for an experiment in grant management that continues as an exemplar of the collaborative approaches that work for Vermont. From this initial agreement to share limited resources has grown a statewide system of support for runaway, homeless, and at-risk youth that serves between 800 and 1,000 youth each year.

Currently, federal funding through RHYA supports Basic Center Program services at eight separate Vermont agencies (under one grant), Transitional Living Program services at nine agencies (under three separate TLP grants) and Street Outreach Programs at six agencies (through two separate grants). These services are typically located in the largest municipalities within Vermont's counties, and are located to be as accessible to youth and families living in Vermont's rural communities as possible. While each program reflects the difference of individual communities and agencies, all thirteen share a common purpose: to serve as an indispensable resource to families experiencing crises and to aid youth on the run, homeless, or who are considering leaving home.

Through VCRHYP agencies, youth have access to caring adults and supportive wrap-around services including individual and family counseling, life skills classes, educational and vocational support, drug and alcohol treatment, mental health counseling, the provision of necessities such as food and clothing, and referrals to an array of other services located within the VCRHYP agencies or the broader community. One of the most important services that VCRHYP agencies provide is safe shelter: an alternative to a couch at a friend's house, the back seat of a car, or a tent in the woods. Be it a 14-year-old experiencing a crisis, whose family needs nurturance and a few days of respite while they can work to settle differences, or a 19-year-old who was told at 18 that it was time to be on her own, regardless of her readiness, VCRHYP services offer an alternative to the uncertainty, fear and danger of life without a place to call home.

The Runaway and Homeless Youth Act provides much more than just funding for Coalition agencies. In addition to being the impetus for the formation of the Coalition, as a recipient of RHYA funding, VCRHYP has received training and technical support through the T&TA system established through the Act. We've also benefited from invaluable direction in the formation of data elements tracked through the Federal Runaway and Homeless Youth Management System (RHYMIS) that has shaped the creation of Vermont's own database for runaway services. Further, before they were removed from the grants process, the performance standards for RHY service promulgated by HHS's Family and Youth Services Bureau (FYSB) provided the backbone for the Coalition's understanding of best practice approaches to service provision to this vulnerable population. As a worker new to the field of youth-work, my introduction to Positive Youth Development came through materials produced by FYSB.

As chair of Vermont's Juvenile Justice State Advisory Group (SAG), I see the services offered through the Runaway and Homeless Youth Act as a vital component of our state's efforts to reduce youth's involvement with the juvenile or adult court system. Our data indicates that nearly half of the youth that VCRHYP members serve come from families with some direct history with the state's child welfare system, and roughly a quarter have had some direct involvement with either that state's JJ or adult corrections system. Roughly 50% have undergone at least some limited mental health assessment, and struggle regularly with education issues. Nearly all of them come from families wrestling with regular family conflict and at least a third voluntarily report a history of emotional, physical or sexual abuse. In short, they are youth and families facing a multitude of economic and social stresses looking for direct assistance. In the absence of this assistance, the youth we serve are apt to continue in a fairly predictable path - leading to continued patterns of criminality for some, depression and the continuity of generational poverty for others. While RHY services are not the lone silver bullet for these youth, for many of them, RHY workers represent the first adults who have ever treated them with the respect they needed in order to begin to see themselves in a new, more hopeful way.

VCRHYP has tried to be a voice for a reasoned understanding of the differences in service delivery between rural and urban communities. It is substantially different to provide services to homeless youth when they have access to public transportation and comparably ample community resources and social networks than it is to provide the same type of services to youth in rural towns with limited or no public transport – youth whose street may be an old dirt road ten miles from town and whose employment, educational and social resources may be virtually inaccessible to them in a moment of crisis. However, despite necessary differences in service delivery and approaches, the field is relatively united in its ideas regarding how to improve the aide we can provide to youth regardless of where they are coming from, or where they would like to call home.

I'd like to take a moment to discuss how some of the improvements put forward by the National Network for Youth would benefit services from my own perspective overseeing programs in Vermont. The National Network for Youth is supporting an increase in the authorization levels. The competition for these grants is incredibly tight and programs that are being funded are operating on the same base grant amounts that they were receiving ten or more years ago. While the costs associated with adequate care rise seemingly daily, a funding approach that supports level funding amounts to an annual revenue loss as the only reward for service. An increase in the appropriation levels would allow for the possibility of future funding increases that could either fund additional programs or begin to make the argument for an increase in the maximum grant awards; either way, more services could be delivered to more youth.

The Network is also supporting an increase to the small state amounts for Basic Center Grants. Vermont is considered a state with a population size that limits our Basic Center Program allotment to $100,000. While Vermont has found ways to maximize that award through effective collaboration, five VCRHYP agencies receive no Federal funding for Basic Center, and several receive little more than the funding required to compensate staff time needed to enter data into the Federal RHYMIS system. An increase in the small state award to $200,000 would be a tremendous benefit to small states, particularly when these grants are shared among multiple communities in an effort to provide comprehensive statewide coverage.

VCRHYP also strongly supports the National Network for Youth's call to increase the lengths of stay for Basic Center and TLP services. The TLP counselors at the VCRHYP agencies are saying that it is growing increasingly unrealistic to prepare even a highly functioning homeless youth for successful independence within the 18 month window allowed under the guidelines for TLP. Rising housing, fuel and food costs, combined with increased competition for low-wage jobs in a struggling economy, make for hard times for a young person trying to make it without support from family. TLP workers report that 18 months is just enough time to stabilize a youth and set them on the right track before program termination precipitates a whole new crisis. The addition of six additional months of service could make an enormous difference to TLP clients struggling to improve credit history, establish positive renter credentials, accumulate a small bank account and maybe even begin the path toward higher education.

VCRHYP also shares the Network's hope that the Federal performance standards be written back into all materials associated with RHY programming. To put it simply, grantees should be expected to explain how they will measure to a universally held set of performance standards in the grants that they write, and HHS/FYSB should be prepared to monitor grantee performance based on the same performance standards. These should set the base standard of care for all RHY grantees regardless of community or service approach.

Among the National Network for Youth's recommendations are a series of national activities and studies that include: requiring HHS to develop a national prevalence count of unaccompanied youth and young adults; requiring HHS to establish research, evaluation and demonstration priorities that are informed by the field; requiring HHS to conduct economic and social studies documenting the benefits to communities who act to intervene by providing supports for unaccompanied youth; and the support of a public awareness campaign to raise the awareness of the needs of this population and of the services available to them. Ultimately, each of these requests is about improving our knowledge and understanding of the field so that we may serve the population better.

Allow me to end with a personal reflection. I came to this field with no personal or emotional attachment to the work, save a desire to do good for my community and sympathy with youth and youth issues. I came from a supportive home with two loving parents that had been high-school sweethearts. I have two brothers who are my best friends to this day. In truth, my experience of family ran tragically counter to many of the youth served by RHY programming. In an effort to support my work, my parents agreed to become trained as shelter parents for the VCRHYP agency that serviced their community. They struggled to identify with some of the challenges that the youth they sheltered were facing, but they stayed with it and have sheltered a number of youth through some very tough times. One young man in particular resonated with them. His father had been in and out of jail and his mother had repeatedly told him that he was worthless and wanted nothing to do with him. This young man's lack of family involvement were severe enough that ultimately foster care was the only viable solution for him, but for a time he was a Basic Center client housed with my parents. This brief 15-day stay established a relationship that lasts to this day. Three years later, they still pick him up every Sunday to take him to Church and have stayed involved in his life, going so far to become licensed foster care providers in order to provide respite support for his current foster family. This youth still struggles with anxiety over going back to live with his father, he still struggles with being a teen in the foster system, and he still worries about what kind of man he will become, but he can do all of this knowing that he has at least two adults willing to wrestle those issues with him. He, and thousands of youth like him are why we need you to reauthorize the Runaway and Homeless Youth Act.

Embargoed: April 29, 2008

## **Testimony of**

Mark Redmond, MPA

Executive Director, Spectrum Youth and Family Services

---

Before the United States Senate Committee on the Judiciary

Hearing on the "Living on the Street: Finding Solutions to Protect "Runaway and Homeless Youth

Tuesday, April 29, 2008

---

Thank you, Chairman Leahy and members of the Committee, for this opportunity to address the fundamental role of the Runaway and Homeless Youth Act in serving young people in our country who are disconnected from family and other supports, many of whom end up living on the streets.

I am the Executive Director of Spectrum Youth and Family Services in Burlington, Vermont, wherewe are the largest provider of services to homeless and at-risk youth in the state. We have been in existence since 1970 -- in fact, Senator Leahy was one of our early board members. We are also a long-standing member of the National Network for Youth.

The Runaway and Homeless Youth Act authorizes three distinct programs. Spectrum is the only nonprofit in Vermont which receives funding for and provides services in all three areas.

The first program within the continuum is Street Outreach. We hire professional, credentialed adults, and college students from nearby St. Michael's College and the University of Vermont and train them to work with this high needs population. Our staff are out every day connecting with the scores of homeless youth in Burlington who are in the abandoned boxcars by Lake Champlain, in the woods near the lake, or living behind restaurants. Our staff know the youth by name, distributing sandwiches, blankets, sleeping bags, gloves, and clothing daily to meet their most basic needs. Our outreach staff use these contacts to build trusting relationships with the youth so that we can get them off the streets and into our shelter.

We also have a drop-in center as part of our street outreach program, right off of the main pedestrian mall in Burlington. Every day of the year, homeless youth can come in and receive a free hot lunch, hot dinner, change of clothing, shower, and access to laundry facilities. There is a free health clinic right next door, run by the Community Health Center of Burlington, where they can see a doctor or nurse. We have four job developers on staff who help kids find employment. We have a full-time teacher to help them get back into high school or take the GED and a part-time staff person who helps them get into college. We have licensed mental health and substance abuse counselors on staff, because we know that mental illness, alcoholism, and drug addiction are prevalent among this population.

The second program model of the Runaway and Homeless Youth Act is called the Basic Center Program (BCP). BCP funds support our 12-bed shelter, which is located above the drop-in center. It too is open every day of the year, and from the moment a youth arrives, the message is, "how can we support you in developing a plan that will get you off the streets permanently?" Our shelter staff also work closely with young people's families to support reunification, if that is possible.

The third program component of the Act is the Transitional Living Program. At Spectrum, this consists of a 9-unit SRO (Single Room Occupancy) building a few blocks away from the shelter. If a young person is in our shelter and cannot be safely reunified with his or her family, he or she then transitions over to the longer-term SRO, where they get a Section 8 lease and their own room. They can stay there for up to 18 months. A few years ago, we developed an aftercare support allowing youth who successfully graduate from the SRO, to receive a Section 8 voucher to take out into the housing market. Others go on to a college dorm, Job Corps, or other safe and stable living situations. Just a month ago, we even had one young man who previously had been homeless -- living in a truck -- leave us successfully to graduate from Paris Island boot camp, as a full-fledged U.S. Marine. Our mission is to help homeless youth develop a plan that will lead to self-sufficiency and independent living.

The Runaway and Homeless Youth Act supports this work, which is why it is so important to reauthorize it before it sunsets in September. I do offer a few recommendations that would strengthen the programs, however: First, the small state minimum for the Basic Center Program should be increased to $200,000 from $100,000. This is currently all that the entire state of Vermont receives, and Spectrum only receives $18,000 of that, making it very difficult to operate a program. Second, the authorization levels for the consolidated account should be $200 million and the Street Outreach Programs should be authorized at $30 million., Spectrum has been level-funded since 1994, and you can only imagine how costs have risen in 14 years while the grant amount stays the same. With more funding available, we can assist youth in exiting the streets and connecting them to school and the workforce. Finally, please extend the amount of time a young person can remain in a Transitional Living Program from 18 months to two years.

Thank you for this opportunity to speak to you today. I look forward to answering any questions you may have.

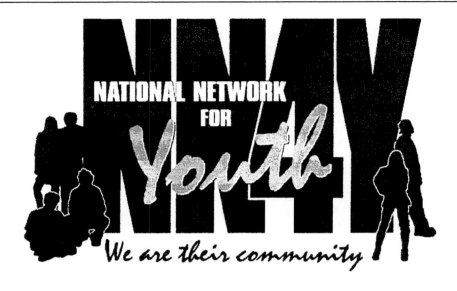

**Statement for the Record of**
**Victoria A. Wagner, MA**
**Chief Executive Officer**
**National Network for Youth**


**before the**
**Committee on the Judiciary**
**United States Senate**


**Hearing on**
*"Living on the Street:*
*Finding Solutions to Protect Runaway and Homeless Youth"*

**April 29, 2008**

Mr. Chairman and Members of the Committee, as President and CEO of the National Network for Youth, I welcome the opportunity to appear before you to discuss solutions for protecting runaway and homeless youth.   Runaway and homeless youth programs were first established by Congress in 1974 to serve as an alternative to incarceration.  In the 60's and 70's, an alarming number of runaway youth were being locked up in unsafe detention centers.  I was among the thousands of youth who had been incarcerated for running away from home and languished in locked custody for a year.

The National Network for Youth is a non-profit membership-based organization with members in each state that collectively serve over 2.5 million youth annually. Founded in 1974 to advocate for the passage of the first Runaway Youth Act, the National Network for Youth is the nation's leading organization on youth homelessness. Last year, the National Network for Youth launched its Place to Call Home Campaign, which seeks to build the conditions, structures, and supports to ensure lifelong connections for runaway, homeless, unaccompanied and disconnected youth.  The reauthorization of the Runaway and Homeless Youth Act is one component of our Place to Call Home Campaign.

## ISSUES CONFRONTING RUNAWAY AND HOMELESS YOUTH

While it is difficult to estimate the number of youth who experience homelessness, evidence suggests that the size of the homeless youth population is substantial and widespread. The U.S. Department of Justice estimated that in 1999, nearly 1.7 million youth under the age of 18 experienced a runaway/throwaway episode.[1]

Youth consistently report family conflict as the primary reason for becoming homeless.  Many are compelled to leave their home environments prematurely due to physical, sexual, or emotional abuse by others in the home.  Further studies have demonstrated that once on the street youth have difficulty meeting their most basic needs and fall prey to further abuses.  In many Communities, RHY funds are the only resources that provide immediate accessible services to young people.

## NATIONAL NETWORK FOR YOUTH'S PUBLIC POLICY PRIORITIES

The National Network for Youth has submitted written testimony outlining our full set of public policy recommendations.  Today, I will focus my oral testimony on our priority recommendations.

**Priority Recommendation #1: Require HHS to develop every fifth year, directly or via contract, a national estimate of the prevalence of runaway and homelessness episodes among youth and young adults.**

In 2002, the Senate Appropriations Committee expressed concern about the lack of research on this high risk population, instructing HHS to develop a plan for estimating the incidence of

---

[1] Hammer, H., Finkelhor, D., Sedlak, A. (2002). *National Incidence Studies of Missing, Abducted, Runaway and Throwaway Children.* Washington, DC: U.S. Department of Justice, Office of Justice Programs, Office of Juvenile Justice and Delinquency Prevention.

runaway and homelessness episodes among youth and to monitor trends. In response, HHS released a report in 2003 which outlined various research methodologies and options for conducting prevalence studies. The report recommended administering studies at regular 5-10 year intervals.

This reauthorization period offers Congress an opportunity to provide leadership and implement the recommendations of the 2003 report by requiring HHS to conduct prevalence studies at five-year intervals. Because runaway and homeless youth are among the most understudied and undercounted populations, there are significant barriers to informing sound public policy and practice decisions.

**Priority Recommendation #2: Reauthorize and increase authorization levels for Runaway and Homeless Youth Programs. The runaway and homeless youth consolidated account, which funds emergency shelter and transitional living programs should be authorized at the $200 million level, and the runaway prevention account should be authorized at the $30 million level**

Runaway and Homeless Youth Act (RHYA) Programs are critical to reconnecting youth to education, work, and caring adults, and in assisting youth in making a successful transition to self-sufficiency. The last federally funded evaluation of RHYA programs demonstrated that the programs reduced drop-out rates; doubled school attendance; increased college attendance; increased employment rates; reduced parental physical abuse; and improved family relationships for unaccompanied youth.

In FY2007, RHYA programs served over 740,000 youth, but only 7% were provided with emergency shelter or transitional housing. According to the federally-administered Runaway and Homeless Youth Management Information System (RHYMIS), 6,800 youth were turned away from the Basic Center and Transitional Living Programs during FY2007. An increase in authorized levels for Runaway and Homeless Youth programs would help communities meet the most basic needs of this vulnerable population of youth and help states in complying with federal law to Deinstitutionalize Status Offenders.

**Priority Recommendation #3: Require HHS to develop performance standards for Runaway and Homeless Youth Act grantees.**

The Family and Youth Services Bureau (FYSB) of the U.S. Department of Health and Human Services have developed performance standards for the Basic Center Program. To ensure higher quality services for youth, the National Network for Youth recommends that HHS develop performance standards for all three RHYA programs. The standards must be fully integrated into the competitive bid process, monitoring, evaluation, and technical assistance. We anticipate that the new performance standards will ensure consistency among providers, serve as a developmental tool for program managers, and increase positive outcomes for youth accessing services under the Runaway and Homeless Youth Act.

**Priority Recommendation #4: Require HHS to develop a process for considering appeals for reconsideration of unsuccessful RHYA applicants.**

There is a critical need for a transparent, formalized appeals process for applicants who are denied funding. There is currently no process for grantees to appeal and essential programs are closed as a result of lack of grant reviewer accuracy. We envision that the appeals process would only be open to a limited group of applicants who score within 5 points of the fundable range and who can demonstrate that the original application included responses to questions that the review panel did not identify.

## SOLUTIONS TO PROTECTING RUNAWAY AND HOMELESS YOUTH

Reauthorization of the Runaway and Homeless Youth Act must be considered just one part of a larger effort to prevent and end youth homelessness. Congress must take bold steps, such as those offered in the National Network's **Place to Call Home Campaign** which includes a comprehensive public policy agenda to prevent, respond to, and end runaway and homeless situations among youth. These steps will bring us closer to making sure that every runaway and homeless youth is connected to a safe and stable home, caring adults, workforce, and education.

We encourage Members of this Committee to support the Place to Call Home Campaign by swiftly reauthorizing the Runaway and Homeless Youth Act; supporting the First Step Forward Act, Senator Schumer's youth reentry legislation; and the National Network's recommended provisions on the issue of deinstitutionalization of status offenders within the reauthorization of the Juvenile Justice and Delinquency Prevention Act, which also sunsets this year. These steps will bring us closer to making sure that each runaway, homeless, and unaccompanied youth is connected to a safe and stable home, caring adults, and opportunities in education and the workforce.

Mr. Chairman, we are deeply grateful for your leadership and support on the reauthorization of the Runaway and Homeless Youth Act, and I look forward to working with you and the Committee to ensure a timely passage.

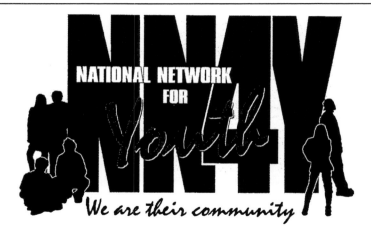

**Written Statement for the Record**
**of the**
**National Network for Youth**

**For the**
**Committee on the Judiciary**
**United States Senate**

**Hearing on**
*"Living on the Street:*
*Finding Solutions to Protect Runaway and Homeless Youth"*

**April 29, 2008**

Mishaela Durán
Vice President of Public Policy
National Network for Youth
1319 F Street NW, Ste. 400
Washington, D.C. 20004
(202) 783-7949 ext. 3109
mduran@nn4youth.org

The **National Network for Youth**, founded in 1974, is a nonprofit membership organization that champions the needs of runaway, homeless, and other disconnected youth through advocacy, innovation and member services. The National Network provides its members and the general public with education, networking, training, materials and policy advocacy with federal, state, and local lawmakers.

The National Network for Youth's membership includes community-based, faith-based, and public organizations that provide an array of services to youth and families in the U.S. states and territories as well as international locations. In addition to service providers, youth workers, youth, and regional and state networks of youth-serving organizations are among our membership base. Members provide a full continuum of core prevention and intervention services to youth and families in high-risk situations, including street-based crisis intervention, family reunification services, emergency shelter, and transitional and independent living programming. Our members also provide supportive services including life skills, health and wellness education, physical and behavioral health treatment and care, education, workforce development, arts, and recreation services to ensure that young people are connected to school, work, caring adults, and their communities. Collectively, National Network for Youth member organizations serve over 2.5 million young people annually.

Last year, the National Network for Youth launched its Place to Call Home Campaign, which seeks to build the conditions, structures, and supports to ensure lifelong connections for runaway, homeless, unaccompanied and disconnected youth. The four cornerstones of the campaign include: 1) Public Policy Advancement and System Change; 2) Best Practices; 3) Public Awareness; and 4) Research and Knowledge Development. The reauthorization of the Runaway and Homeless Youth Act is one component of our Place to Call Home Campaign.

## OVERVIEW OF RESEARCH ON RUNAWAY AND HOMELESS YOUTH

While it is difficult to estimate the number of youth who experience homelessness, evidence suggests that the size of the homeless youth population is substantial and widespread. The U.S. Department of Justice estimated that in 1999, nearly 1.7 million youth had a runaway/throwaway episode.[1] In 1995, the Research Triangle Institute reported a significantly higher number, estimating that 2.8 million youth experience a runaway or homelessness episode over the course of a year.[2]

Youth consistently report family conflict as the primary reason for becoming homeless. Many are compelled to leave their home environments prematurely due to physical, sexual, or emotional abuse by others in the home. Across studies of homeless youth, rates of sexual abuse

---

[1] Hammer, H., Finkelhor, D., Sedlak, A. (2002). *National Incidence Studies of Missing, Abducted, Runaway and Throwaway Children*. Washington, DC: U.S. Department of Justice, Office of Justice Programs, Office of Juvenile Justice and Delinquency Prevention.
[2] Greene, J., Ringwalt, C., Kelly, J., Iachan, R., Cohen, Z. (1995). *Youth with Runaway, Thrownaway, and Homeless Experiences: Prevalence, Drug Use, and Other At-Risk Behaviors*. Volume I: Final Report. Research Traingle Park, NC: Research Triangle Institute.

range from 17 to 53 percent, and physical abuse ranges from 40 to 60 percent.[3] Others are forced out of the home due to parental disapproval of school problems, drug or alcohol use, the pregnancy, parenting status, sexual orientation, or other circumstances of their children.

Regardless of the causal factor, homeless youth, when left to fend for themselves without support, experience poor health, educational, and workforce outcomes, greatly minimizing their prospects for making a successful transition to adulthood.[4] In one study of street youth between the ages of 13 and 17, 57 percent reported having spent at least one day in the past month with nothing to eat, 42 percent had been physically assaulted, and 13 percent had been sexually assaulted.[5] The high levels of victimization and disconnection among runaway and homeless youth often results in involvement in costly public health, social service, emergency assistance, and corrections systems.

## NATIONAL NETWORK FOR YOUTH PUBLIC POLICY RECOMMENDATIONS

The Runaway and Homeless Youth Act (RHYA) is scheduled to sunset in 2008 and merits extension. In addition, new issues have emerged that affect runaway and homeless youth service providers and the young people they serve , and that require a Congressional response. **The National Network for Youth urges Congress to swiftly reauthorize and strengthen the programs and the administration of the Runaway and Homeless Youth Act.** We offer the following recommendations for RHYA reauthorization.

*Funding*

**1. Increase authorization levels for Runaway and Homeless Youth Act programs.** The runaway and homeless youth consolidated account should be authorized at the $200 million level in FY 2009 and "such sums as may be necessary" in each of FY 2010 through FY 2013. The runaway prevention account should be authorized at the $30 million level in FY 2009 and "such sums as may be necessary" in each of FY 2010 through FY 2013.

Runaway and Homeless Youth Act programs play a critical role in reconnecting homeless youth to education, work, and caring adults, and in assisting youth in making a successful transition to self-sufficiency. The last federally funded evaluation of RHYA programs demonstrated that the programs reduced drop-out rates; doubled school attendance; increased college attendance; increased employment rates; reduced parental physical abuse; and improved family relationships for unaccompanied youth.

In FY 2007, RHYA programs served over 740,000 youth, but only 7% were provided with emergency shelter or transitional housing. The other 93% received critical services to meet basic needs through the Street Outreach Program (SOP). According to the federally-administered Runaway and Homeless Youth Management Information System (RHYMIS), 6,800 youth were

---

[3] Robertson, M., and Toro, P. "Homeless Youth: Research, Intervention, and Policy. Fosburg, L. and Dennis, D. (Eds.), *Practical Lessons: The 1998 National Symposium on Homelessness Research.* Washington, DC:
[4] Greenblat, M. & Robertson, M.J. (1993). Homeless Adolescents: Lifestyle, Survival Strategies and Sexual Behaviors. *Hospital and Community Psychiatry*, 44: 1177-1180.
[5] Ibid.

turned away from the Basic Center Program (BCP) and Transitional Living Program (TLP) during FY2007. Thus the most basic needs of homeless children and youth -- namely safe and stable housing -- are unmet, with hundreds of thousands of homeless youth forced to remain on the streets or in precarious housing situations. An increase in authorized levels for the Street Outreach (runaway prevention) account and the consolidated account, which funds residential-based services, would help communities meet the most basic needs of this vulnerable population of youth.

**2. Increase the RHYA Basic Center Program (BCP) allotments for small states and for territories**. The minimum BCP allotment for states with small youth populations should be increased to $200,000. The maximum BCP allotment for U.S. territories should be increased to at least $100,000. **Did you mean to say minimum for states and maximum for territories?**

BCP formula allotments to states with small youth populations are limited to $100,000. This amount makes it difficult for HHS to fund more than one basic center in each such state, even though the geographic swath of many such states tends to be wide. BCP allotments to territories are limited to $40,000. This amount is hardly enough to even serve as seed money for Basic Center Programs to leverage non-RHYA funds.

Basic Center Programs provide critical services that assist states in complying with the Deinstitutionalization of Status Offenders core requirement mandated under the Juvenile Justice and Delinquency Prevention Act (JJDPA). The lack of community based alternatives, such as Basic Center Programs, often results in the juvenile justice system's overreliance on incarceration of status offenders. A recent report released by the Justice Policy Institute concludes that the inappropriate incarceration of status offenders contributes to future delinquent behavior and results in poor educational, health, and employment outcomes.[6] Serving youth in community-based alternatives significantly increases runaway youths' chances of obtaining an education, a job, and a strong connection to caring adults, thus deterring future delinquency.

**3. Permit HHS to redistribute unexpended BCP funds to other BCP applicants for a one-year grant period, after which time the amount should be returned to the BCP general pool for re-allocation**. RHYA grantees and applicants would benefit from greater transparency and standardization in the manner in which HHS reallocates "unrequested" BCP allotments from states lacking applicants to qualified BCP applicants from states that have exceeded the state's allotment.

*RHYA Project Admission and Length of Stay Criteria*

**4. Limit Basic Center Programs provision of shelter services to only individuals who are less than 18 years of age, with an exception for Basic Centers located in states with child-caring facility licensure laws that permit a higher age**. RHYA grantees and applicants would benefit from clarification on the maximum age of youth permitted to receive emergency shelter through a Basic Center Program. Current law permits Basic Centers to provide emergency shelter to youth "not more than 18 years of age," which some interpret to mean ages 17 and

---

[6] Holman, B. and Ziedenberg, J. (2006). *The Dangers of Detention: The Impact of Incarcerating Youth in Detention and Other Secure Facilities.* Justice Policy Institute, Washington, D.C.

under and others interpret to mean through age 18. To resolve confusion in the field, we recommend that the maximum age for emergency shelter services through a BCP be extended to youth "who are less than 18 years of age," which is in alignment with the maximum age used in the formula for allocating BCP funds. However, grantees should be given the discretion to serve youth over age 17 if the child-caring facility licensure law in which the Basic Center is located permits a higher age.

**5. Allow extensions in lengths of stay in Basic Center Programs from 14 days to up to 30 days and in Transitional Living Programs from 18 months up to 24 months, on a case-by-case basis, provided that the state child-caring facility licensure laws permit longer lengths of stay.** RHYA grantees report difficulty in ensuring safe exits for some of their program participants within the timeframes required by current law. Providing grantees with flexibility to keep some of their participants in services beyond the target exit date would allow a greater level of individualized support for those unaccompanied youth at greatest risk of unsafe program exits.

*RHYA Applicant Eligibility, Use of Funds, and Funding Conditions*

**6. Add public entities as eligible applicants for Street Outreach Program funds.** Eligibility for the Street Outreach Program (SOP) is limited to private nonprofit organizations, whereas eligibility for BCP and TLP residential-based services is open to public organizations as well as private nonprofit organizations. Extending SOP eligibility to public organizations would allow public entities receiving either BCP and/or TLP funds to build a full continuum of RHYA services. A full continuum of services within one agency minimizes multiple disruptive placements, which would allow youth to develop positive, trusting relationships with caring professionals.

**7. Clarify that RHYA funds are to be distributed to organizations and not directly to program participants.** The President's FY 2007 budget request included a proposal to reserve a portion of TLP funds for vouchers that would be distributed directly to participants for the purchase maternity group home services. Appropriations Committees in both chambers of the 109th Congress, in consultation with their authorization committee counterparts, concluded that a voucher arrangement was neither authorized by the statute, nor in the best interest of either the pregnant and parenting youth or the youth service provider. Accordingly, the committees rejected the proposal in report language to accompany the FY 2007 Labor-HHS-Education appropriations bills. Current law should be amended to clarify that RHYA funds are to be made available for distribution to youth-serving organizations and not directly to program participants.

**8. Require Basic Center and Transitional Living Programs to have a written emergency management and crisis response plan in place, as a condition for receiving federal RHYA funding.** Hurricanes Katrina and Rita focused national attention on the need to ensure more effective responses to emergencies and crises, including by youth service providers. The 109th Congress recently amended the Older Americans Act and the Promoting Safe and Stable Families Act to ensure that congregate care providers funded through these programs have emergency management and crisis plans in place. A parallel requirement should be established for RHYA Basic Center and Transitional Living programs.

*Federal Program Management*

**9. Require HHS to develop performance standards for RHYA direct service grantees.** At one time, HHS had developed program performance standards for Basic Center Programs and was in the process of developing program performance standards for TLP and SOP grantees. These standards provided guidance to grantees on the minimum expectations of program performance. HHS has suspended standards development due to the lack of clear instruction in the RHYA statute to support their development and implementation.

To ensure high quality services for youth, the National Network for Youth recommends that HHS develop performance standards for all three RHYA programs, in consultation with the field and experts. The standards must be fully integrated into the competitive bid process, monitoring, evaluation, and technical assistance. We anticipate that the new performance standards will ensure consistency among providers, serve as a management tool for program design and development, and improve positive outcomes for youth accessing services under the Runaway and Homeless Youth Act.

**10. Require HHS to develop a process for accepting and considering appeals for reconsideration from unsuccessful RHYA applicants.** As competition for the limited pool of Runaway and Homeless Youth Act funding increases, so does the demand for a transparent, fair, and formalized appeals process for applicants who are denied funding. Every grant season, the National Network for Youth and Members of Congress receive calls from high quality and experienced runaway and homeless youth programs that were denied funding. Currently, the only option for unsuccessful grantees in seeking reconsideration is to exercise rights under the Freedom of Information Act. Unfortunately, this process does not sufficiently address these issues, as it imposes serious lag times and does not authorize the Administration to reconsider decisions. In response to this issue, the National Network recommends that FYSB develop a formal appeals process to ensure fairness and transparency within the administration of grants.

The intent of this recommendation is not to shift FYSB's focus from its current priorities to unnecessary and burdensome administrative tasks. On the contrary, we envision that the appeals process would only be open to a limited group of applicants who score within 5 points of the fundable range and who can demonstrate that the original application included responses to questions that the review panel did not identify. Our members have opportunities to appeal funding decisions on the state and local level and seek a similar avenue on the federal level. Our recommendation allows flexibility for FYSB to develop the appeals process that would work within their current staffing structure and budget.

**11. Add a finding on the applicability of positive youth development to the delivery of services to unaccompanied youth.** Inclusion of a finding on positive youth development in the RHYA statute is important for encouraging grantees to apply strength-based, youth development principles to the development and implementation of their programs.

**12. Add a statutory definition of "runaway youth" identical to the definition of that term in the Code of Federal Regulations.** The RHYA statute does not include a definition of "runaway youth." However, that term is defined in the Code of Federal Regulations (45 CFR 1351.1) as "a person under 18 years of age who absents himself or herself from home or place of legal residence without the permission of his or her family." For the convenience of policymakers, RHYA grantees, and the general public, the current regulatory definition of "runaway youth" should be inserted into statute.

*National Activities*

**13. Require HHS to develop each fifth year, directly or via contract, a national estimate of the prevalence of unaccompanied situations among youth and young adults.**

Current research on homeless youth has major limitations, including a lack of large representative samples, reliable and valid measures, and comparison groups. Because runaway and homeless youth are among the most understudied and undercounted populations, the paucity of empirical evidence creates barriers to informing sound public policy decisions and the development of effective prevention and intervention services.

In 2002, the Senate Appropriations Committee expressed concern about the lack of research on this high risk population, instructing HHS to develop a plan for estimating the incidence of runaway and homelessness episodes among youth and to monitor trends. In response, HHS released a report in 2003 entitled "Incidence and Prevalence of Homeless and Runaway Youth," which outlined various research methodologies and options for conducting prevalence studies. The report recommended administering studies at regular 5-10 year intervals.

This reauthorization period offers Congress an opportunity to provide leadership and implement the recommendations of the 2003 report by requiring HHS to conduct prevalence studies at five- year intervals. The most recent federally funded study on runaway youth, The National Incidence Studies of Missing, Abducted, Runaway, and Thrownaway Youth (NISMART-2), estimates that 1.7 million youth under age 18 left home or were asked to leave home in 1999. While the sample size for NISMART-2 was three times the size of its first administration and therefore provided more accurate information on this youth population, there are still limitations. The most obvious limitation is that NISMART-2 failed to include older homeless youth, given that the sample population was restricted to those under the age of 18. Further, NISMART-2 did not include youth who did not return home and remained homeless -- the most at-risk subpopulation of homeless youth. A more accurate prevalence study must include youth who utilize homeless services, youth who remain on the street, couch-surfers who do not have stable housing, and other unaccompanied youth who do not utilize traditional services. A five-year interval prevalence study will provide policy makers and the field with important information to better serve this vulnerable population of young people.

**14. Require HHS to establish research, evaluation, and demonstration priorities every two years and to provide an opportunity for public comment on such priorities.** The RHYA grants HHS authority to make grants for research, evaluation, demonstration and service projects. RHYA grantees, youth, advocates, and other stakeholders have limited to no input into the identification or prioritization of issues to be studied or evaluated.

**15. Require HHS to conduct, directly or via contract, a cost-benefit analysis study comparing the efficacy of runaway and homeless youth programs to public human services systems, including juvenile justice, child welfare, mental health, public assistance and other systems that youth utilize during emergencies.** While it is intuitive that interventions that resolve homeless situations among youth are more cost-effective to the public in the long-term, there has yet to be conducted an authoritative cost-benefit analysis to demonstrate this assertion. A cost-benefit study would inform federal, state, and local policymakers about the type and level of investments in health and human services programs for children, youth, and families.

**16. Authorize HHS to conduct, directly or via contract, a public information campaign to raise awareness of the unaccompanied youth population and their service and support needs.** Runaway and homeless youth are a largely invisible or misunderstood population. Lack of public awareness of this group of young people, their life circumstances, and the interventions available to support them and end their homeless situations, allows homelessness to persist among the nation's youth.

## SOLUTIONS TO PROTECTING RUNAWAY AND HOMELESS YOUTH

Reauthorization of the Runaway and Homeless Youth Act must be considered just one part of a larger effort to prevent and end youth homelessness. Congress must take bold steps, such as those offered in the National Network's **Place to Call Home Campaign**. The Place to Call Home Campaign includes a comprehensive public policy agenda to prevent, respond to, and end runaway and homeless situations among youth. Proposed legislation addresses reform issues around juvenile justice, child welfare, education, workforce development, teen parenting, homeless assistance, and housing.

We encourage Members of this Committee to support the Place to Call Home Campaign by swiftly reauthorizing the Runaway and Homeless Youth Act; supporting the First Step Forward Act, Senator Schumer's youth reentry legislation; and supporting the National Network's recommended provisions on the issue of deinstitutionalization of status offenders within the reauthorization of the Juvenile Justice and Delinquency Prevention Act, which also sunsets this year. These steps will bring us closer to making sure that each runaway, homeless, and unaccompanied youth is connected to a safe and stable home, caring adults, and opportunities in education and the workforce.

# INDEX

Elementary and Secondary Education Act, 120
elementary school, 14
emergency management, 178
emergency preparedness, 134, 142
emergency response, 206, 210
emotion, 230
emotional, 10, 18, 24, 25, 43, 50, 53, 59, 61, 75, 77,
    80, 140, 156, 157, 162, 163, 169, 171, 172, 194
emotional abuse, 169, 171, 172
emotional disorder, 25, 75
emotions, 210
empathy, 247
employability, 75
employees, 152, 168, 179, 185
employers, 164
employment, ix, 1, 10, 13, 15, 17, 20, 29, 36, 37, 44,
    51, 59, 60, 62, 69, 70, 71, 73, 74, 80, 81, 93, 98,
    106, 108, 114, 121, 140, 170, 171, 173, 174, 181,
    193, 226
employment status, 71
empowered, 139, 251
empowerment, 64, 75
engagement, 21, 48, 61, 64, 66, 68, 94
enrollment, 19, 20, 120, 190
entitlement programs, 66
environment, 2, 48, 52, 57, 64, 67, 70, 71, 78, 79, 91,
    101, 133, 148, 149, 169, 171, 172, 204, 223
environmental factors, 56, 57, 193
ethnic minority, 4
ethnicity, 4, 9, 10, 23, 30, 64, 113, 153, 170
evidence-based program, 36
experimental design, 13, 194
expertise, 117, 137, 146, 158, 201, 203
exploitation, 36, 37, 46, 48, 90, 98, 99, 101, 105,
    116, 125, 130, 174, 189, 194, 197, 198, 200, 204,
    205, 209
exposure, 52, 65
externalizing, 13
externalizing behavior, 13

**F**

fabric, ix, 35
FAFSA, 180
failure, 51
faith, 36, 37, 54, 67, 78, 80, 81, 83, 85, 121, 174,
    175, 188
familial, 22, 69, 171, 188
family conflict, 6, 7, 13, 15, 16, 21, 22, 42, 43, 52,
    54, 55, 63, 68, 74, 104, 113, 169, 175, 190, 243,
    245
family members, 18, 19, 22, 56, 61, 83, 104, 111,
    164, 169, 185, 192, 193, 204, 243

family relationships, 15, 35, 56, 104, 190
family therapy, 57, 79, 92, 93, 192
family violence, 43, 121
fatherhood, 55
FBI, 197, 200, 213, 217, 230
fear, 32, 48, 68, 198
Federal Bureau of Investigation, 200
Federal Emergency Management Agency, 203
federal funds, 107, 108, 166, 177
federal government, 12, 33, 106, 111, 174, 228
federal law, 167, 168, 180, 201
Federal Register, 115, 126, 140, 154
feelings, 53, 221, 239
felony, 172
females, 4, 11, 14, 20, 29, 47, 48, 102, 103, 171
Fest, 95
FFT, 56, 57, 192
films, 239
filters, 232
financial aid, 180, 221
fingerprinting, 216
first language, 249
fitness, 202, 217
flexibility, 66, 69, 79, 80, 177, 250
focusing, 36, 51, 196, 205
food, 7, 11, 21, 37, 47, 65, 66, 71, 73, 74, 82, 105,
    110, 117, 118, 120, 156, 157, 159, 184, 225, 239,
    240
fForeign Operations Appropriations Act, 100
forensic, 199
forgetting, 182, 183
forgiveness, 179
freedom, 30, 62
friendship, 46, 160
frustration, 225
furniture, 17, 71
futures, 194

**G**

gender, 9, 10, 24, 48, 64, 90, 102, 153, 181, 189
gender differences, 24, 90
gender disparity, 189
General Accounting Office, 61
general practitioner, 158
generation, 186, 239
girls, 43, 170, 190, 201, 221
gloves, 241
goals, 13, 51, 56, 58, 62, 63, 64, 69, 70, 71, 73, 83,
    119, 244
God, 229, 233
governance, 136

## S